A Texas Cavalry Officer's Civil War

A TEXAS CAVALRY OFFICER'S
CIVIL WAR

THE DIARY AND LETTERS OF JAMES C. BATES

EDITED BY RICHARD LOWE

LOUISIANA STATE UNIVERSITY PRESS
Baton Rouge

Copyright © 1999 by Louisiana State University Press
Manufactured in the United States of America
First printing
08 07 06 05 04 03 02 01 00 99 5 4 3 2 1

Designer: Amanda McDonald Scallan
Typeface: Galliard
Typesetter: Crane Composition, Inc.
Printer and binder: Edward Brothers Inc.

Library of Congress Cataloging-in-Publication Data:
Bates. James C. (James Campbell), 1837–1891.
    A Texas Cavalry Officer's Civil War : the diary and letters of
James C. Bates / edited by Richard Lowe.
        p. cm.
    Includes bibliographical references and indexes.
    ISBN 0-8071-2372-2 (cloth : alk. paper)
    1. Bates, James C. (James Campbell), 1837–1891 Diaries.   2. Bates,
James C. (James Campbell), 1837–1891 Correspondence.   3. Confederate
States of America.   Army.   Texas Cavalry Regiment, 9th.   4. Texas—
History—Civil War, 1861–1865 Personal narratives.   5. United
States—History—Civil War, 1861–1865 Personal narratives,
Confederate.   6. Soldiers—Texas—Paris Diaries.   7. Soldiers—
Texas—Paris Correspondence. 8. Paris (Tex.) Biography.   I. Lowe,
Richard G., 1942– . II. Title.
E580.6 9th.B37   1999
973.7'464'092—dc21
    [B]   99-14901
                                                               CIP
The paper in this book meets the guidelines for permanence and durability of the Committee on Produc-
tion Guidelines for Book Longevity of the Council on Library Resources.♾

Photograph of William Bramlette courtesy of Paris (Tex.) Masonic Lodge No. 27. All other photographs
reproduced courtesy of Henry and Walter Fink.

for Kathy

Contents

Illustrations

Preface

James C. Bates, a bright young man with sparkling potential, was one of the hundreds of thousands of southern boys who went off to fight the Yankees in 1861. He left his home in Paris, Texas, and joined the 9th Texas Cavalry Regiment, one of the units in future governor Lawrence Sullivan "Sul" Ross's noted Texas Cavalry Brigade. Bates rode thousands of miles during his cavalry service, from the bleak wintry plains of the Indian Territory, across Arkansas, Mississippi, Tennessee, and Alabama, to the mountains of northwest Georgia. In every state he rode through, he and his regiment engaged the enemy, sometimes in small, running skirmishes and at other times in full set-piece battles.

The young Texan went off to war in 1861 because he believed that aggressive northerners were determined to treat their southern brothers as subordinates, not equals. He quoted statements in captured northern letters that further convinced him of this: statements about "teaching the rebels to know their masters," "conquering" the South, and taking southern land for Yankee farms. The destruction of civilian property by Federal armies shocked Bates and confirmed in his mind what the future held for white southerners if the Yankees were allowed to prevail. No honorable southern man, given all this, could stand by and let it happen. Better to see the South destroyed in an effort to resist than submit meekly to the domineering Yankees. Pride, at least, would be saved.

For Bates, the most glaring example of northern hauteur was the Union campaign to free the slaves. As early as the spring of 1862, long before President Lincoln announced his preliminary Emancipation Proclamation in September, Bates wrote that the real aim of the North was to wipe out slavery, an institution that made sense to the young officer and a custom that was none of the North's business. One can easily imagine Bates, who never owned a slave, dealing fairly with the black servants in his Paris boardinghouse (if fairness in a slave system was possible). He was a gentleman, after all. But black southerners, for him and for most white men of the South, were of a different order, a lower order, and the only practical

way for the two races to live together was for the more intelligent and accomplished group to direct the lives and labor of the less intelligent and
less accomplished. If citizens of the southern states were truly equal members of the American nation, then how they handled their domestic
arrangements was no concern of anyone else. The Yankees' meddling in
such matters was not only dangerous to the peace and prosperity of the
South. For Bates, it was another example of their determination to domi-
nate. No free man of the South, no descendant of the Revolutionary
fathers, could allow it.

From his first day in the army almost to his last, he was absolutely convinced that the Confederacy could not lose the contest. Submitting to
"Yankee rule" would be nothing but a form of slavery, he believed, and he
could not conceive of the possibility that his fellow southerners would ever
submit to such a shameful fate. Confederate defeats at Pea Ridge (Elkhorn
Tavern), New Orleans, Memphis, Corinth, and Vicksburg were only de-
tours and delays for Bates. The Confederacy would eventually prevail.

Bates fought in two small engagements in the Indian Territory, at
Elkhorn Tavern in Arkansas, at Corinth and Holly Springs and Jackson in
Mississippi, at Thompson's Station in Tennessee, and at the crossing of the
Etowah River during Sherman's Atlanta campaign in north Georgia. He
nearly froze in Indian Territory, sloshed through overflowing rivers in
Arkansas, suffered with thousands of others in the fetid camps near
Corinth, survived the slaughterhouse at Corinth, received a nearly fatal
wound in Georgia, and endured months of recuperation in Georgia and
Alabama hospitals.

Bates's story reveals a great deal about the hard-riding cavalry of the
western Confederacy, the various battles he lived through, his close rela-
tionships with the three women in his life, and the mental gyrations of a
man who had to square repeated Confederate defeats with his almost naive
belief in ultimate victory. He was directly involved in some of the most important and dramatic moments of the war in the west, and he recorded his
impressions in a detailed diary and dozens of long letters to his mother, his
sister, and his future wife.

Bates's firsthand accounts of the war confirm the general impression of
Texas cavalrymen as a hard-riding bunch—long on aggression and short
on discipline. When they were kept busy with raids and scouts, they were
among the most effective soldiers in the western Confederate armies.
Their charge on a Federal battery at Elkhorn Tavern, across several hundred yards of open ground, was exactly the sort of adventure they envi-
sioned when they signed up for military service. General Dabney Maury

selected the Texans for scouting duties in December 1862 when he could have used men from Mississippi and Missouri. General Van Dorn put the Texans at the front on the attack and at the rear on retreat during his Holly Springs raid. Likewise, the Texans were at the front of Hood's army when it invaded Tennessee in late 1864 and at the rear when Hood limped back into Alabama and Mississippi. Major General Stephen D. Lee, cavalry commander in Mississippi, Alabama, west Tennessee, and east Louisiana, regarded Bates's brigade as the best cavalry in his department. Bates and his comrades were quite aware of their reputation and made conscious efforts to live up to it.

On the other hand, during inactive stretches of the war "the wild Texas boys" could be more of a problem than an asset. When they hanged two of their own men in the first weeks of the war—without trial—their officers must have known that extra energy would be required to handle such soldiers. Shortly after the fall of Vicksburg, dozens of men from the Texas brigade—unhappy with the army's furlough policy, lonesome for home and family after two years away, and bored with the dullness of camp life—simply slipped away to return to Texas. These were men who had nearly frozen on the plains of the Indian Territory, ridden to the muzzles of Yankee cannon in Arkansas, and turned back General Grant's army at Holly Springs. Their sin was not cowardice or softness or defeatism; they were just undisciplined farm boys temporarily dressed as soldiers. Most of them intended to continue the fight west of the Mississippi River after visiting their families. Even when Major Bates was sent out to round them up and return them to duty, some of the men deserted again on the road back to camp. All their dash, their physical courage, and their horsemanship could be wasted if their leaders did not handle them correctly.

Bates also provided interesting insights into the various engagements he witnessed. For example, earlier accounts of the charge on the Federal battery at Elkhorn Tavern have not mentioned that some of the Texans charged on foot. Bates's description of the raid on Holly Springs is one of the few written just days after the event, and it is by far the most detailed of those few. His description of the retreat from the streets of Corinth is especially interesting. He expressed no fear about advancing toward the enemy, but he was certain that every Federal rifle was pointed at his back when he scampered back to the safety of his own lines. Bates's open admission that the Texans had executed some enemies reveals the increasing ferocity of the war in its later stages. His detailed descriptions of his wound and his long recuperation provide unusually specific information about the trauma experienced by soldiers wounded in the Civil War.

The dozens of letters that the young Texas officer wrote to his mother, his sister, and his future wife demonstrate his respect for their intelligence. He did not confine himself to requests for food or clothing, nor did he focus primarily on mundane family matters when corresponding with these women. Instead, he gave them all the latest political and war news he could gather, accurate or not; predicted (sometimes with amazing precision) what might happen next; and included them in his war experience as much as possible. This was their war, too.

By the time his war ended in 1865, Bates was no longer a boy. He was an experienced soldier, worn down with physical injury, memories of lost friends, and unthinkable defeat. Somehow he managed to get through his depression at the end of the war, and he spent the remainder of his relatively short life as a contributing member of society. He became a physician in the late 1860s and spent the next twenty years ministering to the needs of his neighbors in north and west Texas. He married his hometown sweetheart and raised a family of seven children. When he died of complications from his war experiences in 1891, he was only fifty-four.

James C. Bates was well educated, and his letters and diary are generally well written. He often used dashes instead of periods, and other dashes appear almost willy-nilly throughout his correspondence. With the exception of bracketed insertions to clarify meaning, and the imposition of space breaks in long entries, his letters are reproduced here as he wrote them.

All authors incur debts in research and writing, and I owe a great deal to several people who helped me on my way. One of James C. Bates's daughters, Nancy Cate Bates McKnight, preserved his old documents and passed them on to her daughter, Nancy McKnight Fink of Dallas. Mrs. Fink and her sons Walter and Henry Fink made the documents available and answered numerous queries about the Bates family history. Graduate students Jean Stuntz and Kelly Stott risked their eyesight deciphering the faded handwriting of Bates and his correspondents and tracked down elusive bits of pertinent information. Graduate student Cindy Dover, Dr. F. Terry Hambrecht of the National Institutes of Health, and Dr. Ann B. Pearson of Auburn, Alabama, provided information on the hospitals where Bates was a patient. Dr. Hambrecht also educated me about the use of morphine to control pain during the 1860s. Dr. John C. O'Brien, an accomplished surgeon at the Baylor Medical Center in Dallas, helped me to understand Bates's wound and contributed an appendix analyzing the injury. My colleague Jane Tanner, a master editor, made me more aware of Bates's respect for the intelligence of his women correspondents. Another colleague, Randolph Campbell, read parts of the manuscript and offered his usual insightful comments. The Office of Research Administration at the University of North Texas supported my research with two summer grants. My sons and daughter-in-law were not involved in the research or writing, but they at least let me know (or skillfully pretended) that they were interested when I talked about the project. My wife, Kathy, asked questions I had not considered, expertly handled all technical hardware and software problems, and supported me throughout the project. To all of them, my thanks.

Introduction

James Campbell Bates lived in interesting times. A migrant from Tennessee to Texas in his boyhood, he spent his teenage years in the rough-and-tumble frontier environment of Texas. Four hard years of service in the Confederate cavalry left him with a mangled mouth and jaw, a speech impediment, and the lingering aftereffects of wartime dysentery. A medical education at the University of Virginia and Bellevue Hospital in New York and his marriage to his longtime sweetheart after the Civil War launched him on the second half of his life, practicing medicine on the prairies and plains of Texas and raising a family of seven children. By the time he died in 1891, he had fought Indians in present-day Oklahoma, ridden in the most effective cavalry raid of the Civil War, survived several major battles, suffered a painful facial wound, delivered babies and dispensed medicine, and watched his children grow to adolescence and adulthood.

Born in Overton County in middle Tennessee on May 14, 1837, Bates moved to Henderson (Rusk County), Texas, with his widowed mother and older sister while he was still a young boy.[1] His mother took her two children to join her parents and siblings, earlier migrants to east Texas, after her husband died. In 1856, when Bates was nineteen, he and his mother moved to Paris (Lamar County) in far north Texas. They lived with Bates's sister, who had married a prosperous businessman in the small town near the border of the Indian Territory (now Oklahoma). Bates attended country schools. At some point in the 1850s, he was sent back to Tennessee to complete his education at Bethel College, a Presbyterian school in McLemoresville, about one hundred miles west of Nashville. Bates must have been a competent pupil; the government of the United

1. Bates's home county in middle Tennessee was just south of the Kentucky border, but its population was strongly southern in sentiment. In 1860 more than 80 percent of the voters would favor secession. Noel C. Fisher, *War at Every Door: Partisan Politics and Guerrilla Violence in East Tennessee, 1860–1869* (Chapel Hill: University of North Carolina Press, 1997), 189.

States trusted him enough to appoint him a census marshal for Lamar County when he was only twenty-three years old.[2]

One of his fellow marshals recorded information on the substantial home where Bates and his mother lived in 1860. The head of this household was James's brother-in-law, William "Will" Bramlette, a thirty-three-year-old Kentuckian, sometime schoolteacher, secretary of a railroad company, and husband to Bates's sister, Adela. Bramlette and Bates were warm friends and signed their Civil War letters to each other "Your brother" or "Truly your brother." Adela was also very close to her brother, and the siblings exchanged numerous letters during the war. Will's natural brother, Thomas E. Bramlette, was a judge and Union army officer who would be elected governor of Kentucky in 1863. The Texas branch of the family supported the Confederacy during the war; the fact that Will Bramlette owned three slaves in 1860 may have influenced his political leanings.[3]

In addition to Will and the pregnant Adela Bramlette, their four young children, and three slaves, the household also included Bates and his mother, Nancy. "Ma," as James called his mother, must have been a very strong woman. Forty-seven years old in 1860, she had been widowed when her son was only three. She had packed up two young children and moved to Texas when that state was still on the frontier of settlement. Nearly half of the letters Bates wrote during his military career were to "Dear Ma," who did everything possible to provide her son with the necessities and comforts of life. In one of his wartime letters, written after receiving a package of handmade clothing from home, Bates wrote that "Every body [in my company] allowed I must have the best mother in Texas, & I was of that opinion myself." Nancy's strong constitution would enable her, doubtless to her regret, to outlive her children.[4]

2. Obituary in unidentified newspaper clipping (probably from the *Paris [Texas] Herald,* September 1891), James C. Bates Papers, private collection of Henry and Walter Fink, Dallas; Schedule I (Free Inhabitants), Seventh Census of the United States, 1850, and Schedule I, Eighth Census of the United States, 1860, Records of the Bureau of the Census, Record Group 29, National Archives, Washington, D.C. (Microfilm M432, roll 914, Rusk County in 1850, Nancy Bates household; Microfilm M653, roll 1299, Lamar County in 1860, William Bramlette household)—hereinafter cited as Seventh Census or Eighth Census.

3. Schedule I, roll 1299, and Schedule III (Slave Inhabitants), roll 1311, Eighth Census; A. W. Neville, *The History of Lamar County (Texas)* (Paris: North Texas Publishing Co., 1937), 73; Stewart Sifakis, *Who Was Who in the Civil War* (New York: Facts on File, 1988), 69.

4. J. C. Bates to his mother, February [7?], 1863, Bates Papers; James C. Bates obituary, ibid.; Schedule I, roll 1299, Eighth Census. Family tradition holds that Nancy Bates spun the

Packed into a very large house with the Bramlette family, their servants, James, and his mother were two boarders. H. C. Ballinger was a twenty-one-year-old Kentuckian and law student in 1860. He may have been clerking for and studying under the other boarder, Ebenezer Lafayette Dohoney, one of the closest and most interesting friends Bates ever had. Twenty-eight years old, Dohoney was Bates's roommate in Will Bramlette's house and would serve in the same cavalry company with Bates for several months in 1861–1862. A former law student of Bramlette's brother Thomas in Kentucky and a graduate of the University of Louisville law school, he had practiced his profession in Kentucky for a while before moving to Texas for his health in 1859.[5] Quick-witted and sometimes acerbic in his judgments of others, Dohoney would marry the older sister of Thirmuthis "Mootie" Johnson, the woman Bates was destined to wed after the war.

Dohoney, something of a maverick, spoke out against secession in 1860 and went on to a postwar public career as a reformer and outspoken critic of many aspects of Texas life.[6] As a state legislator in the 1870s, he supported a state law that banned carrying firearms in public places, spoke out for woman's suffrage forty years before that reform was adopted, and wrote the local-option liquor clause in the state constitution of 1876. He joined the Greenback Party in 1877, the Prohibition Party in the 1880s, and helped organize the Populist Party in the 1890s. Running on the Prohibition Party ticket, Dohoney lost a race for governor in 1886 when he was defeated by Bates's old cavalry commander, "Sul" Ross. Eight years later he lost another statewide race when he ran as a Populist for chief justice of the state Court of Criminal Appeals. Between political campaigns, he wrote six books, including an autobiography.[7]

Nearly all of the young men who would ride with Dohoney and Bates

---

thread (from family-grown cotton), wove the cloth, and sewed the pieces together to make her son's Confederate uniform. Interview with Henry Fink, Bates's descendant, July 27, 1997.

5. E. L. Dohoney, *An Average American: Being a True History of Leading Events in the Life of Lafayette, Who Was Born in Ky.; But "Went West to Grow Up with the Country"* (Paris, Tex.: n.p., 1907), 9, 28–29, 60; Schedule I, roll 1299, Eighth Census; Ron Tyler et al., eds., *The New Handbook of Texas* (6 vols.; Austin: Texas State Historical Assn., 1996), 2:670–71; Neville, *History of Lamar County,* 185.

6. Dohoney, *Average American,* 70, 74–75, 77–81, passim.

7. Tyler et al., *New Handbook of Texas,* 2:670–71; Neville, *History of Lamar County,* 185; Allene Alverson, "E. L. Dohoney and the Constitution of 1876" (M.A. thesis, Texas Technological College, 1941); Dohoney, *Average American.*

in Company H of the 9th Texas Cavalry lived in Paris and the surrounding countryside of Lamar County. The farms and fields of Lamar were marked by gently rolling terrain, about five hundred feet above sea level, and checkered with pine and hardwood timber and dark-soiled prairies. Settled primarily by immigrants from the upper South, especially Tennessee and Kentucky, Lamar County was part of the north-central plains and prairies of Texas. This region enjoyed fertile soil and adequate rainfall for cotton cultivation, but its distance from the major cotton ports of the state—and the lack of antebellum railroads to connect to those ports—meant that large-scale cotton farming would wait until after the Civil War. Farms in this northwest quadrant of the settled portion of Texas tended to be smaller and more focused on food and grain crops than farms in eastern or coastal Texas, where slaveholding, cotton, and sugar were much more prominent. Similarly, slaveholding families on the plains and prairies were a smaller percentage of the total free population (about 20 percent of all families compared to the statewide figure of nearly 30 percent) and generally held fewer bondsmen than slave owners in the state as a whole.[8]

The upper southerners of north Texas, less dependent on large-scale agriculture and slavery than other Texans, were also less attracted to radical political ideas such as secession. When Republican Abraham Lincoln won the presidency a few months after Bates completed his census rounds, the separatist fever that swept through the Deep South touched more lightly on the prairies of Lamar County. And when the voters of the state were given the opportunity in late February 1861 to accept or reject the secession ordinance adopted in Austin on February 1, more than half of Lamar's voters (55 percent) cast their ballots against separation from the old Union. Dohoney's public statements against breaking away from the rest of the nation put him in the majority in this case. Lamar was one of seven contiguous counties in far north Texas to stand against secession and one of only eighteen among the 122 casting votes to oppose separation. Even so, loyalty to the Union in Lamar County was not unanimous—nearly half of those casting votes in the referendum, after all, had joined with the majority of Texans to approve the secession ordinance.[9]

8. Tyler et al., *New Handbook of Texas,* 4:39–40; *Texas Almanac and State Industrial Guide, 1996–1997* (Dallas: Dallas Morning News, 1995), 217; Randolph B. Campbell and Richard G. Lowe, *Wealth and Power in Antebellum Texas* (College Station: Texas A&M University Press, 1977), 17, 28, 52–55, 85–86, 138–45.

9. Walter L. Buenger, *Secession and the Union in Texas* (Austin: University of Texas Press, 1984), 64–69, 175; Robin E. Baker and Dale Baum, "The Texas Voter and the Crisis of the Union, 1859–1861," *Journal of Southern History* 53 (August 1987): 409, 417–18.

Once Texas officially seceded and joined the new Confederate States of America, majority opinion in the Lone Star State swept most of the doubters and foot-draggers along with the tide of separation. By the time the first artillery shells flew over Charleston harbor in South Carolina in April, thousands of Texans, intoxicated by the exciting prospect of war, rushed to form companies and regiments to defend their homes from the "iron hand of Yankee despotism." Even mavericks and original doubters such as Dohoney caught the fever, as farmers and clerks, blacksmiths and lawyers put aside their peaceful pursuits and picked up the sword.[10]

Among the hundreds of volunteer companies organized in 1861 to defend Texas and the new Confederacy was one formed in Lamar County. A public notice in mid-August informed the men of Lamar that the governor had called on seven counties in north Texas to create a new cavalry battalion of five companies. Volunteers would provide their own arms, horses, and equipment and would serve for twelve months. "Said battalion, when organized, will form a part of an army now being raised in Northern Texas for the defense of her Northern line, and to aid our friends upon the Missouri border." Although the Federal army moving into southwest Missouri was turned back at the Battle of Wilson's Creek (Oak Hills) about the same time the circular appeared, the men of Lamar responded nevertheless and formed their company, the "Lamar Cavalry," for the new battalion. A partial roster of the company for August shows James C. Bates as captain and his fellow boarder, E. L. Dohoney, as sergeant.[11]

This company, organized originally as a state unit, joined several other north Texas companies a few weeks later to form a new regiment (about one thousand men), and the regiment was then officially transferred to Confederate service in October 1861. Nearly three-fourths of the men who would eventually serve in the company were recorded on the original Confederate muster roll of October 14, 1861, and nearly 100 percent (104 of 115) joined by the spring of 1862. They were generally young— 20 percent were in their teens, nearly 90 percent were under thirty, and their median age was only twenty-two. Nine of every ten were from Lamar County, and most of the others were from nearby counties. Reflecting the

10. Buenger, *Secession and the Union in Texas,* 177; Dohoney, *Average American,* 89–90.

11. The circular and roster are in the A. W. Neville Papers, Texas A&M University at Commerce Library, Commerce, Texas. Bates and several other men who would serve in the same regiment during the war had joined a temporary frontier-defense company from Lamar County as early as the winter of 1860–61 to protect the county from Indian raids, so their service in August was not their first experience under arms. Neville, *History of Lamar County,* 112–13.

pattern in north Texas as a whole, natives of the upper South predomi-
nated among the men in the company. Fully half were natives of Tennessee
and Kentucky; 60 percent were from the upper South in general; and only
one-third had been born in the lower South.[12]

As might be expected in a frontier state, nearly two-thirds of the company's volunteers made their living from the soil. In general, the farmers
in Bates's company operated on a small scale. They tilled fewer acres and
owned less land than Texas farmers in general, and the mean value of their
farms was only about 60 percent of the value of farms statewide. Another
14 percent of the soldiers were students, reflecting their youth, and the remaining quarter of the company followed a variety of occupations—merchant, lawyer, teacher, wagon maker, blacksmith, carpenter, and day laborer,
among others. Taken altogether, they fairly represented the makeup of
Lamar and neighboring counties.[13]

Partly because they were younger than the average Texas household
head (and therefore had had less time to accumulate wealth) and partly because they were residents of a less highly developed part of the state, the
soldiers in Bates's company were not as wealthy as the average Texan. The
mean values of the soldiers' real property ($1,745) and overall wealth (real
and personal property combined, $3,339) were substantially lower than
comparable figures for Texas men in general ($2,699 and $6,393). Similarly, only about one-sixth of the soldiers (whether heads of households or
not) owned slaves (compared to one-fourth of household heads statewide), and three-fourths of those soldiers who did own slaves held fewer
than five. Much of the disparity in wealth between the horsemen who rode
with Bates and Dohoney and Texas men in general was owing to the
younger ages of the soldiers. Fewer than half of the soldiers were heads of
their own households, fewer than half were married, and about one-fourth
were still living with their parents. Most of the soldiers in Bates's company

12. These figures and those in the following paragraphs were derived from a database of
information, compiled for this study, from the Eighth Census, 1860, Schedules I and II (rolls
1299 and 1311), and from the Compiled Service Records of Confederate Soldiers Who
Served in Organizations from the State of Texas, War Department Collection of Confederate Records, Record Group 109, National Archives, Washington, D.C. (Microfilm M323,
rolls 56–60). Unless otherwise indicated, editorial identifications of persons mentioned in
Bates's diary and letters are founded on this database.

13. The mean farm value for the soldiers was $1,657, about 60 percent of the statewide
figure of $2,749. Their mean holdings in improved and total farm acreage (56 and 283, re-
spectively) were also lower than statewide means (67 and 544). For regional and statewide
means, see Richard G. Lowe and Randolph B. Campbell, *Planters and Plain Folk: Agriculture in Antebellum Texas* (Dallas: Southern Methodist University Press, 1987), 62–65.

did own property of some sort, whether real or personal, and those who were heads of households were more likely to own property than Texans in general. In short, these young soldiers were still on their way up the economic ladder, but they were not poor or propertyless.[14]

James C. Bates fits neatly into the company's demographic profile. A native of Tennessee, he lived with his mother in a household headed by his brother-in-law. Twenty-four years old when he joined the cavalry, he was not married, and his wealth was modest—he owned no slaves, no real property, and only $900 in personal property. On the other hand, he was well educated, and he circulated among the upper levels of Paris society. His wartime diary and letters reveal him as a politically conscious young man who was keenly aware of the world around him.

14. See Campbell and Lowe, *Wealth and Power in Antebellum Texas,* 28–29, 38, 43–45, 94–95, for statewide figures. For an example of an east Texas cavalry unit that was considerably wealthier than Bates's company, see Douglas Hale, "The Third Texas Cavalry: A Socioeconomic Profile of a Confederate Regiment," *Military History of the Southwest* 19 (Spring 1989): 1–26.

A Texas Cavalry Officer's Civil War

Organization and First Campaign

James C. Bates began his diary in mid-September 1861, after he had joined the cavalry but before his company was officially mustered into Confederate service. His regiment trained for a few weeks near Sherman, Texas, just south of the Red River border with the Indian Territory, then rode off to the northeast to join other Confederate units in Missouri. Before they reached their destination, they were detoured deeper into the Indian Territory to chase down a column of Unionist Indians fleeing toward Kansas. Bates's first few diary entries describe his uncertainty about leaving home, perhaps never to return, and the organization of his regiment.

September 18, 1861 [diary]

This morning started for the rendezvous in company with Jim Poindexter & [Cameron] Givens.[1] Our Company left Paris on the 14th. How many who then bid goodbye to friends—took them by the hand for the last time—perhaps thought as I did, at the expiration of twelve months they would again grasp them by the hand, or perhaps they did not, as was the case with myself, have a full realization of the sad import of those good old words "good bye"—untill after they had been said and those to whom they were spoken were left far behind. Though I did not *then* feel it the *goodby I said last*

1. The rendezvous for the various companies in the new regiment was north of Sherman in Grayson County, about seventy-five miles west of Paris, near the Red River border with Indian Territory. The two men Bates mentions were members of his company and fellow residents of Lamar County. Poindexter was a twenty-one-year-old blacksmith from Tennessee; Charles Cameron Givens was a twenty-three-year-old college student from Kentucky.

night was sadder, than any, save to my dear mother, sister, and other loved ones at home.[2] Mother—sister—are there any other words so full of holy meaning that so fully bring up home and its associations as these? Well! Sad reflections will some times come, but I suppose when we have gotten fully into military harness we will not have many moments for these thoughts.

Left Paris at 11 ocl[oc]k A.M.—took dinner at Mr Burke's—started on our way at 2 P.M.—arrived at Honey grove at dark.[3]

September 19 [1861] [diary]

After having some repairs made on saddles—canteens—we started again. Passed over some beautiful country on way to Bonham. Nothing of interest untill after sunset—when just before us a [little?] North of West, I beheld a most beautiful illusion formed by clouds of various hues singularly thrown together—just above the horizon was a bank of clouds extending from W–NW varying in size form & color as the sunlight was thrown on them with more or less intensity. After looking on this bank of clouds, and a little strip of whitish looking sky under it, which at first glance had nothing more attractive in its appearance than others, we could hardly persuade ourselves that this beautiful & enchanting vision before us was not a reality—that it was in fact a bonafide river [of] pure molten silver flowing on before us. [last sentence illegible]

Although Bates claimed later that he had become a believing Christian during the war, his letters indicate that he was well versed in the Scriptures and accustomed to attending church on a regular basis even before the war began. On the other hand, religion seemed to be only a part of his everyday existence, not something he dwelled on or worried over every day.

September 29th [1861] [diary]

Sunday again, my second Sunday in camp.[4] As our Chaplain is sick we have no preaching today—after reading awhile in my Bible

2. Bates indicates later that he had stayed up late his last night in Paris visiting his sweetheart, seventeen-year-old Thirmuthis "Mootie" Johnson, daughter of a prominent physician in Paris. The Johnson home was next to Will Bramlette's house, allowing frequent and easy contact between the doctor's daughters and the next-door boarders, Bates and Dohoney. Dohoney, *Average American,* 172.

3. Honey Grove is about twenty-one miles west of Paris.

4. This was probably Camp Brogden, a temporary camp of instruction a few miles north

concluded to attend preaching about a mile and a half from here— went & found a goodly number of soldiers from the different companies in attendance—after waiting two hours we were told that the preacher was sick. Saw today the first lady since leaving home. Thoughts of my good lady friends at home came into my mind. Well, if I were at home tonight—wouldn't I go to see—well, no matter who.[5]

September 30th [1861] [diary]

This morning Maj Chilton of McCulloch's army arrived at our camp with authority to muster into Confederate service Col Young's Reg[iment] encamped 4 miles east of here. Our Reg will not be received. It is understood that Y's Reg will be converted into scouting parties on their arrival at McCulloch's.[6]

The young men who gathered north of Sherman were very raw material for a cavalry regiment. Although full of confidence and generally familiar with horses and the outdoors, they had no uniforms, no standard firearms or sabers, no discipline, and no training as soldiers. To distinguish one company from another during drills, the men began wearing colored strips

of Sherman and only a few miles south of the Red River. Homer L. Kerr, ed., *Fighting with Ross' Texas Cavalry Brigade, C.S.A.: The Diary of George L. Griscom, Adjutant, 9th Texas Cavalry Regiment* (Hillsboro, Tex.: Hill Jr. College Press, 1976), 19. For other descriptions of life at this camp and nearby Camp Reeves, see A. W. Sparks, *The War Between the States As I Saw It. Reminiscent, Historical and Personal* (Tyler, Tex.: Lee & Burnett, Printers, 1901), 16; James Henry Davis, *The Cypress Rangers in the Civil War: The Experiences of 85 Confederate Cavalrymen from Texas,* 2nd ed. (Texarkana, Tex.: Heritage Oak Press, 1992), 24–25.

5. Bates is referring to Mootie, his future wife. His diary frequently alludes to her indirectly.

6. Major Chilton was probably George W. Chilton, an outspoken proslavery Kentuckian who had served in the Texas secession convention and was then a major in the 3rd Texas Cavalry Regiment. Colonel Young was probably Cooke County's William C. Young, who raised the 11th Texas Cavalry Regiment early in the war. McCulloch was Brigadier General Ben McCulloch, a legendary Texas Ranger, Indian fighter, and U.S. marshal. McCulloch had commanded the Confederate army that turned back the Federal invasion of southwest Missouri in August at the Battle of Wilson's Creek (Oak Hills), and his forces were then in southern Missouri. For Chilton, see Tyler et. al., *New Handbook of Texas,* 2:83. For Young, see Richard B. McCaslin, *Tainted Breeze: The Great Hanging at Gainesville, Texas, 1862* (Baton Rouge: Louisiana State University Press, 1994), 30, 223, and Marcus J. Wright, comp., and Harold B. Simpson, ed., *Texas in the War, 1861–1865* (Hillsboro, Tex.: Hill Junior College Press, 1965), 115. For McCulloch, see Thomas W. Cutrer, *Ben McCulloch and the Frontier Military Tradition* (Chapel Hill: University of North Carolina Press, 1993).

of cloth on their shoulders—blue for one company, yellow for another, and so on. Their equipment was as unconventional as their clothing. "Double-barrel shot guns were the favorite arms," one private recalled. In addition, "each soldier carried a huge knife, usually made from an old mill file, shaped by the blacksmith and ground according to the fancy of the owner. The horses were a fair average of the Texas mustang type, but not a few were found in the company that had strains of noted blood in their veins. The clothing of the men was light and unsuited for hard service, but almost all wore long boots made of Texas tanned leather with a large flap at the front of the leg to protect the knee."[7]

One of the advantages of camp life in a prosperous countryside un-marked by invasion and the depredations of enemy (or friendly) armies was an abundance of good food. One of the more amusing aspects of camp life was the sight of young men learning to cook for themselves. In later weeks and months, Bates doubtless looked back with fondness at the variety and quality of food available during these early days of the war. His diary also demonstrates Bates's close observation of the countryside. At least in his early army career, he often commented on the terrain and scenery.

Tues. Oct. 1st [1861] [diary]
    After drilling two hours returned at noon and made a sumptuous dinner on boiled beef, buttermilk, sweet potatoes, and bread (corn). After dinner took a ride down in Red River bottoms on the hunt of grapes in company with Raz.[8] I found any abundance of small win-ter grapes, but no large ones. Some of the company bring in grapes of a very large quality—sweet & juicy meet—but a skin so sour that a very few are sufficient to take the skins off our mouths.
    After strolling about amid the brush & vines of the bottoms with-out finding any grapes worth stoping for, we ascended one of the numerous high peaks making out from the hills to the river and had a magnificent view of the river winding along in dense forests like some gigantic red serpent. The scenery beyond the river for 12 or 15 miles is beautiful in the extreme.
    [page(s) missing]
    that there was no getting around it dived into the flour up to my

    7. Sparks, *War Between the States*, 14–15; Davis, *Cypress Rangers*, 24–25.
    8. Raz was probably Erasmus H. Tanner, a twenty-one-year-old private who would later serve as a sergeant in Bates's company.

elbows and after various and sundry mishaps in the way of getting in the ingredients [such] as salt soda I finally got to the stage that I thought fit for the oven—then came out the making out the biscuit after numerous and divers ineffectual efforts to make the first two near the same shape & size I concluded they would not be any better by it—so I contented myself with seeing them all sizes—big little & littler—in fact think them more convenient as suiting the different capacities each one has of storing away a large or small one. Today Capt Townes declared himself a candidate for Major—his opponent Sartain worked himself into a terrible passion on hearing this. thought there must be some skulduggery connected with it to defeat him in particular.[9]

Far away in the distance are to be seen hundreds of small prairies of from 100 to 500 acres in extent with small strips of wood intervening and so much resembling farms in a high state of cultivation that were it not that I *know* the country to be a wilderness I would think it in a fine state of cultivation.

One of the most interesting aspects of mid-nineteenth-century American warfare was the election of officers by the men in the ranks. Americans north and south were accustomed to electioneering and frequent political contests during peacetime, and they had a long-established tradition of electing their militia officers. They saw no reason to change that pattern during a war. Normally, the individuals who had raised the companies and regiments—usually men of some local prominence—were easily elected to company and regimental offices. Some candidates were not above puffing their résumés for political effect. A soldier in the 3rd Texas Cavalry remembered that "the period was preeminently *the* era of the parlor knight. West Pointers, who had never seen West Point, turned up whenever occasion required it. Scarred veterans from Nicaraugua [*sic*] sprung up as if by magic, and the author, alone, formed the personal acquaintance of at least

9. Nathan W. Townes, a thirty-four-year-old lawyer and native of Virginia, was wealthy compared with most residents of the county. He had served with Bates and Dohoney when the company was first organized in August, and he was a friend of the Bates family. He would be elected major of the new regiment about two weeks later and colonel when the regiment was reorganized in May 1862. George F. Sartain, a lieutenant in Company G, was apparently not so popular as Townes. When he lost another election, during the regiment's reorganization in May 1862, he left the army entirely. For Townes, see Neville, *History of Lamar County*, 93; for Sartain, see Compiled Service Records, roll 60.

twelve hundred survivors of the immortal six hundred who charged at Balaklava."[10]

If more than one candidate stepped forward to offer his services, campaigning and wire-pulling often decided the contest. In early October 1861, preparatory to their official muster into Confederate service, the men of the regiment elected their leaders. Bates obviously had his favorites. His appointment to help conduct the elections indicates that he was already considered leadership material by other officers in the camp.

> Wednesday 2nd [October 2, 1861] [diary]
> Well today decides who are to be our field officers—I think the Reg[iment] more interested in the election for Maj than any other of the officers. Either Balte or Sims will make us a good Col[onel]—but rather than have such a man as "good-eze" (Sartain) elected over us I think 1/2 of this company will desert. Col Bowland [Bourland] was over this morning and myself & four others were sworn in as officers to hold the election at our camp.[11]
> 9 P.M. Capt Sims is elected Col of our Reg. Capt Quayle[,] Lieut Col; Capt Townes, Maj—hurrah for "our side." We have beaten Sartain. That's enough glory for one day.[12]

The popular Major Townes had been serving as captain of Bates's company, and his elevation to the rank of major produced an opening for his captaincy. The fact that some men in the company were threatening desertion because of the possible election of this or that new officer indicates

10. Victor M. Rose, *Ross' Texas Brigade, Being a Narrative of Events Connected with Its Service in the Late War Between the States* (Louisville, Ky.: Courier-Journal Book and Job Rooms, 1881), 15. Rose's mention of "the immortal six hundred" referred to the famous charge of the British Light Brigade during the Crimean War.

11. James G. Bourland of Cooke County had been Lamar County's state senator for two terms in the late 1840s. He organized a cavalry regiment to defend of the northern border of Texas at the beginning of the Civil War and was serving as its colonel when he supervised the elections for Bates's regiment. McCaslin, *Tainted Breeze,* 211–12; Wright and Simpson, *Texas in the War,* 122–23.

12. William B. Sims was "a large man and of fine appearance and had a voice equal to the modern fog horn" (Sparks, *War Between the States,* 16). A wealthy merchant of Clarksville in Red River County, just east of Lamar, he would receive a disabling wound at the Battle of Pea Ridge (Elkhorn Tavern) a few months later. Quayle, a native of the Isle of Man, was a former sea captain who had left a judicial bench in Fort Worth to join the Confederate cavalry. Douglas Hale, "Rehearsal for Civil War: The Texas Cavalry in the Indian Territory, 1861," *Chronicles of Oklahoma* 68 (Fall 1990): 231; Kerr, ed., *Fighting with Ross' Texas Cavalry,* 19; Rose, *Ross' Texas Brigade,* 49.

just how undisciplined these young Texans were early in the war. As usual, a certain amount of electioneering preceded the vote. Interestingly, the soldiers voted with their feet by physically gathering around the man of their choice.

Thursday [October] 3rd [1861] [diary]
Today we had an election for Capt to fill the place of Maj Townes. A good deal of dissatisfaction exists among the men on account of Townes running for Major. Some say they will not go under any man in the company—others that if this or that man is not elected they will leave. Aspirants for the office are very numerous. If it were not that there is a possibility of the command being broken up by these dissensions—the tricks & turns & electioneering schemes of the candidates would afford infinite amusement. It is always at the solicitation of *numerous* friends that Candidates offer themselves—& their numerous friends generally turn out to be one or two *particular* friends. I might say with more truth than *some of them* I think that *I too* was solicited by numerous friends that is by four or five. Well after various & divers threats had been made by various & divers persons—as to what they would do under various & divers circumstances these refractory gents were called together and told that the election would be held *that* morning for Captain—and whoever might be elected the Captain to him the whole company must render implicit obedience. Well after a good deal of "fuss & no feathers" we were marched off to an open glade in front of the camps and after the command halt—right dress—front—the next order was that the candidates for captain take their places twenty paces in front when E.L.D. [Dohoney] and H.K.W. [H. Kirke White] stepped out. J.D.W. [Jerry D. Wright] was put in nomination, and was represented by B.(J.) on the command—to *your* respective favorites march[—]a majority was formed in favor of J.D.W. and he was therefore unanimously declared captain of this com[pany].[13]

The lack of discipline among the young troopers was revealed not only in their grumbling and threats of desertion in the midst of elections—these men apparently lynched two of their own number in the early weeks of

13. The new captain, Jerry D. Wright, was a thirty-eight-year-old native of Kentucky, a Lamar County lawyer, and a small slaveholder.

their service! In late October, James K. Bell, the regimental adjutant, was removed from his office and accused of "Abolitionism and bigamy—the latter being pretty strongly proven upon him, the boys *en masse* took him out & hung him & gave his outfit [his equipment] to a poor boy" of the regiment. About two weeks later, W. L. Essy of Company D was "detected in the act of committing a rape upon a married woman in the vicinity of Camp." While regimental officers were pondering what to do with Essy, a crowd of soldiers in the regiment jerked him away from his guards, hanged him, and distributed his equipment to poorer members of his company. Texans, by most accounts, especially their own, made excellent fighters, but they had a great deal to learn about military discipline.[14]

They would require some education before they could determine the best methods of fighting Yankees as well, although they expected to prevail as a matter of course in any personal contests with their northern foes. One member of the regiment recalled that "great was the confidence of the Texas soldier in his own prowess. To whip the Yankees, five to one, was considered the minimum of good fighting." Soldier portraits from the early months of the war often displayed fierce-eyed Texans armed to the chin with shotguns, pistols, and knives. A member of the 3rd Texas Cavalry, a unit that served in the same brigade with Bates's regiment, later recalled the inexperienced troopers of those early days: "An idea may be had of the kind of work the average Texas soldier imagined he would be called upon to perform in battle, by the huge knives carried by many. Some of these knives were three feet long, and heavy enough to cleave the skull of a mailed knight through helmet and all. I think they were never used in the butchery of the Yankees, and, ere the close of the first year's service, were discarded altogether." Lawrence Sullivan "Sul" Ross, a later commander of these troops, reminded his veterans after the war of their early naiveté. He told of one Texan who "had whetted his [homemade knife] till it bore the edge of a razor, and then went out in the woods to practice, and in an attempt to make a grand right and left cut against an imaginary foe, the first whack he made he cut off his horse's right ear, and the next stroke he chipped a chunk out of his left knee, when he immediately dismounted and poked the dangerous thing up a hollow log."[15]

Bates's first surviving wartime letter was written the day after regimental elections. He brought his mother up to date on the regiment's activi-

14. Kerr, ed., *Fighting with Ross' Texas Cavalry*, 2–3; Davis, *Cypress Rangers*, 27; Sparks, *War Between the States*, 18.

15. Rose, *Ross' Texas Brigade*, 18; Sparks, *War Between the States*, 21n (third quotation).

ties, mentioning several Paris and Lamar County men she obviously knew, and reported the rumor that his regiment would be assigned to guard the coast of Texas against Yankee aggression. (Like most wartime rumors, this one would prove unfounded.)

Camp at Round [Brogden?] Springs
Grayson Co—Oct 3d 1861
Dear Ma

As I have an opportunity of sending you a letter by Ben Poindexter I avail myself of the opportunity. As yet we have no intimation as to where we will be ordered. The 9th (Col Young's) Regiment is now being mustered into the Confederate service. Maj. Chilton who arrived in our camp some days ago direct from McCulloch's headquarters—with authority to receive one Regiment and no more. It is understood I believe that this Regiment, Col Young's, will be converted mostly into scouting parties on their arrival there. We had an election yesterday for field officers for our Regiment. Brad Sims was elected Col. Capt Quayle [was elected] Lieut Col and Capt Townes [was elected] Maj. We this morning held an election for Capt—Dohoney and one A Kirk White of our Com[pany] were Candidates. Jerry Wright was also run by some of the Company *and elected*. I don't think he will serve. If he don't we will have to hold another election. Maj Townes has just sent for me to go down to the other camp [Camp Reeves] some three miles from here and I must close. I now think it likely that I will be down home in a week or so. I will write soon as some one will be passing every day or so.
Your Son
J.C. Bates

1 O'clock P.M.

Since writing the above and while on my way down to the other camp I learned that a letter had been received by some one in Young Regiment from Mr Kirby Adj[utant] Gen[eral] at Sherman—stating that we had been received into the Confederate service—and that an officer would be here in the course of a few days to muster us in. Gen Kirby stated that we would most probably be ordered to the Coast. I think therefore that Galveston will be the point of our destination. Maj Townes has concluded since noon to go down home provided he can get permission from the Col—which I suppose he

will do as it will be necessary for us to have ten more men before our Company can be received. As Townes will probably call on you while down he can give you more news than I have time to write.
J.C. Bates

Bates and his comrades spent most of the month of October learning how to become cavalrymen. This involved long hours of drill to train both men and horses to respond to standard commands quickly and uniformly. A. W. Sparks of Titus County remembered, "After the regiment was formed we were drilled mostly in battalions [*sic*], Lieutenant-Colonel Quail commanding the first and Major Townes the second, with Col. Sims always on the field to note the progress of his young professionals." Training at Camp Brogden also included learning the rules of warfare, so the soldiers were sometimes gathered to hear their officers read and explain standard regulations.

> Friday [October] 4th [1861] [diary]
> After Camp duties went through the manual of war this morning—went over to see major Bell of Sims camp and made arrangements to learn saber drill—this evening made me a wooden saber.

> Sat. [October] 5th [1861] [diary]
> After breakfast heard articles of war read—some of the [pages missing]

Bates would not long be satisfied with his wooden practice saber. On October 14, when the men were officially mustered into Confederate service for twelve months, he was elected third lieutenant of his company, making him an officer worthy of a real sword.[16] He apparently visited family and friends in Paris in late October and purchased a saber on his way back to camp. At about the same time, the regiment received orders to proceed to Missouri where they expected to join Ben McCulloch's army in its defense of the northwest frontier of the Confederacy.

16. U.S. War Department, *The War of the Rebellion: A Compilation of the Official Records of the Union and Confederate Armies*, 128 vols. (Washington, D.C.: Government Printing Office, 1880–1901), Ser. I, Vol. 4, p. 144 [hereinafter cited as *OR;* unless otherwise indicated, all citations are to Series 1]; Kerr, ed., *Fighting with Ross' Texas Cavalry,* 230. Kerr's book, a valuable source for the history of the 9th Texas Cavalry, is an edited version of the diary kept by regimental adjutant George L. Griscom, who had access to official unit documents.

Camp Reeve Grayson Co Tex
Oct 26th 1861
Dear Ma & Sister

We arrived safely in camp on Wednesday night about 10 oclk [after our trip to Paris] and found all doing well—with the exception of Dan Hatcher & John Gibbons. Dan has had two or three chills since he had got well of the measles.[17]

I was in Sherman yesterday to get me a saber—got a very fine one for 7<u>50</u>$ [$7.50]. The Infantry Company at that place for Maxey's Reg. leave today for the Rendesvous.[18] I think the first Battalion of our Reg[iment]. will leave camp for a mission on Monday next—our Company will be of the number.

Tell Will [Bramlette] There is no chance to get a position in the Quarter Masters Department as it is full. If he had applied sooner I think he could have gotten it. Earheart's wagon has not got here. A man [missing page(s)]

it this evening some twelve miles below here with only three mules in it, Dave Anderson was driving and as he was drunk when he passed through Warren there is no telling where he has gone to.

We will not get our cloth in time to repair our tents and will have to do so on the road or after we get to Missouri.

I have not time to write more—but will write you again by Dr Earheart.

Very truly yours
J.C. Bates

Bates wrote his mother again the next day, giving further details about the impending move to join McCulloch's army. There is an air of excitement in his letter, indicating his eagerness to get to the seat of war in Missouri. His letters also imply that his brother-in-law, William "Will" Bramlette, was having second thoughts about letting Bates and Dohoney go to war

17. Dan C. Hatcher, a twenty-three-year-old clerk and friend of Bates, had worked with Will Bramlette before the war, surveying lines for a proposed railroad from Texarkana westward to the area near Sherman, Texas. John Gibbons, a second lieutenant in Bates's company, was a twenty-five-year-old native of Tennessee and another of Bates's friends from Paris. He would become one of the wealthiest men in Lamar County by the late 1860s. For Hatcher, see Kerr, ed., *Fighting with Ross' Texas Cavalry*, 231; Neville, *History of Lamar County*, 91. For Gibbons, see Neville, *History of Lamar County*, 143.

18. Samuel Bell Maxey's 9th Texas Infantry Regiment was organized about the same time as Bates's cavalry regiment. Stewart Sifakis, *Compendium of the Confederate Armies: Texas* (New York: Facts on File, 1995), 120; Wright and Simpson, *Texas in the War*, 86.

without him. Although he doubtless would have welcomed Bramlette into the regiment, Bates did find it useful to have an adult male in-law in Paris who could handle his business and legal affairs while he was away. In fact, Bramlette continued to handle Bates's business and tax dealings throughout the war.[19]

Camp Reeve Fannin Co Tex
Oct 27th 1861
My Dear Ma:

I wrote you a few lines by Ed Williams & promised to write again before leaving for Missouri though now I have not much more to write you than I said to you before.

The order for us to start on Monday, was yesterday countermanded, and Wednesday [October 30] is now the day fixed. I suppose by that time we will have every thing in readiness. You would hardly think that we knew this was Sunday if you were in camp a short time. All are as busily engaged at work as on any other day. An express came in on last night from Gen McCulloch stating that the Federal troops, 70,000 or 80,000 strong, were coming down on Ark.[20] McCulloch's and the other divisions of our army in Missouri were falling back into Ark. They do not number more than 30,000 or 40,000 men. It is necessary to concentrate as many troops as possible in northern Ark—to meet the Federal army—hence the reason we are so busy today—getting ready to march.

If Maxey's Reg are anxious for a fight they will have a chance soon, as Col Young says he is going down to propose to muster them in. If they refuse to be mustered in by him it will be because they prefer going to the coast—for the reason they think no fighting will be done there this winter. If they enlisted *to serve our Country* they will not hesitate as to the place they may be ordered or the dangers they may encounter.

19. For Bramlette's role as "agent" for Bates, see the property-tax records for Lamar County during the war years. County Real and Personal Property Tax Rolls (Lamar County), Ad Valorem Tax Division, Records of the Comptroller of Public Accounts, Record Group 304, Texas State Library and Archives Commission, Austin.

20. The Federal army that would eventually invade northwest Arkansas in February 1862 was much smaller than these early reports indicate. Rather than seventy or eighty thousand men, it would include only about eleven or twelve thousand. A brilliant study of this campaign is William L. Shea and Earl J. Hess, *Pea Ridge: Civil War Campaign in the West* (Chapel Hill: University of North Carolina Press, 1992).

I think the number of the federal army is greatly exagerated and the probabilities of a fight rather doubtful, at least this winter: and even if a fight should take place the troops we already have in the field together with about 25,000 militia from Ark that can be called into service on an emergency will be sufficient to whip them.

If Will had come up with us I expect he could have gotten a situation as Commissary for our Reg. As it [is] we will be on the march before this reaches you.

Tell William I want him to get Col Johnson to attend to the case in Miles court in which Howe sued me—I could not be at the trial and I suppose he got judgement against me. If he has I want the suit taken up to the District Court by a writ of *Certiorari*. If the necessary steps are not taken immediately there may not be time before the sixty days expire. A meeting was held about the time I was down at which all the Justices were requested to suspend all civil cases until after the war. If that was done it will not be necessary to do anything more in this case. Tell Will also to make some arrangements if convenient to pay Mr James for bringing up a beef for me to Mr Hatcher. Perhaps Mr Hatcher will pay him in shoes and deduct the amount from the value of the beef. Also to see or send word to old Mr Hathaway to send in ten bushels of wheat to John Falkner— being amount he agreed to give for outfit of our Company. Also see Sam Rucker and get him to accept some orders I drew on him, one at Dr Clements the other at Wright, Wortham & Gibbons—and to attend to my affairs generally.

[rest of letter missing]

A few days after Bates wrote this letter, his company finally rode out of its camp north of Sherman, bound for Ben McCulloch's army in Missouri. Other companies of the regiment left during the next few days, riding northeast up the Butterfield Stage line into Indian Territory (present-day Oklahoma), sometimes referred to as the Indian Nations or simply the Nations.[21] One last long letter before leaving, to his friend and future wife, Mootie, was filled with the idle musings and flirtations of a young man smitten by a pretty young girl. His request that she write him frequently and in detail reveals the serious hunger for news from home that most Civil War soldiers expressed, especially during their first few months in the army. Bates's anxiety that a major battle might be fought in Arkansas or Missouri

21. *OR*, Vol. 4, p. 144; Davis, *Cypress Rangers*, 33.

before his regiment could get there was a common fear among soldiers early in the war. Their eagerness to prove themselves in combat generally abated after their first heavy dose of battlefield gore.

Camp Reeve Oct 29th/61
Miss Mootie Johnson:

   We this morning take up the line of march for Missouri,—say a final goodbye to Texas and her good people hereabouts. *Not* a final goodbye either to Texas, I hope—, but only to these old camps— and before we take leave of Texas I must fulfill my promise to write to you. But even now that I have commenced I have nothing of special interest to write you.

   I do'nt know that others are like myself, but with me there is a vast difference in writing and *conversing*. If the person to whom I am writing could be present, *even to give an occasional nod*, the writing would be comparatively easy. But as you are *not* present I will just imagine you are nodding assent to all I say and proceed.

   We were delayed in Paris untill near noon, on the day we left, and in consequence did not get into camp untill 11 Oclk P.M. Wednesday.[22] If you had seen us laughing, and heard our jokes and jests, after leaving Paris, you *might* have thought we cared little for those we were leaving behind. But I suppose all were like myself, thought that if we did not go to an extreme of merriment we would fall into a worse one—that of sadness and we chose the former as more philosophical, and made an effort to accommodate ourselves to circumstances. We found all in good health in camp except for John Gibbons and Dan H[atcher] both of whom were just recovering from the measles. As John seemed in rather low spirits, I delivered him a good many messages (good ones of course) *more than you sent*. But I thought it pardonable under the circumstances as he seemed *considerably relieved by them*.

   I felt too, a strong inclination to show him a *beautiful picture* I have, but remembering my promise did not do so.[23] I am sure it would have had a more magical effect in bringing about a cure than any prescription the Doctors could have given him—(judging him by myself).

   There was one "Message" however given me by you (with a re-

22. Here Bates refers to his recent visit to Paris and the return trip to camp.
23. Bates carried a small portrait of Mootie with him throughout the war.

quest, if I'm not mistaken, that I would give it to John) that I have not yet delivered, and I hope you will excuse me from doing so. As it was *from your lips* that I received this last parting "Message" (of the kind) on leaving—so you shall be the first to give the "welcome home" when I return—provided always that I may be the fortunate one you may *wish* to welcome first. Such Messages are generally thought but little of when received through a second person consequently no great injustice can be done John by my withholding it; so I have concluded to keep it myself, *for fear I may never receive another*. Besides John will see you before leaving and you can give him one, (not the one you gave me though) in person. But enough on this subject; and I expect you have *thought* the same before reading this far.

I have heard of several marriages in Lamar since coming up. Miss Mollie Womack & John Buck amongst the rest. I have thought for some time that John wished (and needed, as all such "nice young men" do) some one to take care of him, but was a little surprised that Miss Mollie would undertake the task. Or, maybe, those who seem so anxious just at present, to get into the "Noose Matrimonial" think there is more patriotism (or *safety* I wo'nt say which) in remaining at home, than in fighting the battles of their country.

By the way tell Miss Jennie she and Mr R must wait untill we return, as she promised me I should be at the wedding. What marrying and giving in marriage there will be when this war closes—provided it does not last so long there will be none left *to marry*—and provided further if those who may be left are not *too* poor to marry.

As we may be so situated that we cannot hear from you as often as we would wish; and as it would give us (me at least) much pleasure to know what is taking place in Paris *every day*, of interest,—and every event, no matter how small, will possess an interest to us that none can appreciate unless situated as we are—what say you to keeping a *diary*? if not in regular form, at least of making a note of each day's occurrences. As in the beginning I took for granted that you were "nodding assent" to all I wrote, I will now assume that you have no objections to this arrangement—and will therefore expect to read in your first letter all that has been done in Paris, or will be, after your reception of this untill you write—all that others do—all that *you* do—all—no not all but a *part* of your thoughts &c [etc.]. But you probably think I am expecting too much. I will not *ask* you to give me any of your thoughts—though if you do, nothing you may write will be read with more pleasure.

If you but knew with what avidity every thing in the way of "news from home" is devoured—so to speak—by us you would be sure to write *often* and *long* letters when you did write. If you will do as much, I will write *regularly* whether I receive answers to my letters or not.

An express arrived in Camp from Gen McCulloch on last night urging us to march as soon as possible. The Confederate forces were falling back to Fayetteville Ark—where they intended—if possible to make a stand. Gen Wool is reported to have seventy thousand troops, though I doubt this very much.[24] I am very much afraid our Regiment will not be able to reach them before the fight if a fight should take place this winter. Before the arrival of this last express (the first came in some days since) I hardly thought there would be a general engagement before spring; but the last if true leaves little room for doubt that there will. Well if a glorious victory is to be won by our army—which I know *will* be the case if a battle is fought with anything like an equal force on our side—I wish to be present and participate in it, and if we are to suffer defeat I want to be with them in that too.

Well, I expect your patience is wearied ere this, in reading so much to hear so little—so as Pat said "I will bring my letter to a stop."

Give my best wishes to Miss Mary—you may give her *more* than that if she will accept it.[25] Say to her I have not forgotten my promise to write—but will redeem it *soon*, before leaving Texas if possible. And I must not forget Mat.[26] Tell her to study hard—learn fast—and if she does not think Mr Young would object to her corre-

24. Bates apparently had received faulty information about the Union commander. The only Federal general named Wool was John E. Wool, then stationed in Virginia. Ezra J. Warner, *Generals in Blue: Lives of the Union Commanders* (Baton Rouge: Louisiana State University Press, 1964), 573–74.

25. Mary was Mootie's older sister and E. L. Dohoney's future wife. Dohoney described Mary as blond, five feet six inches tall, and weighing 110 pounds. In a presumed compliment, he wrote that Mary's "digestive organs" were so strong that "she developed into a portly woman of 165 pounds in weight." The couple would eventually raise eight children to adulthood. In a humorous characterization of his marriage, Dohoney wrote that "he is a reformer and a crank; she a Christian and a fogy." Dohoney, *Average American*, 173, 174.

26. Mat was Mootie's younger sister.

sponding with a "young gentleman" I would like very much to have a letter from her. As I intended to close this letter some time before this I will now do so by saying good night and sending you many good wishes from
Your Sincerest of Friends
James C. Bates

I said in the beginning of this letter we started this morning which of course could not be, as that time is past. I intended to write *to-morrow morning.* J.C.B.

Another post script! I neglected to say—that in return for your "Diary" I would send you some jottings by the way of passing events &c. I cannot now tell you where to direct your letters—but will give you my address as soon as we arrive at our destination.

Oct 29th '61 Thursday 12 miles [diary]

The long looked for order to march was given yesterday—and this morning at 8 A.M. ocl[oc]k our tents were struck and we took up the line of march. Reached our present encampment at 2 P.M. this evening. Traveled 12 miles. After eating a snack, took a stroll down in the Red River bottom where I found some delicious mustang grapes.

Oct. 30th '61 Friday 15 miles [diary]

This morning about an hour before day—wind shifted around to the north and at sun up a cold heavy mist began to fall which soon increased to a heavy shower and continued to fall at short intervals during most of the day. We have today a foretaste of the weather we may expect in Miss[ouri]. Got to our camping ground at 1 oclk. Built up a fire. Pitched our tents—ate a good hearty dinner and bid defiance to the storm.

Averaging about thirteen miles per day—far fewer than they would routinely travel later in the war—the various companies of the new regiment eventually gathered in early November at Boggy Depot, about fifty miles northeast of their old camp near Sherman. Boggy Depot, the Choctaw capital in the Indian Territory, was a thriving trade center on the Butterfield Stage line. Among the little town's attractions was a trading post where Indians sold trinkets and souvenirs. "The soldiers of the regiment bought quite a lot of these gaudy things and on the march next day presented all the colors of the rainbow in fringes, handkerchiefs, shawls, etc.," one veteran of Company I remembered later.[27]

Saturday 31st Oct Sunday Monday 2nd Nov '61 [diary]

Yesterday and today traveled 25 miles. Got to Boggy Depot at 9 oclk. Passed over some very fine country—mostly prairie and sandy post oak. We are now encamped on Boggy river 1 mile from Boggy. The valley betwixt Big & Little Boggy is the finest I have seen in the [Indian] nation.

Sunday Nov 8th '61 [diary]

After stoping at Boggy several days we resumed our march on yesterday. Today we are encamped 35 miles from B[oggy Depot] on a beautiful little stream on the north side of which rises a tall range of mountains—some 400–500 feet high. After eating a snack started to take some observations. After clambering up over rocks & brush we at last reached the most beautiful summit—the most elevated point where we had a splendid view of the country in every direction. On the very summit stood a solitary tree. After admiring the scenery for some time I concluded that I would occupy a high position in the world one time—look at it from an elevated point once in my life & I therefore took off my arms—firearms I mean & if I did'nt get up as quickly or as gracefully as a squirrel I did manage to clamber up about 30 or 40 feet and had one of the finest views imaginable.

As the men of Bates's regiment rode through the Indian Territory toward their rendezvous in northwestern Arkansas, they had no idea that they were about to be drawn into a deep and long-standing feud among factions of the Five Civilized Tribes of the Indian Territory (the Choctaws, Chickasaws, Cherokees, Creeks, and Seminoles). These tribes, forcibly relocated from the eastern United States before the Civil War, had little reason to side with either the United States or the Confederacy. Indeed, many hoped they could avoid the white man's war altogether. But their close proximity to the fighting in Missouri and Arkansas, their rivalries with and suspicions of each other, and heavy recruiting efforts by both the Union

27. Sparks, *War Between the States*, 22; Pat Carr, ed., *In Fine Spirits: The Civil War Letters of Ras Stirman* (Fayetteville, Ark.: Washington County Historical Society, 1986), 1.

and the Confederacy ultimately drew the Indians into the conflict. For their own reasons, most of the Choctaws and Chickasaws sided with the Confederacy. The Cherokees, Creeks, and Seminoles, however, were divided. About half were not so much pro-Union as they were neutral—they preferred to avoid the aggressive Confederate recruiters in the territory and withdraw among themselves.

In the autumn of 1861, roughly six thousand of these Indians—men, women, children, and all their animals and belongings—gathered near present-day Okemah, about eighty straight-line miles due north of Boggy Depot, preparatory to a cross-country trek to Union-held Kansas. There, they hoped, they could shelter under the protecting arms of the United States Army and avoid the five Confederate regiments raised among their Indian enemies.[28]

The leader of these fugitives was a remarkable chief of the Creek tribe, Opothle Yahola. About eighty years old, he gathered the thousands of anxious Creeks, Seminoles, and Cherokees at his camp north of Boggy Depot and in November led them northward, fleeing the war and their old enemies among the Choctaws and Chickasaws. The leader of the pro-Confederate Indians was Colonel Douglas H. Cooper, a Mississippi planter who had been a Federal agent in the Indian Territory before the war and the man who had raised the five regiments of Confederate Indians. Cooper initially tried to negotiate with Opothle Yahola, but the chief's rivals within the Creek tribe convinced Cooper that Opothle Yahola and his column were a threat to prosouthern Indians and demanded military action. Consequently, Cooper and his Indian regiments (about four thousand men) began a pursuit of Opothle Yahola in mid-November, determined to bring him under Confederate control or drive him out of the territory.[29]

At almost precisely the same time, Bates and his fellow troopers happened to be riding nearby along the north fork of the Canadian River

28. A good summary of the situation in Indian Territory in the fall of 1861 is Hale, "Rehearsal for Civil War," 229–35. For more detailed treatments, see Annie H. Abel, *The American Indian as Slaveholder and Secessionist* (Cleveland: Arthur H. Clark, 1915); Larry C. Rampp and Donald L. Rampp, "The Civil War in Indian Territory: The Confederate Advantage, 1861–1862," *Military History of Texas and the Southwest* 10 (No. 1, 1972): 29–41; Angie Debo, *The Road to Disappearance: A History of the Creek Indians* (1941; reprint, Norman: University of Oklahoma Press, 1967).

29. Sifakis, *Who Was Who,* 478; Richard N. Current, ed., *Encyclopedia of the Confederacy* (4 vols., New York: Simon & Schuster, 1993), 1:409; *OR,* Vol. 8, pp. 5–14; Kerr, ed., *Fighting with Ross' Texas Cavalry,* 3; Davis, *Cypress Rangers,* 35; Hale, "Rehearsal for Civil War," 234–35.

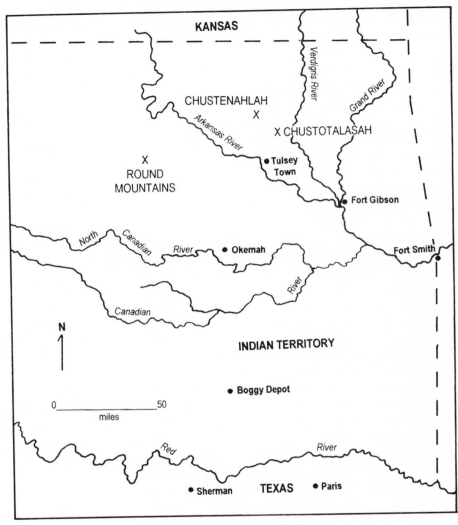

North Texas and the Indian Territory

(a few miles from present-day Eufaula, Oklahoma), and on November 11 Cooper called on Sims's regiment to join him in the pursuit of Opothle Yahola's band.

Nov 11th '61 [diary]

    At 8 A.M. oclk with 500 men under command of Col Quayle and Maj Townes, we started on the march.[30] We proceeded in a NW direction until 4 P.M. in the evening having traveled about 25 miles. Here we halted—fed our horses a little corn—rested an hour & again moved on just at sunset. A messenger came from Cooper saying he was falling back towards us and for us to move on to his camp that night. As some danger was apprehended of an attempt being made to cut us off, the order was given to march in perfect silence —keep in order—ready for any emergency. An advance guard was sent ahead. We moved out at a rapid pace—sometimes in a trot— frequently in a gallop all the rest of the way to Cooper's Camp where we arrived at 12 P.M. oclk having marched about 60 or 65 miles during the day.

When Bates's column finally dragged into Cooper's camp late that night, about forty-five miles south of present-day Tulsa, Cooper's Indians greeted the weary Texans with shouts and the firing of guns. Before the united columns set out in pursuit of Opothle Yahola a few days later, the Indians favored the gawking Texans with a war dance. A private in Company I of Bates's regiment wrote that "a ring was filled with painted Indians, all marching in a side-like manner, stepping high and fast, while they chanted a strange song." Some of the Texans got the spirit and joined their Indian allies, dancing and whooping under the dark skies of the Indian Territory. It is doubtful that Bates sang and danced with the Indians; he regarded them as too strange and undisciplined to be of much use in the coming campaign.[31]

Nov 15th [1861] [diary]

    It was decided at the war talk on yesterday evening that we would today start on a forced march on pursuit of Pothleohola or *Gouge* as

30. Colonel Sims sent only his healthiest five hundred troopers to Cooper's aid. He detoured the other half of the regiment and his supply wagons northward toward the Arkansas River. Hale, "Rehearsal for Civil War," 235.

31. Sparks, *War Between the States,* 26; Kerr, ed., *Fighting with Ross' Texas Cavalry,* 4.

he is classically called.[32] In pursuance to this determination at 8 A.M. oclk we took up the line of march—our little army being composed of 500 men of our Reg—700 Choctaws and 4 or 500 Creeks. The creeks & Choctaws preceded us untill we arrived in the prairie 1 mile from camp—where we all halted to form in regular order of marching—the Creeks in front, our Reg in the center & Choctaws in rear.

We were greeted on our arrival on the field with whoops & yells & screams—such as I never heard before. Most of the Indian faces were painted red with streaks & spots of black presenting a most hideous appearance. After being detained a short time we again resumed our march proceeding in a NW direction untill noon when our course was changed a little more westerly. at 5 P.M. we were halted in the prairie & our company sent 1/2 mile from the road to get corn. We unthoughtedly went up to the house in a gallop & the Indian woman (a widow) living there was so frightened at our approach that she took to the woods. There is no telling how far she went. Took up camp tonight at 8 oclk. If there is an enemy near at hand our Indian brethren will certainly be cut up—have so little order.

Nov 16th '61 [1861] [diary]

At 6 AM again started on the march. Before starting, a piece of white cloth was given to each man to tie on his arm to distinguish him from the enemy. Traveled over poor sandy country—Indian settlement—occasionally sent out a foraging party to kill meat, procure corn, &c. Marched 15 miles & took up camp. After stoping[,] not less than 100 Indians began shooting hogs & cattle untill any man who wanted meat for supper killed a beef or hog & cut a piece out leaving the balance in the woods. If old Gouge does'nt attack us it will be because he is not near at hand and because he is a coward. Two hundred well armed men can rout the whole rabble for this army is no more. if this expedition is conducted according to the usages of military affairs generally then I have formed a very erroneous opinion of how things should be done. I am heartily tired of Indian alliances if all are like [this].

The Texans and their Indian allies, moving generally to the northwest, expected to run up against Opothle Yahola's band at any moment. On

32. Bates, like many of his comrades, was inventive in the spelling of Opothle Yahola's name.

November 17 they received a report that the old Creek chief was nearby, threatening a detachment that had been sent ahead. This was only one of several rumors of contact with the enemy, all of which proved inaccurate. When Bates and his unit were sent off to rescue the supposedly threatened detachment, they got lost and wandered around the prairies for three hours before discovering that the call for help was another false alarm, much to Bates's disgust.

Nov 17th, 1861 [diary]

A council was held last night and as we [are] in the enemy country—it may be in close proximity—it was ordered that the men sleep in line on their arms ready at a moments warning for a determined defense. Think Potheohola not in this section or he would have attacked us. Stood guard on line from 1 AM to 4 AM ready to wake men in case of alarm. After 8 mile march scouts brought in news— had seen signs of enemy. Regiment thrown into twos & fours—& front into line then into column of squadron—com[panies]—platoons—more I think for the purpose of drilling than anything else. Two miles more at a rapid march—halted 1/2 hour. Changed our course to water in a creek near at hand. Just as the last two companies were watering, report of firing in front was received by our company. Capt [Gideon] Smith [of Company B] hurried on but found the alarm to be caused by Indians shooting hogs—turned 2 miles down the river. Camped just after the beating of the retreat at 9 PM. A messenger came in from Col [Daniel M.] McIntosh saying Opotheola was only 6 miles off (Mc[Intosh] had gone 5 miles on ahead). The order to saddle up was given. Reached McIntosh in 3 hours—found Gouge nowhere near.[33]

Opothle Yahola's band had been burning the countryside's grass, crops, and food stores as they fled north, leaving very little for the pursuing Confederates to feed their horses—or themselves. Virtually every Confederate account of this pursuit mentions the shortage of food and forage. One famished Texan moaned that he could eat one of the numerous dead dogs rotting in the wake of the fleeing Indians. "From that moment on I was

33. The Creek colonel Daniel N. McIntosh commanded a Creek cavalry regiment (Confederate) on this expedition. His family was embroiled in a long-standing blood feud with Opothle Yahola. The Texans who galloped to his supposed rescue, including Bates, took a wrong road, backtracked, veered off in another wrong direction, and finally traveled about twenty-five miles to cover less than ten. Kerr, ed., *Fighting with Ross' Texas Cavalry*, 4–5, 23.

hungry," a private in Company I remembered. "I was suffering. I was extremely hungry." The Texans were soon reduced to picking up acorns and chewing on them as they rode across the prairies.[34]

> Nov 18th 1861 [diary]
> Started this morning at sun up. No feed for horses. Cooper would not stop for corn [even though it was with]in 1/2 mile. Marched hard all day—no sign of Gouge—traveled 35 miles. Camped in Gouge's old camp. Some camp fires still burning. No corn for horses. Our bread all out—nothing to eat but beef ourselves.

James C. Bates must have been disappointed with military life at this point. So far, it had been nothing like the exciting stories of courage and boldness that Texans loved so much. He had not yet struck a blow for Texas or the Confederacy. And although he had enjoyed some riveting scenery in his travels, he had also experienced fatigue, hunger, and disgust at some of his allies. But his life was about to become more interesting.

34. Sparks, *War Between the States,* 31–32; Kerr, ed., *Fighting with Ross' Texas Cavalry,* 4–5.

2 Indian Territory

Chasing fugitives across the Indian Territory had not been uppermost in the minds of James C. Bates and his fellow Texans when they volunteered to protect the Confederacy from Yankee aggression. On the other hand, north Texans had always cast a wary eye across the Red River, fearing Indian raids on their farms and villages, so neutralizing a band of Yankee Indians before taking on the legions of Abraham Lincoln made some sense. Corral Opothle Yahola's band first, then off to Missouri.

The Texans and the Confederate Indians chasing after Opothle Yahola finally caught up to the old chief and his band in mid-November, about forty-five miles west of present-day Tulsa. Late on the afternoon of November 19, scouts of the 9th Texas Cavalry spied an enemy vidette stalking them in the distance. When two companies gave chase, the wily fox led the hounds into an ambush. As he fled before them, the scout set fire to the dry prairie grass, sending up clouds of smoke and obscuring the vision of the Texans, already squinting in the gathering darkness. Opothle Yahola's warriors, concealed in the brush and trees in two converging lines of timber, waited as the approaching Texans galloped deeper into the V, too close to be missed by rifles and bows. When the pursuers were within fifty yards of the hidden defenders, the Indians rose up and loosed volley after volley of rifle fire and arrows into the surprised column of Texas horsemen.[1]

1. Sparks, *War Between the States,* 33; Hale, "Rehearsal for Civil War," 238; Angie Debo, "The Location of the Battle of Round Mountains," *Chronicles of Oklahoma* 41 (Spring 1963): 70–104; Charles Bahos, "On Opothleyahola's Trail: Locating the Battle of Round Mountains," ibid., 63 (Spring 1985): 58–59.

The wide-eyed Texans pulled up and wheeled around in all directions, confused by the smoke, the dying light, and the invisible surrounding enemy. Firing wildly, the horsemen could aim only at the flashes from the Indian rifles. Private A. W. Sparks of Company I saw his own captain shot through the head. "The ball that killed him on passing out of his head threw a large wad of his brain upon the sleeve and collar of my coat," Sparks remembered nearly forty years later. Four other Texans fell from their saddles, and the pursuers now became the pursued. Ben Vines, also of Company I, wrote to his wife that "they run us in a place where we had no chance to dodge. We was surrounded with Creaks except one little space where we marched in." Finding that escape was possible only by re-tracing the path they had followed into the trap, the Texans began to back-track. "The enemy was discharging their guns from every side except the side in which we marched in at," Vines told his wife. "We continued firing until we had discharged our guns about three times when we found we was almost surrounded and was compelled to retreat back. We comminced retreating back firing on the enemy until we had went about one half of a mile. When we called a halt and discharged our guns about 3 [more] time [*sic*]."[2]

Meanwhile, the remainder of the regiment, including Bates and the men of Company H, hearing firing in the distance, were coming up to the fight. By now all they could see ahead of them were shadows against the burning prairie. Warren Coffman, who had been guarding the wagon train, was one of the Texans who rode up to assist, but he found only con-fusion: "at this moment was fired on by our men we was greatly confused & giving them our password Texas they run off in the dark   they thought us to be Indians I confess this made me feel curious though. I felt very much like shooting after I was shot at." Not far behind were Colonel Cooper's horsemen, who rode up to the left of the Texans, within sixty yards of the pursuing Creeks, dismounted, and fired by the light of the prairie-grass fire. After fifteen minutes of this exchange, the Creeks melted into the darkness, and the little Battle of Round Mountains was over.[3]

Six days later Bates wrote his mother a long letter, bringing her up to

2. Sparks, *War Between the States*, 34; Benjamin R. Vines to My Dear Wife and babe, No-vember 30, 1861, 9th Texas Cavalry File, Confederate Research Center, Hill College, Hills-boro, Tex.

3. Warren Coffman to William Coffman, December 7, 1861, 9th Texas Cavalry File, Confederate Research Center; Sparks, *War Between the States*, 35; Gris [George L. Griscom] to Dear Herald, November 24, 1861, *Dallas Herald*, December 18, 1861; *OR,* Vol. 8, pp. 5–6, 14; Hale, "Rehearsal for Civil War," 238–40.

date on the regiment's activities since leaving camp near Sherman. Much of his letter repeated information in his November diary, but he also described his experience at Round Mountains. This letter and many later ones to his mother, Adela, and Mootie reveal Bates's respect for the women in his life. Unlike some Civil War soldiers, he did not confine his letters to women to domestic and family matters. He also gave them the latest military and political news, added his own opinions on those topics, and invited their discussion.

In Camp on Ark River
Nov 25th 1861
Dear Ma;

The last letter I wrote you was from Grayson county [Texas]—near a month since: and I expect therefore, that you are becoming somewhat uneasy at not hearing from me before this. I wrote to you from Boggy Depot but the man to whom I gave the letter failed to mail it. Since then I have had no opportunity of sending a letter. After leaving Texas we came on to the north fork of the Canadian [River, near present-day Eufaula, Oklahoma] where we met an express, from Gen Cooper in command of the Indian forces, ordering us to leave our trains behind and proceed immediately by forced march to his camp 75 miles north of there. The express came [at] about 8 or 9 oclk on the evening of the 11th [of November].[4]

Ammunition was at once issued and we were ordered to prepare [missing word owing to tear in letter] rounds of cartridge and two days provisions and in half hour every man in camp was busily engaged getting ready for the march. At 2 Oclk most of our preparations were ready and we lay down and slept untill 4—when we again got up—finished our preparations, got our breakfast, and were on the march soon after sunrise. We moved on in a rapid march—untill 4 in the evening when we halted, fed our horses, took a snack ourselves—and again started intending to take up for the night some 15 miles from there—but after marching 2 or 3 hours we met another express from Cooper saying that he was retreating to meet us—& urging us to hurry on as fast as possible. Although we had already marched some 35 miles—it was determined that we would push on to meet him—expecting either that an attempt would be made to cut us off or that we would find Cooper engaged with the

4. The message arrived on the evening of November 10.

enemy—we had 20 miles farther to go and most of this distance was made in either a trot or gallop at 12 Oclk that night we arrived [at] Coopers camp—having marched 60 miles that day. But after all this hard marching, when [we got] to Cooper's camp—the enemy [had not] been seen near there for some days. Nor indeed had they *ever* been nearer than 25 miles. You may know that we were not a little vexed at riding our horses so hard to no purpose.

But all this time I have not told you who the *enemy* are. They are principally Creek Indians—with the remnant of a few wild tribes together with a few jay hawkers—all headed by one of the Chiefs of the Creeks—his name is *Opotheohola* or as we call him—"Gouge." When our force got into Cooper's camp—amounting to about 500 the balance having been left behind to protect the trains—Cooper decided to pursue old "Gouge" and give him a fight. After resting a couple days—with about a thousand Choctaw[,] Creek & a few Seminole Indians we started in pursuit carrying six days rations with us and leaving Coopers trains to meet ours at that place. If I had time I would give you the particulars of the whole trip. But let it suffice to say that after two days of forced marching [we] came to Gouge's camp—(an old one that he had left several days before) That night (the second one from Coopers [camp]) Col [Daniel M.] McIntosh in command of the [Confederate] Creek regiment who camped six miles in advance of us—sent an express back to us saying that his scouts had come in and reported old Gouge in six miles of him advancing to attack him (McIntosh). This was just as we were going to bed. We were immediately ordered to saddle and mount our horses—and in a few minutes we were again on a forced march. The Choctaw Regiment was before us and the guide with them. In crossing a creek we got lost from them—and as we had no guide—we rambled about over hills and mountains untill after one oclk before we found McIntosh—and when we did find him we found him in no danger. Why he sent back such an express I cant imagine. Old Gouge was then not nearer than 50 miles of us tho' we did not know it at the time.

Well the next morning—although there was an abundance of corn within a mile and a half—Gen Cooper ordered us to start without feeding. We traveled about 30 miles—camped again in one of old Gouge's camps some of the camp fires still burning. Nothing again for our horses to eat for we were by this time out of all the settlements and the enemy had burned all the grass as they retreated.

The next day [November 19] at noon came to the red fork of the Ark[ansas River]—found some cattle that "Gouge" had left which [we] immediately pitched into—(ours had given out the day before). We formed for the fight. The Texas Reg composed the right wing. The Choctaw the center and the Creek the left wing. We saw the smoke from the camp fires rising for about 1/2 a mile up and down a little creek in front of us and in this we supposed we would certainly find the enemy. We therefore advanced as above formed— but found the camp deserted. After crossing the creek—a portion of our Reg. was detached to scour the woods on the left. This portion pushed on rapidly and after coming out of the timber saw the [Confederate] Creek Reg. galloping on about 1/2 mile in advance—supposing that they were in hot pursuit of the enemy. These companies that had been detached from our Reg. moved out and joined the Creeks and in company with them followed on after the enemy— just at sundown we emerged from the timber as we saw them passing over a hill about a mile from us.

Gen Cooper ordered the remainder of our Reg. (in which was our own Company) and the Choctaws to halt. We did so and after remaining there for some time, we concluded that those ahead would soon return as it was then getting too dark to pursue them. Gen Cooper therefore ordered us back to the creek we had crossed to camp. Back there we went and had just taken our saddles off— when word came in that three companies of our Reg were engaged with about a thousand Indians. We immediately saddled again fell into line went out to the prairie and were formed in order of battle. We had scarcely formed when we heard firing—ahead—but it was now so dark that we could not distinguish an Indian from a white man [at] three paces. The firing drew nearer, but we were afraid that if we advanced on them we would be as likely to kill our friends as the enemy—particularly as it was almost impossible for us to tell even in daylight which of the Indians were our friends and which our enemies. It was therefore deemed most advisable for us to remain as we were for a time at least and await events.

The Choctaws had been formed on our left—and rather in advance of us. The firing still drew nearer—& by the light of a prairie burning some half a mile in front of us we could see their passing occasionally. (This prairie had been set on fire by the enemy when they had fled from the camp we expected to find them in.) Our men passed about 1/4 of a mile from us and fell back on the Choctaws on our left who were formed ready to receive the enemy. As soon as the Choctaws opened fire the enemy fled. I neglected to say—our men ran into an ambush—where they were fired on in front and on both flanks. The [Confederate] Creeks immediately fled—and left the Texans to take care of themselves. As there was but one opening left they were forced to escape through it. The enemy were variously estimated at 600 to 1,000. Our men retreated in good order loading and firing as they fell back.

Our Battalion was commanded by Maj Townes[;] our Company [H]—[Captain Gideon] Smith's [Company B] of Fannin [County,] [Captain W. E.] Duncan's [Company F] of Cass [County] & [Captain Joseph C.] Harts [Company E] of Red River [County] comprised this. The other Battalion commanded by Col Quayle—was comprised of Capt [Thomas G.] Berry's [Company A] of Tarrant [County,] [Captain M. J.] Brinsons [Company D] of Tarrant— [Captain J. E.] McCool's [Company C] of Grayson [County,] [Captain James P.] Williams [Company K] of Hopkins [County] and [Captain Charles S.] Stewart's [Company I] of Titus [County]. Our loss was 6 killed and 4 wounded Capt Stewart among the former. The enemy's loss as estimated according to the graves by our Indian allies at over 100—but I suppose not more than 40 or 50.

I have not time to write more—just got to trains this evening. After living on beef for over a week—feel as well as if I had fared sumptuously—only gives us a relish for what we have in camp.[5]

As our scouts (all Indians and Creeks at that) still brot in no news of the enemy and as our horses had been 2 days and 3 nights without a mouthful of anything to eat not even grass and as we ourselves were out of bread and had been for a day or so, Gen Cooper thought it advisable to strike for our trains. The Creeks under McIntosh were for following on; but as we had no idea as to how far the enemy were ahead—it seemed folly to go on with jaded horses. Our Reg and the Choctaws therefore turned to the right about and struck for camp leaving the Creek Reg parleying as to what to do. We recrossed the Red Fork—and had gone a mile or two—when an express came up from the rear and reported Opotheola or "Gouge"—as certainly within six or eight miles of us on the trail that we had been following before turning back. We therefore again wheeled to the right

5. The last two paragraphs of this letter were written on a separate sheet. Judging by the repetition of some information, these paragraphs appear to be part of a different letter. Bates may have sent both letters in the same envelope.

about—and after about 5 hours—we came in sight of the enemy's camp—we were not mistaken this time. The sun was not more than 1/2 an hour high when we were [page(s) missing]

Don't know whether we will be ordered to Gen McCulloch's or into winter quarters. I will have an opportunity of writing again in a day or two and will do so. I don't know whether this is sufficiently intelligible for you to make sense of it or not. I have not time now to look over it to correct mistakes as it is 12 oclk and I must have some sleep. The gentleman who carries this leaves in the morning before day for Sherman. Give my love to all and to yourself. The love of your son,
J.C. Bates

Nov 19th, 1861 [diary]

Started this morning with jaded horses. After a march of fifteen miles came to Red fork of the Arkansas. Poor rolling prairie. No timber on south side. Scrub oak on north. Found some stray stock Gouge had left. Killed them—made a good meal on beef alone. Cooper determined to abandon the chase. Turned our course east. After traveling five or six miles an express came in from Creeks saying that Potheohola's camp was found. After a short consultation we were ordered to right about and proceed at a brisk trot toward the enemy's supposed locality. A prisoner taken today confirms the report of the scouts. Two hours march of ten miles brought us in sight of the enemy's camp. Formed for attack—our Reg on right—Creeks on left—Choctaws in center—proceeded into [enemy] camp—found it deserted. Creeks found some straggling Indians—pursued them. Berry—McCool—Benson's & William's command—thinking they were after enemy followed. Pursued them four miles & suddenly found themselves in an ambush—fired on in front & both flanks—returned the fire & retreated in good order—loading & firing all the time.

After going through woods we were ordered to halt by Cooper—Choctaw regiment formed on left—thinking Creeks & our companies would return in a short time—ordered back to camp—just as we unsaddled—report that our men in advance were engaged with the enemy—retreating—when we were again ordered to saddle.

Proceeded to prairie by companies. Formed Wright's—Smith's—Hart's—Duncan's companies. Choctaws 1/4 mile on left. Just as we got formed heard firing ahead—which came steadily on—saw by light of our fire—our men retreating 1/2 mile off—pursued by enemy—fell back to our left where they were fortunately relieved by Choctaws. As soon as Choctaws opened fire, enemy fled. Just before firing was over we were fired on from the rear. Order was given to right about—was done—but as some doubt existed as to whether these might not be our friends firing on us by mistake we were ordered not to fire. The pass word TEXAS was given but not returned. Col Borland thinks they were part of the enemy attempting to cut off our men who first engaged them but suddenly came on us and were stoped. One half hour after fighting ceased and fight over—bugles sounded. Our troops collected & formed in hollow square—remained so untill all troops collected—ordered back to camp—ordered to sleep on our arms—horses saddled at 10 AM. Alarm given in Creek camp—our men instantly in line—ready for any emergency or enemy. Alarm caused by sentinel being fired on— eight or ten shots returned. At 12 laid down & slept untill 4 PM.

Although the Texans had been surprised and driven back in their first fight, they claimed Round Mountains as a victory because Opothle Yahola had abandoned his camp and retreated during the night. The next day, when the Confederates scouted the northern horizon to find the fugitives' trail, they discovered large stockpiles of food and belongings abandoned by the retreating Creeks. They also found the corpses of some of their comrades, scalped and mutilated by their captors.[6]

November 20th 1861 [diary]

By daylight all men mounted and ready for march. Nothing for horses to eat—only a few blades dry grass—determined to pursue the enemy. Capt [Thomas G.] Berry's Company [A] went ahead to draw enemy out—we followed on but found camp deserted. Creeks composed right—Choctaws center & our Reg left. My squadron left wing—flanked by Berry—[Captain Joseph C.] Hart [and Company E] on one side & N.C. & others on left—again found camp deserted—followed trail several miles. As no signs of enemy seen our horses & selves almost worn out determined to return—in old Potheohola's camp found two of our men taken prisoner by them & beaten to death. Burned & destroyed 15 or 20 wagons with their

6. Sparks, *War Between the States*, 37; Rose, *Ross' Texas Brigade*, 50; Hale, "Rehearsal for Civil War," 240.

contents left by old Gouge. Captured 20 or 30 ponies, 40 or 50 beef and oxen—returned to old camp for night—found some more of our men who had been killed in the fight—making in all 5 men found. Indian graves—one contained sixteen men—saw several others. Thinking by size some 40 or 50 Indians in all were killed. Returned to old camp. Attended to sick & wounded, hauled latter in two of old Gouge's wagons. Moved two miles lower on creek to camp.

Colonel Cooper, overall commander of the forces pursuing Opothle Yahola, about this time received orders from General Ben McCulloch in Missouri to hurry his regiments to the Arkansas border—Federal forces in Missouri were again moving south and threatening northwest Arkansas. Moreover, Cooper realized that his horses needed forage and time to recuperate from their pursuit of the fugitives across the burned-over prairies of the Indian Territory. He therefore turned his little army eastward on November 21, bound for their wagon trains at Concharta on the Arkansas River, about seventy miles southeast of the Round Mountains battlefield.[7] The curious and observant Bates had time to record the sights as he accompanied the column toward Concharta.

November 21st 1861 [diary]

Last night camped on a branch of the Red Fork [of the Arkansas River]. Two hundred horses herded on one acre dry grass. Rested well last night. Breakfasted on beef & coffee. Traveled fifteen miles. Stoped one half hour to rest. After dinner proceeded on march. Passed this evening a couple of Kickapoo graves. They have a singular manner of burying their dead. Instead of burying in the ground, the person is placed in a sitting posture with the back against the stake. A rawhide strap is passed around the body and made fast to the stake. A little pen is then built around the body—higher than the head—with a window in the east & in front of the face so they can see the sun rise. This pen is then filled in with earth—covered—and thus they are left.

Bates and his comrades—and their horses—had not had a decent meal since they left their main column on November 11. Once again they were reduced to scavenging for acorns and wild nuts on their long ride toward

7. *OR,* Vol. 8, p. 7.

Concharta. Occasionally, they appropriated animals and vegetables from abandoned farms along their route, thus explaining Bates's satisfactory meal of November 23.[8]

November 22nd [1861] [diary]
Camped last night on Salt Creek—which is well-named for the water is so salty we could not drink it—even in coffee—so we had to take dry beef alone without even water to wash it down. Found some large over cap acorns today which we devoured like half starved hogs. made a very good dinner today on roasted acorns & beef. Supped on pecans & beef. Traveled twenty five miles.

November 23rd [1861] [diary]
Last night just as we had gone to bed—a very heavy storm of rain came up and we were without tents and with only two blankets each—most of us got well drenched—built up a roaring fire—dried our blankets & slept an hour or two. This morning a stiff norther blowing. Traveled twenty five miles. Took up camp—made a good supper on roasted kid & potatoes. Only fifteen miles to camp.

Finally, on November 24, the gaunt riders of the 9th Texas Cavalry reached their main camp on the Arkansas River at Concharta, about thirty miles southeast of present-day Tulsa. The main attraction of the camp, of course, was plentiful food. The irrepressible Private Sparks of Company I described the scene: "A great heap of biscuits lay on the pan and the skillet was heaped with good brown slices of mess pork, but to my dismay each man was ordered to eat only one biscuit with one slice of meat, then feed his horse five ears of corn and after he had eaten to water him at the river about 300 yards distant, then he could have the second and to feed and water as before. This order, I suppose, was a precaution to prevent us and our horses from over-eating." Despite the inconvenience, Private Sparks managed to gobble down four biscuits and slices of pork. "There were throngs of men and horses going and returning from the water which was kept up to far into the night," he recalled.[9]

November 24th 1861 [diary]
Took an early start this morning and got into camp at 2 pm. One man sent ahead from each mess to have us something prepared to

8. Kerr, ed., *Fighting with Ross' Texas Cavalry*, 6.
9. Sparks, *War Between the States*, 39.

eat. The way we devoured biscuit was not slow. Thought the trains the most welcome sight I had seen for many a day—except some cold bread I found in camp. Those in camp were as glad to see us as we to see them. Wrote a letter home this evening.

After spending the twenty-fifth resting and eating heartily, the regiment traveled east to an abandoned Baptist mission at Tullahassee, a few miles north of present-day Muskogee, for more rest and recuperation. Bates's diary indicates that he had made a great leap, from acorns to apple pies, in only a few days.

November 26th 1861 [diary]
Today moved twenty five miles east near the baptist Mission— passed over some very pretty country—mostly poor. Col Borland [James R. Bourland] & Dr [M. A.] Elliott [assistant regimental surgeon] left for McCulloch's. Encamped on a beautiful hill in a fine grove of timber—a fine spring nearby. Bought some fine apple[s] today at $.10 a dozen. Think I will try my hand at making apple pies.

Rest and apple pies were only temporary pleasures, however, because Colonel Sims's Texans were ordered into the field once more. The Federal threat to northwest Arkansas had abated, making the journey to Arkansas unnecessary for the moment, but cagey old Opothle Yahola had once again done the unexpected. Rather than flee into Kansas after Round Mountains, he had detoured into the Cherokee Nation north of present-day Tulsa. Colonel Cooper was convinced that the old chief would stir up trouble among the Cherokees, so Cooper put his Indian regiments on Opothle Yahola's trail and directed the 9th Texas Cavalry to ride north on a parallel course to the east, along the Verdigris River deep into the Cherokee Nation.[10]

The Texans at the comfortable Baptist mission were not in perfect condition for another long scout. Measles had disabled more men than all of Opothle Yahola's warriors, and the disease would spread through the ranks with increasing severity during December. Others in the regiment suffered from a variety of maladies. Colonel Sims would send only about 260 of his Texans on the expedition. Until they saddled up for the scout, however, Bates and his comrades continued to enjoy the food and warmth of the camp at the mission.[11]

10. OR, Vol. 8, p. 7; Hale, "Rehearsal for Civil War," 241.
11. Sparks, War Between the States, 39; Hale, "Rehearsal for Civil War," 241.

November 27th and 28th 1861 [diary]

Received orders today to march on the 30th. Sixty miles north of here on Grand River—since stoping here [at the mission]—many of the Reg taken sick. Think it is the effect of our late exposure.

November 29th 1861 [diary]

After breakfast concluded we would have a rarity for dinner—namely apple pies. Went to work & amongst us all got up a respectable pie. As these are unusual in camp I was reminded favorably of home. Besides green apple pies we today had various and divers other good things & very much doubt whether there will be a dinner eaten in paris today with so much relish as ours. Capt [W. E.] Duncan [of Company F] came in today from Gen McCulloch's camp. No enemy in the vicinity [of southwest Missouri]—all gone north—we are still in doubt as to where we will winter.

November 30th 1861 [diary]

In obedience to Cooper's command—took up line of march northwest. We are in utter ignorance as to the reason for our being ordered north. It is the prevailing opinion that Col Cooper is afraid of old Potheohola and wants us between him & danger.[12] Marched twelve [miles] & took up camp on Verdigris River. Took a nap on the cold ground & woke up with a bad cold.

December 1st 1861 [diary]

This morning at 4 wind changed to north & by the time we were on the march cold enough to freeze horns off a billy goat. Capt Reeves came in last night and reported Gouge 30 or 40 miles north killing stock—people all running from him. After forming on prairie—a prayer was offered by [regimental chaplain] Rev [T. A.] McIsh—eloquent fervor & full of faith in the justness of our cause. As it was the first prayer I had heard since I left home—many scenes & memories of bygone times were revived. For the first time I was really homesick. As some danger exists of some trains being cut off [we] stoped in some deep hollow or ravine where we would be protected from wind to wait [for] them. Traveled ten miles & encamped

12. Bates, like some of his fellow Texans, respected Opothle Yahola as an able chief and military leader. Private Sparks of Titus County, referring to the Indian ponies captured during the recent expedition against the Creeks, wrote that "each soldier named his captured pony Gouge, in honor to his former associations." Sparks, *War Between the States*, 39.

on Verdigris River. Gouge reported to be in eight miles. Gouge in 30 miles with 3500 men.

December 2nd 1861 [diary]

Marched fifteen miles in a west direction — camped again on Verdigris — at a council of officers — determined to send Col [Sims] with 200 men to prevail on Cooper to let us return to [Fort] Gibson & go into winter quarters.[13] With three days rations they started the next morning.

3rd, 4th, 5th, and 6th December [1861] [diary]

This evening received orders from Col Cooper to move on with all our available men to his camp. Started trains back with the sick. Seventy five men balance of our Reg under Quayle moved on to his [Cooper's] camp and found Sims just returned from a scout. Reports that he approached within two miles of Gouge's camp. Took a prisoner before leaving our camp. Prepared eleven days rations & that with my blankets, pistol, sabre & saddle & myself weighs over 250 lbs.[14]

December 7th 1861 [diary]

This morning with 250 men — [and] about 200 Creeks & some 350 Choctaws took up march to meet Col [John] Drew.[15] Twenty five mile out found he had not come. Encamped in a bottom on bank of Verdigris River.

By December 7 Colonel Cooper's scouts had finally pinpointed Opothle Yahola's band about ten miles north of present-day Tulsa on Bird Creek. Colonel Drew had received word from Opothle Yahola that the old man wanted to negotiate a peace with his pursuers, so Cooper sent some of Drew's Cherokees to parley with the Creek chief the next day. Meanwhile,

---

13. The officers believed the column was too disabled by sickness to continue. Fort Gibson was about ten miles northeast of present-day Muskogee and fifteen miles southeast of the Tullahassee Baptist mission. Davis, *Cypress Rangers*, 39.

14. Bates and his comrades, determined not to go hungry on this scout, packed mounds of food into their saddlebags.

15. Colonel John Drew, sixty-five years old, was a prosperous Cherokee businessman and slave owner. He commanded a regiment of Confederate Cherokees in the fall of 1861. W. Craig Gaines, *The Confederate Cherokees: John Drew's Regiment of Mounted Rifles* (Baton Rouge: Louisiana State University Press, 1989), 16–17.

Cooper's Indians and Sims's Texans converged nearby to await results. While the Confederates paused, more than 400 of Colonel Drew's 480 Cherokees, reluctant to fight their friends on the other side—fled the scene—some to join Opothle Yahola, others to safety at Fort Gibson, and still others to parts unknown.[16]

December 8th 1861 [diary]

Four miles from camp fell in with [Confederate] Creeks who had camped some distance to our left. Moved on some five or six miles— found Col Drew encamped on a small creek with 500 men. Got corn to feed our horses. The first since yesterday morning. Rested an hour or so & moved a mile higher up & encamped. This evening a messenger came from "Gouge" to Col Drew that he was willing to treat with him. Drew therefore sent Capt Dorn to his camp to negotiate a treaty but Gouge's promise like all others he has made was only to deceive.[17] As soon as he had Dorn in his power he threatened to kill him if he did not join his army. Dorn agreed to join on condition he could get leave to return to Fort Gibson for his wife. This permission was given him & he immediately returned to our camp, stated the facts as above & in addition said Gouge intended to attack our camp just before day, tomorrow morning—that Gouge had 7 or 8,000 men—as soon as Drew returned to his camp one mile below ours & made the above statement his whole regiment with the exception of 30 or 40 men deserted his camp some going over to Gouge—others making for home & still others scattered pall mall over the country.[18]

As soon as Cooper received news of this our forces were mounted & formed on the edge of the prairie in front of our camp where we remained on our arms—horses saddled—all night without sleeping. Every fourth man holding the reins—remainder formed in front. After we were formed Col Quayle with two companies proceeded to Drew's camp—found him with only 10 or 12 men—collected a few more in the bushes—brought away all the wagons but left the tents

16. Ibid., 45–46; Hale, "Rehearsal for Civil War," 242.

17. Bates apparently misunderstood the name of Drew's emissary to Opothle Yahola. No one named Dorn was in the delegation that visited the Creek chief's camp. Gaines, *Confederate Cherokees,* 46–47.

18. Actually, the desertion from Drew's regiment occurred before negotiations broke down. In fact, neutrals and Unionists among Drew's soldiers had planned the desertion days earlier. Ibid., 45–47.

& other baggage. The night however passed without any attack being made. What a contrast in this same day, night & year previous to this.[19]

The next day, Colonel Cooper, fearing that his force was not strong enough to attack Opothle Yahola now that most of the Cherokees had deserted, began withdrawing across the prairie to the southeast. As the Confederate horsemen moved down the east bank of Bird Creek, Opothle Yahola prepared another ambush at a place called Chustotalasah (Caving Banks). When the rear guard of Cooper's column trotted past a crossing of the creek, the old chief's warriors, hidden in the brush of the creek bottom, opened on the Confederates with rifles and arrows. This time, Cooper had daylight on his side. He quickly sent the wagons off to the east about two miles and turned his troops to face their enemies to the west. Cooper placed his Choctaws and Chickasaws on his right, Sims's Texans and Drew's remaining Cherokees in the center, and the Confederate Creeks on his left.[20]

The strongest point in Opothle Yahola's position was at the north end of his line, facing the Confederate right. There the stream made a sharp bend through heavy woods and underbrush, affording ample cover for his warriors. In addition, the steep banks of the creek provided a natural earthwork behind which the Creeks could fire with relative safety. From 2 P.M. until about 6 P.M, the battle was hottest around the bend through the woods and underbrush.[21]

At the center and left end of the Confederate line, Bates and his fellow Texans fought a series of small engagements, confronting the enemy in a number of ravines that ran into Bird Creek from the prairie east of the waterway. At times fighting dismounted and at other times on horseback, the Texans and Confederate Creeks finally drove Opothle Yahola's right wing out of the ravines and back across Bird Creek. The Confederates then rode over to their right and joined the fight at the bend of the creek. There too, after a severe contest, the Confederates pushed their enemies through the woods, across the creek, and away from the bottom in a series of small-group engagements. As night fell, Opothle Yahola withdrew to the west

19. Speaking in the third person, Dohoney later wrote, "Of all the nights of Lafayette's [Dohoney's] life, this was the one of greatest suspense and apparently of the greatest danger." Dohoney, *Average American,* 100.

20. *OR,* Vol. 8, pp. 8–10; Hale, "Rehearsal for Civil War," 242–43; Gaines, *Confederate Cherokees,* 49–52.

21. *OR,* Vol. 8, pp. 8–10; Hale, "Rehearsal for Civil War," 242–43.

into the hills behind the creek. Cooper's Indians and Texans likewise withdrew, to their wagon train out on the prairie east of the creek.[22]

The Confederates claimed another victory at Caving Banks because they had driven Opothle Yahola's warriors from their positions in the bottom into the hills west of Bird Creek. Strategically, however, they had failed to bring the Creek chief to heel, and his band continued to roam about the Cherokee Nation during the following weeks.

Once again, Bates wrote a long letter to his mother about a week after the battle, bringing her up to date on the regiment's activities and describing the fight at Chustotalasah in great detail. Part of the letter repeats information he had written in his diary for early December, but his account of the battle is lengthy and reflects his analytical bent, especially his calculations on the likelihood of being wounded in battle. Bates also demonstrates empathy for the followers of Opothle Yahola, a solid historical understanding of the feuds among the Creek Indians, and a prescient suspicion of the Cherokee chief, John Ross, who would within a year switch sides and support the Union.

> Fort Gibson, Cherokee Nation
> Dec 16th 1861
> My Dear Ma;
>   Since writing to you from Concartha [Concharta] on Ark river we have taken another scout of some twelve or fifteen days. But this has not been so severe on us as the other. the weather has been unusually favorable for the season, and we have plenty to eat for ourselves—our horses have fared tolerably well. As you will probably hear all that we have been doing I will try to give you a little history of our rambling through this wild country.
>   After returning from our first expedition we moved from Concartha 25 miles east to the Talahassy Mission. This mission is a large brick building erected by the Baptists for a seminary. There is no school here now however but [it] has been used since we first moved to that vicinity as a hospital. After remaining at the mission two days we were ordered by Cooper to meet him 60 miles north west of there. The next morning with all the men who were able to do duty we started taking most of the wagons with us. On the second day so many of our men were sick that it seemed like folly to go further. Col

22. OR, Vol. 8, pp. 18–19; Sparks, War Between the States, 43; Kerr, ed., Fighting with Ross' Texas Cavalry, 8; Dohoney, Average American, 101–103; Hale, "Rehearsal for Civil War," 243–44.

Sims therefore with 200 men left the trains and proceeded to Col
Cooper's camp to get permission to return to winter quarters. He
failed in this and on the evening of the 7th, we received a dispatch
ordering us to send the trains and sick back to the mission and move
on with the balance of our forces with ten days rations.

Immediately after supper we commenced our preparations mould-
ing bullets, baking bread, roasting & grinding coffee, &c &c. If you
had seen the pile of bread we had baked by midnight, you might
have thought we were preparing a month's instead of ten days
rations. By 2 oclk we had everything in readiness. After finishing I
wrote you and several others letters but doubt whether you have received them or not. Next morning (8th) we moved on to Cooper's
camp and found Col Sims just returned from a scout of two days.
With 200 men he approached within two miles of the enemy's camp.

But I expect you know very little of the enemy we have been
fighting so I will tell you. Optheohola—the leader of the Indians
we have been fighting, is an old *Creek* chief said to be a man of fine
talent, some 80 or 90 years old—and on account of his age and
sagacity possesses almost perfect sway over his followers. He is also
the leader of what is here called the *pin party*. Why called the pin
party I cant say.[23] It is composed chiefly of full blood Indians of
every Nation and tribe with the exception of the Choctaws and
Chickasaws and the members have taken a secret oath or obligation
never to fight against each other. Most of the half breed and many
of the full bloods belong to a party opposed to this and Col Chilly
McIntosh is their leader.[24]

Before the Indians were removed from Georgia Old Optheohola
opposed the treaty by which their lands were sold to the U.S. Col
McIntosh's father was its principal supporter and after they were removed to this country he was murdered—and it is generally believed by the McIntosh party that Optheohola had it done. On this
account and others a bitter feud sprang up between the two parties
and had existed ever since. The McIntoshes have control over the

23. Members of the Pin faction were primarily nonslaveholding full-blooded Indians
who had opposed the sale of their lands east of the Mississippi River to the Federal government. Most of them were sympathetic to the North in the white man's war. Alvin M. Josephy, Jr., *The Civil War in the American West* (New York: Alfred A. Knopf, 1991), 326.

24. Colonel Daniel McIntosh was the son of William McIntosh, a Creek chief who was
murdered in 1828 by followers of Opothle Yahola for agreeing to cede Creek lands in Georgia and Alabama to the United States. Gaines, *Confederate Cherokees*, 23.

[Federal] annuities [to the tribe] and have been accused by Opthe-hola's party of swindling them out of a large amount of it annually.

Both McIntosh and Optheohola are Creeks. The former claims to be and is I suppose a Southern man. The latter is said to be an abolitionist but I think that if he had not been driven by circum-stances to take sides with the north he would not have done so. But it seems he *has* done so and those who sympathize with the north are with him whilst those who are friendly to the South are with McIntosh. Many however have not taken part on either side and I expect that many who are now with us will be so no longer than it is to their interest to be so. I have but little confidence in *any of them* and although old John Ross, the Governor of the Cherokee claims to be a true southern man and is generally represented as such in Texas—still I believe he is a traitor at heart and only wants a favor-able opportunity to show himself such.[25]

But it is impossible for me to give you a true statement of affairs here as I am not sufficiently posted myself-so I will go back to my narrative. On the 7th about noon we took up a line of march in the direction of the enemy's camp & marched 10 miles where we were to have been met by Col Drews Reg of Cherokees—we found how-ever that he was not there. On 8th again moved and at noon came up with Drew's Reg—encamped within 4 or 5 miles of the enemy with 500 men. Our suspicions were aroused by Drews failing to meet us at the appointed place and circumstances proved that they were not without foundation.

We moved a mile higher up the creek and took up our camp. Our entire force was about 450 Choctaws, 400 Creek, 250 of our Reg. and some 500 men under Drew. A Report came into camp that old Optheohola proposed to make a treaty with Col. Drew. Drew sent one of his captains (Van) to Optheohola's camp to negotiate a treaty.[26] about sundown Capt. Van returned to Drew's camp and

25. Seventy-one years old, John Ross, principal chief of the Cherokees, attempted to keep his tribe out of the war in its early months. The Confederate victory at Wilson's Creek (Oak Hills) in August 1861, however, forced him to commit to the Confederacy. Several months after Chustotalasah, he surrendered to Federal forces without a fight, and many of his fellow Cherokees switched sides to support the Union. Bates's doubts about Ross's com-mitment to the Confederacy were well founded. Gaines, *Confederate Cherokees,* 3, 107–12; Grace Steele Woodward, *The Cherokees* (Norman: University of Oklahoma Press, 1963).

26. Bates doubtless refers to Captain James Vann (Company E) of Drew's regiment. Gaines, *Confederate Cherokees,* 47.

reported that Optheohola refused to treat and threatened to kill him if he did not join him. Van says he agreed to do this on condition that he be permitted to return for his wife. Van also reported that Optheohola intended attacking us that night and that he had from 7,000 to 10,000 warriors—all armed with rifles, six shooters and hatchets. Van immediately left the camp with his entire company and told those who remained that they had better get away from there as *they* would be attacked by jay hawkers that night and that *we* would be attacked by Optheohola—and in less than 20 minutes Drew's entire Reg were scattered in every direction most of them going over to Optheohola the balance flying for their home.

As soon as news reached us that Drew's entire Reg. had deserted him we immediately saddled, mounted our horses and moved out into the edge of the prairie, dismounted—formed in line every fourth man holding horses. The Choctaws and Creeks were on our left. In this position we remained until 7 oclk the next morning [December 9] expecting every moment that an attack would be made—but every man determined not to yield an inch of ground. The night however passed off without any attack being made, and you may be sure that daylight was never more heartily welcomed than by us on that morning. A part of our Reg was sent over to protect Drew's wagons and bring them into our camp. As they had to be taken across a very bad creek we did not get them all in untill 2 oclk in the morning. After the return of the scouting parties that had been sent out at daylight—no signs of the enemy being seen we returned to our camp and prepared our breakfasts.

As Col Cooper thought our force too small since the desertion of the Cherokees to contend against Optheohola we commenced moving back in the direction of our trains. The enemy supposing that we would cross Bird Creek (on which the battle was fought) at the same place we crossed going up moved down on the opposite side and took a position on each side of the ford in the brush. Finding however that we would not cross there they made an attack on our Rear Guard from the right. Col Cooper immediately gave the order to "right about" and we moved on to meet them. The Creeks entered the timber and commenced the attack on the enemy right wing. Our Company and two others with them and on *their* right. After about an hour and a half fighting during which time an incessant firing was kept up by both sides the enemy was completely routed here.

The fight being *over* here our companies moved up the creek to the assistance of the Choctaws who with the balance of our regiment were engaged in a hot contest with the left wing of the enemy. The Creeks soon followed us. In the beginning of the fight here the enemy had possession of a house in the edge of the timber and around this the fight raged with the greatest fury. Twice we drove them from it and were each time compelled to retire ourselves. The third time however we succeeded in holding it. The left wing of the enemy with the exception of those in the house fell back and took a position under a creek bank. They were [in]accessible from there [their] rear and each flank being in a bend of the creek—and our only chance of approaching them was through the prairie—being exposed to their fire for about 300 yards and untill we approached to within 50 steps of their line. There we succeeded in getting possession of a little ravine running nearly parallel with the creek bank—and we were in a measure sheltered from their fire.

After nearly an hour fighting here we were ordered by the Col to return to our horses. It was with some reluctance that we obeyed this command for if we had remained half an hour longer we would have driven the enemy away from the mouth of the ravine in which we were and once in possession of that we would have had but a little difficulty in routing them. As it was, we were forced to leave the enemy in possession of part of the field and though others think differently I cant call our victory complete. As soon as our Reg was mounted Cooper called off his force and we moved on down the creek to where we had left our wagons. This was just as the sun was setting.

If we had had one more hour of daylight we would have routed them completely. But in the commencement of the fight we had left our wagons a mile and a half below with a very small guard and as they were in danger of being cut off, we were compelled to draw off and get to them before dark. Our dead and wounded were placed on hacks and wagons and conveyed to our place of camping 2 miles below. As none of us had slept the night before and few the night before that, I lay down as soon as we reached our camping ground waiting only to get a drink of water—and slept as soundly—and felt as secure as I would have done at home.

The next morning Col Cooper with a part of his command returned to the battlefield to see if any of our men had been left on the ground. Only one was found. The enemy had fled to parts unknown. Our entire loss was ten killed and about twenty wounded—

one of our Company slightly wounded. The loss of the enemy, according to the best information we can get, must be near three hundred killed and wounded. It is impossible though for us to judge with any degree of certainty. We know however that 38 or 40 Cherokees were found dead on the field the next morning and that about one fourth or one fifth of the enemy force is composed of Cherokees. Most of the remainder are Creeks and supposing their loss to be in the same proportion, the entire loss of the enemy cannot be far short of 150 killed and the usual proportion of wounded. The Creeks invariably remove their dead from the field as soon as killed. It is a part of their religion never to permit one of their dead to fall into the hands of the enemy—consequently not one was found on the field the next morning.

The following pages of this letter were included with the pages above. This portion appears to be part of a different letter, perhaps enclosed with the one above.

You would not have known that we had slept as soundly and securely during the past night, as we ever did at home. As Genl Cooper thought our force now too small to engage the enemy with any chance of success, we this morning (9th) [December 9] commenced falling back to await reinforcements. As our course lay near the foot of a range of hills on our right all our movements could be seen by Optheohola and he himself remained concealed. Observing our course, he sent his forces down on the opposite side of Bird Creek immediately on our right to attack us while crossing as there was but two crossings in that vicinity and they were both near each other. (We have since learned this from prisoners)—finding however that it was not our intention to cross here after all but our rear guard had passed them they made an attack on this at a distance of 500 yards killing one man.

Gen Cooper immediately gave the order to "right about" and meet them. As soon as they made the attack on our Rear Guard which I think was merely a feint to draw us into the fight—they retreated and took position in the brush—and under the creek bank. One half of our Regiment in which was our company—acted with our Creek allies against the right wing of the enemy—the balance of our Regiment with the Choctaws against their left. Their line was not less than a mile and a half in length. Their main force was on each wing. The battle was commenced on our left by occasional shots from both parties—like warning drops of rain before a shower. As we drew nearer the shots became more frequent and by the time we had dismounted and gotten fairly into the fight one volley followed another in such quick succession that one continuous roar was kept up. This continued for about forty minutes when the enemy retreated back into the bed of the creek—and the firing nearly ceased for a short time.

Soon however they made their appearance higher up the stream, when the four Texas companies present made a charge on them and routed them completely. Finding we had driven the enemy completely from our part of the field we mounted our horses and galloped to the assistance of our friends above. We found them engaged in a contest more fierce if possible than ours had been. The enemy had every possible advantage they could wish—our only way of approaching them being through the prairie—where we were exposed to a heavy fire untill we succeeded in driving them from a ravine running nearly parallel with the creek bank under which they had taken their position. Here we were in some degree sheltered from the heaviest of their fire.

For an hour or more the fighting continued here without any abatement. As the sun was now down we were ordered to fall back to our horses. Col Cooper soon drew off his men and we proceeded down the creek some three miles to our place of camping. After we had retire[d] some distance the enemy

[missing page(s)]

This is my first fight. Our other battle [at Round Mountains] our company was not engaged in. I have always been under the impression that I would be willing for the fight if I should get into one to cease at any moment. But that was not my experience this time. After the first excitement was over—the first few rounds fired—I ceased to have any apprehension whatever of danger. I have often heard men who had been in battles speak of how the bullets whized over and around them but I thought the sound of the bullets was mostly in their imaginations. I have learned however from experience that they were correct. We could even tell by the peculiar whizing noise of the balls whether they were discharged from a minnie or an ordinary rifle. An arrow produces a sound something like a bird flying swiftly through the air.

After all that has been said of battles—the danger &c incured by those engaged in them, in my estimation the *danger is not near so great* as those who have never been in one suppose. It is true that our experience has been rather limited, but in four fifths of the battles fought those engaged in them incur less risk than we have done. We were engaged about three hours and during that time had ten men killed. Estimating the number of enemy at 1,500 (which is a low estimate) and the number of shots fired by each at ten, we find that 15,000 shots were fired at us. As our killed *and* wounded amounted to only thirty you see that only one shot out of 500 had any effect. This may seem like unusually bad shooting, but it is as true of other battles as this.[27]

You see therefore that it only a random shot that kills and we are in much less danger in battle than you may have thought. I apprehend more danger from sickness than from any other cause. I have been taking as good care of myself as possible under the circumstances and intend doing so in future. It is true we have had—and still have a great deal of sickness in the Regiment, but most of it has been brought on by negligence on the part of the men.

So far we have had as fine weather generally as we could desire, tolerably cold but dry, and I think if it continues so for ten or fifteen days we will be in winter quarters by that time. Our winter quarters have been assigned to us at the mouth of Frog Bayou on Arkansas river in Ark. I have found the service so far tolerably hard, though *not as hard as I expected* before entering it. So I have been disappointed, but *very agreeably.* We sometimes have the "blues" but this cant last long—as amongst so many there is always *some fun* on hand. Besides we have so much else to engage our attentions we have but little time to give to desponding thoughts. If I could hear from home and know that you were all well, I believe I would be contented, or at least as nearly as I could be away from home.

Hereafter we can get letters from you at almost any time if directed to Ft Smith. When you write give me *all* the news. We have not heard a word from home since leaving Texas. I want you to write *as* often as every ten days and oftener if you can. I have not written as often as I wished to do from the fact that we have had but few opportunities of sending letters.

27. Bates's observation that hundreds of rounds of small-arms fire were necessary to inflict even one casualty has been seconded by many later veterans and military historians. For examples, see Richard Holmes, *Acts of War: The Behavior of Men in Battle* (New York: Free Press, 1985), 167–70.

From the fact that few of the company supplied themselves with paper my supply is almost exausted as you will find by the way this is written.[28] If you can get them you must send us some late papers. I have not read half a dozen papers since leaving Texas. We are almost entirely isolated from the rest of the world in the way of news.

If there is a prospect of my corn bringing a good price in the Spring I want it sold. Not however for less than 50 cents a bu. My oats I want sold anyway. I suppose I have 75 bushels or more of shelled oats.[29] As Will agreed to let me have these, he taking the [illegible word] oats. If these were placed in the stores there I think they might be sold and pay off some little debts I have there. I don't know when we will draw any pay—but think it will be around Christmas or probably sometime after. Tell Will to write to me. He has more time and better opportunities of writing than I have—and must not wait for me to write first. My best wishes to all my friends—particularly your neighbors on the Clarksville street.[30]
May kind providence guard and protect you all.
J.C. Bates

In addition to the battle account in his letter to his mother, Bates also wrote about the fight in his diary, with one important difference: in the diary he described an incident in which he voluntarily risked his life. Whether he omitted this part of the story in his letter to his mother because he did not wish to alarm her, or for some other reason, is not clear.

December 9th 1861 [diary]
This morning after the return of scouting parties—no enemy being seen—we prepared breakfast. At 11 oclk took up march in direction of trains. After Cherokees went over to Gouge our force too small to attack him. Moved on four or five miles. Some of enemy discovered—trains halted. Head of column ordered right about—formed in column of companies—Creeks on left—Choctaws on right. Enemy's position on edge of bottom on prairie. Creeks on left

28. To cram as much information as possible onto his few sheets of paper, Bates first wrote across the page from left to right then turned the sheet ninety degrees and wrote across the lines he had already penned. This was a common practice among Civil War letter-writers.
29. Bates was not listed as a land owner or farm operator in the 1860 census, but this passage indicates that he must have been renting a plot of land and raising grains near Paris.
30. Bates refers to the family of his sweetheart, Mootie Johnson. The Johnson house still stands at 730 Clarksville Street in Paris.

dismounted—began attack—a part of our Reg with them. After about an hour's fighting they [Federal Creeks] were driven across the creek. This terminated the fight here.

Moved up creek to assistance of right wing, found a constant & heavy firing going on one half mile up & down creek. Dismounted & moved on to the attack. As enemy were hid in brush & behind bank of creek we were very much exposed to their fire. Took our position in a little steam running into the creek. Wherever an Indian head was seen a battle was instantly in or very near same place. Balls whistled over & around us so constantly it made one continuous whiz. After the first half dozen passed over me I ceased to dodge & finally to think anything of them.

After firing from the ravine from 30 or 40 minutes ordered back to our horses. while moving back to them were exposed for 2 or 300 yards to heavy fire but fortunately few were wounded & none killed here. After mounting & forming I saw a wounded man trying to make his escape from the ravine. He was shot in the side & just able to walk. I asked & got permission to go to his assistance. Started in a gallop & called some one else to follow me. Met him about 150 yards from enemy, as soon as I dismounted he sank down on the ground. the bullets came whistling around us as thick as hail. As we were a good target to get shot at—I expected every moment that one of us would be shot down. Two others soon came & we picked him up & carried him amidst a perfect shower of bullets, some passing very near our heads—others striking the ground at our feet—up the hill to our lines.

Gen Cooper thought it advisable to call our men off & get to the trains before night. The bugle was blown & men ordered to mount. With wounded at head of column moved three miles down creek to camp—about 10 oclk got into camp.

December 10th 1861 [diary]

On last night thought an attack was apprehended. I slept as soundly as if I had been at home. two hundred of our Reg were sent on with the wounded to guard wagons & balance of army went back to the battle ground. According to opinion of those who went over the ground about 150 of the enemy were killed.[31] Thirty six Chero-

31. Strength and casualty figures, especially for the Unionist Creeks, are uncertain. Colonel Cooper estimated that the enemy at Chustotalasah included anywhere from 2,500 to 4,000 warriors and that they had lost between 412 and 500 soldiers killed and wounded.

kee were found on the ground. As the proportion of the cherokee were supposed to be about one fifth the above estimate must be nearly correct. The Creeks took all their dead from the ground.

From prisoners taken we learned that Gouge contemplated an attack on us Sunday night [December 8] & actually moved his force within a mile of our camp but as it is supposed that he found out by some means that we were in readiness to meet him he abandoned the idea. Also learned that he supposed we would cross Bird Creek at the point the battle was fought & intended attacking us while crossing but as we passed on by the ford he concluded to have a fight anyway—so he began firing on our Rear Guard. If we had attempted to cross here he would have had us almost surrounded & we must inevitably [have] been cut up if we crossed here. After going over the battle ground to ascertain if any dead or wounded were left, main force joined us four miles down creek at camp.

Two days after the fight, Cooper's command, low on ammunition, turned back toward Fort Gibson. Cooper hoped to convince higher authorities in Arkansas to leave the Texas cavalry under his control—in fact, to send him more Texas regiments—and he also planned to meet with Cherokee leaders at the fort to stiffen their resolve for the Confederate cause.[32] The cold, tired Texans of Bates's regiment, hoping to settle into winter quarters soon, were becoming testy by this time. Bates's second-guessing of Colonel Sims's orders on this march to Fort Gibson reflects his growing impatience with war in the Indian Territory.[33]

December 11th 1861 [diary]

Started wagons with wounded ahead in a S.E. direction—main force moving on S.—twenty two mile to Tulsey Town [Tulsa] where we fed our horses. No sign of Gouge seen—Ark[ansas] river fifteen miles east where we found wagons & advance guard. Got in at camp at 4 oclk. Made me a cup of coffee & went to sleep.

Both sets of figures are almost certainly great exaggerations. Cooper also claimed that the Confederate forces actually engaged included 1,100, of whom 15 were killed and 37 wounded. *OR*, Vol. 8, pp. 10, 16.

32. Ibid., p. 11.

33. Some of the men in the regiment had been skeptical of Sims's leadership abilities ever since the fight at Chustotalasah, when the colonel ordered the men to dismount and attack, saying, "Now, boys, I turn you over to your respective captains, and I will remain out and take care of your horses." Dohoney, *Average American*, 102.

December 12th 1861 [diary]

Leaving Col Cooper's command to follow on[,] our Reg moved on to trains twenty five miles distant. Found on our arrival that five of our Reg had died since leaving camp & some others not expected to live—so thus far nine have died in camp & six have been killed in the field of battle. Found our trains two miles from [Tullahassee] Mission on Ark river two miles from creek [illegible word]

December 13th 1861 [diary]

At 9 oclk last night adjutant came round & said was ordered by Col that all who were able to ride prepare two days ration by morning. Next morning with 400 men, started in direction of [Fort] Gibson leaving train at Mission. Halted by Col [Sims] who condescended to tell us that we were going down to Gibson for the purpose of getting permission to quarter our sick there. Why all the Reg should be called on to do what one man could as easily perform is a mystery. If ever a Reg was cursed with a bigoted self conceited for Col ours is the one. After arriving at Gibson Col ordered fifty men to return for trains. Why did'nt he leave them with the wagons is asked by everyone but answered by none. Oh, deliver me from another such fool as this.

Life at Fort Gibson was much more pleasant than chasing "old Gouge" across the frigid prairies of the Cherokee Nation. Located at the junction of the Grand and Arkansas Rivers, the fort included "a beautiful square, surrounded with small wooden buildings and . . . two bl[o]ck houses made of logs and situated at opposite corners of the square." The neighborhood surrounding the fort was populated primarily by prosperous mixed-blood Cherokees.[34] While at the fort, Bates had time to write letters, read, do some shopping, and see the sights, although the sight of his Indian allies did not fill him with confidence.

December 14th 1861 [diary]

Went up to town & made some purchases. Returned & crossed river to meet trains. Returned to camp, read awhile & wrote some letters. The Cherokee had a grand war dance tonight & their infernal orgies are still kept up—at the close they fire off their guns. Tonight our boys were all asleep when the firing began. As they did

34. Sparks, *War Between the States*, 41.

not know what it was for—it was amusing to see with what dexterity they jumped from under their blankets into their breeches.

Sunday December 15th 1861 [diary]

After breakfast [John] Gibbons and I rode out into the country for fodder for our horses. No preaching in camp this morning. Wrote some letters—read a while and went to bed thinking of home & how I would have spent the day if I had been there—woke up this morning from a pleasant dream.

Monday December 16th 1861 [diary]

Took a ride this morning around the "city" [Fort Gibson] nearly all the houses here were built by the old U.S. C[avalry].—looks like they had been here forty years. Reported in camp that 400 Texans are on the way here from Ft. Smith.[35] Received a Fort Smith Times in which was an account of our fight on the 9th [Chustotalasah] greatly exaggerated in proportion as it gets farther off. A report also that Capt McDaniel one of Gouge's men crossed the Grand river six miles above here with 300 men.

Tuesday December 17th 1861 [diary]

Wrote some letters & sent home by one of our Reg going to Texas on furlough. Heard John Ross—Chief of the Cherokees— make a talk to his people. If he is sincere in what he says he is our friend—this I very much doubt. In the evening he made a talk to the Choctaws nearly a reiteration of the speech he made in the morning.

Among the letters Bates wrote at Fort Gibson was one to his brother-in-law in Paris, Will Bramlette. Bates mentioned the sickness that had debilitated hundreds of men in his regiment. A sergeant in Company D remarked at about the same time that more than 250 of the Texans were down with measles alone.[36] Poor food, inadequate sanitation, close quarters, hard campaigning, exposure to the elements, and lack of previous exposure to childhood diseases combined to enfeeble many young sol-

---

35. Colonel Cooper's request for reinforcements had been granted, and all or parts of five understrength regiments, about 1,600 men (mostly Texans), had left winter quarters in Van Buren, Arkansas, to join in a new pursuit of Opothle Yahola. *OR*, Vol. 8, p. 715; Hale, "Rehearsal for Civil War," 245–46.

36. Kerr, ed., *Fighting with Ross' Texas Cavalry*, 9. The sergeant in Company D, George Griscom, would later be appointed assistant adjutant, then adjutant, of the regiment (ibid., 91).

diers in the first months of the war.[37] Bates's hardy constitution enabled him to avoid the usual maladies, however. He also brought Will Bramlette up to date with regard to the reinforcements coming from Arkansas and expressed once again his suspicions about the Cherokee chief John Ross.

> Fort Gibson
> Dec 17th 1861
> Dear Will,
>
> I wrote to Ma a day or so since, but as the bearer Mr [blank space] intends going through Paris on his way home, I drop you a few lines by him. If he wishes to stop in Paris during the night receive him kindly as he is a soldier in our Regiment.
>
> There is a good deal of sickness in our Regiment at this time. Most of our Company however are well—I have better health than I have had for a year or so—weigh 160# which I think is a pretty good evidence of my health.
>
> You have no doubt received before this a detailed account of our little fight so I will say nothing of it. I expect we may have another soon—but will go with a force sufficient to silence old Opotheyhola for some time at least. 1,400 Texans are on the way to join us from Fort Smith. Another Regiment of Choctaws will be in soon. These with the force we will be able to muster here will give us an army of 2,500 or 3,000 men. Things are rapidly approaching a climax in this section & I think the next battle we have will force all those who have not taken any decided stand (of whom there are a great number) to take sides either for or against us.
>
> Col Cooper and old John Ross have a consultation here tonight. What plans they may agree upon I cannot say. Ross is regarded here by every Southern man with distrust. You need not be surprised to hear that we have trouble with him yet. I hope however it may not be soon. The time for starting on our next expedition has not been made known yet. In a few days though I think. If an opportunity occurs I will write again before starting.

37. A good short treatment of disease in the Confederate armies is in Current, *Encyclopedia of the Confederacy*, 2:754–55. More detailed studies are Horace H. Cunningham's *Doctors in Gray: The Confederate Medical Service* (Baton Rouge: Louisiana State University Press, 1958) and Paul E. Steiner's *Disease in the Civil War: Natural Biological Warfare in 1861–1865* (Springfield, Ill.: C. C. Thomas, 1968).

When you write inclose your letters in two envelopes. Direct the outside one to

G.W. Clark Q.M.
Fort Smith
Ark
The other to J.C. Bates   Company H 4th Reg. Texas Cavalry W.B. Sims Col.[38]
Give my love to all.
Your Brother
J.C. Bates

On the same day that Bates wrote to Bramlette, E. L. Dohoney, Bates's fellow trooper and a former boarder in Bramlette's household, scribbled his own letter, addressed to Will and the pastor of the Cumberland Presbyterian church in Paris, C. J. Bradley.[39] Dohoney provided no new information about the recent fight on Bird Creek, doubtless to the regret of his correspondents, but he did outline the strenuous efforts then being made at Fort Gibson to place the Cherokees in Confederate harness. He also commented on the sickness in the regiment.

Fort Gibson Cherokee Nation
December 17th 1861
Rev. C. J. Bradley & Wm. Bramlette
Dear Friends,
According to promise I write a few lines to acquaint you of our whereabouts & whatabouts. Of the recent Scouts we have taken, & the battles we have fought, you are doubtless sufficiently informed from the many letters already written back. If not I must refer you to the hastily written letters of "North Texan" which appeared in the Paris Press, & upon which you can rely, as containing all the leading facts.[40]

For the particulars of the battle I have already referred you elsewhere. After the fight we fell back to this point [Fort Gibson]—sent to Arkansas for reinforcements, & to Ross for an explanation. Last night Ross arrived at this place, & he & Gen Cooper have had an interview, & a perfect understanding.

38. Bates's regiment, known as the 4th Texas Cavalry early in the war, would be listed as the 9th Texas Cavalry from the spring of 1862 on.
39. Neville, *History of Lamar County,* 108.
40. The first half of Dohoney's letter, not included here, went into great detail to explain the factionalism among the various Indian tribes fighting for both sides.

Today Ross made a speech to the Cherokee people, in which he said that the Cherokee Nation, in mass meeting had determined unanimously to form an alliance with the Confederate States. That Commissioners acting under these resolutions had made a treaty with the Confederate States becoming their friend, & allies—that said treaty had been unanimously adopted & ratified by the general council; & that every provision in it was highly advantageous to the Cherokee people, & that he & a large majority of the Cherokees were as true friends to the South as anybody in the South. He said that the difficulty on the Creek nation he had regarded as a personal one between McIntosh & Opotheyhola & that in the beginning there was no question of North & South in it. He said he had never invited Opotheyhola to lead his forces into the Cherokee nation; that [he] had only invited the chief himself to come, he (Ross) having been authorized by Gen Pike with the consent of the contending parties, to mediate between them, & settle the difficulty, if possible. But[,] said he[,] whether the difficulty in the Creek Nation was personal at the start or not Opotheyhola had made himself the enemy of the Cherokees by invading their territory, & that every Cherokee was in duty bound to make war on him until he is subdued; or makes peace, such as Gen Cooper the Commander of the Confederate forces may require of him. And that he wished the Cherokee to act in harmony with the loyal Creeks Choctaws, Texans & Arkansans in making war on the common enemy of the Confederate States; & that should the Cherokees all prove recreant *he himself would alone die in defense of their soil.*

Gen Cooper then made a short speech saying that he had at one time regarded the Creek difficulty as a personal quarrel between the leaders; but that he now had satisfactory information that Opotheyhola is in league with the North through agents in Kansas, & that it was now clear that this is no longer a personal or party difficulty, but the common war between the North & South. The Choctaws also had a talk with Ross, & it was clearly understood all round that we are all the friends of the South, & are to make war on Opotheyhola as our common enemy.

The reinforcements from Ark, consisting of [Colonel William C.] Young's [11th Texas Cavalry] Regiment[,] a part of [B. Warren] Stone's [6th Texas Cavalry Regiment] & some other forces—are to be here in a day or two. Also a new Choctaw regiment is coming in. As soon as the forces all get in, Gen Cooper will start again in quest of the enemy. The forces already here are ours, the Choctaw—the Creek, & Stanwattie's [Stand Watie's] Cherokee regiment 35 miles above here.[41]

Not more than half our Regiment will be able to go out again; about 200 men are sick & many horses are broke down; we have done some hard service—been greatly exposed, & our regiment is in bad condition. Winter quarters have long ago been assigned us in Arkansas; but we cannot leave here, in fact Gen Cooper is now authorized to retain us & all the forces sent him until this difficulty is settled. So there is no telling how long we will stay here, or whether we get into winter quarters at all or not.

I am enjoying very fine health. So are [Captain Jerry] Wright[,] [James C.] Bates[,] [John] Gibbons, [Dan] Hatcher, [Erasmus H.] Tanner & the Shearons.[42] Providence has blest me with far beyond what I had a right to expect. I have been on every Scout & in every fight—have gone as far as the farthest & done as much as the most, & withal never enjoyed finer health in my life. Our Lamar boys all acquitted themselves with the greatest credit in the battle. They were greatly exposed, but not a man flinched. I never saw as cool a set of men in my life; & I know I never was cooler, & was with them everywhere in the fight, & having no gun myself had an opportunity of watching the action of the men. No distinctions can be made. Every officer & every man was all the time at his post, & did his whole duty. Yours

E.L. Dohoney.

Present my best regards to Mrs Bradley & family to Mrs Bates Mrs Bramlette & family also to Dr [Alfred S.] Johnson's family, & the Paris [illegible word].[43] Please write to me soon & let me know

41. Stand Watie, a fifty-five-year-old Georgia-born Cherokee, was the principal chief of the Confederate Cherokees and a leader of the Ridge faction. A rival of John Ross, he had raised a regiment of Confederate Cherokees early in the war and was serving as its colonel. The only Indian to achieve the rank of general in the Confederate army, he would also be the last southern general to surrender at the end of the war. Current, *Encyclopedia of the Confederacy,* 4:1692–94; Kenny A. Franks, *Stand Watie and the Agony of the Cherokee Nation* (Memphis, Tenn.: Memphis State University Press, 1979).

42. Wright, Bates, Gibbons, Hatcher, and Tanner have all been identified earlier. Andrew J. and Samuel R. Shearon, also members of Company H, were Tennesseans in their early twenties.

43. Alfred S. Johnson, a Paris physician, was the father of the sisters who would later marry Dohoney and Bates. Schedule I, roll 1299, Eighth Census. (Johnson's name was incorrectly recorded as Alex in the 1860 census.)

what is going on in Lamar [County]. I have not heard a word since
I left there. Direct to me at this place. To the care of the Quarter
Master at Ft Smith—to be forwarded by express to this place or our
camp—4th Tex Cav
E.L.D.

Although Dohoney and Bates doubtless enjoyed their days at Fort Gibson,
they would soon be scouting across the freezing terrain of the Cherokee
Nation once again. Opothle Yahola was not finished with them. The two
Texans would follow his trail as far north as Kansas before they were finally
allowed to face real Yankees in Arkansas.

3 To Arkansas and Elkhorn Tavern

The Confederate high command in Arkansas, having granted Colonel Douglas Cooper's request for reinforcements to chase down Opothle Yahola, was determined this time to put an end to the old man's trouble-making in the Indian Territory. About 1,600 fresh troops, hauled out of their winter quarters in northwest Arkansas, rode into the Indian Territory in late December under the leadership of Cooper's superior, Colonel James McIntosh. The latter—a West Point graduate and veteran of the frontier wars against the Indians—came to the Indian Territory himself "to settle matters in the nation."[1]

Ambitious and aggressive, Colonel McIntosh devised an elaborate plan to trap Opothle Yahola in a pincer maneuver: McIntosh would take three of the new Texas regiments north up the Verdigris River (east of the Chustotalasah battleground), and Cooper would lead his old command, plus some of the recent arrivals, northwest up the Arkansas River to a point west of Chustotalasah. Within a week, McIntosh believed, he could crush the dissidents between his two forces and "settle matters in the nation."[2]

Bates and his comrades welcomed the reinforcements from Arkansas, especially an independent company manned by friends and acquaintances from Lamar County. As his column set off on its third expedition against Opothle Yahola, Bates himself was still grumbling about his Indian allies' lack of discipline and Colonel Sims's alleged propensity for show. Bates

1. *OR*, Vol. 8, p. 715; Current, *Encyclopedia of the Confederacy*, 3:973; Hale, "Rehearsal for Civil War," 245–46.

2. *OR*, Vol. 8, pp. 12, 22.

also resorted to a common practice among Civil War soldiers, sometimes called "foraging" or "jayhawking" but otherwise known as stealing food.

Wed. Dec. 18th 1861 [diary]

After breakfast went up to hospital to see our sick. Bought some fine apple cider. Returned to camp & did some tailoring. In evening heard John Ross principal chief of the Cherokees make another speech.

Sat. Dec. 21st 1861 [diary]

Today [Colonel B. Warren] Stone's [6th Texas Cavalry] Regiment came in about 400 men. [Colonel William C.] Young's [11th Texas Cavalry Regiment], [Colonel James] McIntosh's [2nd Arkansas] and [Colonel Elkanah] Greer's [3rd Texas Cavalry] already in as also [Major John W.] Whitfield's [4th Texas Cavalry] Battalion. The troops under McIntosh now number 1,500 or 1,800. [Captain H. S.] Bennett's Company from Lamar came in today. Saw most of my old acquaintances from that county.

Sun. Dec. 22nd 1861 [diary]

McIntosh's command left today at 12 pm for Gouge's camp. They go up betwixt the Verdigris and Grand rivers. Will approach Opotheyhola from the north—in order to cut off his retreat in that direction. Sent a letter to Aunt Tennessee today by a man from English's Company.[3] Sent several others in the last few days to Paris but doubt they will ever reach there.

Mon. Dec. 23rd 1861 [diary]

This morning our Reg or rather 225 of it took up a line of march to join Cooper who is encamped 20 miles from Fort Gibson near Ark river. He has some 1,500 Choctaws & 500 or 600 Creeks camped near him on the west. Saw Wemple this evening—Whitfield's Battalion have gone up to Kiota mission in order to get forage. Wemple says Cooper was yesterday on a big drunk. In fact nearly all his army were on a spree.

3. Thirty-four years old in 1861, Tennessee McDonald Carson was a younger sister of Bates's mother. She had apparently moved from San Antonio to Paris about the time the war began. Schedule I (Free Inhabitants), Seventh Census (Microfilm M432, roll 914, Rusk County); interview with Bates's descendant, Henry Fink, July 29, 1997.

Tues. Dec. 24th 1861 [diary]

Leaving General Cooper this morning we moved up to this place (Broken Arrow) fifteen miles NW of our last night's camp. On the way—Sims marched us around by Whitfield's Battalion in order to show himself I suppose. As we had no meat for dinner I started out with my gun to do my first jay hawking.[4] Succeeded in killing some fine shoats and have enough to roast one for a Christmas dinner.

While Cooper's half of the pincer moved northwest through present-day Tulsa to get behind Opothle Yahola's band, Colonel McIntosh's half rode through ice and snow, circling from the east. On December 26, McIntosh's command finally ran the old chief to ground, about ten miles northwest of the Chustotalasah battlefield. Impulsive as ever, McIntosh ordered a charge against the strongly positioned Creeks, and the Texans charged up a steep ridge. To the surprise of the defenders, the Texans made it up the hill and through clouds of arrows and bullets, firing their shotguns and slashing at every Indian within range. Opothle Yahola's ranks disintegrated under the assault, and his warriors fled to the north, leaving their families and possessions behind. The Battle of Chustenahlah (Shoal Creek) finally eliminated Opothle Yahola's band as a military threat. The fugitive Creeks lost about 250 warriors during the fight and many more as they were pursued northward. Hundreds of their women and children and nearly all their food, animals, and equipment also fell into the hands of the Confederates. The Texans had lost only fifteen killed and about forty wounded.[5]

Bates and the men in Cooper's column knew nothing about the battle until a few days later. On the day of the fight, they were marching through Tulsey Town (Tulsa), still hoping to circle behind Opothle Yahola from the west. Informed by couriers that McIntosh had routed the Creeks, Bates was skeptical. Surely, he thought, McIntosh had fought only a detachment of the dissidents. When it became clear that McIntosh's column from Arkansas had indeed shattered Opothle Yahola's little army, veterans of

4. In their first few months of service, some soldiers felt compelled to admit, rather guiltily, that they had acquired provisions in an unaccustomed manner. Private F. A. Rawlins of the 6th Texas Cavalry admitted to a bit of foraging himself: "We had a big mess of roasting ears today. How we got them is nobodys business." Entry of July 12, 1862, F. A. Rawlins Diary, University of North Texas Library, Denton.

5. For battle reports, see OR, Vol. 8, pp. 22–30. For secondary accounts, see Josephy, Civil War in the American West, 332–33; Douglas Hale, The Third Texas Cavalry in the Civil War (Norman: University of Oklahoma Press, 1993), 80–82.

Round Mountains and Chustotalasah must have silently cursed their misfortune—they had chased the fugitives for six weeks, and suffered mightily in the pursuit, and now newcomers had finished their job for them.[6]

Wed. Dec. 25th 1861 [diary]

Today is Christmas. How differently has this day been spent than
one year ago. Then I was at home among friends—with, it is true, a
dim prospect of war in the future—but few of us thought to be so
soon in the field—but so it is—what may another year bring forth.
Where will we all then be—will we be once more at home or will we
still be engaged in war, bloody strife—will grim visaged war smooth
his wrinkled front—I think not.[7] For a little variety Sims took us out
on the prairie to go through movements that we had done 500 times
before. After drilling an hour or so we returned to camp and whiled
away the day as best we could awaiting the arrival of Cooper who
passed us in the evening. At night as nothing better presented assembled in our tent—to crack jokes, spin yarns—sing songs, thus
passed the time untill 10 oclk at night.

Thurs. Dec 26th 1861 [diary]

At daylight we were on the march. Moved up to Tulsytown
[Tulsa] 15 miles NW. Passed Cooper on our left. Received a dispatch this morning from McIntosh—its nature not made known.
Cooper came up at night—went out this evening & killed a fine
hog. Had to walk about half the time in order to keep warm. Cold
enough to freeze my breath on my mustache.

Friday Dec. 27th 1861 [diary]

Moved up six or eight miles—got some corn—then turned our
course NW in the direction of McIntosh's trains—a mile off Bush
head Creek. Learned from McIntosh's wagon guard that their force
had gone on & attacked Gouge on Thursday. They claim to have
routed them completely. On hearing this Gen Cooper thought it
useless to go farther and camped for the night.

6. George L. Griscom of Company D wrote that the men of the 9th Texas Cavalry were
"very anxious to be concerned" in the climactic fight against Opothle Yahola. Kerr, ed.,
Fighting with Ross' Texas Cavalry, 10.

7. The phrase about "grim visaged war" is from Shakespeare's *Richard III* (act 1,
scene 1).

Sat. Dec. 28th 1861 [diary]

With our trains started this morning to Col McIntosh's assistance as we heard he was still fighting—marched some twelve miles & met McIntosh returning. He reports the enemy completely routed & that it is useless for us to proceed. His loss is 12 killed, 16 wounded. They claim to have killed some 270 enemy. McIntosh passed on down on his way to Fort Smith. Col Cooper however determined to follow the enemy up to the bend of the Ark[ansas River] and destroy all the corn & drive the cattle down to settlements. It is general opinion of our men that McIntosh fought only a small portion of Gouge's force & that the main force is in the Big Bend 25 or 30 miles to the NW. Camped two miles from the battle ground.

Colonel McIntosh, having "settled matters in the nation," led most of the recently arrived Texans back to their winter quarters in Arkansas. Cooper's command, however, spent several more days pursuing the defeated Creeks. Riding across frozen plains and through sleet and snow, the weary, hungry Texans pushed on under gray skies as far north as the Kansas border, perhaps even sliding into Kansas for a while, picking up stragglers and finishing off any who resisted. "There was no game or other food, but ice, wind, snow, sleet and starvation was our experience," Private Sparks complained. Despite the cold, hunger, and discomfort, on New Year's Eve Bates mused about the meaning of it all and speculated about his future.[8]

Sunday Dec. 29th 1861 [diary]

Leaving about 400 men to guard our trains we started on the march in search of the enemy. Moved in a northerly direction four or five miles. Struck Bird Creek where just twenty days ago we laid on our arms all night awaiting an attack from Gouge. Do'nt think I will soon forget that night. Passed around the mountains & found Stanwattury [Stand Watie] encamped gathering up stock, ponies. kept on our march over a very rugged country winding about in order to avoid the worst hills. passed the grave of an Osage Indian. He was buried as all his tribe are—on the surface of the ground with a stone wall built round them and covered over. His horse had been killed by his grave. His bow-arrow & other trinkets were buried with him according to their custom.

8. Sparks, *War Between the States*, 47; Kerr, ed., *Fighting with Ross' Texas Cavalry*, 10–11; Rose, *Ross' Texas Brigade*, 51; Hale, "Rehearsal for Civil War," 253–54.

Mon. Dec. 30th 1861 [diary]

This morning one of Whitfield's Battalion was killed by an accidental discharge of a six shooter. On yesterday two of his men were wounded in like manner. Three squadrons of our Reg, Whitfield's Battalion plus two hundred Choctaws acted as an advance guard today. Marched to every point of the compass today over one of the roughest countries we have yet seen. Marched about fifteen miles & camped in a very fine valley on the headwaters of the Verdigris river.[9]

Tues. Dec. 31st 1861 [diary]

Resuming our march this morning we moved in a northerly direction some ten miles. Passed some camp fires still burning. Since learned a squad of forty or fifty left there this morning. After crossing the creek the head of the column halted to let the rear catch up. While stoped here our scouts discovered four Indians, two squaws & two men. They [the scouts] gave chase—overtook them. One surrendered, the other refused & was shot. The other in the melee escaped. Moved three miles further north. Changed our course west toward the Ark[ansas River]. late in the evening our advance guard took five women & three children prisoners, the men with them running off & leaving them as soon as they discovered our approach. They report the enemy dispersed scattering all over the country. Our guide says we are within eight miles of Kansas. Can see into Kansas from a hill near camp.

A LONG FAREWELL TO EIGHTEEN HUNDRED AND SIXTY ONE. Today one year ago I was at home amongst friends having a merry time over a bowl of eggnog with ———.[10] What unexpected changes are wrought in the short time of one year. In the last year a mighty nation has been rent asunder. The revolution then in its incipiency, a mere speck in the sky is now a giant in proportions, affecting directly or indirectly the whole civilized world. Today advance guard took a number of prisoners, a lot of ponies, and fortunately for all seventeen head of cattle & some dried buffalo meat. All of which will be eaten for supper & breakfast. Still four days from the trains & the four days provisions started with [are] *all* out.

9. It is doubtful that Bates and his fellow troopers reached the actual headwaters of the Verdigris River. That stream rises in east central Kansas, at least eighty miles north of the border with the old Indian Territory.

10. Bates often left a blank space in his diary when he clearly was referring to his sweetheart, Mootie, back in Paris.

The Battle of Chustenahlah and the pursuit of the survivors over the wintry plains of the Indian Territory is one of the saddest sagas in the history of the Creek Nation. Those who came through the battle and eluded the Texans still had to contend with food shortages, separation from family members, and bitter cold. Those who straggled to safety in southeastern Kansas found little immediate help from the U. S. Army or the Federal government. During February and March alone, nearly 250 Creeks died in their new camp, and dozens of others had frozen limbs amputated to save their lives. (Opothle Yahola himself, survivor of many hardships in a very long life, would die in 1863.)[11]

Bates and the pursuing column of Confederates turned west on New Year's Eve and then southeast along the Arkansas River toward their base camp at Fort Gibson, still sweeping up scattered fugitives here and there. As usual, the observant and curious Bates was never too busy to soak up local customs and lore about the Indians. Once again, the Texans, far from their supply wagons, suffered from hunger; some ate a horse, and Bates foraged for stray grains of corn. When they came upon abandoned farms and fields, however, they fared somewhat better. When they finally reached Fort Gibson, they must have marveled at the luxury of female company, music, and eggnog.[12]

> Wed. Jan 1st 1862 [diary]
> Last night a norther commenced blowing. This morning advance guard took some prisoners, cattle & buffalo meat dried. The beef & meat a lucky haul for us as we have nothing to eat besides these. A long way from our trains. If the first twelve days of the year are an index to the whole year, we will certainly not suffer from gout the first month. The dawn of this year is certainly not inviting whatever the close may be. Oh, that this day might be the beginning of a new era in our history—that with the new year peace & tranquillity might begin to reign once more.

> Thurs. Jan. 2nd 1862 [diary]
> Last night a drizzling rain fell most of the night freezing as it fell.

11. Edmund J. Danziger, Jr., "The Office of Indian Affairs and the Problem of Civil War Indian Refugees in Kansas," *Kansas Historical Quarterly* 35 (Autumn 1969): 261–64; Debo, *Road to Disappearance*, 152; Hale, "Rehearsal for Civil War," 254.

12. By January 1, Bates's regiment could count only 677 men on duty, about two-thirds of their original number. Many, too ill to ride, had been left behind at various camps. *OR*, Vol. 8, p. 28.

This morning our top blankets as stiff as a plank from the ice.[13] As officer of the day had command of the advance guard. About noon came on the long-looked for Ark river. Found an old trail of considerable size making down the river. Was probably made when they [Opothle Yahola's band] retreated from Round Mountain. Took down the trail passing a large camp every mile or two. Have been deserted two or three weeks. Late in the evening discovered three Indians. Made their escape across the river. A half mile further down discovered a camp—made a charge on it. All but two made their escape up the bluff. There intercepted seventeen women & children & one man trying to make their escape. Moved on a mile or so. Camped for the night. Nothing but a little scrap of dirty buffalo meat left for breakfast & to eat tonight. Better however fast a little in order to rest our digestive organs. Some have nothing to eat. Whitfield's men killed a colt tonight & ate it. After mounting & putting out guard—parched a handful of corn in the ashes I found this morning.

Friday Jan. 3rd 1862 [diary]

As we were not troubled this morning with getting breakfast— have nothing to eat—got an early start. About noon came to an old deserted house. Discovered a cow & some poor hogs. Instantly a dozen or more hungry men were after each hog & fifty after the cow. These soon shot—cut up & tied behind our saddles. Some built a fire & went to cooking. A few miles further found plenty of hogs & some corn. We feasted tonight on roast pork. Where we camped on Xmas Day—Broken Arrows—takes its name from an Indian legend. Soon after the red men came to this section of the country a pale face wandered from his tribe & was found hungry & cold by an Indian maiden who took him to the camp of her father. There he remained for a time when a mutual passion sprang up between them but the father refused to give his blessing. He refused to give his daughter to the pale face. Mimalela at last yielded to the entreaties of her lover & consented to fly with him to his own native land but Mimalela's father pursued and at this place overtook them. Maddened with rage he determined to take the life of the one who had robbed him of his Mimalela. The last but one arrow was taken from his quiver and shot

13. "On one day and night the sleet fell and accumulated on guns, sticks, and all objects to a thickness of more than one inch," Private Sparks remembered. Sparks, *War Between the States*, 47.

at him yet the pale face stood with folded arms still unharmed. The father called on the great spirit to strike the pale face down if this last arrow should fail him. The instant the arrow sped from the bow a thunderbolt from the great spirit descended but instead of killing the pale face it struck the arrow breaking it in the middle—one half falling on the east, the other on the west side of a beautiful little rivulet running by. These were turned to stone & having continued to grow untill now they are each about ten feet long and one foot in diameter. Resemble very much a large arrow. The father took this as evidence of the unjustness of his opposition—relented—they were married. Many may now be found claiming to be descendants of Mimalela and the pale face.

Monday Jan. 6th 1862 [diary]
    A march of twenty miles brought us to the Ark river [near Tulsa] where we camped [on January 4].[14]

Tuesday Jan. 7th 1862 [diary]
    Arrived in Gibson about twelve miles [i.e., within twelve miles of Fort Gibson]. Traveled eighteen miles found most of the boys able to be up. there have been many deaths in the Reg since we left—none in our command.[15] Been absent fifteen days on the scout. With Eb [Dohoney], John [Gibbons], & Dan [Hatcher] called on the Misses, heard some very good music. Drank some fine eggnog, had a pleasant chat of an hour or two & enjoyed myself finely. First house I have sat down in since leaving home.

Almost immediately upon arriving at Fort Gibson, the regiment was ordered to pack up and move east to Arkansas, their original destination when they had left their camp of instruction near Sherman in late October. Now, finally, they might be able to do some good for the Confederacy, they hoped. Bates and many of his comrades certainly were glad to leave the Indian Territory. Private Sparks wrote that "We left the Indians with great rejoicings and none seem inclined to remain in the B. I. T. or beautiful Indian Territory."[16]

    14. Kerr, ed., *Fighting with Ross' Texas Cavalry,* 11.
    15. Although Bates's diary indicated that no men of Company H had died, Private Sparks wrote that while at Fort Gibson, "our flag was nearly always at half mast and a funeral possession [procession] was of daily occurrence. In the grave-yard southeast of Fort Gibson are buried many of the 9th Texas Cavalry." Sparks, *War Between the States,* 49.
    16. Ibid.

Lieutenant Bates, accurately recalling his history lessons, noted that the day of departure from Fort Gibson was the forty-seventh anniversary of Andrew Jackson's victory at the Battle of New Orleans. Contemplating a long winter of leisure, Bates even began thinking of visiting his family and friends back in Paris. Securing one of the prized furloughs granted after the regiment reached Arkansas, he set off on a long, cold ride back across the Indian Territory to Paris.

Wed. Jan 8th 1862 [diary]

Were ordered to start on the march this morning to Horse head Bayou [in Arkansas]—our winter quarters 120 miles from here—accordingly by 8 oclk all were in readiness.[17] We were in motion. The thought of once more leaving these Indians & getting amongst white people had made me feel very much like I was going home. Today forty seven years ago the last & greatest battle of the war of 1812–14 was fought. Would that today the last battle of this war might be fought.

Thur. Jan 9th 1862 [diary]

Traveled today over a hilly broken country—fifteen miles recrossed the Ark[ansas River]. One of the finest bottoms & timber here I ever saw. Saw standing in the door of a house a half mile back one of the finest looking women I have ever seen in the nation. Think I will come back to this section when the war is over as I understand there are a number of wealthy young ladies living in this vicinity.

Fri. Jan 10 Sat Jan 11th 1862 [diary]

Yesterday & today have traveled thirty five miles. Yesterday over a very rough broken country—today have had a good road but most of the country is sandy prairie. We are camped tonight eight miles from Fort Smith.[18] The nearer I get to winter quarters—more I am in notion of going home. Heard this evening there was a package of letters at Ft. Smith for us. Think I will get one from ———.

17. From Fort Gibson the regiment would ride about eighty-five road miles southeast to Van Buren, on the Arkansas side of the border with the Indian Territory. The winter camp at Horsehead Creek was about fifty road miles farther east of Van Buren. Kerr, ed., *Fighting with Ross' Texas Cavalry,* 11–12.

18. Fort Smith, Arkansas, was about seven miles southwest of Van Buren.

Sunday Jan 12th 1862 [diary]

had hardly finished my "notes of the day" last night when some of Capt [H. C.] Bennett's Company [the Lamar Cavalry] came in from Ft. Smith bringing a letter from Ma & one from ———. Felt almost like I had just paid a visit home. Ordered not to go through Ft. Smith on account of small pox. Passed through Van Buren & camped in two miles of it. Permission was given by Gen McIntosh to furlough four privates & two officers from each company.[19]

Monday Jan 13th 1862 [diary]

Went into Van Buren last evening to write the furloughs of our men—determined to go myself about Sunday. Got everything in readiness last night. Started for home this morning. Detained in Van Buren untill afternoon. Went over to Ft. Smith in the evening. Got our furloughs signed by Gen McIntosh. Went with Lieut Wright to see some ladies.[20] Had a fine time generally.

Tuesday Jan 14 Wed. Jan 15th [1862] [diary]

Yesterday and today traveled sixty five miles. Staid last night at McDaniel's thirty two miles from Ft. Smith. Tonight at Capt Riddle's. Last three days so cold could not ride but few miles untill we had to walk to warm ourselves. Traveled today mostly through a valley—mountains on each side. Poor country thinly inhabited. Passed over two or three of the Seven Devils—have not got to the big devil yet.[21]

19. Colonel James McIntosh, not yet a general, would be promoted on January 24. The mischievous Private Sparks of Company I and some of his comrades celebrated their return to town life and its temptations by getting drunk, "notwithstanding heroic efforts of the officers to keep us sober." Sparks, *War Between the States,* 49; Ezra J. Warner, *Generals in Gray: Lives of the Confederate Commanders* (Baton Rouge: Louisiana State University Press, 1959), 203.

20. This may have been Ewell M. Wright of Company B. In their letters and diaries Civil War soldiers, as one might expect from gentlemen of the Victorian era, were notoriously indirect and even evasive about sex. Whether the women Bates and Wright visited were ladies in the polite sense of the word or something else was not specified, but nowhere does Bates mention any female kin or acquaintances in the area of Fort Smith. Muster roll, Company B, in Kerr, ed., *Fighting with Ross' Texas Cavalry,* 215; Thomas P. Lowry, *The Story the Soldiers Wouldn't Tell: Sex in the Civil War* (Mechanicsburg, Pa.: Stackpole Books, 1994), x, 5–8.

21. The Seven Devils is a series of steep sandstone ridges in the Ouachita Mountains of southeastern Oklahoma. Seven Devils Mountain is in modern-day Haskell County, about forty miles west-southwest of Fort Smith.

Thurs. Jan 16th 1862 [diary]

Breakfasted this morning at 5 oclk. As soon as we could travel we were on our way. Traveled twenty miles by noon. While waiting for our dinners the lady received the news that her husband had been killed at Ft. Smith a few days ago by falling down a flight of stairs while drunk. Poor woman, the blow was hard enough without her sorrow being made ten fold more bitter by knowing how he died. This war will give an aching heart to many a wife widowed and children made orphans—but near despair must be the bitter grief of those who mourn some loved one dead & a drunkard.

Friday Jan 17th 1862 [diary]

Traveled forty five miles today over some of the worst road we have had yet. Crossed the *biggest*—the *rockiest highest steepest* and last of the Seven Devils. In fact the last one was *the* very devil. Got to our stoping place just at dark & as a cold rain was just setting in. Got the first good supper since leaving the train.

After a hard five-day ride of about two hundred miles through the wintry hills of the Choctaw Nation, Bates and his unnamed companions rode into Paris on the afternoon of January 18. Arriving without advance notice, Bates was overwhelmed by the female attention showered on him in Paris. His mother, his sister Adela, Mootie, and other women of the neighborhood probably looked upon the returning soldiers in a new light now that they had "gone to war." Bates recorded no diary entries during his month in Paris—there seemed no need to write down the events at home—but he and his comrades doubtless enjoyed plentiful food cooked by more expert hands than usual, admiring glances from lady friends, and numerous opportunities to tell and retell stories about their pursuit of "old Gouge."

Sat. Jan 18th 1862 [diary]

Started at sun up. A cold mist falling untill noon, crossed the Red River at 10 AM. Met several old acquaintances—got into Paris at 4 oclk—not looking for me at home—soon after I got in several of my lady friends called. Either they were glad to see me—or else I had so changed or it had been a long time since I had had a lady to look at me it seemed they were all looking at me at the same time. I felt like I had rather face a battery of cannon than so many bright eyes at the same time. After an absence of four months in camp, home &

home comforts have a zest that none can appreciate who have not tried it. I have one short month to stay at home. Will this be the last? I hope it will not.

While Bates and his comrades enjoyed life in Paris, their regiment continued about fifty miles east of Van Buren and set up a winter camp on Horsehead Creek, a tributary of the nearby Arkansas River and about seven miles west of Clarksville. Log cabins (built in rows by company), chimneys, stoves, and other luxuries "were much more comfortable than a blanket in the snow or even a tent," a sergeant in Company D remembered. In fact, "but for the daily routine of feeding our stock[,] Guard mountings &c we would get lazy." Private Sparks of Company I, always ready for entertainment, remembered that "the only sport we had at this camp was horse racing, in which we tried the speed of some of the Arkansaw stock to our sorrow. One little gray horse belonging to an old hayseed beat one of our best horses." The cozy, drowsy camp at Horsehead Creek sprang to life on February 16, however, when word arrived that Brigadier General Samuel R. Curtis's Federal army in Missouri was moving toward northwest Arkansas. Within a day the regiment had packed up, saddled up, and was traveling north to join General Ben McCulloch's main army near Fayetteville.[22]

On the same day that the regiment moved out of winter quarters to join McCulloch, Bates was making his farewells to his mother, sister, Mootie, and Paris friends. He knew nothing of the excitement coursing through his regiment as he saddled up for another long, cold ride back to camp.

Mon Feb. 17th 1862 [diary]

My leave of absence has expired—one month passed & it hardly seems a day. This morning I bid good bye to the loved ones at home. Will it be a last goodbye? Something seems to whisper that it was. A presentiment which I hope may only be produced by the fear that it may be the last.

22. Kerr, ed., *Fighting with Ross' Texas Cavalry*, 11–12; Sparks, *War Between the States*, 50. Curtis's army of eleven thousand men occupied Springfield in southwest Missouri on February 13 and continued into northwest Arkansas. Meanwhile, Confederate Brigadier General Ben McCulloch's regiments combined with Sterling Price's Missouri militia to form an army of about seventeen thousand men, under the overall command of Major General Earl Van Dorn, in the Boston Mountains just south of Fayetteville. For the entire Pea Ridge campaign, see Shea and Hess, *Pea Ridge*.

Tues. Feb. 18th 1862 [diary]

Started this morning with a cold sleet with the prospect of it continuing all day. Riding in the sleet with the blues is no pleasant business. Stoped at an execrable looking shanty—& got supper—fat bacon—corn bread & corn meal, coffee about 9 oclk. Traveled twenty five miles.

Feb 19th 1862 [diary]

Got an early start this morning, ground frozen hard as a brick. Traveled forty five miles today and stayed at a worse looking place if possible than on last night—on the line road from Mineral Hill. We are seeing some of Arkansas now.

Thurs. Feb 20th 1862 [diary]

Our road today lay over the poorest and most completely God forsaken country I ever saw. Do'nt think the inhabitants here know anything of this war. In fact do'nt think they know anything. Cant imagine why the roads in Ark are so narrow unless it is because they are stretched so. At any rate the miles are all very long.

Friday Feb 21st 1862 [diary]

Rode hard today untill noon & found we were only twelve miles in a direct line from where we started this morning. Called at a house near by to get some water. While looking at the mercury in a thermometer banging against the wall, Briggs came up & asked what it was & I told him. After looking at it awhile he remarked that a friend of his had one larger than that—it would set green wood on fire.

Bates and his party found the road back to camp longer and harder than the one to Paris, and they rode a full week before reaching their regiment's winter quarters near Clarksville, called Cantonment Slidell by the men in honor of the land owner.[23] As soon as he arrived, he sat down to write letters to his mother and Mootie. By then, the regiment had trotted off to the north to join McCulloch and Price south of Fayetteville. Within a few days, Bates and most of the remaining men in the regiment followed them.

23. Sparks, *War Between the States*, 49–50.

Cantonment Slidell Ark
Feb [24?] 1862
Dear Ma:

This evening about 4 oclk we arrived at our quarters—several days before getting here *we* learned that our Regt had been ordered to join Gen Price at Fayetteville, or Boston Mountain some distance this side of there—we consequently found our quarters nearly deserted—only a few men left to take care of the baggage, Government stores &c. This evening we received an order from Gen McCulloch to join him immediately—we start tomorrow morning—will not reach his camp until the day after tomorrow

you will doubtless hear very exaggerated reports of the State of affairs here. The nearer we get to the army—the less cause is there for alarm. The latest news we have from there is, that at Cross Hollows some distance beyond Fayetteville a little fight had taken place in which we lost 3 men & the enemy over 100. This was on Tuesday last the day we left home. Since then Price had fallen back to Boston Mountain—below Fayetteville—and will there make a stand. His and McCulloch's forces combined will amount to 20 or 25,000. The federal force is variously estimated at from 30 to 75,000.[24] The pickets have been fighting every day for a week—our troops are said to be eager for a fight and confident of success if the enemy can be induced to attack us at Boston Mountain as it is a very strong position. I am of opinion the fight will be over before we will be able to get there if there is a fight at all. Many here seem to think the enemy will not attack us at all. The Militia have all been ordered out here—and are joining price as rapidly as possible—six or eight thousand will join him in the course of this week. There are but a few of our company left here—all but the sick will go with us tomorrow.

I have no time to write more to-night but will as soon as we get to the army. I hope the enemy will give us a fight. I want us to make amends for the defeats we have suffered in the East.[25] If we win a vic-

24. Both sides frequently overestimated the size of the enemy's army. Here Bates overestimates the size of both forces. The Federal army in northwest Arkansas numbered about eleven thousand men; the Confederates, about seventeen thousand.

25. Always interested in the overall progress of the war, Bates kept himself informed about events in other theaters. The defeats he mentions were probably the Federal army's occupation of various points along the coast of the Carolinas and Georgia in late 1861 and early 1862. Unlike some men on both sides, Bates generally did not exaggerate victories or down-

tory it may cost us the lives of many men—but they cannot die in a nobler cause. If it should be *my* fate to fall with others you shall never blush to hear how I fell. I have not and *will not* forget my last promise to you.[26] My love to all. Direct as heretofore to Ft. Smith.

JC Bates

Cantonment Slidell
Johnson Co Ark Feb [24?] 62
Miss Mootie Johnson
Dear Friend:

One week since this evening (I believe however since I think of it, it was in the "wee small hours anent the twal" on *Tuesday*) I told you "good bye." Tonight 250 Arkansas miles intervene between us. As much as I have seen of Ark—the worst has remained until the last. Our route to this point has been over Mountain after Mountain from the time we crossed the line untill we arrived at camp which was late this evening. If the Arkansas troops are one half as rough as their country they need but to show themselves to a Yankee to make him run. As a fair specimen of the hills and hollows we have crossed over—and of the people and where they live—I will tell you what I [letter torn and sentences missing]

I have heard of long roads without a turn, but this is the longest I have seen without a *straight* place. But enough about Ark.

We start tomorrow morning by day light for Gen Price's army. Our Regt with the exception of a few sick are already there. A fight is hourly anticipated. Whether we will get there in time to take part or not I do'nt know but hope we will. Gen Price has fallen back to Boston Mountain 80 or 90 mile N W of this place where he will make a stand. His force is 20,000 or more—that of the enemy not known but considerably greater. A little fight occurred on last Tuesday in which we lost 3 men—the enemy over one hundred—so says report. We also have a report that [James H.] Lane and Opothleyhola are coming down into the Creek nation, but this is not gener-

---

play defeats when he had solid information. His disappointment with the incomplete victory at Chustotalasah is an earlier example.

26. His mother had apparently made Bates promise not to expose himself to danger unnecessarily.

ally credited.[27] My kindest regards to Mrs J[ohnson, Mootie's mother] Miss Mary and Mat [Mootie's sisters].

March 1st 1862 [diary]

Several days have elapsed & I have made no notes. In fact I got sick of Arkansas & everything connected with it. Got to our winter quarters last night and stayed there.[28] Found our Reg had been gone several days. Started this morning with those of the regiment who had been left behind. Stayed tonight at Storm's winter quarters.

March 2nd 1862 [diary]

Leaving this morning we took the nearest by roads leading to Boston Mountains as we learned a fight was expected immediately. Marched untill night & was told we could get forage on the mountain. Found it all gone & had to turn back two miles.

March 3rd 1862 [diary][29]

Before sun up on the march—& about 3 PM arrived at McCulloch's headquarters—stoped awhile with Bennett's corn—went on to our camp at the foot of the mountain—found nearly all the boys out foraging.[30] The enemy still at Cross Hollows [just south of the Missouri border]. My Company out near Fayetteville on picket guard [about forty miles south of the Missouri border]. Started before breakfast so have had nothing to eat all day.

March 4th 1862 [diary]

Ordered by Van Dorn (who came in yesterday) to prepare ten days rations last night, but as we had but two days rations that was all we could cook—so we started with that.[31] Camped tonight one

27. James H. Lane, Republican senator from Kansas, had been pressuring President Lincoln since the beginning of the war to allow him to lead a slave-liberating invasion from Kansas to Texas. Opothle Yahola and the Creeks, of course, were in no condition to go to war again in the winter of 1861–62. Josephy, *Civil War in the American West,* 350; Patricia L. Faust, ed., *Historical Times Illustrated Encyclopedia of the Civil War* (New York: Harper & Row, 1986), 424–25.

28. Bates mistakenly wrote "last night" when he meant "last week."

29. On March 3 the designation of Sims's Texas regiment was changed from the 4th to the 9th Texas Cavalry. Kerr, ed., *Fighting with Ross' Texas Cavalry,* 13.

30. Bates and the men in his party apparently borrowed forage for their horses from Captain H. C. Bennett's independent company of cavalry from Lamar County.

31. Major General Earl Van Dorn, forty-one years old, was a West Point graduate, a vet-

mile from Fayetteville. I was sent out this evening in command of a foraging party—found corn & oats—took what we wanted—gave a receipt for it.[32] Saw no Feds.

By March 5 the leading edges of the two opposing armies were beginning to make contact a few miles north of Fayetteville. While the main body of Van Dorn's Confederate army moved north from Fayetteville by the road toward Bentonville, hoping to loop around to the west of the Federal army and to its rear, some of the Texas cavalry were sent up a parallel road a few miles to the east to distract Federal attention. As Bates's diary makes clear, the 6th Texas Cavalry did most of this work. After demonstrating and drawing enemy eyes toward them on the parallel road, the Texans slipped over to the other route and proceeded north ahead of the main body of Van Dorn's army.[33]

March 5th 1862 [diary]

Our pickets stayed in Fayetteville last night with four pieces of artillery. Here Price's command took the right hand, so we took the left leading to Elm Springs—seven or eight miles from Fayetteville. [B. Warren] Stone's [6th Texas Cavalry] Reg went on in advance to attack the enemy & draw out their cavalry. Our Reg, [William C.] Young's [11th Texas Cavalry] & [Elkanah] Greer's [3rd Texas Cavalry] in ambush on the right of the road. Waited there several hours but they did not come. Stone's Reg [rode] within two miles of their camp and captured seven wagons loaded with corn and thirty six prisoners. Finding we could not draw the enemy out—ordered to mount & proceed to Elm Springs where Price had already arrived by

eran of the Mexican War, and a friend of his fellow Mississippian, Confederate President Jefferson Davis. When Generals Sterling Price and Ben McCulloch found it impossible to cooperate with each other, Van Dorn, commander of the Confederacy's Trans-Mississippi District, took command of their combined forces. Current, *Encyclopedia of the Confederacy,* 4:1651–52; Robert G. Hartje, *Van Dorn: The Life and Times of a Confederate General* (Nashville, Tenn.: Vanderbilt University Press, 1967). See also Dabney H. Maury to Colonel William Preston Johnston, June 10, 1876, in *Supplement to the Official Records of the Union and Confederate Armies,* ed. Janet B. Hewett, Noah Andre Trudeau, and Bryce A. Suderow (47 vols. to date; Wilmington, N.C.: Broadfoot, 1994–), 1:558–60.

32. Hapless civilians caught in the path of any Civil War army were often deprived of food and forage despite their protests. If the expropriators considered them loyal, the civilians were given receipts for later reimbursement.

33. *OR,* Vol. 8, p. 303; Shea and Hess, *Pea Ridge,* 63–64.

a different route. All we get for our horses here is by jay hawking. Often the last ear of corn is taken from families who are bound to suffer in consequence.

General Van Dorn hoped to make a quick dash northward and capture Bentonville, about twenty-five miles north of Fayetteville. From there, he thought, he could swing around to the east behind Curtis's Federal army and cut its supply line to Missouri. On March 6 he sent James McIntosh's cavalry, including the 9th Texas, and Sterling Price's Missouri militia up toward Bentonville. In addition to circling behind Curtis's main army, the Confederates hoped to bag a detachment of the Federals still loitering in Bentonville. The tardy retreat of Brigadier General Franz Sigel from the little crossroads town almost resulted in his isolation from the rest of the Union army. General McIntosh's cavalry had an opportunity when they reached the southern outskirts of Bentonville to gallop directly northeast a few miles and thereby cut off Sigel's command from the main Federal army. Instead, McIntosh, thinking the enemy might retreat to the west, led his horsemen to the northwest, swinging around Bentonville in a clockwise manner and allowing the little German general to retreat eastward to safety. To compound McIntosh's error, he then got lost as he swung around the town and veered north, away from his target. When he finally wandered east and happened upon the rear of Sigel's column, McIntosh's bone-weary and half-frozen troopers were too tired and strung too far out to heed his command to charge. The result of all this was that Van Dorn's attempt to get behind Curtis was now detected and Sigel survived to fight another day.[34]

Bates's diary entry for March 6 describes the movement through a snowstorm toward Bentonville, the swing around the west side of the town, and the botched and belated charge on Sigel's command. Unfortunately, Bates lost his diary somewhere along the road that night (he later recovered it) and therefore made no diary entries describing his participation in the coming battle of Elkhorn Tavern (Pea Ridge).

March 6th 1862 [diary]

Learning there was a body of federal cavalry at a mill [Osage Mill] eight or ten miles distance, our Brigade was ordered to march at 4 AM and try & surprise them. A few minutes after 4 we were on the march—a bitter cold wind blowing from the north occasionally a

34. Shea and Hess, *Pea Ridge*, 68–72, 76–77.

heavy fall of snow. Had to walk nearly all morning in order to keep warm. On arriving at the Mills found the Feds had left last night at midnight in direction of Bentonville seven miles distant. Pushed on to that place. Gen Price & his command going to the same point by a different route. We moved on when we came in sight of Bentonville on left of Gen Price. When within a mile of the place several dark columns of smoke shot up from different parts of the town. We afterward learned that these were large stores in which the feds had their supplies & did not have time to remove them. We were told by an old lady who kept a sort of a hotel that Siegel was at dinner when we were discovered approaching across the prairie two miles distant. He jumped up from the table—ran upstairs & watched us with his glass untill we got within three fourths of a mile when he got a good look at our flag, as it was blown out by the wind. He ran downstairs & remarked, "it is de damn *Secesh* boys, we best be git away quick" & forthwith jumped on his horse & got away on double quick.[35] Gen Price moved on to the right of town (east) and succeeded in getting in range of the rear guard of the dutch [*i.e.*, German-speaking Federals]. A sharp little skirmish ensued here in which we killed several enemy, wounded a good many & took some prisoners. Our loss was a few horses killed and several men wounded. A running fight was kept up for some time.

Our command under Col McIntosh went on to the left of bentonville in order to prevent the escape of the enemy in that direction, but we learned soon that they had already gone. Col McIntosh received an order to move on to the left & intercept the enemy at a point three or four miles distant. We moved on rapidly & soon came in sight of the enemy, but owing to some mismanagement or misunderstanding of the command[,] when the order to charge was given it was not obeyed except by a few of McIntosh's & Sim's Regiment.[36] I do not think McIntosh's command was heard or understood—by the Cols of the different regiments. In fact I know they did not. I am satisfied but few if any of the entire command knew where we were going or the object of our move. Coming suddenly on an enemy as we did—without warning or without expecting it

35. General Sigel did indeed watch the approaching Confederate cavalry with his field glasses before hurrying his command east out of Bentonville. Whether Bates recorded the general's exact words is a different matter. Ibid., 70.

36. Part of the 3rd Texas Cavalry did hear the command and charged Sigel's rear units. Ibid., 76–77.

threw us for a short time into some confusion, but to effect any good it was necessary that Col McIntosh's command should have been executed with promptness & that we should act in unison. This however was not done but a few only of our men charging—consequently by the time we were formed again it was too late to effect any good—as their batteries were so planted that we could not charge them without great loss. We therefore moved as rapidly as possible back to Bentonville & when we got there we ascertained for the first time that Gen Price had been fighting the enemy as they retreated.

On the 6th of March lost this book & did not get it back again for a long time. Battle of Elk Horn & events following have also [been] lost. March 20th 1862

Although Van Dorn's plan to circle behind Curtis's Federal army was no longer a secret, the Confederate general did have his men, or some of them—Price's Missourians—astride the road to Missouri behind the Federals. General Curtis, not one to lose his head in a tight situation, simply turned his army around to face the Confederates coming down from the north. Because Van Dorn had plunged ahead with little regard for the condition of his men and horses, he found his cold, hungry, and weary army strung out over several miles on the morning of March 7. Rather than wait for McCulloch's contingent to catch up to Price's men, Van Dorn simply ordered Price to move south down the Telegraph Road toward Curtis while McCulloch's command, miles to the west, approached the Federals from that direction. Essentially, the battle became two different fights two miles apart: Price attacking from the north and McCulloch, with McIntosh's cavalry, attacking from the west.

Bates's regiment was with McIntosh's cavalry in McCulloch's wing. As McCulloch led his command eastward along a country road late that morning of March 7, hoping to link up with Price, the Confederates were startled by a barrage from a Federal battery on their right across an uncultivated field. The solid shot came crashing through the Texas cavalry, killing at least ten men and wounding others. After the Texans regained their composure and some order, General McCulloch directed three Texas regiments, a Texas battalion, and an Arkansas battalion—about three thousand men—to face right and form for a charge against the guns and about five hundred Federals. Colonel Sims's 9th Texas Cavalry was one of the regiments wheeled into line for the charge.[37]

---

37. Ibid., 95–99.

When the bugles sounded, away they went, through the horse-high weeds, toward the Federal battery and its cavalry support. A captain in the Arkansas battalion described the charge: "At the sound of the bugle we began to advance in a walk, then a trot; when we had covered about 1/2 of the distance, the charge was sounded; our horses were put to full speed & we rushed right in among the Federals, our men being armed mostly with double-barreled shot-guns, loaded with buck shot. By reserving our fire until we were among them, then firing both barrels into their ranks, then clubbing our guns, the effect was terrible." A private in the 9th Texas Cavalry later boasted that his regiment was first to the battery. "The 9th Texas being the nearest to the battery were the first to reach the guns and Company K, the center and guide company of the regiment, was the first to plant a flag on that battery."[38] Another soldier in the 9th Texas was even more specific: "Our color bearer, Hyram Duff, was the first man to the battery; he jumped upon one of the guns and waved our battle flag over it." The Federals, outnumbered six to one and shattered by the momentum of the charge, were almost helpless. An Iowa cavalryman near the Federal guns was shocked by the carnage. "In every direction I could see my comrades falling. Horses frencied [sic] and riderless, ran to and fro. Men and horses ran in collision crushing each other to the ground. Dismounted troopers ran in every direction. Officers tried to rally their men but order gave way to confusion. The scene baffles description."[39]

The thrilling and successful cavalry charge—the sort of moment that many young Texans had dreamed of when they joined the army—was about the only positive development for McCulloch's wing of the army. Not long afterward, General McCulloch himself was killed when he rode ahead of his lines to reconnoiter. Soon after, General McIntosh, second in command, was mortally wounded, and Colonel Louis Hébert, third in command, was captured. The entire Confederate command structure in the western battle was lost, and for the remainder of the day the Confederates on that wing milled around without orders, waiting for some direction,

38. Private Sparks described the banner as "a small brownish red silk flag, in the center of which was a crescent moon and thirteen five-pointed silver stars. It was trimmed with silk fringe and was attached to a dark mahogany colored staff with a gilded spear head at the top" (Sparks, *War Between the States*, 53). A likeness of this flag, often called a Van Dorn battle flag, is in Alan K. Sumrall, *Battle Flags of Texans in the Confederacy* (Austin: Eakin Press, 1995), 42.

39. *Confederate Veteran* 4 (May 1896): 163; Shea and Hess, *Pea Ridge*, 100; Carr, *In Fine Spirits*, 33; Sparks, *War Between the States*, 53; Samuel B. Barron, *The Lone Star Defenders: A Chronicle of the Third Texas Cavalry Regiment in the Civil War* (1908; reprint Washington, D.C.: Zenger, 1983), 67–69.

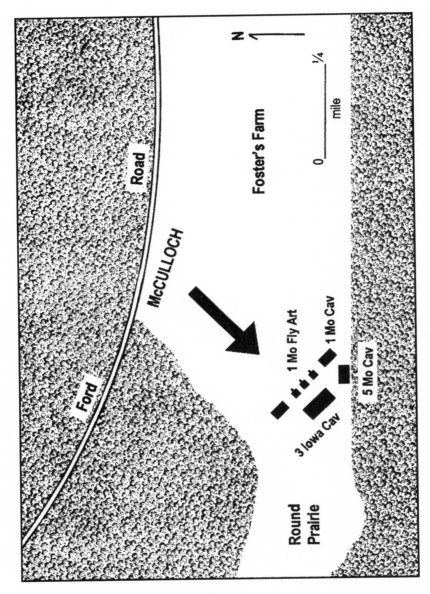

The Charge of McCulloch's Cavalry at Elkhorn Tavern

finally retreating to the northwest. The battle raged more furiously on the eastern wing, where Price's regiments grappled with Curtis's Federals around an old tavern. Union artillery fire and Confederate ammunition shortages finally compelled Price to withdraw around midday on March 8, leaving General Curtis with an impressive victory against a larger foe and clearing Missouri of Confederate armies for most of the war.[40]

Because Bates had lost his diary, the only accounts he wrote of the Battle of Elkhorn Tavern (Pea Ridge) were in letters to Mootie and his mother. The incomplete letter to his mother laments Van Dorn's decision to go on the offensive, blames the defeat of the western wing of the army on the deaths of Generals McCulloch and McIntosh, and raises the suspicion at least that Van Dorn bore responsibility for the failure of the entire campaign. The letter to Mootie provides a brief but colorful account of the charge against the Federal battery, adding new information that does not appear in previous accounts: part of the Texas cavalry charged through the overgrown field on foot. Bates's lament that Van Dorn's artillery had to withdraw on the second day of the fight for lack of ammunition adds weight to the view that Van Dorn's staff work and logistics had been bungled.[41] Expressing a view shared by many other Texans, Bates also believed that the infusion of more Texans into the Confederate army would solve most of its problems.

[March 15?, 1862]
[Van Buren, Ark.]
[page(s) missing in Bates's letter to his mother]
Most persons seem to think that If his [General McCulloch's] advice had been followed we would not now have to make the humiliating confession that we are defeated. His policy was to fight there on Boston Mountain [south of Fayetteville]—to choose his own position—and let the enemy make the attack. I think Siegel's move north was only a feint to draw us out to make the attack.[42] Gen McC said before we went into the fight that we would be whiped if we

---

40. Barron, *Lone Star Defenders,* 69–70; Shea and Hess, *Pea Ridge,* chaps. 5–13.

41. According to Van Dorn's chief of staff, an incompetent ordnance officer had sent the ammunition train fifteen miles away from the front line. Maury to Johnston, June 10, 1876, in Hewett, Trudeau, and Suderow, eds., *Supplement to the Official Records,* 1:565, 566.

42. Sigel's tardy withdrawal from Bentonville, not regarded by Sigel or his superiors as a feint, had nothing to do with Van Dorn's decision to swing around the rear of the Federal army. Bates, like many Confederates, was trying to understand how the Confederates could have lost a battle to mere Yankees.

attacked the enemy in his position. He said too if forced to fight against his judgement he would make a desperate stand and either conquer or die on the field—Gen (or Col) McIntosh was also killed—The loss of these two men was, I think the principal cause of our defeat—for several Regiments were awaiting orders from them—to assist other Regiments—but they were both killed near the same time—and we waited in vain ignorant of the cause why the order did not come untill it was to late. The army censure Gen Van Dorn very much for mismanagement generally—but as I do'nt *know* that he is deserving of censure—I say nothing.[43]

I sat down to write but a few lines only as I have had but a short time to write in. I have been ordered out on Picket guard and must close. I don't know that you can read this scrawl for I have written in a great hurry—nothing to write on and not much to write with—will write again soon. I do'nt think there is a probability of the enemy coming down here soon.

I have just stoped writing to read your letter brought in by Lafayette Means a few moments ago.[44] Ten new recruits came in today from Lamar and were sworn in this evening. We now have 106 rank & file in our company. The health of the company is generally good. John Gibbons is at our winter quarters. Left in charge of things there. Dohoney has been in Ft. Smith since we left the Boston Mountain in pursuit of the enemy.[45] He came down for some clothing and was retained by Maj Clark—and so did not go with us—I have not time to say more at present. Give my love to all the family and do not forget to present my best wishes to my good friends Miss Annie Miss Mary and Miss Moot—I have not had time to write since leaving our winter quarters on our way up—but think we will have more leisure for several weeks at least. Truly your son
J.C. Bates

43. Historians have agreed with Van Dorn's soldiers that the Mississippi general botched the whole campaign. He drove his army relentlessly without regard to logistics or fatigue, ignored the need for a competent staff, cut his army off from its supply wagons, and selected the wrong ground for a fight. Shea and Hess, *Pea Ridge*, 311–12.

44. Lafayette Means was a thirty-one-year-old farmer from Nacogdoches County and one of several new recruits who joined the regiment the day Bates wrote his letter.

45. Dohoney missed the fight at Elkhorn Tavern. His only contribution to the cause was to command the honor guard that fired the salute at General McCulloch's burial at Fort Smith. Dohoney, *Average American*, 107; Cutrer, *Ben McCulloch*, 311.

Van Buren Ark
March 16*th* 1862
Miss Mootie Johnson
Dear Friend

On this good sabbath morning, as we have no preaching in camp, and as I cannot in consequence, use the time to better advantage than by writing to you, I will do so, not that I have any thing of special interest to write but more to fulfill my promise than any thing else.

I need not say much in regard to our recent battle. I suppose an official report of it will be published soon by Genl Van Dorn. If so, the full particulars of the fight will be given by him. As I was engaged in the fight on Friday only, and saw but little of it except on that day—I could not if I wished, give you a detailed account of the whole. I will only say—that on Friday about noon—near an hour after the fight had commenced by Gen Price on the left wing—we discovered the enemy advancing on our division—Gen McCulloch immediately ordered us to prepare for a charge & form a line of battle. This was instantly done. The 5th Squadron—(our company and Capt [Gideon] Smith's [Company B]) were ordered to dismount and make the charge on foot—as the undergrowth was so thick betwixt us and the enemy we could not get through with sufficient speed on horseback. (I should have stated above that the enemy had planted a battery of rifled cannon in an old field on our right supported by a Reg of Infantry and large body of Cavalry—and it was this we were preparing to charge).[46] As soon as the charge was sounded the whole Reg—on foot and on horse—with a yell more savage if possible than we had been accustomed to hear from the Indians—rushed on amid grape and canister and bomb shell—with such irresistible force to the very mouth of the cannon—that the enemy seemed perfectly terror stricken—and in five minutes were in utter confusion—completely routed—running in every direction and leaving their cannon in our possession. Amidst loud huzza's our company flag was unfurled over the cannon. Our loss in this charge was six or eight killed and fifteen or twenty wounded. We were formed several times after this to fight awaiting orders from

46. The Federal battery had no infantry support, only parts of three cavalry regiments. Shea and Hess, *Pea Ridge*, 96.

Gen McC[ulloch] but we waited and waited in vain, ignorant of the fact that his brave spirit had long since taken its flight to another world. The death of Gen McC lost the battle to us on Friday.

Saturday morning the firing was opened with the dawn of day and was continued with partial successes on either side untill about 9 Oclk. At this time our batteries began to be withdrawn. I asked the reason and received the same reply from all—out of ammunition. The last battery passed us and with it went every hope of a victory that day. Although the firing with small arms still continued and no order had *as yet* been given for us to fall back I felt that it would soon come. The suspense and intense excitement of the two hours previous had been so great that it was actually a relief to me to know the fight would terminate. I have often thought it would be bad enough to *look on* while a battle was being fought and much worse to engage in it, but if I could have my choice I had rather be actively engaged in *ten* battles than look with folded arms on *one* other such as this. If engaged *actively* we have *no time* for reflection if not engaged we can do nothing else *but* think.

Our army was *not* whiped but the fight ceased for the want of ammunition—we fell back in perfect order—the enemy being well satisfied to let us depart without an effort to annoy us. But I have said more of the battle than I had intended. The enemy are still some sixty miles north of this [and] show no indication of an advance in this direction.

Eben [Dohoney] was not in the fight—he was retained at Ft. Smith for Garrison duty—Jno G[ibbons] too was left in charge of our winter quarters. One of our company had his horse shot under him[,] another wounded in the arm but not badly.

Mr Chisum has just called at my tent on his way to Tex. and as he is waiting rather impatiently I must close this scribble. Before the next battle I hope we may have at least ten thousand Texans in our ranks. Yesterday ten from Lamar were sworn into our company—we now have 106 rank and file. Our Col distinguished himself greatly in our fight.[47] In fact, our Reg gets the credit of having done more fighting than *all the balance* of the cavalry—which is really true. Say to Miss Mary I will write to her soon as I will also to you. I have not

---

47. Bates had a much higher opinion of his colonel now that Sims had led the regiment in the charge. In fact, Sims had been severely wounded in the right arm by grapeshot during the charge and was disabled for life. Kerr, ed., *Fighting with Ross' Texas Cavalry,* 14, 28; Rose, *Ross' Texas Brigade,* 51.

forgotten my promise and hope you will not forget yours—to write
whether we receive letters from each other or not.

Very truly your Friend

J.C. Bates

our loss as far as we have been able to ascertain is near 120 killed &
many more than that wounded. The loss of the enemy is near four
hundred so say those who returned to bury the dead.[48]

In their first fight against "real Yankees," the horsemen from Lamar experienced mixed results. They had charged an enemy battery across open
ground, captured it in fine style, and ground its defenders to dust. On the
other hand, their most popular general was dead, their colonel was disabled, and, owing to blundering by higher-ups, they had lost the battle.
Bates and his comrades could only mutter about the need for more Texans as they retraced their steps through the gray, wintry Arkansas mountains to their winter camp at Cantonment Slidell near Clarksville.

48. Overall Federal losses were near 1,400: 203 killed, 980 wounded (some mortally),
and 201 missing. Confederate casualties, possibly underreported, were about 800 killed and
wounded and 500 or more captured. Shea and Hess, *Pea Ridge,* 270.

 **From Arkansas to Corinth**

In their first five months of Confederate service, Bates and the soldiers of the 9th Texas Cavalry had chased fugitive Indians across the Nations, fought two small engagements in the Indian Territory, captured an enemy battery in a classic cavalry charge, and admitted defeat in the largest battle yet fought west of the Mississippi. They had also suffered from hunger for days on end and ridden, walked, and slept in snow, sleet, and bitter cold. They had already experienced more combat and hard service than some regiments, confined to garrison duty, would encounter in the entire war. In the aftermath of Elkhorn Tavern, they would wind through the back roads of northern Arkansas on an aborted mission to strike behind Federal lines in Missouri. Then, in an attempt to turn back the Union tide flooding south through Kentucky and west Tennessee, they would also participate in the last great transfer of Confederate troops across the Mississippi River.

The regiment spent the latter part of March preparing for a raid into Missouri—horses had to be shod, wagons repaired, commissary stores stockpiled, and bullets moulded. Bates found time to write a letter to his mother and give her the sad news that his friend Cameron Givens had died of disease. The next day the men elected Dohoney the new company captain to replace Jerry Wright, recently appointed regimental commissary officer. Bates faithfully supported his friend Dohoney for the captaincy, but he made it clear in his diary that he might have won the honor for himself had he pursued it. Instead, Bates gave up his former position as third lieutenant and was elected first lieutenant. A day later the men of the company were surprised and happy to welcome into camp a contingent of civilians from Paris; they had come 250 miles through hard country with wagons to carry off the many wounded they expected to find after the battle at Elkhorn Tavern. Bates would have liked to return to Paris with his friends, but duty called him in another direction. All in all, the last days of March were busy ones for Bates and his comrades.

March 25th 1862 Tuesday [diary]

On yesterday went down with Dan [Hatcher] to see our sick— Jo L [Joseph Loyd] & K.B found them improving.[1] On our way back stoped to see John [Gibbons] & Eb's [Dohoney's] Ark sweet-hearts—(the Misses Colthorpe) found them very pretty, sensible & agreeable girls. Spent an hour with them very pleasantly. I think it would have been better if I had not gone for it only increased my de-sire to see others whom it is impossible for a time at least to see. On taking leave, we gave them a hearty shake of the hand promising to call if we should ever get in reach—they promising to give us their prayers for our safety & the success of our cause. GOD BLESS ALL THE WOMEN.

Cantonment Slidell Ark
March [26,] 1862
My Dear Ma

As I have an opportunity of sending a letter to Texas this morn-ing I drop you a few lines. Our Regt has been here for the last week. But will leave tomorrow. Where we will go I cannot say. It is my *im-pression* that we will go north of this—probably—near the Missouri line. Most of the Cavalry have left Van Buren and are moving East-ward. I do not know their destination—as the movements of the army are kept strictly secret. Since the death of Gens McCulloch & McIntosh the army has been reorganized. We are in the second brigade commanded by [Brigadier] Gen [Thomas J.] Churchhill.[2]

1. Joseph Loyd, nineteen years old, was a native of Tennessee and a Lamar County team-ster before the war. The man identified as K. B. could not be identified in company records. (The initials may have been incorrectly transcribed from the diary.)

2. The 6th, 9th, and 11th Texas Cavalry Regiments formed a new brigade on March 17. Brigade commander Thomas J. Churchill was a Kentucky native, a veteran of the Mexican War, and the former postmaster of Little Rock, Arkansas. He would serve as Arkansas's gov-ernor in the early 1880s. *OR*, Vol. 53, pp. 796–97; Warner, *Generals in Gray*, 49–50.

I expect you will hear very exagerated accounts of our late battle. From several of our men who were captured in the fight and have made their escape and just got into camp we have been able to learn — with some accuracy I think — the number killed and wounded on both sides. Our loss in killed was about 350 — wounded & prisoners near 1000. The loss of the enemy, according to their own admissions, was near seven hundred killed & about 1500 wounded — we have upwards of three hundred of their men prisoners. There is a good deal of dissatisfaction in the whole army with Gen Van Dorn. It is the impression of many — in fact of nearly every one — that we would have gained the last fight if he had not ordered a retreat. Gen Raines of Missouri told him he was the only man in the army who was whiped.[3]

We have a great deal sickness in the Regt though not of a very dangerous character. The first death that has occurred in our company — was on yesterday evening about 5 Oclk. Poor Cam[eron] Givens lives no more.[4] He was a good soldier — a brave man a true christian and he will be missed and his death lamented by all the company. It will be better for him *where he is now*. He will be buried this evening with military honors.

I sent one hundred and twenty five dollars home by Ben Forney a few days since. After paying what I owe there if there should be any more remaining than you want for your own use — tell Will to take up a note Dr Clement holds on Dohoney. He will return the amount to me here. Dohoney left an approved account against the estate of Mr Pearcy — with Dr Clement as collateral security. He wishes Will to get that and collect it if possible.[5]

We will have to elect another Capt in a few days. Our comissary has resigned and Capt Wright will be transferred to that department.

3. James Spencer Rains, a brigadier general in the Missouri State Guard (militia), was arrested for his disparaging remark about Van Dorn, but many veterans of Elkhorn Tavern, still stinging from their defeat, quoted General Rains to explain their misfortune. Bruce S. Allardice, *More Generals in Gray* (Baton Rouge: Louisiana State University Press, 1995), 190–91; Shea and Hess, *Pea Ridge*, 260; William Clyde Billingsley, ed., " 'Such Is War': The Confederate Memoirs of Newton Asbury Keen" (Part 1), *Texas Military History* 6 (Winter 1967): 252.

4. Givens, a twenty-three-year-old Kentucky native, had ridden with Bates to their first training camp north of Sherman the previous September.

5. Will Bramlette was handling the affairs of both Bates and Dohoney while they were away from Paris.

I have not time to write more at present but will write again the first opportunity. Direct your letters to me hereafter in Churchhill's Brigade (Second,) Sim's Regt. Send them to Little Rock to be forwarded to me as above. Give My love to all.
J.C. Bates

March 26th 1862 Wednesday [diary]

For the past two days all has been bustle & confusion getting ready for the scout. This evening an election was held to fill the vacancy caused by the resignation of Capt Wright who is made comissary—I was solicited by a large number of the company (at least half) to run for Captain but declined in favor of Dohoney—as I thought he was entitled to the office. I told them I would be satisfied with 1st Lieut to which office they elected me over T.A. Perkins. I.A.J. also ran for 3rd Lieut but was beaten by only one vote—D.C. Hatcher being elected. John Fowler was elected in Ian's place (2nd Sergeant)—over Gabbard—had a severe chill today.[6]

March 27th 1862 Thurs [diary]

This morning made preparations to start on a scout to Springfield (Mo). Do'nt know the object of it unless to get in above the enemy burn their railroads & destroy other property or it may be to draw the enemy out of Ark. It is evidently intended that we make some bold daring move as we have but little baggage & can move rapidly. At 11 oclk Reg called out for inspection & horses not fit for scout condemned—very unexpectedly. This evening several of our friends from Paris came in—Will Bramlette & several others. Having as we expected they would a very exaggerated account of the battle, they came up with hacks to haul the wounded home. Fortunately none of those who came found wounded friends. In the afternoon our comissary stores arrived & were issued. At 4 pm the Battalion (450) started, the balance of the brigade having gone on in the morning. I got permission to remain with my friends & join the command in the morning.

6. T. A. Perkins would remain a private in the regiment for the rest of the war. Fowler, the new second sergeant, was a twenty-year-old Texas native still living with his parents and attending school at the time of the 1860 census. John N. Gabbert was a twenty-seven-year-old Kentucky-born saddler. I. A. J. could not be identified in company records. Kerr, ed., *Fighting with Ross' Texas Cavalry*, 232.

March 28th 1862 Friday [diary]

Remained untill 8 am this morning with our Paris friends and having bid them goodbye started to join the command. Oh, how I wished that I could return with them—but duty calls me elsewhere and even if I could obtain leave of absence I would not. Came up with the Reg at dark having ridden forty miles over a very rough road.

The Texas brigade left Clarksville in late March and rode north over narrow, rocky, curving roads through the sparsely settled mountains of northern Arkansas. Each day Bates found the roads worse than the day before. George Griscom of Company D recorded a particularly hard patch of ground to cover on March 29: "ascend the main peak by a zig zag road up an almost perpendicular hill side—it requiring the whole of each Company to assist their respective wagons up the steep—& they have 6 mules each & *contain only* cooking utensils." Bates was not impressed with some of the people in this part of Arkansas—they seemed poor and ignorant, and their loyalty to the Confederacy was likewise suspect. After a week and 135 twisting miles, the Texans crossed the line into Missouri and stopped briefly at Forsyth, about forty-five road miles south of Springfield.

March 29th 1862 Sat. [diary]

Of all the rough roads I have ever seen this is the worst. It beats Ark itself. Do'nt think our trains will get much farther than this (8 miles from our last camp). Tonight we were ordered to make the trip to Springfield in eight days—three have elapsed & we are not fifty miles. At noon today I thought we had seen some rough road—but I had not then seen the Ozark Mountains. I will not be astonished at any sort of country I see in Ark hereafter. There is only one redeeming feature of this country, viz the water. I drank frequently today merely because the cool clear springs gushing from the rocks looked so delicious & tempting. marched untill 8 pm & camped at the foot of the mountain fifteen miles from Jasper [Arkansas]. Trains not up—go to bed supperless.

March 30th 1862 Sun [diary]

Sunday morning yet we are again on the march—I wonder if the Sabbath is as little respected by the northern as the southern army. Marched seven or eight miles & overtook the regiments of the Brigade—took up camp untill tomorrow. Although Sunday—I got

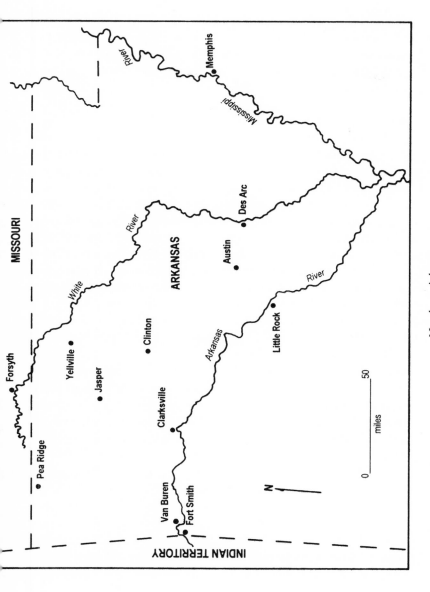

Northern Arkansas

Lieut Hatcher to assist me—& with some tools borrowed from the miller close by patched my boot. Think they will last me untill I get to the trains. The Miller's daughter is the prettiest little girl I have seen in Ark. In the evening distributed some ammunition to the men & made myself some cartridges.

March 31st 1862 Mon [diary]

The country for the last two days I thought was as poor & rough & rugged as could be but our road today was over a country the poorest, roughest I have *ever* seen. Newton Co is certainly the fag end of the Southern Confederacy and it is a slander even to ark to call Jasper a town. There are but six or seven houses & the inhabitants are principally women & children—the former ragged & dirty & the latter more so. The women gaze at you from the doors—one hand over their eyes—the children climb the yard fence shut one eye & look at you askance with the other. No courthouse, no church— no schoolhouse—no nothing—yes I am mistaken one thing is conspicuous—a jail. Traveled twenty five miles our course north.

April 1st 1862 Tues [diary]

At nearly every house we have passed for the last few days a number of women & children have been collected to see us pass & at one house there were twenty eight children—the families of three brothers-in-law who had taken them all to one place & gone themselves to war. Every mile or so today have seen handsome & intelligent looking ladies who by some act or sign gave us a welcome. Marched about fifteen miles today over the best country I have seen in Ark. Rained a perfect flood last night but managed to keep dry by making a tent out of a blanket. Reported we have gained a great victory at Corinth, Miss.[7]

April 2nd 1862 Wed [diary]

Ordered last night to pack four days rations—& with this left the trains this morning & marched thirty five miles over a barren rocky country. About morning crossed the Missouri line. Camped at Forsyth on White River. River so swollen—last night's rain—impassable. Think we had best swim the river as we learn from men just

---

7. The victory at Corinth was another rumor. The only activity in that vicinity in March was the slow gathering of Confederate forces from other parts of the South. E. B. Long, *The Civil War Day by Day: An Almanac, 1861–1865* (Garden City, N.Y.: Doubleday, 1971), 904.

from Springfield that there are but few troops there (12 or 1500). While passing a very nice house today eight young ladies came out on the Portico & sang Dixie for us. I was ordered out last night four miles from camp in command of picket guard. To while away the time & keep myself awake I am now (3 oclk am) by the light of a few twigs jotting down these notes—wonder if they wont be read by some yankee.

While at Forsyth the Texans received orders to abandon the raid on Springfield and turn toward Des Arc, Arkansas, about 240 road miles down the White River to the southeast. There, nearly twelve thousand trans-Mississippi cavalry were being gathered for transfer east of the Mississippi River. Major General Ulysses S. Grant's reduction of Forts Henry and Donelson in northwest Tennessee in early February had opened a dangerous crevasse in the Confederacy's northern border, and authorities in Richmond were rushing as many regiments as possible to concentrate at Corinth in northeast Mississippi.

Bates would find very little to commend Arkansas on his two-week journey down the White River toward Des Arc. The country looked poor, and the people were of uncertain loyalty. "I want it distinctly understood," he wrote in his diary, "that I am not fighting for any such country as this—or any such people." Once his brigade finally left the mountains, they found themselves in the midst of flooding creeks and rivers. To make matters much worse, as the Texans approached Des Arc, rumors began spreading through the brigade that they would be dismounted and forced to serve as infantry before their transfer east of the Mississippi River.

April 3rd 1862 Thurs [diary]

   General Churchill received orders from Gen Van Dorn to turn back & report himself at Yellville forthwith.[8] Came in from picket this morning & drank a cup of coffee & felt much better. Bought some apples this morning & ate a few, gave the balance to the boys. March thirty five miles today & at night found no forage for our horses. Our trains came in late last night having turned across to this road yesterday. Our course today is a little south of east. Our road today is still over barren hills & mountains. The report that the confederates had gained a victory in Miss is today contradicted—God grant that the first report may be true.

8. Yellville, Arkansas, is about forty straight-line miles southeast of Forsyth, Missouri.

April 4th 1862 Friday [diary]

As we had no forage last night we moved on in advance this morning untill we got some corn—fed & fell in the rear—marched five miles & camped on a beautiful little creek four miles west of Yellville nearby. All the men in this section are at home—not seeming to care which way the war terminates—think they will be with the strong party. They profess to be with us as we are here—but if the North had possession of this country they would be good Union men. Country still barren & rocky, course East, population sparse. Bought a little black flour & shorts [shortening?] today—made splendid bread compared with coarse corn-meal unsifted.

April 5th 1862 Sat [diary]

Came on in advance of the Reg to have some [horse] shoeing done but found all the shops engaged by other regiments. Found Yellville, Ark an average Ark town, no goods of any description only a few drugs in it. Country still as poor as ever—I want it distinctly understood that I am not fighting for any such country as this—or any such people. Saw Parson Bone today & rode awhile with him. He is still of opinion that Rev Mr Bone is a smart man. Requested to sign a paper recommending Col [B. Warren] Stone as a suitable man for our Brig. Gen. Col S is a drunkard & therefore disqualified for any position in my opinion.[9]

April 6th 1862 Sun [diary][10]

Sunday again—a beautiful bright sunny—sabbath this has been & always on *such* a Sabbath I do long to be at home with the loved ones—at Sunday school to see the bright shining faces there, & at church to see the faces there, not smiling perhaps but equally as cheerful & pleasant—assembled to do homage to Him who holds the destinies of nations as well as individuals in his hands. Though I

9. B. Warren Stone, a native of Kentucky and a lawyer in Dallas before the war, had raised the 6th Texas Cavalry early in the war and served as its colonel at Elkhorn Tavern. Unpopular with his men, he would lose his office when his regiment elected Lawrence Sullivan "Sul" Ross to replace him as colonel in May 1862. Bates, who had little patience with the inebriated, obviously was not among Stone's admirers. Tyler et al., *New Handbook of Texas,* 6:110.

10. Bates could not have known it as he wrote his diary entry, but on this same morning the Confederate army that had gathered at Corinth, Mississippi, attacked Grant's troops at Pittsburg Landing in southwest Tennessee, opening the bloody carnage of the Battle of Shiloh.

have felt toward God as a *Christian* must feel—still when so many
instances of his power or wisdom & goodness are visible every day[,]
when I *see* & *enjoy* so much that can be given by his hand only—I
can but feel a sort of reverential awe at his power & wisdom—& for
his goodness & mercy a feeling very near akin to the *love that makes
men Christians* steals over me & for a time at least I feel as much
gratitude for these gifts as I suppose a *sinner* can feel. Marched eighteen miles—passed through Burrowville—a very sorry place about
100 greasy dirty looking individuals—all out to see us pass by.
Houses nearly all log huts. Ladies waved their gingham handkerchiefs at us as we passed. Carried forage for our horses two or three
miles. Camped on Buffalo Creek in rich valley of land. Bought some
molasses & milk this morning—Quarter master paying off Capt
[Thomas G.] Berry's command [Company A] for seventeen days—
four months still due.

April 7th 1862 Mon [diary]
     Marched eight miles—camped at foot of Boston or Ozark
Mountain on Cove Creek—Searcy County—three fourths of men
here are Union—have been quiet since heard we were coming
through—forage for horses plenty—left eight men behind to have
horses shod—left John Gibbons sick also left Dan Hatcher four days
ago with foundered horse & could not keep up—little uneasy about
him—our cook left behind today—have to do our own cooking—
commenced to rain about noon—as we were getting dinner rained
so fast couldnt get the dough still enough to bake—so poured it in
as batter. Got some milk—first since leaving Texas.

April 8th 1862 Tues [diary]
     Ordered last night to be up at 3 & be ready to march at 5—was
up & ready but did not start till 7 as we were ordered to rear today.
Ascended Ozark Mts which is not near so bad as where we crossed
going up—but few houses on mountains—they only huts—do'nt
think an honest man could live on it. Marched twenty miles—
camped at Clinton—a dirty muddy place in junction of the two Red
rivers. Nothing in town but a doggery & Ark tavern.[11] A cold rain
still falling since 5 this evening. Takes one company of men to guard
the grocery to keep men from getting drunk.

11. Clinton is about sixty-five road miles south of Yellville. A doggery was a cheap saloon.

April 9th 1862 Wed [diary]

Rained nearly all night—river so swollen had to go three miles above to a shallow ford. Enough of whiskey obtained by some means to make about 100 men drunk—four or five fights & a dozen quarrels the consequence. Received money for our Co for two months and seventeen days—just finished paying them off. Dan Hatcher not yet come in. Reported in camp our forces evacuated Pocahuntas[.] Federal pickets in Clarksville—Gen [Albert] Pike had a fight with the feds & killed 500 in Cherokee Nation.[12] Country still poor—marched fifteen miles   had frost last night & on the 4th also.

April 10th 1862 Thurs [diary]

Marched eighteen miles. Soil poor & sandy with usual growth—scant & poor population. Boys left behind to have horses shod came in—say they were watched narrowly in cove valley while they remained. they think most of the people there are union. Several men arrested today for jay hawking pigs horses chickens &c. One man who lost a horse came to our Reg to look for him—seeing Lieut G standing by rode up to him—told him his business & remarked "Judging by your appearance I thought you would be likely to know something of my horse if he is in your Reg"—Lieut G looked rather blank, not knowing whether the fellow meant he looked like a thief or some important personage in the Reg.

April 11th 1862 Fri [diary]

Began to rain this morning at 6 just as we started—& continued without intermission untill noon—nothing but a blanket to put around me & was soon wet to the skin, my boots full of water—most disagreeable day we have had for a month—visions of home—a bright glowing cheerful fire, kind friends—& innumerable comforts rose in my mind & for once—I wished to be at home. Marched eighteen miles—wagons five miles behind—nothing for supper—little for our horses—built up a roaring log fire—dried our clothes & blankets. made a tent large enough for Capt [Dohoney] & myself—& as the rain has ceased think I will sleep finely—take every thing as a matter of course.

12. Pocahontas is in northeastern Arkansas. The rumor about Pike was unfounded.

April 12th 1862 Sat [diary]

Got up this morning feeling as well as if I had slept in a palace—have nothing for breakfast but still not nearly as hungry as have been—ordered to return to our wagons & cook two days rations—leave the wagons behind; company all returned—I remained behind to take care of baggage. Col [Quayle] asked me to have dinner with him—glad to accept as I am a little hungry.[13] At 2 pm started to Desarc—Cypress creek out of its banks one half mile wide over bottom from one to two feet deep. Nearly every man had a plunge in the water before we got over. One end of bridge washed away—jumped our horses off in four feet of water—marched four miles further & camped in Austin.[14]

April 13th 1862 Sunday [diary]

Last night Ed Williams Capt Patterson & several other of our Paris friends came in to see us from Whitfield's Legion camped nearby—had a chat of an hour or so about old times. Had breakfast & ready to start by daylight—waiting for the Reg to come up—we got ahead of them yesterday & camped by ourselves—the last twenty five miles the worst road I ever saw—horses frequently in mud & water up to saddle skirts—Cant imagine how our wagons will get over this road soon—impossible to keep company together—every man takes his course either in road or woods as suits him—country low—flat—soil very good. Passed some very large farms—saw some pretty women who waved their handkerchiefs at us. Got with our trains from winter quarters tonight. Most men well—some left sick on way up. march twenty five miles—camped five miles from Desarc—think we will be dismounted.

The rumors about the dismounting of the cavalry regiments gathering near Des Arc proved to be true. Forage for their horses was scarce at their destination near Corinth, so the men were dismounted with the promise that they would be remounted when the situation allowed. Still, this order was a great disappointment to the Texans, who regarded the cavalry as the

13. Lieutenant Colonel William Quayle served as the 9th Texas Cavalry's commander after Colonel Sims was wounded at Elkhorn Tavern. Quayle would be replaced as colonel one month later. Kerr, ed., *Fighting with Ross' Texas Cavalry*, 16.

14. Austin, Arkansas, is about thirty road miles northeast of Little Rock in the center of the state.

natural home of Texas men. Indeed, when they were called upon to defend their state and their new nation from the Yankees in 1861, Texans had signed on for mounted service in a ratio of 2.4 to 1 compared with the infantry. This contrasted even with other trans-Mississippi states, whose citizens joined infantry units in larger proportions. George Griscom recorded that "the Regt are not very well pleased but submit." Bates wrote his mother that "a good deal of dissatisfaction was manifested by some but when they found it would be of no avail they acquiesced with as good a grace as possible." A member of the 3rd Texas Cavalry described his regiment's reaction as "utter astonishment." They considered Van Dorn's order to dismount them "a breach of faith, totally at variance with our contract, yet the men being impressed with a correct idea of the critical condition in which recent reverses had placed the Confederacy, yielded their own inclinations . . . and complied."[15]

Bates, like most of his comrades, regretted the order to dismount, but his ardor for the Confederacy was strong enough to outweigh his disappointment. He was willing to fight for southern independence in any arm of the service. While his regiment made arrangements to send its horses back to Texas, rumors floated through the camps around Des Arc that the Confederates had won a great victory near Corinth. This was another unfounded rumor: the Confederate army had in fact lost a bloody struggle on the banks of the Tennessee River north of Corinth, in the woods surrounding a little church called Shiloh.

April 15th 1862 Tues [diary]
Ordered this evening to move down within a mile of Desarc. Order from Van Dorn read dismounting us temporarily—only for the emergency. Think the emergency will last the remainder of our term. Some dissatisfaction but most of the men are willing to do *anything* for the best. I had rather remain cavalry—but am willing to serve my country in any capacity in which I can be most useful. Our camping place is much better than the last one. Heard this morning that Island 10 has been taken with 1,500 men, several steamers and many cannon.[16]

15. Kerr, ed., *Fighting with Ross' Texas Cavalry,* 35; Rose, *Ross' Texas Brigade,* 63, 64; Stephen B. Oates, *Confederate Cavalry West of the River* (Austin: University of Texas Press, 1961), 26–27.
16. On April 7 Major General John Pope's small Federal army captured Island No. 10 near New Madrid, Missouri, thereby gaining Union control of the Mississippi River as far south as Fort Pillow, Tennessee, only forty road miles north of Memphis.

Desarc Ark
April 15th 1862
Dear Ma & Sister

Mr Robins leaves this morning for Texas & as he will be in Paris soon after he gets home I drop you a line by him. I have not written you since Will left for the reason I have had no opportunity of mailing a letter. We left winter quarters on the day he got there on a scout into Mo. The object of the trip up there was to ascertain if there was any federal force at Springfield of consequence—and if not to make a dash on to that place destroy all the federal property there of which there was nearly $2,000,000 in comissary & quartermaster stores—ammunition, ordinance &c and make our escape to Pocahontas [in northeastern Arkansas]. When we got to Forsyth however we found White River so swolen by recent rains we could not cross. The evening we got there too we met an order from Gen Van Dorn to report ourselves at this point forthwith.

From spies sent on in advance we learned that there was but a small Federal force in Springfield, and we could have destroyed an immense amount of property. The main body of the Federal army is still in the vicinity of Sugar Creek in Benton Co. [near the Elkhorn Tavern battlefield]. [Torn section] & Regt is much improved since leaving winter quarters. We have lost three men however in the last month. One of them C.C. Givens died a day or so before Wm [Bramlette] came up. The other a few days after. Another died in Van Buren in the hospital. All new recruits. Most of the sickness we have had has been among the new recruits—the old members of the company being generally well. I had one chill before Wm came up & one or two after—but am now in as good health as I have been in since I left Texas.

The news of a victory gained by the Confederates—near Corinth has been confirmed. It may not be and I think is not, as complete as reported, still there is no doubt but that it has been decided. I think the fate of the Confederacy will be decided on the Miss. River and that too within less than three months. Lincoln admits in his special message to Congress that he thinks they will be compeled to acknowledge the independence of the cotton states—but says they must hold—Virginia Tenn & Mo at any cost.[17] Much depends, in

17. Contrary to Bates's statement, Lincoln never admitted or predicted that the Union would be broken.

my opinion all, on the next battle to be fought on the east bank of the Miss. It will be such an one as has never been fought on this continent. [one line missing] Tenn.

The greater portion of Price's force has already left this [torn section] on boats—and are still leaving every day.[18] The Cavalry are being dismounted and their horses either sent home or kept at the expense of the government as the companies prefer. The order dismounting our Regt was this morning read to the men. A good deal of dissatisfaction was manifested by some but when they found it would be of no avail they acquiesced with as good a grace as possible. We have determined to send our horses to Lamar Co. Some will send their horses to their friends there and five men are detailed to take charge of the remainder (graze them).[19] If Wm has any use for mine he can take him and use him   take good care of him & get him fat if possible by the time I may need him. The order is for us to be dismounted temporarily—but I am of opinion that it will be for the remainder of our term. It will be at any rate for whatever time this army may be needed on the Miss[issippi River]—and I think that will be for the war. The order applies only to Twelve Months Men.[20] We still receive the pay of cavalry. I do not know how long we will remain at this place. Probably not more than one or two days, possibly a week.

[top of page missing] Some time since [torn section] Forney one hundred and twenty five Dollars for which I have his receipt. I will send by Mr Robins two hundred Dollars more. I hardly know what to advise you to do with it. I think however if Wm knows of a *good* piece of vacant land he may buy a land certificate and locate it. If I were there to attend to them I would invest all my wages in [live]stock of some kind.

I have but a few minutes in which to write—as we have much to attend to and little time to work in. I will prevail on Mr Robins if I

18. Along with the trans-Mississippi cavalry regiments, Major General Sterling Price's Missouri State Guard and other infantry units also crossed to the east side of the Mississippi River. Oates, *Confederate Cavalry,* 36–37.

19. Private Sparks of Company I was detailed to accompany the horses of his unit to north Texas. His account of the trip is in Sparks, *War Between the States,* 56–58.

20. The day after Bates wrote his letter, the Confederate Congress passed a national conscription law converting all "Twelve Months Men" (i.e., volunteers for twelve months' service) into "Thirty-Six Months Men." Men such as Bates, who had originally signed on for one year of service, were now legally required to serve for three years. Albert Burton Moore, *Conscription and Conflict in the Confederacy* (New York: Macmillan, 1924), 14, 308.

can to call and see you. He has been with us several weeks and can tell you more than I have time to write. I have not received a line from home but once since I left, although men have been passing frequently from Paris to the Regt. Do you write at all or have you quit entirely.[21] I will write you again before leaving here. Direct your letters to me at Little Rock—to be forwarded to me in *Van Dorn's Division—Churchhill's Brigade.*
Nothing further to write you now but remain your &c
James C. Bates

I have concluded to send but one hundred & fifty dollars by Mr Robins as I may need the remainder. I will draw some more in a day or so & send it by T. A. Perkins.

Desarc Ark
Apr 16th 62
Dear Ma;
  I wrote you by Mr Robins on yesterday. Today we start our horses to Texas and I write you again though have nothing of interest to communicate.
  Troops are still being sent off as rapidly as possible. you may expect to hear before the expiration of a month of a great battle on the Miss[issippi River]. I don't know if we will join the main army under [General P. G. T.] Beauregard [at Corinth] or be sent to some other point. We still continue to receive cheering news from our army at Corinth. I hardly think all the good news can be untrue. Last night however we heard of some reverses at Island No 10. Whether they true or not I cannot say—I fear they are. Our horses leave today for Texas. Tell Will to have some of my oats & corn brought up & feed my horse well for two or three weeks. If he does not want to use him he can turn him over at any time to those in charge of him.

April 17th 1862 Thurs [diary]
  Today our horse in charge of a detail of seven men left for Texas—it seemed like parting with an old friend to see my horse leave. He has carried me so long & so willingly—& through so

21. Bates, like many soldiers on both sides, occasionally lost patience with the home folks, thinking they were not writing often enough. Later missives indicate that family and friends were writing more letters than he was receiving. Some messages from both directions apparently never reached their destinations.

many dangers that I was loath to give him up. If I should live through the war I will keep him for the noble service he has done. Ordered to cook five days rations & be ready tomorrow morning to leave on the steamer—appointed ordnance officer for the Reg this morning & have been busily engaged making out a report of the number, description &c of our army.[22]

The transfer of trans-Mississippi Confederates to the east side of the Mississippi in April and May 1862 was truly a large undertaking, and it was the last of its kind for the remainder of the war. In addition to Sterling Price's Missouri militia and other infantry units, sixteen regiments, one battalion, and three companies of cavalry milled around the river landings, ready for departure to Tennessee and Mississippi. Altogether, more than twenty-two thousand Confederates—about half cavalry—made the trip.[23]

After reluctantly turning their horses over to men detailed to lead them back to Texas, Bates and his fellow troopers climbed the gangplanks onto crowded steamboats for the journey down the White River and then up the Mississippi to Memphis. The river cruise offered a welcome change of scene after months of traversing frozen prairies and icy mountain passes on horseback. The observant Bates recorded much of the scenery in his diary. Upon arrival at Memphis, he immediately began visiting army offices to outfit his regiment with the ordnance that might be required for their new war east of the river.

April 18th 1862 Fri [diary]

This morning we moved on the boat.[24] Our Reg, 700 men crowds it from stem to stern—ten or twelve boats are still at the wharf taking on troops. Desarc presents quite an animated appearance—wagons drays, cannon—horses soldiers, citizens crowd every street. As each boat swings off from its moorings & turns its prow down the river cheer after cheer is given by those leaving, & those still behind manifest their impatience to be off—by giving still louder cheers.

22. The regimental ordnance officer was responsible for procuring firearms, ammunition, and necessary appurtenances such as cartridge boxes for his unit.

23. Oates, *Confederate Cavalry,* 36–37.

24. The steamboat that carried the regiment downstream, the *Victoria,* was built in Pennsylvania in 1858. A 400–ton sidewheeler, it was 222 feet long and 32 feet wide. Kerr, ed., *Fighting with Ross' Texas Cavalry,* 36, 84; Paul H. Silverstone, *Warships of the Civil War Navies* (Annapolis, Md.: Naval Institute Press, 1989), 180.

April 19th 1862 Sat [diary]

A mist of rain falling nearly all day—made good speed today passing several boats on our way down—White River is entirely out of its banks. Occasionally we see houses on banks raised on blocks & pillars—to get them above high water—the water is over some of the floors.[25] Been making out Pay Rolls today—find it a troublesome job—our staterooms poorly ventilated & I slept out on guard last night on my blanket. I believe that nearly half of the Reg are at this time 9 pm engaged in gambling.[26]

Desarc Ark
Apr 19th 62
Dear Ma:

We leave this morning on a steamer for Memphis. Our horses were started on yesterday to Texas. I cannot say how I will like Infantry but am willing to go any way in which I will be of most service to my country. We have but little marching to do & as it would be almost impossible to procure forage for our horses, I think we will be better dismounted.

I have but little news to write more than I gave you on yesterday & the day before. I send by Lieut Calaway sixty dollars. I sent you one hundred & fifty by Mr Robins & one hundred & twenty some time previous by Ben Forney. Of this amount retain for your own use as much as you wish. If Aunt Tenn is in need of any give her as much as you think proper. Give my kindest regards to Miss Annie R. & Miss Mary & Moot—tell them a letter is due each of them from me; but I have had so much to attend to and so little time in which to do it I have positively had no time to write. I may have a day of leisure on the boat & will devote that to writing to my many good friends in Paris. My love to all the family.
Truly your son
J.C. Bates

The late news at this point is contained in the inclosed army paper.

25. Sergeant Griscom wrote that "the whole country is now under water & in most places the people are living in the second story of their houses—yet they cheer us as we go by, especially the ladies." Kerr, ed., *Fighting with Ross' Texas Cavalry*, 36; Barron, *Lone Star Defenders*, 81; Billingsley, " 'Such Is War' " (Part 2), *Texas Military History* 7 (Spring 1968): 44.

26. If Bates ever joined his comrades in drinking and gambling, he did not admit it in his diary or letters.

April 20th 1862 [diary]

A cold disagreeable mist still falling on the back water from the Miss & the boats run slow. Some splendid farms completely submerged in water. Finished our muster & pay rolls. About 10 am came into the great father of waters [the Mississippi River] & as it was out of its banks it seemed like emerging from a little rivulet into a small ocean. Arrived at Memphis about 2 pm. As we passed different boats on the wharf—loaded with troops it seemed every man was trying to split his throat cheering. As we passed through the city on our way out to camp—the ladies—God bless them—From the windows & doors of every dwelling we passed for two miles waved handkerchiefs or flags. Many as we passed came out to the streets & threw us beautiful bouquets & baskets of flowers. [27] It seemed almost like coming amongst a different race of people—so much more interest being manifested by the ladies of Tenn than those of Ark.

April 21st 1862 [diary]

Raining again—I have been in the city all day trying to get ammunition for our Reg—have not yet succeeded. Firing heard in direction of Fort Pillow. Have been unwell for several days past.

April 22nd 1862 Tues [diary]

Went in again today for ammunition—failed to get it. Still raining & Miss river still rising. Boats coming in constantly with troops. Road so muddy out to camp will stay in city tonight.[28] Went to Hospital in which our sick are. Ladies are gliding about in every room like ministering angels sent to watch our sick & wounded soldiers. Saw many of the federals wounded in the battle of Shiloh—they received the same kind of treatment as our own wounded. Many of them say they will never take up arms (again) against the South.

April 23rd 1862 [diary]

Immediately after breakfast went again to the chief of ordnance[.] my requisition not yet approved. The request of the last

27. A private in the 6th Texas Cavalry had been similarly impressed when he arrived two days earlier. Memphis, he noted, "is a large and handsome city full of flowers and beautiful women." Entry of April 18, 1862, F. A. Rawlins Diary.

28. The regiment camped in the eastern suburbs of Memphis. Kerr, ed., *Fighting with Ross' Texas Cavalry*, 36.

three days is again repeated "come again." Having nothing else to do consumed most of the day in visiting places of interest to me in the city. Those possessing most interest to me was the iron works, of which there are several, & the cannon foundry—have seen some as good sabres bayonets & other articles from the novelty works as are made any where. Several pieces of brass cannon at the finishing houses are the finest I ever saw. Several pieces of very large caliber have been cast & are being bored & mounted. Also saw a number of 13 inch mortars just finished. Late in the evening went again to Ordnance Department—again put off. Been a wet cold disagreeable day still raining & has rained for so many days back that I can hardly remember when it did'nt. As the mud is nearly knee deep from here to camp and almost as deep after I get there, think I will try a crowded hotel again tonight. Heavy cannonading still heard in the direction of Fort Pillow.

Bates finally squeezed his regiment's ordnance supplies out of the Confederate bureaucracy in Memphis in late April. The receipt he signed listed the following items:

5,000 buck-and-ball cartridges
2,000 Sharps rifle cartridges
2,000 cartridge holsters
25,000 shotgun caps
550 gun slings
50 cartridge boxes
50 cap boxes
50 waist belts
1 keg powder[29]

This list indicates that the men of the 9th Texas Cavalry, like most western horsemen, were armed primarily with shotguns, although a minority used smoothbore muskets and rifles.

Bates wrote a long-delayed letter to Mootie the same day, painting an upbeat picture of the troops at Memphis and relating some exaggerated secondhand stories about the recent Battle of Shiloh. He recognized by now that the engagement on the Tennessee River had been a defeat. He

29. The list of ordnance stores is included in Bates's file in the Compiled Service Records (Microfilm M323, roll 56).

also repeated gossip about various Texas officers and units and mentioned what must have been a favorite topic of conversation among the troops, the recent conscription law passed by the Confederate Congress.

One day later the men of the regiment climbed onto railroad cars at the Memphis depot, the engines of the Memphis & Charleston Railroad jerked forward, and the 9th Texas Cavalry steamed eastward toward Corinth, ninety miles away. The recent riverboat trip had been slow and leisurely; the junket by rail must have seemed positively astonishing by contrast—a mile in only a minute and a half! Some of the farm boys from north Texas were seeing a great deal more of the world than ever before.

April 24th 1862 Thurs [diary]
    At the Ordnance office again—had the satisfaction of finding my requisition approved—sent my wagon to the boats & had it loaded—got a wagon at the government stables to haul out my guns. Met Maj Townes who told me we had received an order to take the cars [the train] for Corinth at 6 oclk[.] sent the guns to Depot & went out to camp—found them just moving into depot. I was left in charge of those behind till wagons returned. The men had hardly left their camp before they were filled with scamps ready to steal any thing they could lay hands on. they succeeded in laying hands on my sharp shooter & disappeared with it[30]—with Capt Sims took supper at Mrs Wynns who has shown great kindness to our Reg, especially to the sick.[31] She says her niece & herself have visited the Hospitals daily for the last six weeks taking two or three of their servants with them to assist them in cooking for, & waiting on & setting up with the sick. Ladies of memphis who have never soiled their hands with labor have done & are still doing a noble part for our sick. If gratitude will repay their kindness they receive it from all.

Memphis Tenn
April 24th 1862
Miss Mootie Johnson
Dear Friend
    When I wrote to you last from Cantonment Slidell I little thought that my next letter would be from this place. But so it is. In

30. Bates had apparently armed himself with a Sharps rifle or carbine, a breech-loading weapon effective at up to six hundred yards. Mark Mayo Boatner III, *The Civil War Dictionary* (rev. ed.; New York: David McKay, 1988), 735.
    31. This was probably J. W. Sims, the regiment's assistant quartermaster. Kerr, ed., *Fighting with Ross' Texas Cavalry*, 211.

time of peace we do not know one day where our "Star of fortune" may land us the next. How much more difficult it is even to guess at coming events in these "exciting times of war." I have sometimes wished I could lift the veil that hides the future from our view and get a glimpse of the hidden Mysteries yet undeveloped[,] Mysteries that we await with so much impatience to see unraveled. But it is best for us that we cannot.

Events are coming—will be upon us before the expiration of fifteen days—which I would like much to know the result of—as the fate of the Southern Confederacy will be in a measure decided by them. It seems indeed that Baldwin's prophecies are—in some respects being fulfilled—and that the battle of Armageddon is not as far distant as we supposed one year ago. If the combined armies of the North & South meet in pitched battle in the valley of the Miss— it will be more terrible in its results than that which decided the fate of Bonaparte at Waterloo. I have not a doubt of the result—of the next battle to be fought here unless the Federals receive large reinforcements.

The troops here are in fine spirits and eager for another fight. While marching from the boats to our camp at this place we were greeted with cheers and huzza's from the crowd assembled to see us pass. Our way was strewn with flowers thrown by the fair hands of the patriotic ladies of Memphis. He who would not fight for a cause in which so many ladies have enlisted with their whole souls have hearts too craven to resist oppression from *any* source. I hope there are not many such in the Southern Confederacy.

Capt. Hill of [Samuel B.] Maxey's [9th Texas Infantry] Regt was in our camp this morning on his way to Texas—having been discharged. He gave us some items of interest relative to the battle of Shiloh. Says our loss was from five to seven thousand killed & wounded—not more than three hundred prisoners. No arms lost. While the loss of the enemy according to their own admission will not fall short of fifteen thousand killed & wounded & about five thousand prisoners—and twelve to fifteen thousand stand of arms.[32] We whiped them on the first day—but on the second they received fifty thousand reinforcements under Buel—and to use a popular, or at least a common, phrase our forces "fell back" in other words were

---

32. As usual with such camp stories, estimates of enemy losses were exaggerated and friendly losses were minimized. Federal casualties at Shiloh comprised about 1,750 killed, 8,400 wounded, and 2,900 missing. Confederate figures were roughly 1,700 killed, 8,000 wounded, and 1,000 missing. Boatner, *Civil War Dictionary,* 757.

whiped.[33] They retreated however but a short distance and in good order.

The proportion of officers killed was unusually large—one Regt (5th Tenn) having 9 captains & seventeen Lieuts killed. Maxey's Regt, or a small portion of them were in the battle—and according to Capt Hill "did *some* fighting." Maxey is a Brigadier Gen—*but his old Regt is not in his Brigade.* I have seen and conversed with several of his men—they all rejoice at his promotion—because they say— *it removes them from under his command.* Men who were his warmest friends before leaving Texas are now most bitter in his denunciation. Two hundred fifty of the Regt have died or been killed by negligence as some of them say—since they were organized. Capt Hill says another battle may be expected there (at Shiloh) soon. I do not much think the fight will be there.

For two days past and now while I write, heavy cannonading may be heard in the direction of Fort Pillow—thirty miles above this on the Miss river. We have received no news as to the result. The Federals have a large number of Gun Boats besides a heavy land force to cooperate with them. They rely mostly on their gun boats as they are almost shot and bomb proof—less than a thirty two pound ball having no effect on them.

I might give you some items that would interest you with regard to the movement of our troops and gun boats—if *permitted* to do so. I will send you some papers containing the latest news *made public.*

A conscription law has recently been passed by Congress according to which all men between the ages of 18 & 85 are to [rest of letter missing][34]

April 25th 1862 Fri [diary]

We did not expect to get off last night—not being able to get all our baggage to the Depot untill 3 oclk—at which time I lay down to snatch an hour's sleep. At 5 we were up & loaded on our bag-

33. Major General Don Carlos Buell's army of 25,000 (not 50,000) men reinforced Grant during the battle.

34. The Conscription Act of April 16, 1862, made all white males between eighteen and thirty-five years of age subject to a national draft for three years of service. Those men who had previously joined for twelve months of service were now required to remain in the army for thirty-six months. As compensation, these twelve-month men were allowed to reorganize their regiments and elect new officers. Moore, *Conscription and Conflict,* 14.

gage—at 6 all was ready—& at 7 a shrill whistle announced we were ready to move off & by the time we were out of the city we were speeding along at the rate of thirty miles per hour. Occasionally on an incline grade of several miles we would make a mile in one and one half minutes—which most of the boys thought *pretty tall* travelling compared with riding on horseback. The road for about twenty miles lay over a beautiful & finely cultivated country from every house in sight of the road flags & handkerchiefs were waved as we passed—& frequently ladies were standing by the road—as we passed they would throw a shower of beautiful flowers & bouquets on us the receipt of which was acknowledged by such shouts as only Texans can give. On account of having to stop so often we did not get to corinth untill after dark. Country for the last half of the distance poor, low—flat.

As more and more trains pulled into the Corinth depot carrying regiments from all parts of the Confederacy, General P. G. T. Beauregard's army doubled in size, to roughly 66,000 men. Some of the rough-hewn Texans were impressed with the real Confederate uniforms, "all aglitter with brass buttons and gold lace. . . . I never had seen anything like it before," one trooper remembered. Situating, feeding, and supplying such numbers was a formidable task. "The roads for miles around were crammed and jammed with wagons, carts, ambulances, caissons and artillery carriages," a physician in the 3rd Texas Cavalry exclaimed. The 9th Texas Cavalry (now dismounted) had other worries as well: they had to learn to fight as infantry. Bates and his fellow officers spent many hours in the bleak, muddy fields around Corinth, mastering new commands and maneuvers and passing their freshly learned lessons on to their soldiers.[35]

Making their job all the more difficult were crowded camps, sinks (latrines) placed upstream from drinking sources, and unhealthy water, so foul smelling that the horses refused to drink it.[36] A trooper in the 3rd Texas Cavalry described it as "a mean, milky-looking fluid." Soldiers by the hundreds and thousands came down with a variety of illnesses, especially typhoid and dysentery, which debilitated them for weeks or months on end.[37] "Fully one half of the men were prostrated by camp dysentery," one

35. Barron, *Lone Star Defenders,* 83; Hale, *Third Texas Cavalry,* 110.

36. Faced with the murky liquids at Corinth, Bates must have thought longingly of the sparkling spring water he had enjoyed in the mountains of northern Arkansas.

37. "Dysentery and diarrhea, which deplete and dehydrate the body and leave the patient susceptible to other illnesses," struck Civil War soldiers more often than any other malady,

Texan recalled. "Day by day, the ranks of the men on duty grew thinner and thinner. The hospitals were crowded, and thousands were sent to asylums far in the rear."[38]

If Bates occasionally felt discouraged, he quickly put such thoughts out of his mind and expressed his determination to fight to the end, even if it meant the destruction of the South. He would have none of the "tyranny" with which the Yankees intended to saddle his people. For Bates, this was a war about freedom and slavery—not the enslavement of black people but the North's intended enslavement of southern white people. If southerners submitted to the rule of "the invading vandals of the north," they would be nothing but slaves themselves.[39]

April 26th 1862 Sat [diary]
    Consumed principal part of the day in moving camp lower down the road to higher ground—clearing off streets & parade ground. No drill today. Troops still coming in on every train—no rain for three days past—some indication of it today.

April 27th 1862 Sun [diary]
    Will hereafter have dress parade at *7am* camp drill at 9 am *officers drill at 2pm & Battalion drill at 4pm.*

In the back of his diary, Bates jotted a schedule of drills. Whether the schedule was followed at Corinth or earlier is not clear, but it gives a fair picture of the hours the men spent learning to be soldiers:

AM
Reveille and Roll Call	4 1/2 oclk
Dress Parade	5 1/2 oclk
Guard Mount	6 oclk
Officers Drill	6 to 7 oclk

and Confederates suffered more frequently than their enemies. Judith Lee Hallock, " 'Lethal and Debilitating': The Southern Disease Environment as a Factor in Confederate Defeat," *Journal of Confederate History* 7 (No. 1, 1991): 53.

    38. Barron, *Lone Star Defenders,* 89; Rose, *Ross' Texas Brigade,* 65.

    39. Bates fit the profile outlined by James M. McPherson in *For Cause and Comrades: Why Men Fought in the Civil War* (New York: Oxford University Press, 1997), 13, 21. The young officer invoked the spirit of the founding fathers of the United States to justify the Confederacy's resistance to outside "oppression."

Company Drill	7 1/2 to 9 oclk
Comp[any] Off[icers'] Recitation	11 oclk

PM

Battalion Drill	4 1/2 to 6 1/2 oclk
Dress Parade (Brigade)	6 3/4 oclk

April 28th 1862 Mon [diary]

After dress parade made out a requisition for ammunition &c with a detachment of thirty men went to the ordnance department & had it carried up to camp. Will Long of Maxey's old Reg was over to see us today also Willie Williams.

April 29th 1862 Tues [diary]

After attending drill & parade spent an hour in tailoring & sewing up rents, sewing buttons on, &c. This [war] is a troublesome business & if we can have peace on *honorable* terms God grant how soon it may come—but otherwise *never do I wish to see it.* I had rather see the sunny South with all its substantial wealth destroyed by the invading vandals of the north than submit to their rule—and if the people of the south have not lost the energy & determination of their sires we *will* gain our independence & be freed from the yoke of tyranny.

Corinth Miss

May 2nd/62

My Dear Ma:

As I have just learned a gentleman leaves here for Texas this morning I take the opportunity of writing by him. We are encamped two miles from Corinth on the Memphis and Charlston rail road—the main army being entrenched on the east and north of the place. Active preparations are being made by our Genls for the coming conflict. The Federals [torn section] gaining a victory here—and they are determined, as far as I have had an opportunity of judging, to win this fight at *any cost*—and it may and doubtless will cost us many lives—but *all* are sanguine of success because, as I said before, in this fight hinges, in a great measure the fate of the Southern Confederacy. All the troops that can be spared from other points are being concentrated at this place and our force will be—*sufficient.*

[torn section] and long before this reaches you the fate of many a brave man will be sealed. If I should be one, *I am not afraid to die*—and perhaps realize *some* of the bright hopes of a year ago. still if he who holds the destinies of nations wills that I should fall I am ready to lay my life down for my country. [torn section] Whitfield's Regt (in which is Patterson's company) is also near us. They have a good deal of sickness in camp. Troops who came out last spring are suffering considerably with sickness whilst those who have been out since fall are generally well.

I have not time to write more—would send you some more money but don't know the man who will take this. Tell Will to be sure and invest the money I have sent in something. Tell Miss Mary—the capt [E. L. Dohoney] is well and of course looking well. Jno Gibbons Dan H[atcher] & Capt Wright are all well. [Rest of letter missing]

The Federal army that had won the Battle of Shiloh in early April was now under the command of Major General Henry W. Halleck, a scholarly and cautious officer known more for his books on military science than for any great battles he had won. Determined to follow up on the victory at Shiloh, he assembled three separate Union armies—110,000 men altogether—for the drive on Beauregard's army at Corinth. In late April the outer edges of Halleck's slow-moving behemoth began to make contact with the Confederate regiments ringing Corinth. A series of probing encounters in early and mid-May seemed like battles to some of the soldiers, who had never seen so many people in such a small space. But a full engagement of the two armies would not come for another five months.

Bates's regiment, now numbering about 650 men, was hauled from its tents and put into line on more than one occasion in early May. It seemed that any one of these faceoffs might erupt into a full-scale engagement, but each time one or the other army pulled back.[40] Bates described two of these encounters in a letter to his sister.

In Camp Near Corinth
May 9 1862
My Dear Sister:
    I wrote to Ma a few days since but another opportunity of sending a letter is presented and I will not let the opportunity slip. A day

---

40. *OR*, Vol. 10, Pt. 2, p. 489; Thomas Lawrence Connelly, *Army of the Heartland: The Army of Tennessee, 1861–1862* (Baton Rouge: Louisiana State University Press, 1967), 176.

or so after writing to Ma we were ordered out with three days rations. I thought the fight pretty near at hand—we marched some two or three miles out in the direction of our rifle pits where we were halted and remained untill evening—and then returned to our camp. We could hear at intervals during the day—cannonading in the direction of Purdy (our left wing) some ten miles from Corinth (NW). We have since learned that nothing material was accomplished—the fighting having all been done at "long tom" with long Toms, in other words with cannon.

On the Monday following we were ordered out on picket guard. Our col not understanding the directions we were to take, marched us within one mile of the enemy's left wing at which point they were said to be sixty-thousand strong. Here we remained untill evening when some of our scouts—who had been out reconoitering found us and informed us of our close proximity to the enemy & consequent danger. As we were four or five miles in advance of our main army we did not feel very easy untill we had moved to a safer distance which we were not long in doing. As we remained out three days longer our provisions ran short & we paid as high as 75cts pr lb for bacon & 25 cts for *very small* "dodgers" of corn bread tolerably "high living" I should say.

On the evening of the fourth day out—about sun set, we were ordered in to Corinth—10 miles which place we reached at 12 Oclk that night. We were too tired to think of eating if we had anything to eat, so we droped down on the ground & slept soundly untill morning [May 9], when Gen Van Dorn's entire command was ordered out to attack the enemy's left who were reported to be advancing in force. Five miles [east] from Corinth—we formed our lines of battle & advanced in column of Divisions—each Division forming a separate line—the 1st in front &c we were in the second. We moved on a mile or more when the enemy's advance was discovered & one of our batteries opened on them—& soon drove them from their position. They fell back 1/2 mile & took position in some heavy timber and underbrush, their batteries in rear. Two of our batteries (on the right and left) kept up a constant fire of grape and shell and under cover of this the first division was ordered forward to make the attack.

They moved on two or three hundred yards in "double quick"—disappearing in the underbrush—and for a few minutes the excitement along our line was intense[,] all eager to take a hand in the fray.

Presently a few sharp reports from the rifles of our advance skir- mishers were heard and all again was still. We knew that when the si- lence was again broken it would be by a tremendous volley from the entire line on both sides. But a few minutes elapsed before it com- menced and for a short time it was terrible. We received the order to move on and the whole line started on the run. Before getting to the timber we heard the shouts and huzzas of our men, & we were or- dered to halt. In a few moments we saw the horses of the Federal Cavalry running in every direction and we knew that *some* of them had been made to bite the dust. Our advance division pressed for- ward driving the enemy before them—for a mile or more keeping up a continuous fire most of the time.

The enemy's force was generally estimated at about ten thousand —we had about twenty thousand out though not more than one fourth of them were engaged. We took 50 or 60 prisoners 6 pieces of cannon some small arms—2,000 or more, knapsacks of clothing —camp equipage &c.[41] The loss of killed and wounded was small on both sides, I think about equal from the best information I have. The enemy had thrown this force forward for the purpose I suppose, of throwing up embankments—rifle pits &c as they had brought a few loads of picks & spades with them. They also had a telegraph wire running back to their main army which we destroyed. After driv- ing them back across a swampy creek—our Genls I presume, did not deem it prudent to pursue them further and we returned to camp. To one not accustomed to see such large bodies of men together our force might have seemed large enough to fight the whole Northern army. But the two armies here have grown to such gigantic propor- tions that our little fight is only termed *sharp skirmishing.*

As the gentleman who will carry this may not be able to get off for several days I will add more if anything of interest occurs.

Bates clearly believed a major battle, one that might decide the fate of the Confederacy, was inevitable in the near future. But the two armies sparring on the outskirts of Corinth would not come to grips with each other for several months. By that time the lieutenant's military career would take some major turns.

---

41. General Halleck reported to Washington that part of his army had been driven back to its main line in the action Bates described in his letter. This small engagement is sometimes called the Battle of Farmington. *OR,* Vol. 52, Pt. 1, pp. 248–49.

5 Reorganization

While the two armies at Corinth threw occasional light jabs at each other for several weeks, the soldiers in the Confederate camps engaged in the time-honored practice of electing their leaders. The new conscription law allowed the so-called twelve-month regiments to reorganize and elect new officers. In addition, those soldiers who were younger than eighteen or older than thirty-five and those officers not reelected were allowed to return to their homes. Colonel Sims's wound at Elkhorn Tavern had disabled him, and he would have to be replaced. In addition, some of the soldiers were determined to remove officers who had not proved themselves good leaders since the original elections in October. For much of the month of May, the men divided their time between forming lines of battle for one alarm or another and electioneering in camp.

Bates, who had been elected third lieutenant in October and first lieutenant in March, had demonstrated leadership capacity. He was intelligent, a strong believer in the Confederate cause, efficient in carrying out his duties, responsible, and courageous. His rescue of a wounded comrade under fire at Chustotalasah doubtless revealed to the satisfaction of all that he would lead rather than follow his fellow Texans when danger threatened. When the men cast their votes for captain on May 10, Bates was elected without opposition, a revealing endorsement of his leadership qualities. His military career thus took a new direction just as he marked his twenty-fifth birthday.

His friend Dohoney, ambitious for higher office, submitted his name for the lieutenant colonelcy, but for one reason or another—perhaps Dohoney's late entry into the contest, perhaps his sharp tongue—he was not elected. Instead, Dudley W. Jones, a young man who would prove himself many times over, assumed that position. Bates's next letter to his mother (a continuation of his May 9 letter to his sister) outlines the results of the election and passes judgment on some of his fellow soldiers.

May 10th 1862

Dear Mary

On yesterday I wrote to Sister [Mootie] but Dr Apling not having started I will write again. On yesterday we received an order to reorganize in compliance with the conscription act passed by congress at its last session. In obedience to the order at 10 Oclk today each company went into an election for company officers. They also balloted for field officers, but no one has as yet been elected. The balloting will be resumed in the morning.

The election in our Company for company officers went as follows. For captain your unworthy brother—no opposition.[1] 1st Lieut J.C. Gibbons—Sen [senior] 2nd [lieutenant] D.C. Hatcher—Jr. 2nd [lieutenant] R.I. Jennings—Orderly Seargt J.L. Fowler—2nd Seargt E. H. Tanner.[2] The remainder you do not know. Dohoney ran for Lieut Col but too much caucusing & wire working had been done before he announced himself. Our former adjutant D. W. Jones was elected Lieut Col. He is a clever well meaning man but utterly incompetent to fill the position.[3] Our Maj[,] Dodson of Tarrant County[,] is not much better.[4] The fact is we have no men in the Regt capable of filling the position of field officer except Lieut

1. This part of the letter was sent to both Bates's sister and his mother. In any case, he is referring to himself as the newly elected captain.

2. Gibbons, Hatcher, and Tanner have been identified previously. Robert I. Jennings was a twenty-five-year-old farmer and native of Tennessee. He would be killed four months later at the Battle of Iuka. J. L. Fowler, only twenty-one, was a Texas native still living with his parents before the war. He would be wounded and captured the following September.

3. Contrary to Bates's assessment, Jones would prove to be a superior officer. Only twenty-two years old, he distinguished himself in the following months and was promoted to colonel in 1863. Veterans of the 9th Texas Cavalry remembered Jones as a courageous and effective leader. For some reason—perhaps Jones's defeat of Dohoney for the lieutenant colonelcy—Bates disliked Jones, and the new captain would not warm to the new lieutenant colonel for many months. Tyler et al., *New Handbook of Texas*, 3:979–80; Rose, *Ross' Texas Brigade*, 149; Kerr, ed., *Fighting with Ross' Texas Cavalry*, 210.

4. J. W. Dodson of Company A was elected major at this time and later served briefly as lieutenant colonel of the regiment. See the roster of regimental officers compiled by the unit's adjutant in Kerr, ed., *Fighting with Ross' Texas Cavalry*, 210.

Col Quayle who is going home—soon—& Maj Townes. Maj T. has announced himself as a candidate for Col. His opponent[,] Capt [M. J.] Brenson of Tarrant Co[unty and Company D], is not only an ordinary man as to capacity but a *drunkard*.

Sunday [May] 11th The balloting for Col was this morning resumed.[5] Maj Townes withdrew misname & on the third ballot Capt [Gideon] Smith of Fannin Co[unty and Company B] was elected. I think it probable that another election will be ordered—as the general impression seems to be that the law of Texas—by which we are governed in the elections, will not admit a new candidate after the first ballot.[6] I think it doubtful whether our Col elect will be able to stand an examination by the Military board of examiners or not. All officers elected in the reorganization have to undergo a rigid examination and if found incompetent are rejected. I have been told that *sixteen* were rejected from [Samuel B.] Maxeys old [9th Texas Infantry] Regiment.

Whether I will be able to stand the test or not is yet to be tried. In fact I am not very particular as to whether I am passed or not as officers not *reelected* & passed will be relieved from duty for the remainder of our twelve months or long enough to go home for a time. If it were not for the members of the company I would procure a transfer to some other Regiment. The boys say if I leave I will have to take them with me, or they will desert. If we are refused another election for field officers, we will make an attempt to have them appointed. If we fail in both we will have to submit—provided I ca'nt get a transfer of the entire company. I am heartily tired of this Regiment.[7]

Monday [May] 12th—We have various rumors this morning of skirmishes on yesterday[,] the advances of the enemy—the taking of 6,000 federal prisoners &c. None of which I put any reliance on. I believe *nothing* I hear in camp—in fact rarely ever listen to these rumors. If you at home would believe only what you *know* to be

5. No candidate for the office of colonel had received a majority in the first day's balloting. Ibid., 38.

6. Smith's election was soon overturned by General Van Dorn, and Townes was eventually selected the regiment's new colonel. Ibid., 210.

7. Bates's disappointment at the election of Jones over Dohoney and, briefly, Smith over Townes, was probably the source of his alienation from his old regiment. His willingness to separate from the regiment may have been a factor in the transfer of his company to a different regiment a few weeks later.

reliable you would be spared much unnecessary uneasiness of mind. There has been some sickness in our company since we have been at this place. Jno Gibbons[,] Eb.[Dohoney,] Dan [Hatcher]—& Ras [Erasmus] Tanner have all been on the sick list for a week or ten days—but are all improving.[8] I am not near so fleshy as when I left home but still have excellent health—have no fear of being sick as I am careful not to expose myself in any way. We have orders to march from here at 3 Oclk so I must leave off. I will write the first opportunity. My love to Ma[,] Will[,] the children and your self.
J.C. Bates

Two days later, Bates again found himself standing in line of battle with his company, waiting for orders. Taking advantage of a lull, he sat down and scribbled a letter to Mootie on paper taken from a Federal knapsack after the skirmish at Farmington on May 9. He was alarmed at the information he had been reading in captured correspondence and northern newspapers. Those sources convinced Bates that the people of the North were not fighting, as they claimed, only to restore the Union, but to subjugate the southern people and free their slaves. Bates was already convinced that he and his fellow Confederates were fighting to protect their freedom from northern tyranny; these documents only intensified his commitment to a prolonged armed struggle.

Camp Churchill Clark
Corinth Miss May 14 / 62
[To Mootie Johnson]
    On our return from picket guard yesterday evening, tired, and hungry and *sleepy,* I droped down in the tent thinking I had never been so greatly exhausted before and requested not to be disturbed for anything. Soon after Dan H[atcher] came to my tent with a bundle of letters for Company H. In an instant I was up, and having found three letters for myself (two from you & one from home) all thought of weariness was forgotten in the pleasure of reading them & by the time I had finished I was ready for another
    Although these letters were some time in finding me they were still as welcome as if written but a few days before. I can well understand the suspense you were in from reports received of our fight at

8. Dohoney later claimed that he nearly died at Corinth. Dohoney, *Average American,* 109.

Elk Horn. But I hope you have learned ere this to believe *nothing you hear* unless it is substantiated by evidence that cannot be doubted.

You need not believe *any* of the reports you may hear of the battle soon to be fought here, untill they come from those whom you know. There are several men in our Regt & some in our company who will be relieved from duty immediately after the battle who will proceed forthwith to Tex. From these you will get the first reliable news.

Well—this is the third time I have been interrupted since commencing this letter. This morning I had just written "My Dear Friend" when the call to Dress parade was sounded. I laid aside my paper got the company in line moved out on the parade ground— & after parade began again, but was in a few minutes called out to discharge our firearms.[9] This over I took up my paper to "try again" but had not written a dozen lines when we received an order to march forthwith—throwing our knapsacks on our backs we were soon on the march & were halted at this place, formed in line of battle, with the order to rest in our places. I am now siting in front of my company "penciling" these lines not knowing whether you or a Yankee will read them, doubtful if either.

Two days since [actually, on May 9] we had a sharp skirmish with the advance of the left wing of the "feds" in which we drove them back about two miles taking 57 prisoners, 6 pieces of cannon, a large lot of knapsacks, &cc. This paper on which I write is part of the "booty." A large number of letters fell into our hands. Such expressions as "quelling the rebellion" "wiping out slavery and the South" "teaching the rebels to know their masters" &c were very common. Some even had selected farms on which they intended to "settle" when they had "conquered us."

I once thought that the mass of the northern people were ignorant of the true cause of this war. Ignorant of the fact that the subjugation of the South & the extinction of slavery was the prime object in view with Abe Lincoln & every other abolition leader in the north. But when so many public journals of the North boldly proclaim *the abolition of slavery* to be the object of this war, it is hard to believe that the most *credulous* & *stupid* even of the Northern

9. During wet weather, which could foul the gunpowder in their weapons, the men were occasionally required to fire their muskets, rifles, and shotguns to ensure that they were in good working order.

masses could still be in ignorance.[10] And if this be the motive for the war—and I have not a doubt of it, we can we *must* do nothing else but "conquer a peace" and teach *them* that we *have* no masters. Even if defeated here—of which I have no fears—we have got thousands of men with the *will* and the *nerve* to rally and come again—and make every inch of their progress south cost them a life.

[May] 16th   We received an order last evening to return to our camp leaving 1/4 of the brigade out on pickets. Several days since we received an order to reorganize—by electing company and field officers. Our election for Col was pronounced void by Gen Van Dorn & we will therefore ballot again tomorrow. Capt Smith of Fannin County was elected. If Maj Townes will consent to have his name run we will elect him—I think. Esqr Hunt who will be the bearer of this is impatient to get off so I must close. I have no news of interest to write you—not much probability of a fight for some time yet—and there may be none at all The enemy seem afraid to attack us in our position. If they do we will defeat them *without a doubt.*

Dan H[atcher] sends regards to you   Jno G[ibbons] I know would, but he is not up yet. Our mess have all been a *little* unwell for several days—but all are improving. My good wishes to Miss Mary, [and] Mat "the rat." I will write again in a few days if an opportunity of sending a letter occurs.
Very truly Your Friend
J.C. Bates

Like you when you wrote last I have no ink and must therefore write with a pencil.

The remaining days of May were filled with orders to form lines of battle and counterorders to return to camp. Occasional skirmishes flared here and there around Corinth, but still the two armies did not come to grips with each other. Bates still expected a major engagement, but he was invariably disappointed. He repeated his suspicions about northern war aims to his brother-in-law, Will Bramlette, and urged him to join the army by accepting the post of regimental quartermaster.

10. President Abraham Lincoln would not announce emancipation as a war aim until the following September, but Bates was certain he had divined northern intentions well before Lincoln's preliminary Emancipation Proclamation.

May 21st 1862 Wed [diary]

For a long time I have "made no notes" every day the same—
monotonous round—varied only by a few skirmishes. On the 9th
we attacked—drove in the advance of the enemy—our loss very
small—theirs heavy—we did not receive a single check—as stated
by Gen Pope in his account neither was a single disabled—as he
stated. This evening we are ordered out—at 5 oclk—I have heretofore thought a fight very improbable when we were ordered out—
but now I do'nt know why I think *we will fight before returning*. If
so many a brave man will be sent to the spirit world—before we return—ambitious men will have an opportunity of displaying their
bravery—& patriots to die for their country. In any profession "The
paths of glory lead but to the grave."[11]

May 22nd 1862 Thurs [diary]

Marched out five miles S.E. of our camp last night—owing to the
large force & the darkness our Brigade which was in the rear did not
get up till after midnight. Tired and weary & sleepy I droped down
on my blanket & slept soundly untill morning. The head of our column was on the move before daylight—& one continuous stream
kept pouring along untill 11 oclk before our Brigade started—
marched on untill the rear was within two miles of Farmington when
we were halted & commanded to about face & return to camp—
various reports prevailed as to the cause of our turning back—one
that the enemy were not to be found—another that they were found
too strong to be attacked with our force—another that Gen [Brax-
ton] Bragg was ordered not to make an attack if the enemy were on
the opposite side of Chambers Creek as there was but one good
crossing & the enemy had possession of that. I think the latter sup-
position the most probable. Whatever the reasons for our turning
back I suppose they were good ones. The men seemed eager for the
fray & were consequently disappointed that we did not have a brush
with them. Came into camp hungry but weariness overpowered
hunger so I droped down & slept untill night.

May 23rd 1862 Friday [diary]

Leaving one fourth of the command out in front of the camp to
guard against surprise the remainder returned to their tents. If the

11. Bates's diary and letters occasionally reveal his solid education in English literature.
The line quoted is from Thomas Gray's "Elegy Written in a Country Churchyard."

enemy had but known our camps were left so exposed what an opportunity they would have had to sweep everything before them on
yesterday. Nothing occurred today except some picket fighting in
which we drove them back without loss on our side. Cannonading
heard at intervals during last night on our left wing.

May 24th 1862 Sat [diary]

[Major] Gen [Thomas C.] Hindman today had a brush with the
enemy. He drew them into ambush—killed many & took many prisoners.[12] A number of prisoners were taken today "with bells on."
Suppose their object was to lead our men to believe they were cattle
or horses belled—dodge about through the brush—make what dis-
coveries they could—perhaps pick off a few of our pickets. But our
men were up to a few yank tricks & having discovered them
"bag[g]ed" the whole party. An attempt was made today by a party
of Feds to capture the train of cars from Memphis but their design
was discovered. Nine of them killed & some taken prisoner. Some
sharp cannonading in direction of Farmington.

Camp Churchill Clark
May 1862
Dear Will:

Yours of the 26th ult by the hand of Capt Sarfley[?] was received
several days since.

The long expected battle at this place has not come yet but may
at any day. I have no fear as to the result. I am satisfied of one thing
—it will be the most desperate & bloody & terrible battle that will
be fought during the war—at any rate if it is not little can be determined as to the result of a battle by indications seen before it. From
all I can learn Gen Halleck is determined to regain what he lost at
Shiloh and our whole army from Beauregard down to the lowest
subaltern are equally determined not only to hold every inch of
ground we may have—but to make the defeat of the enemy more
terrible than at Shiloh.[13] The men of our army are fully aware of the

12. Bates was misinformed. General Hindman was on his way from Corinth to Arkansas
to take command of the Trans-Mississippi District in late May 1862. Diane Neal and Thomas
W. Kremm, *Lion of the South: General Thomas C. Hindman* (Macon, Ga.: Mercer University
Press, 1993), 117–18.

13. Uncharacteristically, Bates had reverted to calling Shiloh a Confederate victory even
though he had earlier admitted it was a defeat.

importance of a victory here and hence the confidence all feel as to the result. Defeat to us, however, is not an impossibility. We *may* be defeated. If we are it will be by overwhelming numbers only.

Heavy skirmishing still continues almost daily, and with few exceptions the results have been decidedly in our favor. I do not think the day of the great battle can be prolonged many days. It will probably be fought and you will have news of it before this reaches you.

If we are defeated here the war, with the South, will have only *begun* in earnest. It was a long time before I could be induced to believe that this war was waged for the extinction of slavery—and although they might have started out with the intention only of "crushing the rebellion" and though they *still claim* that as their object it is evident to my mind that the real purpose of the war is to "wipe out slavery."

Letters written by the Yankees—and by their friends at home—have fallen into our hands here after the skirmishes that have occured here daily and the general tone of *all* of these is that the *South will soon be conquered* (not the rebellion crushed) and that slavery will be in consequence forever wiped out—and the power of the South crushed for all time—and this is the tone not only of the letters of the soldiers but of almost every northern journal that I have seen and I have seen many.

But stronger evidence than any of these, is the action of the Northern army—wherever they have gained possession of any of our territory. Every single Negro within reach of the Northern army—who would listen to their seductive promises have been persuaded to run away—and many of them *forced* to go. To some of these they have given free *passes* and sent north. Others they have in their camp—cooking[,] working on their rifle pits &c. Negro is not the only property they steal. Every thing of value belonging to Southern men household furniture — farming utensils — horses cattle hogs &c and every species of private property is destroyed wherever they go. Corn, wheat & bacon are taken wherever they find them, even to the last grains of corn & the last pound of bacon from defenseless women & children, leaving them to starve or make their way South as best they could.[14] Such is their policy here and such will be the fate of the whole South unless we drive him back

14. Of course, Bates had earlier written that Confederate soldiers often took the last ear of corn from their own civilians. But to Bates, the sin was more wicked when committed by the Yankees.

from our soil—and make them feel some of the horrors of war by taking the war into their own country.

You tell me not to reinlist untill I come home—I had already done this before I got your letter. Our entire army—as I wrote some time ago—reorganized in accordance with an act of congress. (The conscription act). By the provisions of this act Officers not reelected will be relieved, and have an opportunity of going home. I would have taken advantage of this and gone home for a while—but the boys in the company would not hear of me leaving. I think after this fight I will have an opportunity of going home as recruiting officer for the Regt.

Maj Townes has been elected Col. of our Regt. and is anxious to have you for Quarter Master. As the office will pay you well, and you can serve your country in that capacity as well as any other—& much *easier*, I would like for you to accept the position. Jere Wright says he is going home as soon as released & he can take charge of your business. Some doubt exists as to whether surgeons, Q.M.s [quartermasters] & comissaries will be released by the conscript act—or whether the newly elected Cols [colonels] have the right to appoint new staff. As soon as this question is settled you will have the offer of the Q.M. Department—or would have if Maj T[ownes] was assured you would accept. At least so he told me—when I applied for the position for you. Capt Dohoney declined to run for Capt at the reorganization. He announced his name for Lieut Col. on the day of the election and would have been elected, I think, if he had announced himself a week sooner. He intends going home as soon as he gets off.

If you invest the money I have sent home in land, *I want it all in Ma's name.* If any of Howe's property can be come at attend to it for me. Tell Aunt Tenn she can have as much of my corn as she wishes to use—she can probably pay for the hauling in corn. If she has received no money from San Antonio and stands in need of any, let her have some and I will remit the amount to you the first opportunity. If you stand in need of corn [rest of letter missing]

Company and regimental elections were made official on May 26, and some of the newly elected officers such as Bates must have wondered whether they were up to the task. Those who had not been reelected began leaving the camp near Corinth to return to Texas. Dohoney went back to Paris, where he married Mootie's sister Mary later in 1862. He served as an army commissary agent in Paris, resumed the practice of law, and eventually turned to politics, where he maintained his reputation as a maverick for the rest of his life.[15] Lieutenant Colonel Quayle, the former sea captain and Tarrant County judge, had declined to stand for election, probably owing to illness, and he too turned to politics after the war, serving in the Texas senate and later in the Missouri state legislature.[16]

May 25th 1862 Sun [diary]
And such a Sabbath as we have not had for a long while. A holy calm & quiet pervades today so unusual for a camp that it seems peace had begun her reign once more—& that our armies have forgotten their avocations—"grim visaged war has smoothed his wrinkled front" for the day in awe of him who "turns the tide of war."[17] It may be that this is the calm that always precedes the storm—the precursor of the terrible conflict that may begin at any moment, & in all probability will begin before another Sabbath. In the forenoon scribbled to my good friend Miss M—J— [Mootie Johnson] & in the afternoon listened to an excellent sermon by our chaplain. Lieut Col Quayle left today for Texas.

May 26th 1862 Mon [diary]
Yesterday the officers not reelected at our reorganization received their discharge & some of them left for home—others will remain untill after the battle. Called on [Brigadier] Gen [Dabney H.] Maury to know if those exempt by the conscript act are to be discharged immediately—he had received no order to that effect—so they will have to remain a while longer. Today the newly elected officers enter on the discharge of their duties. I feel my inability to take command of a company but intend, as far as I am able to do *my whole duty* without fear or favor. Oh, I know I will make *some* enemies but can make all who wish to do right—my friends.

While the Confederates reorganized their regiments and elected new officers, General Halleck's massive Federal army, now more than 100,000

15. In his autobiography Dohoney does not mention his defeat for the lieutenant colonelcy, remarking only that he was "discharged on account of physical disability." Dohoney, *Average American,* 109.

16. Tyler et al., *New Handbook of Texas,* 2:670–71, 5:383.

17. Bates remembered his Shakespeare as well as his Thomas Gray. His reference to "grim visaged war," which he used on more than one occasion, is from *Richard III* (act 1, scene 1).

strong, inched closer to Corinth. By May 25 Halleck was ready to loose his heavy guns on the Mississippi railroad town, and Bates's diary entries in late May reflect the new intensity among the Union gunners. Bates did not realize at first that General Beauregard, greatly overmatched, had decided to evacuate Corinth and move his army farther south into Mississippi. Instead, the new captain at first interpreted signs of movement as preparations for an advance. Within a few days it became clear that the Confederates were giving up the railroad junction at Corinth.[18]

May 27th 1862 Tues [diary]

Our Brigade received an order last night to be in readiness to march this morning at 4 oclk & report to [Major] Gen [Samuel] Jones at 5—which we did & as I anticipated were ordered out on picket.[19] The Brigade we relieved had a little brush with the enemy's pickets on yesterday—not much damage done on either side. At sunset received an order from Gen Jones to send in all Q.M.'s [quartermasters], Comissaries & Ordnance officers with ten men & a commissioned officer from each company. It is my opinion from this order that preparations are being made for an advance movement— & that we will attack the enemy in his position. Received news this evening of three glorious victories in V.a. [Virginia][20]

May 28th 1862 Wed [diary]

Everything is this morning quiet on our wing—but on the extreme left can hear cannonading. As yesterday passed without a brush with the pickets guess we will have it today. As I anticipated this morning the fight has opened—at 11 oclk sharp firing was heard in the direction of our pickets & continued for one half hour. After it ceased—a silence of one half hour—firing again by pickets. At the first firing our Brigade & the one in advance formed a line of battle. At 12 noon the battery on our left which sweeps the country north

18. Connelly, *Army of the Heartland,* 176–77.

19. Major General Samuel Jones, a Virginia-born West Point graduate and former instructor at the military academy, commanded the First Division of Van Dorn's Army of the West. The 9th Texas Cavalry at this time was in the Third Brigade of Jones's division. Warner, *Generals in Gray,* 165–66; *OR,* Vol. 10, Pt. 2, p. 551.

20. Bates may have been referring to Thomas J. "Stonewall" Jackson's victories in the famous Valley campaign of the spring of 1862. See Robert G. Tanner, *Stonewall in the Valley: Thomas J. "Stonewall" Jackson's Shenandoah Valley Campaign, Spring 1862* (Garden City, N.Y.: Doubleday, 1976).

of the M&C R.R. [Memphis & Charleston Railroad] opened firing slowly for one half hour—during which time our Brigade was ordered back in rear of the battery some two hundred yards. We had not been in position long before the enemy's batteries opened with hollow shot, their fire being directed principally at our battery—some of the shot however struck & bursted very near our line—others cut the timber over our heads. Only one man hurt—that slightly by a falling limb. Firing on both sides ceased at 1 pm resumed again by our batteries—the enemy soon replied—no damage done us so far—2:30 pm firing again commenced.

Though no one is yet hurt by the enemy a distressing accident occurred to Col Townes who received a severe wounding in the leg by the accidental discharge of a shot gun.[21] Two other men slightly injured by the same shot. It passed entirely through his leg, fracturing the bone badly. So much for carelessness. 4pm After a short silence firing again opened & now as I write, the heavy thundering sound of the artillery reverberates along these hills with terrific splendor. Suddenly the artillery on our left is hushed, but in a moment another sound reaches us which if not as terrible to listen at is tenfold more effective & destructive   it is the sharp cracking of small arms—they increase in rapidity—till presently—one continuous roar comes up from the little valley before us—continuous about ten minutes then ceases—then comes on the breeze a loud shout—but who from—is it a signal that the enemy has been repulsed? or have our forces been driven back, this is the shout of a victorious enemy. Oh, this terrible suspense 'tis worse than to be actually engaged in the battle. Heavy cannonading has been heard at short intervals since noon on our left—sometimes apparently along the entire line for five or six miles—occasional shots still exchanged by our batteries—sometimes by small arms in front.

May 29th 1862 Thurs [diary]
    5 AM Our forces drove the enemy back last evening only two or three wounded. At 12 last night our Reg moved forward some three

21. On his third official day as colonel, Townes was accidentally wounded when another soldier inadvertently stepped on a loaded shotgun that had been left on the ground, discharging the weapon and injuring Townes and at least one other man. The colonel, who was wounded in his knee joint, had to leave the regiment for treatment and recuperation and never returned as its field commander. Kerr, ed., *Fighting with Ross' Texas Cavalry*, 39; Sparks, *War Between the States*, 272.

hundred yards & took a position behind our advance battery to support it. The ring of the rifles of our sharp shooters in advance warns us that the enemy is still about. learned last night that the enemy were handsomely repulsed—on our center. 10 am The enemy has planted a battery one half mile in front of us in a field & opened fire. Our batteries are replying. 10 1/2 [10:30] another battery opened on us from the right[.] both throw elongated hollow shot[.] some of these burst very near our lines—others explode in front & shower their missiles amongst us frightening a few of the most timid but hurting no one as yet. The enemy's pickets attacked (Greer's [3rd Texas Cavalry] Reg) ours at 9am & after a sharp engagement were driven back. Our loss 5 killed—15 wounded. 12 M firing very slow—we have one man slightly wounded by a shell. The left wing generally quiet—a cannon now & then—with a few volleys of musketry.

Judging by some indications I have seen today & yesterday I think we are preparing for an evacuation of this place & I now think that instead of an attack being intended our forces are thrown out here only as a blind to the enemy to draw his attention while the evacuation is going on. If this is true the next twelve hours will tell it. 4 pm the enemy's batteries & ours still playing on each other. We had three men wounded & three horses killed a half mile in the rear of us by a shell. A column of the enemy were discovered moving across the field in rear of their batteries & both of our batteries (eight guns) "let loose the dogs of war on them" which must have done considerable damage as the shells (36 pounders) were seen to explode in & around their ranks—throwing them into utter confusion—Most of them taking to their heels in every direction for the timber to get out of sight.[22]

Another round was then fired by our batteries at a house occupied by the feds in front of their batteries & a half mile from ours— & the white smoke had hardly belched from the mouth of our cannon when they were seen darting out the doors & windows & scampered off behind a little hill nearby. With an eye glass we could see where two shells had passed through the house. The enemy's batteries which had been silent for some time now opened upon us &

22. Bates again quotes Shakespeare, this time *Julius Caesar* (act 3, scene 1): "Cry 'havoc!' and let loose the dogs of war."

ours immediately paid their respects to them—but few rounds had been fired when a well-aimed shot from one of our rifled 24 pdr's struck one of the enemy's guns, smashing it to atoms. Our guns now had to cease firing for the want of ammunition—two caissons were dispatched to Corinth for another supply. The enemy's also soon ceased & they withdrew into the timber, the firing having ceased.

7 oclk Col [Lawrence Sullivan "Sul"] Ross [commander of the 6th Texas Cavalry Regiment] came to us & ordered us to join the Brigade which we did & moved on toward our camps—found all the troops in rear of us had left. My suspicions of the last few days that we were going to evacuate Corinth were now confirmed. We made no halt at our camps—but moved on down the left of the [Mobile & Ohio] Rail Road.

In a skillful and deceptive movement, General Beauregard pulled his divisions out of Corinth on the night of May 29 and retreated south toward Tupelo before General Halleck realized what was happening. Thus, the major battle that Bates had been predicting for weeks was delayed for another four months, and the Confederates were allowed to pull back farther into Mississippi with little interference. Halleck finally had his railroad junction, but Beauregard still had an army in the field.[23]

May 30th 1862 Friday [diary]
    Marched all last night, only stoped occasionally to rest. Waded several little creeks—& swamps—owing to the extreme darkness— the sky being cloudy—we could not see a man in front of us except on open woods & our progress was rather slow & tedious—by daylight we had marched twelve miles—after resting one half hour moved on four miles further & camped for the day. Having had but little to eat for the last two days we were almost completely exhausted. We were glad to fall down anywhere in the shade & fall to sleep.[24] Our comissary started out to hunt some beef & in the after-

23. Connelly, *Army of the Heartland*, 177–78.
24. On this march, the Texas horsemen were learning the travails of the foot soldier. Walking while carrying a firearm, blanket, and other equipment was much slower, and more tiring, than riding. A private in the 6th Texas Cavalry recorded his fatigue on a later, similar march near Corinth: "I am completely tired out and exhausted and sore in every limb. To day as I was marching along, [I was] so weak I accidently stumbled and fell flat on the ground." Entry of September 6, 1862, F. A. Rawlins Diary.

noon brought in one. We made a hearty meal on beef roasted on sticks—without bread—washing it down with a little water.

About 8 oclk we heard what we thought at the time was heavy cannonading eight miles before us—but learned this morning that two Regs of federal cavalry had made a dash into Boonville & set fire to a train of cars on which was some boxes of shells—& these exploding—was the supposed cannonading[25]—about 1,500 of our sick were also on the train & as they had no arms were at the mercy of the enemy. They were marched out to the road—formed in four's ready to be marched off but just at this juncture—while the fed Cavalry [end of diary]

Bates's diary ended abruptly on May 30. Whether he discontinued his daily entries because of the press of his new duties as captain or for some other reason is not known. From June 1862 on, he recorded his army life only in the letters to his family and friends in Paris.

Bates had little activity to report during the summer of 1862. The war in northern Mississippi entered a long lull, giving the Confederates time to organize and recuperate from their stay in the sickly camps of Corinth. A letter to his mother in early June indicates that his regiment had taken up new quarters about six miles east of the main Confederate army at Tupelo. Now that the men had escaped the bad water, crowded camps, and disease at Corinth, and now that they had access to higher ground and plentiful food, their health was improving.

The brigade to which the regiment belonged had also been reorganized in early June. The 6th and 9th Texas Cavalry, the 3rd Arkansas Cavalry— all still dismounted—and an Arkansas battalion of sharpshooters were now brigaded under the command of an acting brigadier general and friend of General Van Dorn, Charles W. Phifer. Their new commander would spend a great deal of time training "the wild Texas boys" as infantry, and they resented him at first. "We hated him to start on for no other reason than that he was a soldier and methodically correct in all of his commands and movements," Private Sparks remarked years later. "He worried with us, he stormed at us, he cursed at us, he put us to severest tests, he punished us, and was finally rewarded by pronouncing us the best and most efficient Brigade of the army."[26]

25. Booneville is about twenty miles directly south of Corinth.

26. Sparks, *War Between the States,* 274. George Griscom indicated that General Phifer established a higher level of order ("Strict orders read & a new discipline to be enforced")

Crawford, Lowndes Co Miss
June 11th 1862
My Dear Ma:

I have just met with a gentleman on the cars on his way to Texas and I take the opportunity of sending you a few lines by him. I came down to this place [south of Tupelo on the Mobile & Ohio Railroad] this morning in search of the baggage belonging to our Regt. which was sent off on the cars before the evacuation of Corinth. I succeeded in finding most of it, but a telegraphic dispatch has just been received from Gen Bragg ordering it to be kept in this place. From some indications I have seen I judge we will move still further down in this direction. Our army—or most of it, is eighty miles above here at Tupola [Tupelo]. We May however remain—where we are.

Telegraphic dispatches from Richmond dated the 9th say we are still victorious there.[27] Heavy skirmishing still goes on, though no battles have been fought since Saturday & Sunday week ago. There was some little fighting at Chatanooga on the 8th & 9th.[28] Gen Mitchell's force was at that place with a force of some 10,000. Our forces there are *sufficient*.

Tell Dohoney we have *another* Brig Gen—O. [*sic*] W. Phifer is his name.[29] I have not seen enough of him to say how I will like *him*.

The health of all my company and of all the troops in fact is much improved since leaving Corinth. Men are coming in daily from the hospital. Our Brigade is stationed at Mooresville six miles east of the main army—we have a beautiful—high camping ground and what is better are entirely removed from the remainder of the army—have been living finely on vegetables, chickens milk butter &cc. I hear the

---

and considerably more drilling than the Texans might have preferred (Kerr, ed., *Fighting with Ross' Texas Cavalry*, 40).

27. Bates is probably referring to the Confederates' successful defense of Richmond during General George B. McClellan's Peninsula campaign of the spring and summer.

28. Federal Major General Ormsby Mitchel launched an artillery and infantry attack at Chattanooga, on June 7, but Confederate defenders repelled the assault. Long, *Civil War Day by Day*, 223.

29. Charles W. Phifer, twenty-nine years old, was an honors graduate of the University of North Carolina and a veteran of the famed 2nd U.S. Cavalry Regiment and its wars against the Indians in Texas. Phifer doubtless hoped to duplicate among his "wild Texas boys" the discipline he had known in the 2nd U.S. Cavalry. Allardice, *More Generals in Gray*, 181.

cars coming up & so must close. Give my kindest regards to friends
& the family.
J.C. Bates

heard from Col Townes yesterday   he is improving—will be able to
be on his watch in two or three weeks—My health is better now
than since I left Ark   think my march down here improved me

A long string of Confederate defeats in the winter and spring of 1862—at
Forts Henry and Donelson, Elkhorn Tavern, Island No. 10, Glorieta Pass
(in New Mexico), Shiloh, and New Orleans—did not discourage Bates.
The stakes were high enough for him to look past these setbacks toward
ultimate victory. Confederate prospects must have appeared much dimmer
to his sister back in Paris, however, for she apparently expressed some
melancholy thoughts in a letter to the young captain. He proceeded to lecture her sternly in his next communication, chastising her for her defeatist
attitude. Bates was the most dangerous sort of enemy to the Union—intelligent, well educated, courageous, physically hardy, burning with re-
sentment of the Yankees, and deeply committed to Confederate victory.[30]

Camp Near Moorsvile [Miss]
June 16th 1862
Dear Sister:
    Your letter of 12th u[ltimo, i.e., the previous month] has not
been answered yet because I have written two letters to Ma since
that time—& have not had time to write more.
    You begin by saying—of all the gloomy people you ever saw you
are the gloomiest. Why all this gloom? What is there to depress the
spirits of the people of Paris more than any other? No where that I
have ever been on this side the Miss[issippi River]—are the people
as much depressed as you seem to be. You permit your imagination
to conjure up a thousand dangers & difficulties & causes for trouble
that have no existence in reality. You ask what have we to encourage
us? Have you so soon given up all hope of establishing our indepen-

30. Young, educated, slaveholding officers who had reached maturity in the 1850s provided the "emotional core" of Confederate nationalism in the eastern Confederate army, according to historian Gary Gallagher. Although Bates did not own slaves before the war, he
lived in a slaveholding household, reached maturity in the 1850s, was well educated, and provided a western parallel to the officers in Lee's Army of Northern Virginia. Gary W. Gallagher, *The Confederate War* (Cambridge, Mass.: Harvard University Press, 1997), 96–111.

dence? Have the reverses that we have met with been sufficient to crush every hope of success[?]   I admit there is *some* cause for despondency—but cannot say with you that we have nothing to hope for. It is true the Federals have possession of many of our important points of [torn spot] of the Miss—but if they should over run our entire country they would still not have us *subjugated*.

Did the patriots of 76 despair of success when England had possession of every town and village & river—& had overrun every colony & had every point completely blockaded? Did their hopes of winning their independence waver even when reduced to the barest necessities of life & often to the point of starvation. When their money was exhausted, their credit gone, their means of subsistence barely sufficient to maintain life, their ammunition exausted—did they lay down their arms in despair. Or did they not rather redouble their efforts at each new reverse and determine that every defeat should only inspire them with fresh courage to meet & fight the enemy at any odds.

It is true we labor under many difficulties and disadvantages—we have many privations and hardships to undergo—but even if the South, for the next two years, should suffer reverses as she has, during the last six months, our condition would still be far better than the colonies at any period of the war. We still have a currency that answers all our purposes—we have an abundance of provisions—we have arms and ammunition—we have as good an army, as to *material*, as Napoleon ever had. Are we less *men* than the patriots of 76. Have we less powers of endurance than they? Have we less energy & courage and perseverance? Are we less patriotic? Have the men of the South so degenerated that a few reverses & defeats are sufficient to make them sue for peace? I think not. We have men as brave and daring as were in the revolution—& they only want the opportunity & the right sort of men to lead them to prove it. A people as strong as we, & possessing such a country as ours, can *never* be subjugated if they will but remain united in the determination to win their independence.

You ask, again, what are victories without friends. Let me ask in return what are friends with *slavery*?[31] You may reply that slavery will not be our fate—but I tell you that if the South fails we will be

---

31. Bates refers to the "slavery" that a victorious Union would impose on the people of the Confederacy.

reduced to a state of slavery in all but name. Already the Confiscation act has passed one house of the northern Congress—an act for the emancipation of the negroes came near passing the same house.[32] The whole northern press, in the ultra abolition states, are clamoring for the abolition of slavery. They have nearly ceased to talk about a restoration of the union. They now speak of "subjugating" and "conquering the South" of "teaching the Southern Rebels to know that the slaves they own *are of right* and *shall be* their equals." They say "Let them (the negroes) have their freedom if they can win it, *even though it be over the corpses of their masters and the ashes of their ruined homesteads.*" But I will clip a few articles from some northern papers I have & send you. These papers are fair specimens of all I have seen north of Kentucky. We get them frequently and with rare instances they teem with taunts & jeers & threats of what they will do with the property & *the people* of the South when they shall have "subjugated" us.

Shall we for one moment in the face of all this, think of taking upon our necks such a yoke as our "northern masters"(?) would certainly place upon them if they get the power? That power I hope they will never get & to prevent them from getting it, we have only to be united and determined. I do not doubt of ultimate success. If you would look upon the bright, one half as much as you look on the dark side of the picture you would be more hopeful. I do not suffer my mind to become gloomy over any reverses or misfortunes, at any rate not long at a time. What good does it do us? It *cannot* mend matters—but only tends to aggravate them. Do not suffer your mind to dwell on the dark—but accustom yourself to look on the bright side. Persevere in this one week and you will be astonished at the change in *your own* feelings & in *others* that your mood would have an influence on. I think it is your *duty*—(as it is of others) not only for your own sake, but on account of those who are associated with you—to make an effort to appear cheerful at all times—& making the *effort* to appear so will soon really make you feel so.

Well, I did'nt intend, when I set out, to write you a "lecture" al-

32. The Second Confiscation Act, adopted by Congress in July, allowed the Federal government to seize the property of Confederate soldiers and civilians, including slave property. These liberated bondsmen would then be "forever free." Bates interprets the law as further proof that supporters of the Confederacy can expect no mercy from their Yankee enemies. James G. Randall, *Constitutional Problems under Lincoln* (rev. ed.; Urbana: University of Illinois Press, 1964), 278–79, 288–89.

though I do'nt know but you needed it for writing such a gloomy letter—so I will drop this subject as there is already more in it than you will believe.

The army since Capt Dohoney [left] has fallen back to this place. If you will take a map and look about the center of Itawamba Co Miss you will see where our army is camped. Our Brigade is 8 miles East of the [Mobile & Ohio] rail road—at Moorsville placed here I suppose as a sort of outpost or picket. We have a very pleasant high situation entirely removed from the main army. Although we have more picket duty to perform here than if we were with the army—I still prefer being here on account of health & of having an opportunity of getting into the country occasionally where I can get some good milk and butter.

We have lived finely since we have been here, though at tolerably high rates 50 & 75cts each for chickens 50cts for butter 25cts pr qt for milk 2$ pr bin for Irish potatoes—but these I consider cheap. Clothing of every description is enormously high—good hats 10$ boots from 15 to 25$ good casimer pants from 12 to 20$—coats none here. Brown domestic 75cts & 18 pr yd—& scarce & every thing else is about the same proportion. There is little cloth made in the country here on account of the difficulty of obtaining cotton cards—& woolen also.[33] These are a very necessary article which I suppose you do not now get in Texas. A portion of my clothing was burned at Corinth—and I have not yet been able to replace them. I have still enough to last some months yet—if I should not loose it.

I am afraid our troops will find it a difficult matter to obtain a sufficiency of clothing for next winter. I suppose however our chief quarter master will have foresight enough to prepare for this in time. From the prospect as far as 150 miles below this we will certainly not want for bread. Latest news from Richmond represent every thing quiet before the city. No indications of another fight.

It is my opinion the federals will not follow us down here. I think we will have no fight untill we advance on them, as to whether we will do that or not I am unable to give even a probable conjecture. Gens [John C.] Breckinridge & [Sterling] Price are now in Rich-

---

33. Cotton and woolen cards were used to clean and disentangle fibers preparatory to spinning. The cards were usually made of closely set rows of wire teeth fastened to a sturdy backing.

mond. What they have gone there for I do not know. We have various rumors but none are likely to be correct.[34]

Mr Henry Bingham (Susans father) is engaged in carrying letters to & from Texas (from the army) at 50cts each. You may appropriate as much of my money as you like to paying postage on letters to me. I would frequently give *ten Dollars* for a letter direct from home. My health is *provokingly good* of late. If I were bad I might get a discharge. Maybe I will send this by Dr Sayles—if [W]ill can [see] him he can get the latest news.

Give my kindest regards to all my friends. I would write to some of them but the Dr is waiting for this letter & I must close.

My love to all the family
As always your affectionate brother
JC Bates

The young captain could be gravely serious when he detected Yankee duplicity or Confederate defeatism, but he could lighten his mood very quickly when he corresponded with Mootie, now eighteen years old. The day after he scolded his sister, he wrote to Mootie and described the daydreams he indulged in during this summertime lull in the war.

Camp Maury Miss
June 17 / 62
Miss Mootie Johnson
Dear Friend:

Although I have written to you two or three times since receiving an answer to any of my letters, I will write again, as I have an opportunity of sending this by one of my *non* conscripts—who will be discharged this evening.

How little one year ago did I think that today I would write you a letter especially from this place. But so it is. We can form but an improbable conjecture one day where the next may find us, or at least, situated as I am it is so with me. I have been relieved from duty today, and as it has been a deliciously cool, pleasant morning, I have

34. Price went to Richmond to lobby President Jefferson Davis for command of the Trans-Mississippi Department. Breckinridge did not go to Richmond in May or June 1862; he was in Mississippi and Louisiana during those months. William C. Davis, *Jefferson Davis: The Man and His Hour* (New York: HarperCollins Publishers, 1991), 461; William C. Davis, *Breckinridge: Statesman, Soldier, Symbol* (Baton Rouge: Louisiana State University Press, 1974), 315–17.

been laying in the shade of a great old oak in front—not of my tent, but of where it would be if I had one—dreaming day dreams and building air castles, and wondering where the star of my fortune will take me next, wishing too, that I could change the famous line of Bishop Herbert "Westward the Star of Empire takes its way" to westward *My guiding star* takes its way.[35]

That cannot be at present however, but still it is often times a pleasure to make wishes which we know at the time cannot be realized. I can sometimes find almost as much pleasure in "dreaming with my eyes open" as if the circumstances by which I imagine myself surrounded were really true, and the persons I suppose present were so in reality. I do not know whether others possess this *dreaming faculty* to the same extent that I do or not. I am glad that I have it for I have whiled away many hours very pleasantly that otherwise might have been tedious. It is true these hours might have been spent with greater advantage to myself by thinking on subjects of a more practical nature, but is questionable whether I would have done so or not, had I not been dreaming, for I am not much given to *practical* thinking. Nature or somebody else has given me a *mental* structure of such a character that it is not often that I can get [torn spot] thinking systematically.

We have been in our present encampment ten days—will remain here probably during part of the summer. We have various reports in regard to the enemy. The last is that they are following our example and evacuating Corinth.[36] Our Genl's I suppose are posted as to their movements, but we "smaller fry" know nothing more than we can gather from that very (un)reliable news bearer 'dam rumor.

35. "Westward the course of empire takes its way" is a line from George Berkeley (not George Herbert), *On the Prospect of Planting Arts and Learning in America* (1752). Berkeley (1685–1753) was an Irish philosopher, poet, and bishop who attempted to found a college in the New World. John Quincy Adams, in his *Oration at Plymouth* (1802), quoted Berkeley, but changed the word "course" to "star," and Bates may have been more familiar with the Adams version. Frank N. Magill, ed., *Magill's Quotations in Context* (New York: Harper and Row, 1965), 1120 (with thanks to Vicki Betts, University of Texas at Tyler).

36. When General Halleck's Federal army marched into Corinth in late May, the northern soldiers slid into the same unhealthful environment the Confederates had abandoned. Diarrhea was so widespread in Union camps that the malady was labeled "the Evacuation of Corinth." Indeed, one reason Halleck did not pursue Beauregard's army deeper into Mississippi was his fear of exposing his men to even more sickness in the hot, humid interior of the state. James M. McPherson, *Battle Cry of Freedom: The Civil War Era* (New York: Oxford University Press, 1988), 488.

The latest piece of intelligence we have from the aforesaid, (Madam Rumor) is to the effect that England France & Spain had recognized our independence [and] that these three powers had submitted six or seven different propositions as to the Federal & Confederate Government's as a basis for the adjustment of existing difficulties, (what these propositions are Rumor does not say) another rumor is that the Feds have evacuated Memphis & N[ew] Orleans, that an armistice of 60 days has been agreed upon—and finally—no not finally for there is no end to rumors,—we have it fresh this morning that negotiations for peace are now pending—and we will not get to fight (or run) any more.[37]

I merely give you these for what they are worth—without indorsing, or believing *a* [torn spot] of them myself. I have been in camp so long I have learned to believe nothing I hear and but little I see. Three or four months in the army would do you at home a vast deal of good in one respect—it would teach you the absurdity of giving any credit to the numberless wild reports you hear from the army—and you would thereby be spared much uneasiness which you may now suffer on account of absent friends and relatives.

Inclosed you will find some clippings from the latest papers I have. If I can procure any papers of later date I will send them to you. Tell Miss Mary I have been waiting patiently for a letter from her for lo, these many days. I hope she will not forget me entirely after the Capt [Dohoney] gets home. I heard from your old sweetheart Geo King a few days since. He is clerk I believe in the Q.M. Department of Grier's Regt. I saw, too, Si Quisenberry a short time since. He had a good deal to say about you and Miss Mary— thought he could whip half a dozen Yankees if you were present to "inspire his heart and nerve his arm to deeds of valor"—and who could'nt. I have three or four other letters to write this morning and must close. Present my regards to Dr & Mrs J[ohnson, Mootie's parents]—and to Miss Mary and Mat and accept the best wishes of Your Sincere Friend
J.C. Bates

The drowsy days of summer, unmarked by any significant action or movements of the army, afforded Bates the luxury of writing more often than

37. As Bates suspected, these were only rumors. No foreign nation ever extended diplomatic recognition to the Confederacy, and Federal armies did not give up Memphis and New Orleans. Such stories were repeated in Confederate camps for most of the war.

usual, short notes containing little or no significant news—although to his mother, any news was important. Very few of her letters to Bates made it back to Paris for safekeeping, but one, reminding him of his spiritual responsibilities, has survived. Not forgetting more earthly concerns, his mother also provided a recipe for an antidiarrheal concoction.

Camp Maury Miss
June 26th 1862
Dear Ma:

Although I have written several letters home within the last few days, I write again, not because I have anything new to write, but because you get so few of my letters & I have concluded to write, by every body I find going to Texas if it is daily. I have had the mumps for a week past, but will be able for duty in a few days. With that exception my health has been very good since we left Corinth. Some few of the company are still sick but nothing serious.

It is rumored in camp that Genl Price has telegraphed Genl Bragg that another battle has been fought at Richmond in which our forces were victorious. No particulars given. I doubt the truth of the report. There is little doubt now but that the principal part of the Federal force at Corinth are moving Eastward. Consequently I think our next move will be in that direction.

I received a note from Col Townes this morning. He says he is doing well, his wound healing rapidly, will be able to go on his crutches in a week or ten days.

I have not time at present to write more—*be sure* and write often. My good wishes to Eb [Dohoney]—tell him to write—tell Capt Wright I would like to hear from him.

My love to all.
Your Affectionate Son
J.C. Bates

Paris Texas
July 14th 1862
Dear James

Mr Bingham is here and sayes he will leave Texas for the army. wee are all delited at the chance of sending letters to you   wee have written many letters and sent by Persons going   I suppose you never received them   your Sister wrote you last week by Cpt Rone   he belonges to [William C.] Younges [11th Texas Cavalry] Reg   the health of the country is verry good   crops look badly owing to the drouth   we have had no rain in two months   only [unless] it rains with in ten days there will be no corn raised—more then half the corn in this county is ruined   your wheat only made from two to five bushels per acre   there is egreat deal of old corn in the country if the people could kep it but texas is now under martial law   General Hindman has sent twelve hundred head of Missoura horses in to this county and ordered them to be fed on corn   the qr Master that has charge of them has set the price on corn fifty cents per bushel   sayes if the people refuse to let it goe at that price he will press it

arumor has just reached here that Vandorn's Division will be moved on this side the Miss[issippi River]   I hope it is true   oh how wee would all rejoice to know you were all safe on this side once more   wee hear so many reports that I believe nothing I hear good or bad   the knewes reached here afew days ago of agreat battle Richmond one at Holly Springs another at Vicksburgh in which we were victorious and that England France & Spain had recognized our independence and requested hostilites to sease for sixty days [and] that our Generals many of them had gone to Richmond and an armistice was agreed to   all of those patriotic clamorous stay at home fighters believed it all   declared wee would have peace in less than three months—our soldiers here under Pike have reorganized under the Conscript [law]   evry officer in Talors Regment was leten [let go] but one   that was George Provine   John Buck was elected Capt in Griffin's place. Miner run for Major and was beaten   Col Johnson for the same office   he hate was badly beaten.

I am proud to hear you sustain yourself so well   the men that have returned home from your company speak in the highest termes of you both as an officer and a gentleman that you are untiring in your efforts to relieve the sick and distressed   oh my son no Mother ever loved their Son more than I or would be prouder to know they had discharged their duty towardes their fellow man.

I fear the most important duty of all you neglect   your duty to your god   in one of your letters to mee you said if you fell you would die in a good cause   oh my dear child don't suffer your self for one moment to think the cause however good would save the sole. Washington fought in a good cause [and] was as brave soldier as ever lived he was a christian   he trusted in god alone   my son choose that good part that can nevver be taken from you   it wi[ll] ennable you to bare up under the many hardshipes and trials you will have to encounter   reflect seriously you are surrounded by many dangers and should you be called suddenly away as many of your comrades are nothing could console mee for your loss but to know that you had gone to rest

wee have heard of the death of John Holeford   he died of fevor was out of his head all the time of his sickness   his Mother is almost deranged   Alvis Rion writes that Doct Snow has been missing since the evacuation of Corinth   supposes he was taken prisenor   Peterson is a candidate for State atorney also enroling officer for the conscripts   some say they will nevver be enroled by him.

your sister & Dohoney both received letters from you last week Col Fowler got one from John the first he has heard of him since he left Arkansas   the old man has been nearly crazy about him. when you write mention as many boys as you can conviently as you write oftener than most of them   Bill Scotts [mother?] comes evry weak or too thinking she can hear from him in some of your letters.

I want you to have your picture taken the first opportunity and send it to mee. Mr Bramlette has just returned from Auston   he brought fifteen hundred dollars of your aunt Tenns Money to her   it had been deposited there   it is Confederate money and no one wished to borrow it   he is at alows [a loss] in what way to lay it out your money all reached here you sent   I gave your Aunt Tenn ten dollars[,] ten dollars to Dr Johnson   your debts [are] over one hundred. . . . Mr Bramlette has laid out in land about [four hundred dollars.]   [With the] twenty dollars I used[, this] is the way it has been laid out   Mr Bramlette has not sold your horse yet   I think horses will be dull sale   you have plenty here to feed him or perhaps you will kneed him again   he has not sold any of your corn yet   I guess it will bring a good price this fall. he declined exepting [accepting] the appointment of quarter master   he wrote to Col Townes some time ago   I think he would be doing his family a great injustice were he to leave them now   besides your aunt Tenn has no one now to depend on

I want you to write what kind of clothing you want for next winter   be sure to mention every article you will kneed[,] over shirts cotton and flannel shirts cotton and flannel drawers wollen and cotton socks coat pants & how many of each kind you will kneed   let mee know in good time as it will all have to be manufactured at home   there is nothing to be bought in the country not even spun thread and but few can make any cloth owing to the scarcity of cotton cards—will you kneed blankets

this letter is paid for   I mention it that you may not pay again   the family all send their love to you Miss Lue Bywaters & Miss Gertrude Latimore is here to day   Gertrude is much prettier than she was when she went to school here   it is generally believed that Dohoney and Miss Mary will marry soon   I doe not believe. So he almost lives there yet he positively declared ther is no engagement existing between them. She was on the eve of going to Marshal on avisit when he came home   she declined going   well if they doe not marry it will not be her fault nor the familys either   I believe I have given all the knewes—may God bless and keep you is the constant prayer of your Mother
N C. Bates

I send you a receipt [recipe] for flux or diarea   equal portion peppermint laudanum camphire and brandy   mix a bottle an keep it by you if you posibly can[38]

At some point in June or July, Captain Bates's military career took another significant turn. His Company H was transferred from the 9th Texas Cavalry to the Arkansas battalion of sharpshooters (generally used as skirmishers) in his brigade. No evidence indicates that Bates requested the transfer, but his sour attitude toward the new young lieutenant colonel of the 9th Texas, Dudley W. Jones (now in command of the regiment since the wounding of Colonel Townes), probably did not dispose Bates to resist the change very forcefully. In fact, his well-drilled company may have been sent over to the new unit precisely because of its precision and discipline. The prickly young captain apparently got himself into an early scrape with his new battalion commander, but shortly thereafter the battalion was consolidated with another to form a new regiment much more to Bates's taste.

The regiment's commander, Erasmus "Ras" Stirman, had charged the Federal battery with Bates's Texans at Elkhorn Tavern as a member of an Arkansas cavalry unit. Only twenty-three, Stirman was from a wealthy and prominent family in Fayetteville, Arkansas. General Braxton Bragg had recently brought Stirman's battalion up to regimental size and Stirman up to

---

38. Bates may have complained of diarrhea in letters that have not survived. He would suffer from the lingering effects of chronic diarrhea after the war.

the rank of colonel. The Arkansas officer took great pride in his new regiment. He wrote to his sister, "I am now a Colonel and have ten as good Companies as there is in the Army of the West. I now have a regiment of Sharp Shooters. I have them all uniformed in Gray with Caps and well armed and equipped in every respect not bragging to much, but you just ought to See them on Battalion Drill or on parade, we are exempted from all duties except drills."[39]

Bates's last letter of July was addressed to his sister. He gave her his personal impressions of Generals Braxton Bragg and Sterling Price, indicating his preference for the latter, and brought her up to date on the progress of the war in other theaters. (Bates apparently read every newspaper and dispatch he could find to stay informed about the overall conduct of the war.) He took another verbal swipe at Lieutenant Colonel Jones and described—in terms favorable to himself, of course—his initial set-to with his temporary battalion commander. Like many officers at much higher levels in the western Confederacy, Bates was quick to take offense at perceived slights from his superiors.

In Camp Near Tupola [Tupelo] Miss
July 26th 1862
My Dear Sister;

    For two or three months I have waited for a letter from you, but none have come since the one I received through T.J. Sarfley[?]. Have you not written since then? I can hardly think it—yet I should get *some* letters if you have written as often as I have. Letters are still received from Texas, by our Regt through the mails & if you will direct them to be sent via Natches—Helena—Gains Landing—or some other point on the Miss[issippi River]—where communication is not interrupted by federal gunboats—they will still come. The best plan however, is to send them by hand if possible to be mailed *east* of the Miss.

    We moved our camp a few days since to this place. We have better water, but not as good a camping ground as the place we left. We have done but little drilling since we have been here most of the time having been occupied in Brigade, Division, & Grand Reviews.

    Day before yesterday I saw on review most of the officers of note left with this portion of the army. I had a good look at the great ar-

39. Carr, *In Fine Spirits*, foreword (no page number), 48 (quotation); "Col. Erasmus I. Stirman," *Confederate Veteran* 22 (May 1914): 226; Bates's file in Compiled Service Records, roll 56.

tillerist—Gen'l Bragg at present in command of this department.
He looks to be about 40 years old—is near six feet high—had
square shoulders & a full deep chest & is so straight that he leans
backward a little. I should think about my weight—(I only weigh
139 lbs now). His hair is tolerably gray—large keen blue eyes—
long, heavy, straight eyebrows which are completely united over his
nose—large mouth—thin lips always seeming to be tightly com-
pressed. He is altogether a fine looking man.

Genl Price was also on the field—& decidedly the finest looking
man in the army—he is very large—full six feet two inches high—
weighs 200 lbs or more—florid complexion a full, round, benevo-
lent, kind dignified looking face—a high broad forehead gray hair—
nearly white — heavy eye brows highly arched — large bluish
gray eyes[,] nose a little aquiline—mouth large lips neither thick nor
thin—but *appear* thin when he is not in conversation—because they
are then tightly closed. Genl Bragg, in appearance haughty—proud,
& rather forbidding—on the other hand, the first glance at Genl
Price inspires respect, esteem, and confidence. Genl Bragg can only
be approached by officers of superior rank—and his army will obey
him through *fear.* Genl Price will listen as readily and with as much
respect to a *private* as to the highest officer under his command—
and his men will do any thing he commands them to do purely for
the love and respect the[y] have for him.

General Bragg is the right sort of man to command a *Regular*
army, Genl Price a *volunteer* army.[40] As all our troops are volunteer
you can form a pretty correct opinion as to how each are liked by
their men. Several other Maj Genls were in the field—but have'nt
time now to say more about Genls.

I see no indications at present of the army of the west leaving
here—and I do'nt think it will untill our army in Virginia is again
put in fighting trim and some general plan of operation for the future agreed upon.

You may expect to hear before a great while of some stiring
events about Chatanooga in East Tenn.[41] The feds are concentrat-

40. Braxton Bragg, a graduate of the military academy at West Point, had a well-deserved
reputation as a stern disciplinarian. Sterling Price, known as "Old Pap" to his men, was a former politician and an accomplished glad-hander. It is not surprising that a volunteer soldier
such as Bates might prefer the blustery, good-natured Price to the forbidding Bragg.

41. In late July, General Bragg took about half the army in Mississippi on a roundabout
rail trip to Chattanooga; from there, he intended to strike into Kentucky. Bates's brigade

ing a considerable force in that section and I expect will make an effort to retrieve their waning fortunes. If they get possession of that
country they will have the key to all Georgia—North Alabama—&
North Carolina & will besides cut off communications with this section & the East. I hardly think however our Genls will loose sight of
so important a point as that. We already have a considerable force
around Chatanooga—sufficient I expect—to cope with Buell.

Forrest & Morgan's cavalry have been doing some good work in
a small way.[42] The former captured Murfreesboro—some two weeks
since—with 1,200 prisoners—2 Brig Genls ([T. T.] Crittenden &
[Colonel William] Duffield) a considerable amount of comissary &
quartermaster stores &cc. He then entered Lebanon [and] captured
a few prisoners—alarmed the Nash*villans* considerably & afterward
turned his course—South.[43] Col Morgan also had a brush with the
enemy at Tompkinsville Ky—killed a few captured some—and at
last account the mortal dread of the Texas Rangers had penetrated
Yankeedom even to Louisville. If we had more of such men as Forrest and Morgan—Tenn & Ky would soon be disinthralled.

Moorsville
27th We have just gone through another review and inspection this
morning—Sunday—and as I have an hour or so of leisure I will finish my letter. My Company is still in a Battalion of Skirmishers and
I suppose is destined to remain here. If Col Townes had been here
we would now be with our Regt [i.e., the 9th Texas Cavalry]—but
as Col Jones seems to be afraid to speak to a Superior officer much
less to *demand* his rights and the rights of his men we must quietly
submit.

If my company had not been *so well drilled,* I think we could have
gotten out [of the sharpshooter unit] a few days since—as old

remained in its camp near Tupelo with the other half of the army, about 32,000 men. Connelly, *Army of the Heartland,* 197–99; McPherson, *Battle Cry of Freedom,* 515.

42. Bates is too conservative in his assessment of General Nathan Bedford Forrest and
Colonel John Hunt Morgan. Their cavalry raids through middle Tennessee and Kentucky in
July immobilized a Federal army of forty thousand men and halted its movement toward
Chattanooga. McPherson, *Battle Cry of Freedom,* 513–14.

43. At little cost to his own command, Forrest captured twelve hundred prisoners, several artillery pieces, and considerable equipment at Murfreesboro. Brian Steel Wills, *A Battle from the Start: The Life of Nathan Bedford Forrest* (New York: HarperCollins Publishers,
1992), 74–76.

"*Tige*" (the Genl) said the only difficulty was that there was no other company so well drilled, and he could not think of putting raw men in place of this company.[44] Although this was quite complimentary to the company I was very sorry to hear it. If we had a man possessed of some gentlemanly principles to command us I would prefer remaining in the Battalion. But he [the unnamed battalion commander] is a perfect lickspittle for the Genl and is so much afraid of doing something *wrong* that he never does anything. He is another Butler on a *very small* scale.

I have nothing, however, to complain of for my company. No mistreatment so far. On one occasion when we first came into the [sharpshooter] Battalion he [the battalion commander] used me badly and I told him so. I told him at the same time that I had rights which I held as sacred as the political rights for which we were fighting, and I was as ready to lay down my life for the one as the other—that I had as soon be shot by sentence of a court martial as made a Slave of and a little rather,—that he might shape his acts according to what he thought me and my company would submit to—and if he did'nt *know* what we *would* submit to, his first act of tyranny would learn him.

Since then, although nearly every other man in the Battalion has been punished for some thing—not one of this company has ever been, as the boys say "put on roots." But I have said more of our "grievances" than I am in the habit of—and will drop the subject. I think we will be able to take care of ourselves.

I went down to see Col Townes several days since but failed to see him as he had a few days before left for Maj Bennetts (a brother to Judge Bennett[)], I learned however that he was doing well, cannot walk yet without a crutch but can bear some weight on his leg.

I had a distinguished visitor on yesterday—who spent the day with me. It was no less a personage than T Jefferson Crooks. I have met him frequently since we have been this side of the Miss[issippi River], and he has always ben *very* friendly and sociable. I understand he makes *a good* soldier and however bad a man may be otherwise, if he is a good soldier (*there are a very few who are*) I have some respect for him.

Genl Bragg left yesterday for Chatanooga and Genl Price assumes

44. Old Tige was either Bates's brigade commander, acting brigadier general Phifer, or the division commander, Brigadier General Dabney H. Maury.

command here. I hope we may remain under his command. If we do, there is a remote probability of our returning west of the Miss[issippi River]. I would feel, anywhere west of the Miss, like I was getting in the neighborhood of home.

The recent reverses of the federal army before Richmond has opened the eyes of the North to the fact that the South is not to be conquered and the rebellion crushed in as short a time as they had hoped.[45]

Lincoln has made a call for 300,000 more men. From all I can gather from Northern papers he will have to resort to drafting before he gets.[46] He cannot get his armies again organized—before Oct—and the campaign of the summer may therefore be considered at an end—at least as to the progress of the Feds South. I would not be surprised from some movements going on—If Price's army— (now called the "army of the Tenn") moved northward in the direction of Corinth in a short time. There is but a small Federal force now at Corinth—most of them having gone East—as I wrote you I thought they would. We have nothing late from Virginia. Everything quiet there from last account.

I wrote you some time since that I thought I might get furlough this fall—but I now have b[ut] little hope of that. I have *nearly* co[nten]ted myself to remain untill the war is over—but will go home if I can get leave of abscence.

29th Dr Gentry leaves this evening and I will close. My good wishes to my friends—I cant write to all. Tell Ma to let Aunt Tenn have what money she needs   also to use *as much as she wishes* herself. Tell her not to want for *anything*. I will send some more money the first opportunity. *Be sure and write often* to your affectionate brother

J.C. Bates

30th Dr Genry the bearer of this lives in or near Black Jack Grove. He will return in six or eight weeks from this time and will bring letters to us *if sent* to him as above   *do not fail to write often*. No fur-

45. General Robert E. Lee's Confederate army had turned back McClellan's Federals from the outskirts of Richmond in late June and early July in the Seven Days' battles.

46. President Lincoln did call for 300,000 new volunteers on July 2, and the Union did resort to a form of conscription when the 300,000 were slow to sign up. McPherson, *Battle Cry of Freedom*, 491–92; James W. Geary, *We Need Men: The Union Draft in the Civil War* (DeKalb.: Northern Illinois University Press, 1991), 27–28.

ther news this morning except some vague rumors. I send you a few clippings from the latest papers I have. My best wishes to Dohoney.

In only two months, Bates's military career had taken two major turns. He had been elected captain of his company in May, giving him command of about one hundred men. Then, partly because he was so successful in drilling his men, the captain and his unit were transferred to a smart new Arkansas regiment of sharpshooters, whose main responsibility was to act as skirmishers. His deep commitment to the Confederate cause allowed Bates to make the adjustments smoothly, after a brief dustup with an interim commander. Stirman's sharpshooters and Bates's Texans would serve together for three more months, through two battles, before the men of Lamar returned to their original unit and their beloved horses.

James C. Bates in 1861

Bates in 1865. He had this photograph taken in Vicksburg
shortly after the end of the war.

Thirmuthis "Mootie" Johnson, Bates's wartime sweetheart and future wife. Bates carried this image with him during the war and mentions it several times in his letters.

Nancy McDonald Bates, James Bates's mother. The photograph appears to date to during or soon after the war.

William Bramlette, James Bates's brother-in-law, friend, and
frequent correspondent. The image is probably from the late
1860s or the 1870s.

Dudley Jones, colonel of the 9th Texas Cavalry and Bates's
commanding officer

Bates as a medical student, 1867

Bates in his later years

Mootie Johnson Bates in 1907, at age sixty-three

A leather-and-wood trunk used by Bates during the war

6 Northern Mississippi

While Robert E. Lee's Army of Northern Virginia fought and maneuvered from Richmond to Cedar Mountain to Manassas in July and August, Braxton Bragg's Confederate army swung over by rail from Mississippi to Chattanooga. These Confederate movements set the stage for a proposed multitheater invasion of northern soil in the late summer and early fall of 1862: Lee would slice through western Maryland into Pennsylvania, Bragg's and Edmund Kirby Smith's armies would march into Kentucky from east Tennessee, and Van Dorn and Price would leave Mississippi and cut through west Tennessee, perhaps as far north as the Ohio River. If all went well, the people and farms of the Confederacy would be relieved of destructive hordes of soldiers, Kentucky and Maryland would be welcomed into the Confederate fold, antiwar elements in the North would be encouraged and strengthened, and Britain and France might be persuaded to intervene in the war.[1]

While high officials in the Confederate capital at Richmond and generals in the various southern armies pored over maps and planned the grand offensive of 1862, the men in the ranks in northern Mississippi continued to drill and prepare for the next campaign—where and when it might be, they had no idea. Even Bates, who read every newspaper he could find and took pride in understanding the war as a whole, was not sure where he and his friends might go next.

1. McPherson, *Battle Cry of Freedom*, 515–16, 534.

Camp Near Tupola Miss
Aug 9th 1862
My Dear Ma:

Your kind letter of date July 14th was received four days since. You can well imagine my joy at receiving a letter from home, when I tell you it was the first I heard from you since May. I received a letter from Cousin Kittie several days before, but not a word was said about any of you—and I was becoming somewhat uneasy in consequence. I have written to you by Allen Brackeen—who was discharged from this co[mpany] a few days ago, but as he is very feeble & may have to stop on the way I will send this by Bingham.[2]

We moved our camp on yesterday. Our present encampment is the best we have yet had, being on high ground—& well shaded. We have as good water as I could wish for, an abundance of good apples, green corn, peaches, &c & what is much better I have engaged milk as long as we remain here and as long as we have "peach cobbler" and sweet milk, I want nothing better.

My Company is now in a Regt of Sharp Shooters. The old Battalion we were in, & Brooks' [battalion]—which Dohoney will remember—having been consolidated and a Regt formed of the two. Our Company must either be considered a very worthless or a very valuable "concern" by the rapidity with which it changes hands, & whether above or below "par" we are at least "advancing" a little being the Second Company [i.e., Company B] in the Regt. Our Col, Sterman, is I think, all a gentleman, and I believe the company will be if they are not now, satisfied. I cannot say how long we will remain here, probably a month possibly not two days.

When we move at all I am of *opinion* our course will either be toward Corinth or the Miss river—but tomorrow something I see or hear may change my opinion. The "common herd" of soldiers are literally and emphatically "know nothings." We have no late news of interest. I will send you some late papers if I can get them.

Several hundred Yankee prisoners came in yesterday—nine captains in the number. They were captured betwixt here and Corinth and on the Memphis & Charleston R Road. The *little* victories we have gained recently if put together would make a considerable bat-

2. A native Texan, Brackeen was a nineteen-year-old laborer on his family's farm in Lamar County. He was discharged from the army owing to illness.

tle. Dispatches from Vicksburgh say the federal fleet have left that place—one portion going north the other down the river.[3] Some new move may be looked for as [Major General Samuel R.] Curtis' army or a portion of it, has crossed to this side the river & has been reinforced from Memphis. They probably design making a land attack on Vicksburgh. I think if they do, they will get hold of the "wrong horn"[—]that is it wont be an *Elkhorn*.[4]

Give my good wishes to all my friends. *Tell* them I would like to hear from them oftener than I do. It is a little discouraging to write once or twice a week and get letters once in two or three months. Ask Will if he is so much occupied that he has not time to answer my letters. My health has been *very* good for the last two months although I am getting as lean and tough as the beef we eat. My love to the family to Aunt Tenn Eliza & Clint.

J.C. Bates

Two days later Bates wrote to his brother-in-law, Will Bramlette, discussing the war in its broadest terms. The captain's letter brings Bramlette up to date on the latest war news, expresses once again his willingness to fight as long as necessary, and recommends that the Confederacy match the Union's call for more troops by drafting younger boys and older men. Bates repeats his complaint that northerners are dissembling by claiming to fight only for restoration of the Union; he is sure that the abolition of slavery is at the root of the Federal war effort. Although he was not involved in planning the Confederacy's grand offensive, Bates's predictions about southern strategy are close to the mark. He ruefully remarks that the 6th Texas Cavalry is about to be remounted and takes another swipe at Lieutenant Colonel Dudley Jones by implying that Colonel Townes would have the 9th Texas Cavalry remounted as well if he were in command. Finally, Bates suggests a business deal to his brother-in-law: selling Texas cattle to the Confederate army. The slow days in camp obviously allowed Bates's mind to wander over many topics.

3. Two fleets of Federal gunboats and mortars shelled Vicksburg from late June to late July, but the city's defenders, situated on high ground, suffered little damage. The river fleets then abandoned the project and returned to New Orleans and Memphis. Boatner, *Civil War Dictionary*, 870–71.

4. Bates's play on words alludes to the fact that Curtis was the victorious Union general at Elkhorn Tavern.

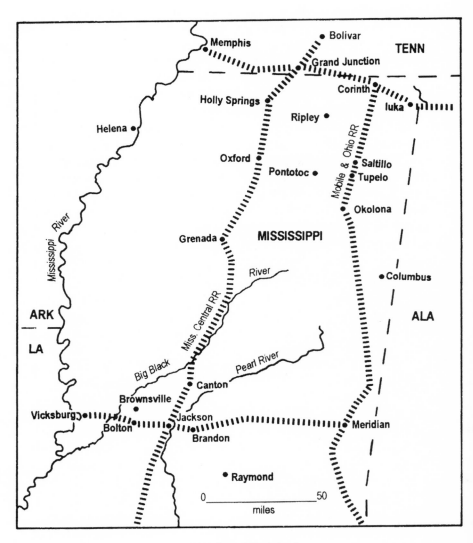

Northern Mississippi

Camp Near Tupola Miss
Aug 11th 1862
Dear Will:

Although I have written Several letters home during the last week, so few from some cause reach their destination, I have concluded to write again as I have an opportunity of sending a letter direct to Paris. I don't know that you are as anxious to hear from us as we are to hear from home—but take it for granted you *are* & therefore write often.

The news received Several days ago of an engagement at Cumberland Gap—in which our forces were victorious, is today confirmed.[5] No particulars as yet. We have heard nothing from Baton Rouge the last two days and I am inclined to think we have not gained much there.[6] The famous little gun boat Arkansas received a shot in her machinery which rendered her unmanageable and she was blown up to prevent her falling into the hands of the federals and this is the end of the Confederate "Navy" on the Miss[issippi River].[7] But if our navy is gone—our army is today stronger than at any time during the war. Still we are not strong enough. Lincoln has called for 300,000 more troops and these he will get—if not by volunteering he will get them by draft. It seems to me the south will be compeled to raise a corresponding force to meet these. The number of conscripts under the present law will not be sufficient, and I am inclined to think the law will be so changed as to include all over 16 and under 40 or 45 years of age.[8] This change is being urged by all the newspapers and I do'nt see how else we are to raise the requisite force.

5. Cumberland Gap, in far northeastern Tennessee, would not be abandoned by Federal forces until September 17, as a result of Bragg's and Kirby Smith's invasions of Kentucky. Long, *Civil War Day by Day,* 268.

6. A Confederate column of about 2,600 men under Major General John C. Breckinridge attacked the Federal garrison at Baton Rouge on August 5, but the heavy guns of U.S. riverboats drove the Confederates away. Davis, *Breckinridge,* 318–24; Current, *Encyclopedia of the Confederacy,* 1:141.

7. Breckinridge's attack on Baton Rouge was to have been accompanied by an attack on Federal riverboats by the Confederate ironclad ram CSS *Arkansas.* But the ram's engines failed just as it drew within sight of Baton Rouge, and the crew set it afire. Current, *Encyclopedia of the Confederacy,* 1:55, 141.

8. The Confederacy eventually went even further than Bates suggests. In early 1864 the government in Richmond began drafting men between the ages of seventeen and fifty. Moore, *Conscription and Conflict,* 308.

I think the prospect of foreign intervention or aid, if it ever existed, has long since passed and we must now, as we should have done from the commencement, rely on our own strength and resources for success. That we will *finally* succeed I entertain not a single doubt—provided we remain united. I do not however look for peace soon. Another year *may* bring it—but I think it probable that two or three years will be necessary to convince the great yankee nation that they cannot subjugate the South. The acts of the northern congress & the orders of their generals & from the war department for the last three months, all furnish conclusive evidence that every hope and all desire of restoring the union *as it once* was, is gone—if indeed they ever had any such hope or wish and they are only fighting now—to subjugate the South—to free our slaves—to gratify their feeling of hate, to get revenge for their failure, so far as forcing the South back in the union, and last, but by no means *least,* for the rich prospect of plunder held out to their soldiers if they succeed. Moreover they cannot give us peace without recognizing our independence and that would be, they say, yielding everything for which they had spilt so much blood—and wasted so many millions of Dollars to retain and disgrace them in the eyes of the world. The cupidity of the yankees will cause them to make a desperate struggle before giving up as rich a slice of their territory as the South.

But these are only "speculations" of mine, and while speculating for want of any thing better to write I'll give you what I think is the programme our Genls have marked out. First then Genls [Robert E.] Lee & [Joseph E.] Johns[t]on & [Thomas J. "Stonewall"] Jackson are to attack McClellan & Pope "in detail" before they get reinforcements—whip them and make their way on to Washington or at least in that direction.[9] Secondly Genl Bragg is to attack Buell at Chatanooga and if he defeats him push on towards Nashville, and draw the federal forces from Memphis[,] Corinth and other points along the Miss river[,] and lastly after a portion of the forces along the Miss river are drawn off the army of the West under Van Dorn & Price will push forward[,] take Corinth & Memphis in "their victorious career" and take as their motto "on to Cincinatti" at which

9. Lee's army would strike and defeat John Pope's Federal army at the Battle of Second Manassas (Bull Run) in late August, before McClellan's army arrived from the Virginia Peninsula to reinforce Pope. Rather than move on Washington, however, Lee began his first invasion into western Maryland. John J. Hennessy, *Return to Bull Run: The Campaign and Battle of Second Manassas* (New York: Simon & Schuster, 1993).

place we expect to eat our Christmas dinner provided Abraham has no objections. Forrest & Morgan in the meanwhile will clear the way for us.[10]

But I must close—as the bearer of this is waiting. Col Ross has succeeded in getting permission to mount his Regt (Stone's old Regt) [the 6th Texas Cavalry]. If Col Townes were here, we too I think would be mounted, but it will be too late before he will be able to do anything. Col Townes was improving a few days ago when I heard from him last.

Ma says Aunt Tenn has some difficulty in loaning her money. If you are willing to try the experiment—I will borrow the money for a time—pay the interest and we will buy a drove of beef cattle & drive them either to [Thomas C.] Hindman's or [Albert] Pike's army [in Arkansas and the Indian Territory]—that is you will have to do the driving & buying as I cannot be there. If Paterson has beef cattle & will sell them at reasonable rates buy from him. Government pays from 10 to 15 cts per lb here for beef and while we were in Ark from 5 to 8 cts. If you can get the beeves reasonably I know it will pay well. Some beef contractors here drive from Texas. I wish you to write as often as convenient. My kindest regards to all. All the company *present* are well but one (Wilson Davis).[11] The army here in excellent health.
Truly your brother
J.C. Bates

In late August the brigade that included Stirman's sharpshooters and the dismounted troopers of the 9th Texas Cavalry moved to yet another camp, this one closer to Tupelo. Bates was still uncertain about the army's future movements, thinking its destination might be Corinth to the north or Vicksburg to the west. He also had more sad news for the home folks in Paris—Dan Hatcher, one of his closest friends in the army, had died of disease.

Bates—affectionate to his family, loyal to his friends, intelligent, and well educated—was nevertheless a product of his time and place. He regarded slavery as a necessary and legitimate institution and resented north-

10. Bates's predictions about the armies of Bragg, Van Dorn, and Price, and especially his wording with regard to Forrest and Morgan, almost duplicate the language of Bragg himself, leading to the conclusion that Bates must have read some of Bragg's statements. "Abraham" is President Lincoln. McPherson, *Battle Cry of Freedom*, 515–16.

11. Wilson Davis was a twenty-three-year-old Texas-born farmer in Bates's company.

ern criticisms of the South's "peculiar institution." He seemed also to have resented efforts by southern slaves to raise themselves out of what he considered their proper role in society—as silent and submissive servants. His August 27 letter to his mother reflects these attitudes and demonstrates once again how even men with many admirable qualities could hold to ideas considered evil by many of their own generation and by later generations. In the same letter in which he writes so movingly about the death of his friend, Bates heaps scorn and sarcasm on other men he does not know. The story about the slave and his master has all the earmarks of rumor and exaggeration, but it was likely to stir the emotions of men who feared the emancipation of the South's slaves.

Just before he sealed his letter, Bates learned from Lieutenant Colonel Dudley Jones of the old regiment that the 9th Texas had permission to send for its horses in Texas. Presumably, Jones told Bates this because the captain's company would consequently be transferred back to its regular place in the cavalry. No words could have been sweeter to the ears of Bates and his comrades from Lamar.[12] Texans and horses seemed a natural pairing to these men, and, in Bates's words, "the boys are half crazy to get them." Perhaps to the captain's surprise, the young lieutenant colonel had indeed managed to get his regiment remounted, and Bates's hard attitude toward Jones seemed to soften thereafter.

Camp Armstrong Miss[13]
Aug 27th 1862
My Dear Ma:
    The probabilities of a letter reaching you by mail are so remote since the federals have again threatened Vicksburgh, that I hardly know whether the slim chance this has of reaching you will repay for the writing, but as it costs but little time and labor I can only make the experiment.We occupy the same camps we were in when I wrote

12. A petition from Major J. N. Dodson of the 9th Texas Cavalry to the Confederate Secretary of War illustrates how desperate some of the Texans were to be remounted. Dodson feared wholesale desertion unless the regiment was returned to the cavalry: "We are horsemen by trade and by profession, and policing and scouting the country was our occupation at home, being from the stock raising prairies," Dodson wrote. "We are healthy, hardy and efficient upon horseback, and ailing, unhealthy, tender, dispirited, and inefficient on foot." The petition was probably never sent to Richmond. Misdated 1864 when first published, the document can be found in "Dismounted Cavalry," *Confederate Veteran* 37 (November 1929): 411–12.

13. Camp Armstrong was apparently a few miles nearer to Tupelo than the camp at Mooresville. Kerr, ed., *Fighting with Ross' Texas Cavalry,* 40–41.

last some ten days since. Judging by the signs I see I think we will move from here betwixt the 1st & 15th of Sept but the direction we will take is more than I know at present. It is my impression that we will either move north or west[.] if north we will have to drive the federals before us [and] if west we will meet with less opposition. We have various & conflicting reports from the federals at Corinth—one that they are evacuating[,] another that they are reinforcing.

Some deserters who came in yesterday say they had a general row several days since about the everlasting "nigger." They say a federal Captain went to a man's house near Corinth—took all his negroes into camp—dressed one big buck up in a federal uniform[,] mounted him [and] gave him a sword & pistols—sent him to his master's house with a squad of men & he, the *negro* ordered one of Lincoln's minions to take his master & *handcuff* him & take him to camp. The man was put to cooking for his nigger—the nigger did'nt *like* his *breakfast* & kicked his master—the master did'nt like the kick & knocked the niggers ivory down his throat. Some good union patriots hard by undertook to assist cuffy: others thought a nigger was yet a nigger if he was some kin to old Ham(lin).[14] Hence the general row which resulted in 40 or 50 broken noses & about 300 desertions. So say these deserters.

We have heard so little from V.A. [Virginia] of late & that little so unsatisfactory that we commonly conjecture what is going on. I would not be surprised if in my next I could give you the news of another battle there—probably others besides it. I do not know why it is, but I have a presentiment that the next engagement there will not go well with us.[15]

Our forces at Chattanooga are still advancing, and from all I can learn a fight with Buell within the next week or so is not improbable. Morgan is again on the wing; dashing on the enemy where he least expects it. He captured Gallatin 16 miles from Nashville a few days ago—1,300 prisoners—destroyed a large amount of government stores—the depot—blew up the Tunnell, & destroyed several Rail road bridges.[16] Forrest is also gone and we may expect soon to hear of his daring feats.

14. Bates's pun refers to Lincoln's vice president, Hannibal Hamlin of Maine.

15. Bates's hunch was wrong. The Second Battle of Manassas, fought just a few days after his letter, was a smashing victory for Lee's Confederate army.

16. John Hunt Morgan's Confederate cavalry captured Gallatin, northeast of Nashville, on August 12. Long, *Civil War Day by Day*, 250.

We are still in the Regt of Sharp Shooters, doing as well I suppose as if I were in our old Regt. In fact if Col Townes does not return I would prefer to remain here. I have learned of late to accommodate myself to circumstances—to do when in Rome as Rome does and am therefore tolerably content anywhere. As our Col is a man of some talent and withal a gentleman I do not doubt but we will do as well here as elsewhere.

Since I wrote to you last, death has taken from the Company our best and most valued member—Dan Hatcher. Never was I so pained to hear of the death of any one not a near relative. We did not know how highly he was valued—or how much he was loved untill death claimed him as her own and took him from us.

Jno Gibbons went down to the hospital where he was but got there only in time to hear that he had just died. And when he returned although I knew instinctively what reply would be given to my inquiry about Dan: when the answer was made, *he is dead*, I felt as though I had just heard the announcement made of the death of a brother, and more eyes were wet with tears than mine, eyes unused to being dim[m]ed with tears of sorrow. Dan's death has made a void that will not soon be filled at least with [illegible words]. I can say honestly and candidly that Dan was one of the most honorable, honest—high minded & best hearted men I ever saw. There were few his equal and *none better.*

You asked me to mention as many of the Company as I could. Well that would take too much space since I *could* mention all of them. Jno Gibbons is not in good health, has not been for some time, but his illness is not so serious I suppose, that a smile from Miss "Mat" or Miss "Lizzie" or Miss Moot would not restore him again to health. Judging him by myself he would have to be sick "nigh unto death" if beyond the reach of such a life restoring [blank space] as a "sweet smile" from any of the ladies of Paris—including Miss Nellie. But as much as I would like to see some of the young ladies, one hour *at home* would be worth a *month* any where else. Give my best wishes to all my friends—I would still like to hear from them occasionally but cannot *insist any longer* on their writing. Give my love to Aunt Tenn, Eliza & Clint.

Write often—write by mail, I will get the letters after a while.
Affectionately Your Son
James C. Bates

After writing the above I was sent for by Col Jones & informed that he had been ordered to send a man to collect our horses—and I have added a few more items in the few minutes I have had to write this morning. I do'nt know what or how I have written them—for I have had to answer about 50 questions per minute about our horses—the boys are half crazy to get them.

Jno Fowler is well at present. Bill Scott, Sam Griffith Dick & Jack Shearon also.[17] In fact there is no one *sick* at present—a few cases of diarrhoia of light form the only diseases we have.

Bates was so excited about the prospect of returning his company to mounted service that he wrote a second letter the same day to his mother and another to Will Bramlette, forwarding detailed instructions about the return of the horses and riding equipment. Bates, like Jones, was led to believe that the remounted regiment might be reassigned to the Trans-Mississippi Department of the Confederacy, more good news for the Texans. This proved to be only wishful thinking by General Sterling Price, however, for the regiment spent the remainder of the war east of the Mississippi River.

Camp Tupola Miss
Aug 27th 1862
Dear Ma:

Our Regt has just received orders to send to Texas and have our horses collected and Capt [Thomas G.] Berry [of Company A] starts tomorrow for that purpose. If you have my horse yet, have him in readiness. Capt Berry will notify the parents & friends of the members of the Company by hand Bills or otherwise, of the time & place at which the horses will be collected and received by him. I suppose the horses of each Company will be collected at some particular place and kept there untill we cross the river, which I hope will not be many months. Lt. Col Jones tells me that Genl Price said to him on yesterday that we would cross the river soon if some unforeseen accident did not prevent. As soon as we cross men will be sent from each Company to bring our horses to us.

If you have my horse I want him in as good order as possible. If you have sold him—tell Will to get him again *at any reasonable* cost.

17. Fowler, Scott, Griffith, and the Shearons were all members of Bates's company.

I have *tried* him, & *know* that there is no better. If he is sold tell Will to buy me another—5 or 6 years old 16 hands high, dark bay or brown—heavy made & active. I also want the same *saddle I sent home*—or one as *near like* it as possible, a good *stiff bit* bridle single rein, with hitch rein, the bit to be attached to the head stall with *snaps* so that the bridle may be used as a halter. I also want a p[ai]r of saddle Bags, get Falkner to make them—tolerably large covered with patent leather. Also get Mr. Hatcher to make me a pr boots no 8—double soles & upper—good calf skin—leg to reach to my knee, or higher[,] not clumsy—but as *nice* a boot as he can make. If you can have any of my clothes made by the time the horses are sent, do so, but don't undertake to make them yourself. I would prefer to buy them. If you have any cloth for a coat send it without making. If there is such a thing as a good overcoat in Paris I would like to have one.

Mark whatever you send me—saddle[,] saddle bags—bridle &c & have every thing securely fast to the saddle.

If there is any thing else I may want I will write you again soon & let you know what it is. Tell Mr Hatcher I have $1200 of Dan's money. All he had left. He left some other effects which I will have sold. I forgot to mention this in my letter to him. I will send his Daguerreotype by Sam Davis who is discharged from this co & will start in a day or so.
JC Bates

[August 27?, 1862]
Will

I wish you to attend to procuring the things that I have written for. If you have used all my money borrow some from Aunt Tenn & I will pay her a good int[erest] & return the money in a month or so. We have not been paid any in near four months & I have none at present to spare to send home. We will be paid shortly.

If you can get the money from Aunt Tenn for a time, I wish you to send me *two* horses—one besides the yellow if you still have him—provided you can get *good ones*, in *good order*. Capt Berry may not call for the horses for some time and you need not therefore be in any great haste. In fact I will not be *at all disappointed* if we remain on this side of the river—and remain too, as infantry. Col Jones however told me this morning that Genl Price assured him we would certainly cross the river soon, & in case we do I want every thing in readiness.

I should not be surprised if this impression was put out to induce the federals to withdraw a portion of their forces from this to the other side of the river—and give us greater chances of success here. If it is the intention of Genl Price to cross the river—I predict we will have some hard fighting to do first, and that at no very distant day—and I think we will have the fighting to do whether we cross or not. The next news you get from here will probably be of one if not of three great battles—in Virginia—E Tenn—& one somewhere north or west of this.[18] I do'nt think we will remain here *longer* than ten days. We have no news of much interest. I will send you some late papers if I can get them. Hand the enclosed note to Col Townes if he is at home. I have not heard from him for some time—but understand he has gone home.

If you know of any who would like to join this co say to them we can receive 15 or 20 men yet.

Truly Yours

J.C. Bates

Bates wrote another letter to his mother about the same time, either late August or early September, but the first four pages are missing. The part that survives indicates that he had been spending his own money to help clothe the men in his regiment. This was doubtless the sort of behavior that inspired admiration and respect among his men. He also comments on the high price of good food but makes it plain that the nourishment was worth every penny he spent on it. Bates lodges a complaint against stay-at-home men who were released from the army when it was reorganized in May. Soldiers in the ranks often berated those who stayed close to their firesides while others suffered in the field. In fact, some of the loudest supporters of conscription were soldiers already serving in the army.[19] Bates reserves his greatest contempt for another civilian, his congressman, who apparently took credit for things he did not do.

draw my pay for a month or so & as I have but 125$ concluded it would be best to keep it. There is four months pay due the privates two of which they will draw in a few days. I have spent a good deal

18. Bates is doubtless referring to Lee's army in Virginia, Kirby Smith's and Bragg's columns in east Tennessee, and Price's force in northern Mississippi.

19. Bell Irvin Wiley, *The Life of Johnny Reb: The Common Soldier of the Confederacy* (Indianapolis: Bobbs-Merrill, 1943), 342–43; James I. Robertson, Jr., *Soldiers Blue and Gray* (Columbia: University of South Carolina Press, 1988), 39.

of money since I left Corinth, Buying clothes for the men & myself and also something to eat for my self & *mess*. I came to the conclusion that I could never get entirely well on the diet we were able to get from the government & determined to spend all my wages for something to eat rather than running the risk of dying with chronic interitis a disease that carries off three fourths of the soldiers who die in camp.[20] We pay 2/ [25 cents] pr qt for milk—6 to 8/ [75 cents to $1.00] for butter—8 to 12/ [$1.00 to $1.50] for peaches & apples—4 to 8/ [50 cents to $1.00] for chickens[,] & other thing in same proportion, watermelons *only* 5$ for the largest size —we eat but few of these mainly because we cant get them— money paid by a soldier for vegetables &c is never misspent even at exorbitant prices.

Jno Gibbons is still in bad health & will [stay?] so as long as he remains in the army. Jno Fowler—the two Shearon boys—Sam Griffiths Bill Scott & in fact all the company who were from Paris are well. Jno Gabbart wishes Will to see Tim Williams & get Tim to buy him a horse—bridle (stiff bit) & saddle & saddle blanket—also a pr of boots No 8—*large*—Mr Williams to pay for these things out of money he has of John's & also call on John Falkner for money if he (Mr W) has not enough for these purposes. He wants a horse 5 or 6 years old 16 hand high dark bay or brown—a Texas or Spanish saddle—& high top boots. His name on all these things & well fastened to his saddle. I should have written about these things in my last letter & *may* have done so but do not now remember.

If crops are as near a failure in Texas as I have heard Will had best keep my corn for his own use if he has not already supplied. I want Aunt Tenn to have a portion of it.

We have no news of much interest. No Battle had been fought as yet in Virginia or E Tenn, and the prospect now is that there will be no battle in Tenn as Buell was retreating a few days ago. There is no guessing even what will take place within the next ten days in E Tenn. We are expecting every day to hear of another great battle in V.a. I am very fearful Pope & McClellan will form a junction of their forces & finally prove too much for us.

What has become of those gentlemen who left Corinth so pre-

---

20. Bates uses the word enteritis to refer to the various intestinal disorders—especially diarrhea and dysentery—that had afflicted the army, especially since they arrived at Corinth.

cipitately a few months since. Are they still permitted to prowl round Paris while better men are fighting for them. Has Bill Wright been in Paris since he first went to Congress.[21] In a speech in congress on the bill for the extension of the conscript law he said he had not been in Texas since its passage, but had "Mingled freely with the tens of thousands of Texans at Tupola["] (this place) from his portion of the state & had not seen a dozen now amongst them all who opposed it. If he has ever been at Tupola a single *hour*, to say nothing of three months, I have never heard of him.

My good wishes to my good friends who think enough of me to write. Write often send your letters by mail via Marshall & Vicksburgh. Love to all the family.

Your son

J.C.B.

Captain Bates invariably welcomed soft, warm words from home, but Eb Dohoney was always available to scald a few hides with his sharp tongue and pen as well. Now back in Paris after failing to defeat Dudley Jones for the lieutenant colonelcy, Dohoney brought Bates up to date on the war in the trans-Mississippi region in late August. Dohoney must have been amazed that the Confederacy had survived as long as it had, given the sinkholes of incompetence and vanity he detected in its army.

Paris Texas

Aug 28th 1862

Dear Friend

Yours of August was received a few days since & read with great pleasure. I was surprized that you had rec'd neither of the three letters I have written you. Especially that the one sent by Bingham did not come to hand. And as you have read nothing from me, I had better first address myself to matters of business duty &c, about which I have already written, & afterwards recur to matters of local & historical interest if I have space.

I will recapitulate in brief order what I can now think of. First Mr Hatcher wants you to write to him about Dan, & what his real condition is; & I think you ought to have done so sooner; although I

---

21. William B. Wright was a native of Georgia and a prominent lawyer in Paris. He had been elected to the Confederate Congress in October 1861. Tyler et al., *New Handbook of Texas*, 6:1092.

have explained to him that Dan was off at Hospital, & that probably you knew no more of his condition than the old man himself, & that in my opinion accounted for you not writing of him.[22] Mr J. Beard wishes (& very anxiously) to know whether you can tell him what has become of his son John W. Beard. When last heard from, he was at or near Holly Springs at a hospital.[23] Old man Givens wants you to obtain the letter that is due C.C. Givens, if it will not be more trouble than it is worth.[24] Bowden wants Smith Compton to send him the money for the shotgun Givens had, or an obligation similar to the one he has from Givens, which binds to return the gun in good order, or its value. Geo Wright wants pay for Willy Smith's horse[25]—Bapano's are half distracted to get Bob Sike's horse back[26] —ask Bob whether he wants the horse returned, or prefers paying for him—they prefer the horse.

[Hiram] Duff has recently obtained a discharge from some of the various commanders of Details here & now claims pay up to present date.[27] How does he now stand on your roll? You will see that I drew his money for Jan & Feb, & reported him absent without leave for March & April, & drew nothing on that roll. What has since been done, & how does he now stand? He was discharged as being over 35 years of age. T.M. Reed is also discharged for physical disability, & referred to Comp[any] Roll for settlement.[28] Wants you to draw his money & send—will send his duplicate &c &c.

Newt Stevenson requested me to say that he & Rin[?] had fell in with the detachment here under one Maj Estes & took up line of march last Saturday—all our boys not discharged are along.[29] The

22. Word of Dan Hatcher's death had not reached Paris by the time Dohoney wrote.

23. John W. Beard, a twenty-five-year-old farmer and Alabama native, was wounded at some point in the war, but his military records do not indicate the date.

24. C. C. Givens had died in March while the regiment was still in Arkansas.

25. Two J. W. Smiths served in Bates's company, but it is not clear whether either was the one Dohoney refers to.

26. Robert Sikes was a twenty-nine-year-old private in Bates's company.

27. Duff, the soldier who had waved the company flag over the captured Federal guns at Elkhorn Tavern, had been a private in Bates's company but had returned to Paris when he was released owing to age under the terms of the conscription law.

28. T. M. Reed, twenty-five years old, was a member of Bates's company who was discharged for illness in August 1862.

29. N. E. Stephenson, a twenty-six-year-old farmer and Alabama native, was listed as a deserter in the company's military records. Major Estes may have been William E. Estes of the 32nd Texas Cavalry. For Estes, see Wright and Simpson, *Texas in the War,* 28.

Detachment is now stopped in Bowie county I believe, & a general squable going on.[30] Whitfield's agents claim his men to be remounted, & Col Griffith also claims Stone's [6th Texas Cavalry would be remounted], while Estes, a *blamed fool,* refuses to give them up.[31] At last account Griffith was going to have Estes arrested, & the devil is to play generally. Estes in my opinion has no more authority than I have over any of them, & Capt Sims ought to take the 9th Tex detachments & go on with them.[32] They have had these detachments in camp at Morris Springs ever since I got home trying to get off, & they are yet in Texas.

First [Thomas C.] Hindman the *great Proclamating General* of ctr. Kansas assumed authority, & ordered Col Diamond to take charge of them, & bring to Little Rock.[33] Then came Lins Griffith & others with orders from Tupelo. Then up popped Maj Estes claiming to be the ranking officer of *horse detachments*—sent home a searg-majer in charge of horses, & at the reorganization elected Major. The whole matter was referred to Gen [Henry E.] Mccullough, being in his Military District & he decided in favor of the aforesaid Estes, & now he [Estes] refuses to give up to later orders, & officers who come for the detachments & horses of their Regt.[34]

---

30. Apparently, some men of the regiment were in Paris and trying to return to service when they ran into a jurisdictional dispute among various officers.

31. John W. Whitfield of Lavaca County, Texas, a native of Tennessee, had raised "Whitfield's Legion," a unit of cavalry that was later transformed into a regiment (the 27th Texas Cavalry). John S. Griffith was a Maryland native and Kaufman County resident who had raised a company in the 6th Texas Cavalry. He had been elected lieutenant colonel of that regiment when it was reorganized in May. The officious Major Estes was evidently interfering with the efforts of these regiments to send their men and horses to Mississippi. For Whitfield, see Warner, *Generals in Gray,* 333–34; Tyler et al., *New Handbook of Texas,* 6:945. For Griffith, see Tyler et al., 3:339; Kerr, ed., *Fighting with Ross' Texas Cavalry,* 91.

32. Captain J. W. Sims, assistant quartermaster for the 9th Texas Cavalry, was apparently in command of the men returning to that regiment.

33. Major General Thomas C. Hindman, commander of the Trans-Mississippi District in the summer of 1862, exerted great efforts to put as many men as possible into the army in his department, thus perhaps explaining his order to divert the Texas horsemen to Arkansas. Colonel James J. Diamond of Cooke County was an officer in the 11th Texas Cavalry. For Hindman, see Neal and Kremm, *Lion of the South,* 120–24. For Diamond, see Tyler et al., *New Handbook of Texas,* 2:628.

34. Colonel Henry E. McCulloch, the brother of Ben McCulloch, was overall commander in north Texas in the summer of 1862. Faust, *Historical Times Illustrated Encyclopedia,* 458–59; *Tyler (Texas) Reporter,* June 19, 1862, p. 1.

Paris has been cursed for the last two months with more *military swell heads* than Tupelo itself. Q M [Quartermaster A. S.] Cabbell [of the 7th Texas Cavalry] & his numerous retinue in town, & Estes camp at Morris Springs. A great many troops have lately left & are leaving Texas for the Ark Army.[35] Regts sworn in last Spring are just getting out, & such as have been raising in the Spring are not yet organized viz Demors & Goulds &c.[36] There is an awful delinquency somewhere—surely not in Government certainly not in the men who promptly volunteer—must be in the *pretended great* ones who raise them & go on to Richmond for commissions. Men from Texas have been commissioned to raise Regts & are now Cols, whom I would not appoint 1st corporal in a company of mine, Waterhouse of Jefferson & Bass of Sherman & numerous others.[37] But this is a politician's war, & partizans favoritism must have the spoils.

The word here is that the West now is again "On to Missouri." But in my opinion if the war goes on, & *go on it must* before Christmas we like Mcclellan will fall back not to the Junction of the Chicahominy but to the bank of Red River—"to improve our lines."[38] I now predict that if the attempt is made our army will be driven out of Mo [Missouri], & there being nothing to eat from the valley of the Mo [River] to Red River, we necessarily fall back on that as a base of supplies. Again the principal supply of our army beef goes from Texas; the Federals will make a determined effort to cut off these supplies, & unless our Army is again victorious at Richmond, a Federal Army will be in Northern Texas before Spring.

35. Several Texas regiments raised in the spring of 1862 marched toward Little Rock in the summer. Most of them would later be organized into John G. Walker's Texas Division. See Norman D. Brown's introduction to Joseph Palmer Blessington, *The Campaigns of Walker's Texas Division* (1875; reprint Austin, Tex.: State House Press, 1994).

36. Charles DeMorse, a native of Massachusetts, organized the 29th Texas Cavalry in 1862. Robert S. Gould, a North Carolina native and member of the Texas secession convention, raised a battalion of cavalry that would serve in Walker's Division. For DeMorse, see Tyler et al., *New Handbook of Texas*, 2:591–92. For Gould, see ibid., 3:258.

37. Richard Waterhouse, a Tennessee native, raised the 19th Texas Infantry Regiment, Walker's Texas Division, and served as its colonel. Thomas C. Bass of Sherman was a Mississippi native and an outspoken advocate of secession. He raised the 20th Texas Cavalry Regiment and served as its colonel. For Waterhouse, see ibid., 6:841. For Bass, see ibid., 1:408–409.

38. Confederates often made sport of Federal general George B. McClellan's use of euphemisms to describe a retreat.

Hindman the *Great Proclamator,* who in his vanity & multitude of his "Orders" even issued one against *Saying* & *believing lies* (the unnatural man to try to reverse the *regular order of things*).[39] Hindman the *aforesaid* had been superseded in the Little Rock throne by one Carolina Holmes, & the aforesaid Tommy [Hindman] now acts as second fiddle & takes the field to lead the army nearly ready to go into Mo.[40] Why in the name of all common sense did they not send Price instead of Holmes & take Hindman away. In the battle of Cotton plant [Arkansas] it is said some of the Texas troops did not fight the Federals, but were all the time looking for Hindman to shoot him.[41] Price is the only man who can lead an Army into Mo with any possibility of success. Gen Pike has resigned, & Cooper is commanding in the Indian Department. Our Army is now at & about Ft Gibson living on or about half rations. The Federals lately came down [and] took Ft Gibson but finding nothing to live on returned hastily to Kansas, taking with them John Ross chief of Cherokees & many of his relations. His enemies over there say he is a traitor— probably so—[42]

The *distinguished captain of the Lamar Artillery* charged by 104 of his men—with taking their coffee & bacon—making false muster —& other things too tedious to mention—has been arrested— court-martialed, & has come home—his friends say honorably acquitted, & on 30 days furlough but how it is the public yet know not.[43] *I have a shrewd suspicion of how it may be.* The notorious [il-

39. General Hindman's energetic and sometimes heavy-handed efforts to mobilize men and resources for the defense of Arkansas alienated many civilians, including Dohoney. Dohoney, *Average American,* 130; Neal and Kremm, *Lion of the South,* 118–35.

40. Theophilus H. Holmes, a fifty-seven-year-old native of North Carolina, was a West Point graduate, veteran of the Mexican War, and successor to Hindman as commander of the Trans-Mississippi Department. Warner, *Generals in Gray,* 141; Neal and Kremm, *Lion of the South,* 134.

41. General Hindman was not present at the small engagement at Cotton Plant (Cache River), Arkansas, on July 7, so Dohoney's claims about murderous soldiers were incorrect. Neal and Kremm, *Lion of the South,* 131.

42. Ross's willingness to cooperate with Federal forces did not surprise Bates, who had questioned Ross's loyalty to the Confederacy for months.

43. James M. Daniel, captain of the Lamar Artillery, was a native of Virginia; brother of the controversial editor of the *Richmond (Va.) Examiner,* John Moncure Daniel; and nephew of Peter V. Daniel, a justice on the United States Supreme Court before the war. John D. Perkins, *Daniel's Battery: The 9th Texas Field Battery* (Hillsboro, Tex.: Hill College Press, 1998), 5.

legible word] [J. S.] Stewart has got himself made Capt of a
Comp[any] of Sharp-Shooters for Maxey's Brigade. Goodrich 1
Lieut, Dan Latimer & Jno Bennett 2nd Lieuts. Tom Littlejohn is
Capt. Ras Mosely 1 Lieut & Bayles & Belmer lieutenants of a Com-
pany for Demorse. Lion Hearnan is also a Capt of a Company for
Demorse's Regt.
[E. L. Dohoney]

In early September the army around Tupelo, now numbering about fifteen
thousand and commanded by Sterling Price, began moving toward
Corinth, fifty miles to the north. General Bragg had directed Price to engage the Federals at Corinth, thereby keeping them away from Bragg's
route to the Ohio River.[44] Bates fired off at least four more letters before
his regiment tramped up the road toward the Yankees. The first continued
his excited instructions about the return of his horse and equipment. Two
letters to Will Bramlette reported lopsided Confederate victories in Virginia and Kentucky. The fourth complained again about the lack of mail
from home and reported the unhappy news that still another of Bates's
close friends, John Gibbons, was leaving the army. Slowly and steadily, his
circle of prewar companions was shrinking.

Camp Armstrong Miss
September 3d 1862
My Dear Sister
    Not to let an opportunity pass I write you again today—but
about all that I can say that will be of interest to you is that we are
all, or nearly all, well, our sick list comprising those only who have
long since learned to play the "old soldier" and are daily put down
sick without questioning.
    I wrote to you several days since by Capt Berry—of our Regt—
who goes to Texas for our horses—or his business is rather to collect the horses of the different companies and hold them in readiness
for us if it should be our good fortune to cross the Miss river as now
contemplated. I wrote to Will to keep my horse if he had not sold
him, and intended to say to Will to get him again at any reasonable
cost in case he was sold but I had so many letters to write for others
and was so hurried in writing for myself that I don't remember
whether I did so or not. I have tried him sufficiently and know his

44. Connelly, *Army of the Heartland*, 225, 228.

value. Horses bring almost fabulous prices here and I was told by a gentleman just from Texas that that they are equally high in Arkansas.

None but good horses will be received and I am afraid some of the company will have some difficulty in getting horses at present prices. Every effort should be made by the parents and friends of the boys here to procure good horses for them.

Our's gets the praise of being the best drilled, and disciplined company in the Regt—and if we should be mounted I still want it to preserve its good name—and it will be difficult to do this on shabby ponies. I wrote by Capt Berry for most I will need that can be brought from home. I neglected to mention one thing which might be of considerable service in case we were forced to "change our base" rapidly viz—a good pair of spurs. I do'nt suppose they can be had in any of the stores there and if not have a small pr Mexicans spurs made by some good smith. If I am not mistaken the bridle bit I sent home was broken on one side—if this cannot be mended I would like to have a small, light, stiff bit made. I wrote to Will to borrow the money from Aunt Tenn, if he had none of mine, to pay for these things. I would have sent money by Capt Berry—but have some doubt about being able to [rest of letter missing]

Camp Armstrong Miss
[Sept ? 1862]
Will

The following order was read to us on yesterday evening on dress parade
Genl Orders
No 27 By direction of the War Department the Maj genl comdg communicates to the Army of the West the following glorious intelligence from the army in V.A.

"The enemy attacked my left under Jackson on Thursday & was repulsed. He attacked my right under Longstreet on Friday and was repulsed. On Saturday I attacked him with my combined armies and utterly routed the combined armies of Pope & McClellan on the plains of Manassas
Robt E Lee"
Gel Lee was in pursuit of the enemy on yesterday.
    Sterling Price Maj Genl
    Comd Army of the West

We have since received telegraphic dispatches confirming the above. Genl [Dabney] Maury has just sent us another *order* saying dispatches were received from Chatanooga this morning & that Genl [Edmund Kirby] Smith attacked [William] Bull Nelson and utterly routed him.[45] Nelson is retreating & abandoning his Comissary & ordnance stores & Smith is in pursuit. Two Kentuck Regiments laid down their arms and came over to Genl Smith. Kentuckians are coming in here [every] day. These two victories [torn spot] will be followed up soon by one more brilliant over the enemy north of us won by the army of the West. I have not time to write particulars as this mail closes in a few minutes if it has not already. I will write again in a day or so. Yours &c

J.C. Bates

Camp Armstrong [Miss] Sept 4 [1862]
Will

We have just received the glorious news of the defeat of Genl Pope by Genls Lee & Jackson on the old Manassas battle ground. Our loss ten to fifteen thousand, Pope's twenty to thirty thousand.[46] Pope in full retreat towards Washington & old "Stonewall" in pursuit.

We leave here in a few days & the Yankees north of us will have a chance to retrieve their waning fortunes or else give us another example of the facility with which they can "change their base." When I get the particulars I will write again. The above was telegraphed to Genl Price.

Yours &c
J.C. Bates

We have just had some additional news by telegraph—leaving no doubt of our forces having gained a complete victory. The last news

---

45. Major General Edmund Kirby Smith led one of the two Confederate columns penetrating Kentucky from east Tennessee. On August 30 Smith's twelve thousand veterans smashed seven thousand green recruits under Major General William "Bull" Nelson at Richmond, Kentucky, only seventy-five miles south of Cincinnati. Connelly, *Army of the Heartland*, 214–17; Shelby Foote, *The Civil War: A Narrative* (3 vols.; New York: Random House, 1958–74), 1:650–53; McPherson, *Battle Cry of Freedom*, 517.

46. As usual, the numbers were exaggerated. Union losses were about sixteen thousand; Confederate, about nine thousand. Boatner, *Civil War Dictionary*, 105.

by telegraph—reports 60,000 prisoners captured. This is of course an exaggeration of the facts—but still there is room for a great victory.

Camp Armstrong Miss
Sept 6th 1862
Dear Sister:

As we leave this place in a few hours I drop you a few lines not knowing how long it may be before I have another opportunity.

I have looked in vain for a letter from some of you untill the last hour is nearly passed yet no letter has come. Do you write? Others get letters and why cannot I? I have written to some of you weekly ever since we have been here & received from home *one* letter since May. A large mail comes in from Texas nearly every day which seems to indicate that there is still free communication by mail.

In consequence of continued bad health Jno Gibbons has sent up his resignation on certificate of disability—if it is accepted he will leave for Texas in a few days & can give you all the news, and more, than I can write. Judging by his appearance I think he is taking the dropsy & does right in resigning. Jno has been a good officer and all will regret to see him leave. I am the only officer who started out with the company yet remaining with it. It is my intention to remain with the company as long as it remains and return with it.

We still continue to receive cheering news from V.A. but as yet have no particulars. It is rumored in camp that a telegraphic dispatch has been received saying McClellan had fallen back to Arlington Heights & it is supposed that Pope is trying to hold Lee in check untill McClellan gets his forces in a position to defend Washington. I am of opinion that we will have some hard fighting before we get in sight of Washington.[47]

We have had no news from Chatanooga for two days and I am afraid the news of the defeat of Buell was only given in anticipation of that event occuring.

I will write again in a few days and send the letter to Jno Gibbons at this place as he will probably remain here several days. I send you

47. Lee's Confederate army turned away from the defenses of Washington and crossed the Potomac River into western Maryland in early September.

the latest telegraphic news I have. I have subscribed for a Mobile paper and sent to you. Let me know if you receive it.

My good wishes to Capts Wright[,] Dohoney & other friends, tell them I would like to hear from them.

Your brother

JC Bates

Since writing the above I have concluded to send it by Lieut Gibbons as he will probably start in a day or so.

Sterling Price's Army of the West moved out of its camps near Tupelo in early September to distract the Federals at Corinth, perhaps by making a dash into west Tennessee. Phifer's brigade—including Stirman's Sharpshooters and the 9th Texas Cavalry—trudged up the road early on the morning of September 6. Still not accustomed to long marches on foot, the Texans suffered in the late summer heat—"our feet blistered & backs sore from the weight of knap & haver sacks—Very Hot." After twelve miles of this undignified torture, the brigade halted at Saltillo. The next day they moved into a nearby camp abandoned by other troops, where they remained for a few days before resuming the march on September 11.[48]

During the lull at Saltillo, Bates wrote two more letters to Paris. He and his comrades were receiving so much good news from the armies in Virginia and Kentucky—some of it accurate—that Bates could hardly contain his high spirits. It appeared finally that the Confederacy was on the verge of winning the war. The father of his dead friend, Dan Hatcher, apparently had some quarrel with Bates (perhaps the lack of frequent updates on Hatcher's illness), but even that could not dim the bright glow surrounding the Confederacy in the late summer of 1862.

Camp near Saltillo Miss

Sept 9th 1862

My Dear Ma:

As Lieut Gibbons has not yet received his leave of absence & may not for several days I will send this by another person going to Texas this morning. We have received so much and such glorious news from all our sources that the whole encampment is about delirious

48. Kerr, ed., *Fighting with Ross' Texas Cavalry*, 41.

with joy and excitement. I wrote to Will a few days since sending him Lee's dispatch after the second victory at Manassas and also dispatches saying Bull Nelson had surrendered his entire army to Gen Kirby Smith.

This last has been fully confirmed and we last night received the glorious intelligence of the capture of Cincinatti by Gen Smith at 10 A.M. on last Saturday.[49] We have but few particulars yet. Genl Smith met a small force four miles from Covington but only fired one round when they surrendered. He then proceeded to Covington [Bates meant Cincinnati] & demanded the surrender of the city giving the authorities two hours to surrender in. The Mayor asked four which was granted & at the expiration of four hours the proud city the "queen of the west" was surrendered to the "Rebels" with the immense amount of government stores contained in it.[50]

Genl Phifer told me last night these dispatches came officially to Genl Maury—& there was no doubt they are true. He also informed me a dispatch was captured a few days since from Buell to Rosencrantz [Rosecrans] in which the former urges the latter to meet him in Nashville as speedily as possible, saying if they did not effect a junction of their forces speedily both would be attacked and destroyed in detail.[51] I also heard last night from a citizen just from the neighborhood of Corinth that the Yankees had had another fight amongst themselves at that place about the niggers in which near two hundred were killed.

I have not time to write more as the bearer of this is waiting for it. We will resume the march again in a few days & I think will either go in the direction of Nashville via Corinth or make directly for the Miss river.[52] Genl Bragg is pushing on toward Nashville. Genl Breckinridge is moving up the central road. We had a report last night that

49. The news about Cincinnati was wrong. Kirby Smith's army did not cross the Ohio River.

50. Covington, Kentucky, across the Ohio River from Cincinnati, was approached by Kirby Smith's army in mid-September, but neither Covington nor Cincinnati surrendered to the Confederates. Foote, *Civil War*, 1:654; Long, *Civil War Day by Day*, 267.

51. Major General William S. Rosecrans was commander of Federal forces at Corinth, Mississippi. He did not join Buell at Nashville because Rosecrans was under pressure from Sterling Price's army, which was approaching from the south.

52. Sterling Price and the Texans may have been dreaming of crossing to the trans-Mississippi region, but the Confederate high command expected them to defeat Rosecrans at Corinth and reclaim west Tennessee from Federal control.

he attacked & whiped the enemy at grand junction.[53] I doubt this. I will write again in a few days.

Your affectionate son

J.C. Bates

Genl Phifer also informed me last night that Maury had received a dispatch saying Genl [Stonewall] Jackson had crossed the Potomack at Leesburgh & was threatening Washington from the north.[54]

Camp near Saltillo Miss
Sept 9 1862
[To Mootie Johnson]

Yours of the 23d ult was received on the evening of the 8th inst. That day will long be remembered by me as one of the most joyful I have known for many long months. Returning to camp late in the evening, hot tired & hungry (you were not mistaken in your recollection of my appetite) I lay down for a few moments to rest myself before sitting down—*not* to peach cobbler & sweet milk—but to my bacon & cornbread, and while resting the mail for our old Regt was brought in, and when I was told there were letters for every company but mine, I began to wonder why it is that some of *our* friends did not write, or whether in fact we *had* any friends. I came to the conclusion that our friends were to say the least, very negligent and careless; and this, added to some little bad news I had been reading, made a pretty good foundation for an attack of that to me most to be dreaded of all enemies, the "blues." Fortunately before I succeeded in "working myself into a *miserable state of fix*" I heard some of the boys drawling out [four illegible words] "all about the fight at Manassas" &c and in the hope of finding something to divert my mind from the "old folks at home" (and from other folks too) I bought a paper and proceeded to *devour* its contents.

I plunged into the battle of Manassas (the description of it I mean) and had forgotten I ever had a home or friends or SH [sweet-

53. General Breckinridge had not captured Grand Junction, about fifty miles east of Memphis. In fact, Breckinridge's small force was still gathering at Jackson in central Mississippi, preparatory to a dash by rail in a different direction, to Chattanooga. Davis, *Breckinridge*, 326–27.

54. Lee's army did cross the Potomac River in early September, but it was marching north toward Pennsylvania, not east toward Washington.

heart] when Col Jones sent me something to read from one of the person's *not* named above. I need hardly tell you the newspaper was droped "instanter," and the battle of Manassas and *every body* else was forgotten in the pleasure I found in reading your letter; which with the newspaper raised my "spirits" about 50 degrees, and before I had finished reading the interesting news (whether your letter or the paper was most interesting you can easily judge) more than *twice* over, Genl Phifer came in bringing news fully confirming the capture of Nelson's entire army, stores arms; &c by Genl Kirby Smith. On the strength of this the aforesaid "spirits" *riz* about 25 degrees more. Before we had fairly commenced rejoicing over the above one of Genl Maury's aids brought in the glorious intelligence of the capture of Cincinnatti Ohio by the same invincible Kirby Smith. I thought this was too good to be true so went down to learn of Genl Phifer how the intelligence came in. He informed me it was telegraphed to Genl Maury as official, and there was no doubt but that it was correct.

You may be sure this additional news raised the spirits in the thermometer of my "feelinks" to the boiling point, and they accordingly run over and found vent in a loud "whoop hurrah" for every body. Throwing up one's cap and whooping like a savage is not a very dignified proceeding for a captain even, but as I had the example of a Genl, several Colonels, and various and divers other "Grey coats" I concluded my dignity would not be compromised much by letting out some of my pent up feelings. So like the little boy who accidently whistled in school I opened my mouth and it just "hollered" itself. We also received news that Genl Breckinridge attacked and defeated the enemy at Grand Junction. This I do not credit. We also have it by telegraph that Genl Jackson had crossed the Potomack at Lee's burgh and was threatening Washington City.

It cannot be wondered at that all this good news coming in less than half an hour should produce such joy and excitement as was seen in our camp. Nor is it a great matter of wonder that I—even I—should forget, in the excitement of the moment, to eat my supper. Yes all the disappointment of the last three or four months was fully compensated by the reception of the glorious news & of your letter. Even the loss of my supper was not regarded much, especially as I did'nt think of it untill breakfast next morning.

You begin by hoping I wo'nt think you presumptuous in writing before receiving a reply to your letter. Let *me* hope you were not serious in thinking or seeming to think that I could entertain such a thought—after so often requesting you to write whether you received my letters or not. I believe I promised you, and Miss Mary, to write regularly whether I received letters from you or not.

Well after answering your last letter I waited a sufficient length of time for a reply, but as none came I wrote you again. Still receiving no letter from you I wrote the third letter since receiving yours. But when the time came to write the fourth—I doubted the propriety of sending it. As *all* my letters except two to Miss Mary had reached their destination, there was a fair probability at least that *some* of mine had reached you and you might in consequence think *me* presumptuous in writing the fourth time. I thought too if you *had* received my letters a correspondence all carried on by *one party* could not be *very* interesting and I had better therefore wait untill I heard whether you had received my letters or not. Why my letters do not reach you I cannot imagine. You say you were disappointed in not receiving a letter by Mr Bingham. I confess I *should* have written, & would have done so but for the reasons given above—that they possibly might not be welcomed. You say too that Miss Mary claims a letter due her from me. Say to Miss Mary I have written *twice* to her one at Corinth & once at Moorsville since receiving one from her and the letters are therefore due me. But not to be exacting I will still continue to write.

Sept 10th

I commenced to write on yesterday evening but owing to the darkness I was forced to stop (I have no candles at present & bacon grease is too scarce to make a "poor folks lamp of.") Early this morning we were ordered out on Division review which lasted untill noon & now having made a hearty meal on some of the aforesaid bacon & cornbread washed it down with some good old hard cider I am ready to finish my letter.[55]

I very much regret Mr Hatcher thinks I acted badly in regard to Dan. I cannot doubt his love for Dan but *can* say that he did not esteem him more highly than I did. I suppose you have heard before this that the great reaper, Death, has cut him down—that his spirit has winged its flight to a better world than this—to a *truer father*

---

55. Private Rawlins of the 6th Texas Cavalry mentioned that one of the brigades in the division review had four fifers and eight drummers leading the march. Entry of September 12, 1862, F. A. Rawlins Diary.

than it ever had on this. Amongst ten thousand young men one could not be found *better* than Dan was and few his equal. The army is *the* place to try "what sort of stuff men's souls are made of" and if ever Dan was found wanting, I do not know it.[56] If he had been my own brother I would not have regretted his death much more. I esteemed him highly before we became soldiers together — but never learned to *love* him untill I saw him severely tested by the severe ordeal of a soldier's life. To those who *knew* him he needs no eulogy — & those who *did not* know him cannot know his worth. The bugle has just sounded the "preparation for march" I will finish after packing up.

Sept 25th I said just above that I would finish my letter after packing up. Well! it has not taken all this while to pack up my "traps" — they are not so numerous as that, but after getting everything in readiness for a start—I had to draw my rations, issue ammunition— draw clothing for the men &cc & by the time this was finished 9 Oclk had come—it was raining—the wind blowing so hard a candle would not have burned if I had any—and as we started the next morning at 4 oclk I had not time to write. This is the reason you have not received a reply to your letter sooner. I have since had no opportunity of mailing a letter even if I had had an opportunity of writing.

It is true, what I have written above is somewhat out of date— especially what little news there is in it—but as you insist that I write *long letters*—I send you this partly in answer to yours of the 23 ult, partly to "fill up" (you will find I have nothing better to write) but *principally* because it is too valuable to throw away. I expect you will be in a quandary as to whether *it* in the last sentence has a reference to the reading matter, *or* to the *paper* on which it is written.

Your letter of the 29th Aug was received several days since. I hardly expected a letter from you so soon, but it was nonetheless just as gladly received as if I had not heard from you for a long while. It made me feel too like I had been doing you an injustice in supposing you had not written and I now take it all back — own up — and promise as you wish, to be as good a *boy* as circumstances will allow — but am not willing to promise to be a *very little* one as I

---

56. Bates is paraphrasing Thomas Paine's "These are the times that try men's souls. The summer soldier and the sunshine patriot will, in this crisis, shrink from the service of their country," from Paine's introduction to a series of pamphlets, "The American Crisis" (1776).

am at present quite small enough. I hope *you* may be a *good* girl, but will not ask you to be a little one as that would be a physical impossibility.

If this letter meets with as many stoppings on the road as it has since I began to write, it will be a long while on the road. Not less than half a dozen times have I been called away on some other business. Several items of news or rumors rather, in the first part of my letter have proved to be unfounded. Cincinnatti has *not* been taken by Genl Smith—neither has Grand Junction by Breckinridge. Old Stonewal had not crossed the Potomack at the time I first wrote but has since & probably now has possession of Baltimore.[57] We have nothing however, but rumors from V.a. nor in fact from anywhere else.

[September] 26th Well the fates *have* decided that this shall be an unfortunate letter. If I can't finish at this "sitting" I'll quit. My ideas have been so "obfuscated" by the thousand and one things demanding my attention for the last day or so that I hardly know half the time what I meant.

Lieut Gibbon's health has been failing for some months & as it is probable he will not be able for duty for some time you may look for him home soon. He has already sent up his resignation. It has not yet been approved by Genl Price but I suppose will. I regret he has to leave. He has been a good officer & will be much missed. I have just received three other letters from Paris & as you have doubtless long before this thought that it was time for me to say "enough, it is finished" I will close this miserable scrawl with the promise to do better in the future—*if I can.*

We take up the line of march in two hours—where I cant say— & I must try to scribble an answer to my other letters. Will write again the first opportunity.
Very Truly Your Friend
"Capt Jimmy"

Pretty certain *you* wont ask for another long letter.

---

57. By the time Bates wrote the last part of his letter, Lee's army, including Stonewall Jackson's corps, had fought the Battle of Antietam (Sharpsburg) on September 17 and then returned to northern Virginia. See Stephen W. Sears, *Landscape Turned Red: The Battle of Antietam* (New Haven, Conn.: Ticknor & Fields, 1983).

Except for a few long-range skirmishes on the outskirts of Corinth the preceding May, Bates and his friends had not fought the Yankees since the defeat at Elkhorn Tavern in early March, six months earlier. In the interim the men of Lamar had reorganized their regiment and elected new officers; Bates had been elected captain; his company had been transferred to a regiment of sharpshooters; and the men had spent a long summer training in the camps of northern Mississippi. Their next six months would be much different.

 Corinth

Sterling Price's Army of the West, under orders to distract the Federals in northern Mississippi while Braxton Bragg marched into Kentucky, left Saltillo on September 11, 1862, and moved toward Iuka. About twenty miles southeast of Corinth, the prosperous village of Iuka was manned by a small garrison of Federals and sat astride the Memphis & Charleston Railroad. On September 14 Price's fifteen thousand Confederates chased the surprised and outnumbered defenders out of the little town and gobbled up mountains of quartermaster and commissary stores left behind by the Federals: "wagons, flour, crackers, corn, salt, & other necessities & many luxuries—& plenty of the latter," Sergeant Griscom recorded in his diary. "Got full rations of Bacon & Crackers (Captured)."[1]

Ulysses S. Grant, the overall commander of Federal forces in west Tennessee and northern Mississippi, saw Price's movement to Iuka as an opportunity to bag the old Missourian's whole army. Grant sent two columns to do the job—eight thousand soldiers under E. O. C. Ord and nine thousand under William S. Rosecrans. As it turned out, Price escaped the trap after some hard, close-in fighting on September 19.[2] Phifer's brigade, including Stirman's Sharpshooters and the 9th Texas Cavalry, played no significant role in the battle at Iuka. A soldier in the 9th Texas Cavalry remembered that "a few shells fell among us, lost but few." George Gris-

1. Kerr, ed., *Fighting with Ross' Texas Cavalry,* 42; Peter Cozzens, *The Darkest Days of the War: The Battles of Iuka and Corinth* (Chapel Hill: University of North Carolina Press, 1997), 56–57; Foote, *Civil War,* 1:716–18; McPherson, *Battle Cry of Freedom,* 522–23.

2. Cozzens, *Darkest Days,* 63–66, 74–117, 133; Foote, *Civil War,* 1:717–19; McPherson, *Battle Cry of Freedom,* 522.

com reported that "our position was in sight of the battle & could see it all." If Bates described the battle in any of his letters, they have not survived, but he would have had little to write in any case.[3]

After slipping through Grant's trap at Iuka, Price led his two divisions along a curving route to the south and west toward Ripley in late September. Bad roads and driving rain storms made the march miserable for the men in the ranks, especially the dismounted Texans, unaccustomed to slogging through knee-deep mud. "I think nearly every man fell down from one to a dozen times" during one rainy night, a Missouri soldier complained. Sergeant Griscom of the 9th Texas Cavalry was amazed at how heavy wet blankets could be on the march. Price's army joined Van Dorn's at Ripley on September 28. This combined force, the Army of West Tennessee, comprised three divisions and about twenty-two thousand men under the overall command of Van Dorn.[4]

General Van Dorn planned to strike the Federal army at Corinth, but only after a diversionary march north into Tennessee. Then, before the Federals could be certain which garrisoned town was his prey, he would race southeast to Corinth and assault the earthworks on the northwest side of town. On the twenty-ninth the one division Van Dorn had brought to the new army tramped north out of Ripley toward the Tennessee line. At daylight the next day Price's two divisions followed. Phifer's brigade (in Dabney Maury's division) reached the Tennessee line on October 1, and the next day it accompanied the rest of the army on its twenty-mile dash toward Corinth.[5]

Waiting for the Confederates at Corinth was General Rosecrans's army of twenty-three thousand. Rosecrans had a powerful edge in the coming contest: his army occupied the strong defensive works built by the Confederates back in the spring. These works, expanded by Rosecrans, included an outer line of forts, gun emplacements, and trenches, more than a mile from the center of town, and a stronger inner line of works at the edge of Corinth. Outside the earthworks were wide expanses of felled trees (abatis, in military parlance), arranged so that the branches pointed outward toward the Confederates.[6]

3. Sparks, *War Between the States,* 274; Kerr, ed., *Fighting with Ross' Texas Cavalry,* 43; Carr, *In Fine Spirits,* 48. The only casualty in Bates's company was 2nd Lieutenant Robert I. Jennings, a twenty-six-year-old Tennessee native and Lamar County farmer.

4. Cozzens, *Darkest Days,* 135–37, 327–28; Kerr, ed., *Fighting with Ross' Texas Cavalry,* 43–44; Foote, *Civil War,* 1:719–20.

5. Cozzens, *Darkest Days,* 136–37, 140; Kerr, ed., *Fighting with Ross' Texas Cavalry,* 44.

6. Cozzens, *Darkest Days,* 145–46, 155; Current, *Encyclopedia of the Confederacy,* 1:414.

On the unusually warm morning of October 3, Van Dorn sent his three divisions crashing through the felled timber and against the outer line of Federal works. Phifer's brigade attacked from northwest to southeast, in the center of the Confederate line. In the blistering heat of midday, Rosecrans's brigades buckled under Van Dorn's assault, abandoning their guns and streaming back toward the second line of defense more than a mile away. The Confederates came whooping after them, but these Federals were veterans, and they took up four successive positions before finally retreating into their inner earthworks at dark.[7]

After resting on the battlefield that night, the Confederates resumed the fight before dawn with a thunderous artillery assault. Then, at 10 A.M., Van Dorn threw his infantry once again against the Federal line, now even stronger because more compact. Although many of Van Dorn's regiments were shattered when they reached the earthworks, some units, including Stirman's Sharpshooters, crashed through the Union defense and rushed toward the streets of Corinth itself. Colonel Stirman described the assault:

> The bugle sounded & with fixed bayonets we advanced reserving our fire. It was not long until the abattis had broken our line in to fragments, but we kept up the advance. The Federals were on their breastworks firing at us; when we had reached within 50 yds of their line the order to fire was given. We were up close & they were so thick that we simply cut them into shreds. The charge was sounded & we rushed at the works and with the bayonetts swept them from the field.[8]

Stirman's Sharpshooters and units from another brigade then pushed through two Illinois regiments along the tracks of the Mobile & Ohio Railroad and sliced into the streets of Corinth. Indeed, the sharpshooters planted their flag in front of the Tishomingo Hotel, a much photographed site after the battle. But the Federals threw in their reserves, Van Dorn did

---

7. Cozzens, *Darkest Days,* 165–220. A Minnesota colonel to the left of Bates and his men reported that "the heat, during the engagement of my command, was most intense, said to be 108 degrees in the shade." Alonzo L. Brown, *History of the Fourth Regiment of Minnesota Infantry Volunteers During the Great Rebellion, 1861–1865* (St. Paul, Minn.: Pioneer Press, 1892), 132. Also see William S. Rosecrans, "The Battle of Corinth," in Robert Underwood Johnson and Clarence Clough Buel, eds., *Battles and Leaders of the Civil War* (4 vols.; New York: Century, 1887–88), 2:748.

8. Carr, *In Fine Spirits,* 52. Also see *OR,* Vol. 17, Pt. 1, pp. 185–86, for a Federal officer's account of this charge.

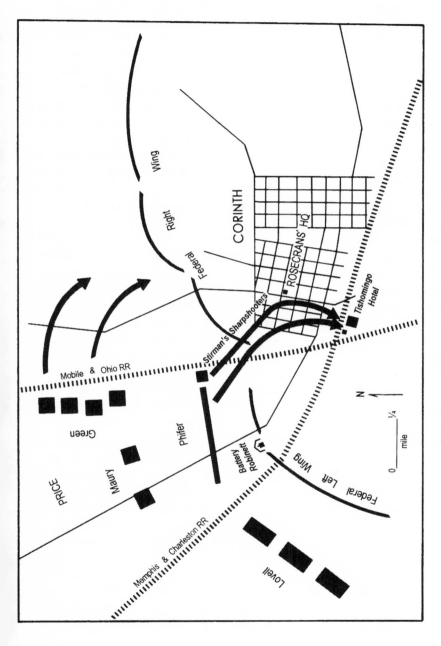

The Charge of Stirman's Sharpshooters at Corinth

not, and the most advanced Confederates, including Bates and his company, were forced to retreat back over the ground they had just won. Some of the sharpshooters jumped on Federal horses tied up at the hotel and galloped off to the northwest. Others, including Bates, had to fall back on foot. An Iowa soldier watched the withdrawal: "I could not help but pity these poor fellows who thus went into certain and sure destruction here. They had been cut to pieces in the most intense meaning of that term. Such bravery has never been excelled on any field." Corinth was saved for the Union, and Van Dorn had lost another battle.[9]

The battered Confederates turned away from the bloody fields of Corinth that afternoon, retracing their steps north and west toward the Tennessee line. The next morning, just north of the state line, their path crossed a wooden bridge over the twenty-yard-wide Hatchie River. Just after some leading units of Van Dorn's army crossed the bridge, they ran upon a fresh column of five thousand Federals coming down from Tennessee. The outnumbered Confederates, including Stirman's Sharpshooters and the 9th Texas Cavalry, began to backtrack toward the bridge, but the Federals captured nearly three hundred before they could get across. George Griscom of the 9th Texas Cavalry wrote that "all those who had crossed the river [were] forced to run a very narrow risk of their lives in getting back, hundreds swimming Hatchie river & many being taken prisoners."[10]

The tide turned once the Confederates were back on the high ground east of the bridge. Now the Federals came forward to cross the bridge and were mowed down by General Dabney Maury's artillery and infantry. One of the attackers wrote that the rebels "lined every available point on that [east] side of the river." The Federal line "was struggling against a storm of lead and iron, which swept the entire length and breadth of the bridge." Colonel Stirman's sharpshooters were well placed to turn back the Federal advance: "Our men would lie down and would not be seen until the enemy were within 75 yards of our line. We would allow them to approach until we could see the whites of their eyes, then without exposing ourselves in the least we would pour volley after volley into them, cutting them down like grass. No men on earth could stand such fire. Our men were all fine shots and nearly every shot must have taken effect. I never saw such slaughter in my life." Maury's crippled division, including Stirman's regi-

9. Cozzens, *Darkest Days,* 221–72; Carr, *In Fine Spirits,* 52; Rosecrans, "Battle of Corinth," 2:749; Foote, *Civil War,* 1:723–25.
10. Kerr, ed., *Fighting with Ross' Texas Cavalry,* 47; Cozzens, *Darkest Days,* 278–92.

ment and the 9th Texas Cavalry, held off four times their number for six hours, disabled nearly six hundred Federals, and allowed Van Dorn time to find a different route of retreat.[11]

Van Dorn accompanied his defeated army away from Corinth and the Hatchie River to Ripley and then westward to Holly Springs. Only when the Army of West Tennessee reached safety there did Captain Bates have time to write home to Paris. His first letter was to his mother. He began by telling her he had no time to recount the battle, then, as usual, he wrote page after page of detailed description. He was very proud of his company and regiment—they had fought as well as the best—but he also had a new-found respect for his enemies: "union men *will fight*," he wrote. Page after page, the words poured out. This was no small-scale engagement on the frozen plains of the Indian Territory, nor was it long-range skirmishing as at Corinth the preceding spring. This was bigger even than the battle at Elkhorn Tavern. Bates and his company had advanced as far as any Confederates into the streets of Corinth and had been in the hottest of the fight at Davis Bridge. This was worth some paper.

> In Camp near Holly Springs
> Miss Oct 12th 1862
> My Dear Ma;
> As you will be uneasy on my account, after hearing of the recent battle at Corinth, (I suppose you will get rumors of it before this reaches you) I avail myself of the first opportunity to drop you a line that you may know I have escaped unhurt.
> I have not time to give you a description of the battle—& such a description as I could give would not be very interesting anyway. Let it suffice then to say that on the 3d inst the combined forces of Genls Van Dorn & Price under the command of the former attacked the enemy at Corinth & drove them before us at every point—& when dark put an end to the fight for the day we were in sight of Corinth—on the night of the 3d we lay on our arms within 300 yds. of the breast works & siege guns of the enemy. About 4 oclk on the morning of the 4th heavy cannonading was commenced & kept up by both parties untill after sun up—the huge siege guns making the very earth & trees around us tremble.
> Little else was done except skirmishing untill 9 oclk when a

11. Letter in *Chicago Times,* reprinted in *New York Times,* October 17, 1862; Carr, *In Fine Spirits,* 53; Cozzens, *Darkest Days,* 278–92.

general advance was made by Price's Division of the army. We drove the enemy into their breast works at every point—& about 11 oclk we were ordered forward to attack these.

The timber had all been cut down in front of their breast works for 3 or 400 yds—this lay crossed in every direction—& presented such an obstacle to our advance that we were compeled to move slowly—but notwithstanding these obstacles we moved steadily amidst the most terrific volleys of musketry & thunderings of artillery that I have ever heard.[12] Bombs burst before, behind & over us. Grape shot canister—& buck shot rattled around us like a terrific hail storm—& besides these it seemed that the air was literally filled with Musket & rifle balls.[13] When the bugle sounded the charge our men gave one loud shout & started on the run—clambering over logs & creeping under brush—firing & loading as fast as possible but still moving on, & by the time our foremost men were within twenty steps of the breast works the last Yankee was leaving in hot haste. Before we had time to form our men again—a line of federal infantry emerged from the ravine's not a hundred yards in front of us—& presently another in their rear. We could see those whom we had just driven from the breast works running over the hills in wild confusion—their officers trying to rally them but with little effect. We knew that cut up as were our forces & at the moment disorganized we could not hold our present position without support. We looked anxiously for the assistance that *should* have been placed immediately in our rear—but looked in vain. We kept them at bay for half or three quarters of an hour—untill it seemed like madness to attempt to hold out longer against such fearful odds & we were therefore ordered to fall back. This we did in as good order as possible—but having no line on which to fall back we were thrown into some confusion. We had not got our men rallied & formed again when the retreat was ordered.

Why we did not have the necessary support I cannot imagine— especially as Van Dorn's men had scarcely fired a gun during the

12. Sam Griffith of Bates's company wrote that "we had to crawl through brush and cut timber for hundreds of yards, under a galling fire." Mamie Yeary, comp., *Reminiscences of the Boys in Gray, 1861–1865* (1912; reprint, Dayton, Ohio: Morningside, 1986), 287.

13. George Griscom of the 9th Texas Cavalry wrote that his regiment "took position & lie down in line & take the most terrific fire shaking the very earth & cutting the trees all around us." Kerr, ed., *Fighting with Ross' Texas Cavalry*, 45.

whole fight.[14] I never before heard of a whole army being thrown into a *single* line of battle—& having to charge & *hold* such works as the federal breast works—when it was known that the enemy should as a matter or course bring his reserve against us before we were ready to receive them. It is my opinion if we had had the proper support at the moment we got possession of their lines & guns that we would today be in Corinth the *victors* instead of being *here* the vanquished for there is no use denying the fact that we have been beaten—& badly beaten. We were not defeated however because the men did not fight—for men never fought more bravely or desperately—but for the *want of generalship*.

Our Brigade got into the edge of town & the one on our right [Brigadier General John C. Moore's brigade] went further—that on our left not so far. Genl Hebert Division was still to our left & also drove the enemy from almost all their works—Van Dorn's troops [i.e., Lovell's division]—were to the right of our (Maury's) Division —with no enemy but a few skirmishers to oppose them. It looked hard indeed that Price's men should be forced to yield all that they had fought so bravely & desperately to gain—when 8,000 men were laying & had been laying on their arms in idleness for near two days—who could have been brought to our support in fifteen minutes. But either fate or *Mr* Van Dorn so willed it & we were helpless.

When the order was given to fall back and I saw one after another of the enemy's works given up to them again—when I saw how many of our brave men had poured out their lifeblood to possess that which we were then abandoning—& that all this blood had been spilled in vain—and when I began to realize that the day was lost—& that this retreating from the enemy's works was but the terrible acknowledgement of our defeat—when I saw all this—such a sickening sensation came over me—such an utterly hopeless sinking of the heart—as I have never before felt & trust may never again. It seemed that every conceivable disaster & evil attending a defeat was suddenly spread out vividly before me & I *realized* it all instantly. It may seem strange, but I actually forgot for a moment where I was.

14. Bates refers to the failure of Major General Mansfield Lovell's division to move against the Federals and provide relief to the other two divisions of the army. In fact, Lovell was the target of curses throughout the army, even among his fellow officers. Cozzens, *Darkest Days,* 271–72, 306.

It was not long however before the Yankees brought me to my senses—& although two minutes before I would'nt have given a snap of my fingers for my life—those two minutes were quite sufficient to make me as willing to save my life as any others.

Our Col (Stirman) Maj [Robert M.] White of the 6th Texas & myself remained behind for a few moments—gave the yanks a parting salute with our six shooters over their siege guns—and as they gained the line of breast works not twenty yards to our left we turned our backs to the enemy to take care of No 1. I do not know how it is with others but as long as I *face* the enemy I can *stand* and fight them or *move forward* without feeling much if any fear—but as soon as I turn my *back* to them—& march in retreat, I have a strong inclination to run—especially when bullets & grape & bombs come crashing around us as they did at Corinth. While charging their breast works I did'nt think much about getting shot, but while leaving them I could'nt avoid looking back every step or two to see if the whole Yankee line was taking aim at my back in particular. But if they did they fortunately missed their mark & I hope will never have the same target to shoot at again—the same side I mean.

But I am making this letter much longer than I expected so will go back to the retreat. This was begun as soon as Price's forces were drawn off & reformed—Van Dorn covering the retreat. We moved some 8 or 10 miles that evening stoped about 4 oclk—& remained untill morning. The next morning we resumed the march & when the advance (Maury's) Division were within five miles of Hatchie [River] which is 20 miles from Corinth we received an order to move forward with all possible speed as the enemy were making an attempt to head us off here & burn the bridge across Hatchie river. (We have since learned that this force came down from the vicinity of Memphis—but our cavalry is utterly worthless & we consequently knew nothing of their coming untill they were in a few miles of the bridge)[15] We started on the "double quick" but so nearly exhausted were we by the two previous days fighting & marching that the enemy were on us before we had time to form after crossing the bridge. We were therefore ordered to recross the

15. The five thousand Federals had come down from Bolivar, Tennessee, to cut off Van Dorn's retreat from Corinth. Ibid., 280.

bridge—but as the bridge was narrow & we had to cross under a heavy fire we had a good many cut entirely off & captured.[16] Our Regt being on the extreme right & farthest from the bridge suffered most.[17]

After recrossing the bridge we took a position some distance back—the enemy followed—attacked us—but we kept them back for nearly two hours—untill nearly every round of ammunition was exhausted. Our Division went into the fight at the bridge with from 50 to 60 rounds to the man & came out with none at the expiration of two hours. You may judge from this as to how desperate the fighting was. From here we were ordered back half a mile to get a fresh supply of ammunition. By the time we were in our new position the ammunition had come—we were again supplied & ready for them. They however showed no disposition to renew the attack & as we were too much exhausted to do so both parties lay quietly in their positions—with an occasional artillery duel, untill Van Dorn's troops, who were fresh, came up from the rear.

We moved back several miles—took another road & continued the retreat. About an hour by sun [Brigadier] Genl [John] Villepiege Division—(a part of Van Dorn's force) attacked them—drove them back across the river & captured near 300 prisoners—as soon as night came he drew off—followed us & we were molested no more.[18]

I have seen no official report of our loss, but taking this Brigade as an average it will be in the neighborhood of 1,500 in killed, missing, & wounded. This Brigade however suffered much more than

16. One soldier in the 9th Texas Cavalry narrowly escaped death before he could recross the bridge. "A grape shot struck my [shot]gun and cut one barrel in two and knocked me back, I believe, thirty feet. It deadened my arms and hurt my head and breast so bad that I could not get upon my feet. I could not crawl and I just had to wiggle behind the horse that stood near by." His senses soon returned, however, and when they did, "I jumped up and got my piece of a gun and flew." Sparks, *War Between the States*, 275–76.

17. Bates means that Stirman's regiment suffered more than other regiments in Phifer's brigade. Indeed, the sharpshooters accounted for 71 of the brigade's 131 casualties at the bridge. *OR*, Vol. 17, Pt. 1, p. 383.

18. The Texan with the shattered shotgun pitched in with one of the Confederate batteries raking the bridge. When the battery withdrew, he later wrote, "I fell in with the advance of the enemy and asked for something to eat[.] I was told that they had nothing to eat but powder, and as I had partaken of a sufficiency of that article I stepped to one side and quickened speed and finally come upon some of our stragglers." Sparks, *War Between the States*, 276.

any other and the above estimate may be too great.[19] Our Regt suffered more than any other that I have heard of, and my company more than any other in the Regt in wounded but not so many in killed.[20] Our Regt went into the fight with 321 men—our entire loss 167 in three days fighting—a little more than half.[21] It is needless for me to say anything in praise of my "boys." Their thined ranks sufficiently attest the fact that union men *will fight*—whatever prejudiced parsons— self conceited *Generals* or such old grannies as their wives may say to the contrary. I have as brave boys (I will not say the bravest) as Texas affords & will again do honor to old Lamar if opportunity occurs.

I must not forget our old flag—though torn & tattered & faded. In the three days of fighting, although about 18 inches was torn off the end & lost—there is *fifteen* bullet holes through the flag & *three* through the staff—& besides this a large rent made by a piece of a bomb. *Three* color bearers were shot down & the fourth now carries it. If I should live through the war I would want no brighter monument than this faded flag to decorate my parlor walls—(Provided I ever have a parlor).

I went into the fight with 45 men and came out with 25. Loss as follows. Killed 3d Lieut P G Mosley. Wounded—Seargt J L Fowler left side of neck—Corpls S Dider, in left shoulder & chin—J M Birmingham[,] right temple—Privates L A Crow in right shoulder— J T Mowry in right side Sam Neathery in left hand—R Sikes in left ankle. The above are severely, but not dangerously wounded. J T Robinson wounded in abdomen I do not think will live. The wound of Wm Yates in the right side is also very severe—but the surgeons say will recover.[22]

The following received only flesh wounds & may be considered comparatively slight—viz J M Clampett in right foot—J M Caveness

---

19. In fact, the devastation had been much worse than Bates suspected. Van Dorn lost nearly 4,900 men at Corinth and Hatchie Bridge. Maury's division accounted for more than 2,500 of the total. Phifer's brigade of Maury's division lost 567 men killed, wounded, and missing, but John C. Moore's brigade of 1,900 men lost nearly 1,300—so Bates's belief that his brigade had suffered most is incorrect. *OR,* Vol. 17, Pt. 1, pp. 381–84.

20. Bates's regiment lost more men (167) in the two engagements than any other regiment in his brigade, but at least four other regiments in various brigades suffered more total casualties than Stirman's Sharpshooters. The 35th Mississippi Infantry in Moore's Brigade (Maury's Division) lost 489 men and was virtually destroyed. Ibid.

21. More than one-third of the men who assaulted the works at Corinth were killed, wounded, or missing by the end of the battle. Cozzens, *Darkest Days,* 305.

22. Robinson died of his wound, but Yates survived another year, then he too was killed.

in right thigh—J T Henderson in back & right knee—B F Means in left arm—Wm Simmons in left side of neck—J F Williams left hip— Jno Gabbart severe flesh wound in right arm—W J Wilson whom I had forgotten to name above severely wounded in right shoulder.[23]

The Missing are as follows Lieut S A Griffith—is a prisoner— has been heard from[24]—J F R Williams[,] M N Thomas—W B Carico—J P Norris—J B Johnstone—H H Miller & W Bourland are missing & supposed to be prisoners. The fate of those missing will be known in a few days as all prisoners taken are to be paroled in two days from time of capture. J L Fowler, R Sikes—S Dider— W J Wilson & Wm Yates we were forced to leave at the hospital at Corinth for the want of ambulances in which to haul them—the other wounded were all brought down with us. Those left will receive good attention as our surgeon was left with them. Tell Col Fowler he need not be uneasy about Jno his wound is not at all dangerous. You must make known to the parents & friends of those wounded—the character of their wounds if you can possibly do so—as I can not write to all. If Capt Dohoney will take the trouble he can see or send word to most of them—ask him to do so for me.

Oct 14th Well! as you will see I commenced to write this two days ago intending to send it off by J J Martin who was discharged from this Co[mpany] on that day.[25] But I had to go out on review before finishing the letter & Martin left before I came back. I gave him his discharge two days before his time was out—knowing you would be anxious to hear from us—& he promised faithfully— pledged *his honor* (all he had) that he would wait untill every body in the Co who wished to do so had time to write. Instead of doing this he sneaked away without waiting for a *single* letter—when too, in order to accommodate him I quit writing this letter to make out his papers. Well we don't miss such as him & shed but few tears when they leave. We have no use for men who value their own

23. All the men named in this paragraph survived their wounds at Corinth and Hatchie Bridge.

24. First Lieutenant Samuel A. Griffith, a Tennessee-born clerk in Lamar County before the war, was captured at Hatchie Bridge. His brief time as a prisoner apparently had no lasting effects on his health, for he would live to be one hundred years old, dying in 1938. Yeary, *Reminiscences of the Boys in Gray,* 287; Ron Brothers, comp., "Confederate Veterans Who Died or Are Buried in Lamar County, TX," Lamar County, Texas, World Wide Web page on the Internet (http://gen.1starnet.com/civilwar/csadead.htm).

25. Martin was a thirty-seven-year-old schoolteacher from Smith County. He was released from service under the terms of the conscription act because of his age.

worthless necks too much to risk them in battle—& shirk every duty possible. I sincerely hope he will serve his country better at home than he has in the army. The true reason he left was that he thought we would have another battle soon—& he did not have the courage to risk his carcass in it. As he will certainly hear what I have said about him he may & doubtless will, in revenge, use his tongue in slandering me *there* as he has others *here*. If he should, inform me of the fact—*I have a way to stop it.*

I have no late news of interest to write you—have seen no late papers. The Ft Donnelson prisoners & also those captured at Island 10 have reorganized and are at Holly Springs & near there.[26] I do not know how long we will be in this place. Think we will make a stand at Holly Springs if the enemy should move against us. I understand Van Dorn has been superseded in this department—by some man whose name I have forgotten [Major General John C. Pemberton]. I sincerely hope this may be true. Van Dorn *may* be a good general—but the people & the *soldiers* have lost confidence in him—& implicit confidence in a general is half the battle.

I have not time to write more & you have hardly time to read more I do'nt expect—unless it was more worth reading—will write you again as soon as we get a little more settled. If Will is at home or should come home before our horses are ordered to us (& it may be that we will not get them at all) tell him he must make some arrangements to send my horse & other things that I have sent for as I may not draw any more money soon. Tell Nannie she must try another letter to me I would like very much to have one from her.

My love to Aunt Tenn & the family. Direct your letters hereafter to Holly Springs Miss.
Your affectionate son
J.C. Bates

Genl Pemberton is the name of the [man] who superseded Van Dorn.

Three days later Bates wrote to Mootie. Characteristically, he acknowledged defeat at Corinth but looked past that to ultimate victory. Historians who argue that Confederates lacked the will to win the war have never

---

26. Five thousand Confederates captured at Fort Donelson earlier in 1862 had been exchanged, and they joined Van Dorn's army at Holly Springs. Cozzens, *Darkest Days,* 316–17.

read the letters of James C. Bates. He indicates that he was nearly captured at the bridge over the Hatchie River and also mentions that, for the first time, he was commanding a regiment, albeit temporarily because of injuries and absences among his superiors.

Camp Near Holly Springs
Oct 15th 1862
Miss Mootie Johnson
Esteemed friend,

Several discharged soldiers leave this morning for Tex—by whom I can send this direct to Paris & I avail myself of the opportunity to drop you a line or two, hastily.[27]

Since writing to you last I can assure you we have seen some stiring times—a good deal of hard marching & three days of the hardest fighting that it has been my fortune to engage in. From present indications I am inclined to think we will have an opportunity soon to regain what we have lost & retrieve our waning fortunes. If the enemy should move against us here, we will be able to meet them under more favorable circumstances than at Corinth & I have no fears as [to] the result. The fight will be a desperate one—*but we will win it*—the fact is we *must* win it—for the disaster resulting from a defeat here would be incalculable.

One year ago yesterday we were sworn to the Confederate service. I little thought then that one year would find me at this place. I did not even think that it would find me in the army. But here I am with the prospect of remaining a long while yet. The last year has passed I do not know how. It seems but a dream—a blank in my past life. Nothing I have seen or done seems real to me—unless indeed I except what fighting I have done & I can assure you there has been quite enough of reality in that. There was no *dreaming* there. One year ago tomorrow evening I spent an hour *very pleasantly*—(so my "notes" say) in the company of Miss Mary & yourself. Where will my guiding star lead me a year hence? I *hope* to the same pleasant spot.

The Fort Donnelson Divisions have been reorganized & are at Holly Springs—at least most of them are. I suppose your brother Tom was exchanged with the others—if so you have heard from him

27. The 9th Texas Cavalry and Bates's company released men over thirty-five and under eighteen years of age in mid-October, one year after they had signed up for Confederate service. These releases were specified in the conscription law of April 1862. Kerr, ed., *Fighting with Ross' Texas Cavalry*, 48.

long before this.[28] I would have taken a look for him before this—but have been confined closely in camp, as we are liable to be ordered to march at any moment—& I have come to be so important a personage of late that my presence with the Regt is indispensable—(Our Lieut Col & Maj were both wounded in the battle at Corinth—our Col is absent—& the command of the Regiment for the time devolves on me).

If we remain here for a few days I will make an effort to find Tom—for I would like very much to hear his experience. If I had not done some pretty fast running at the battle at Hatchie I would have had a chance myself to take a peep into a northern prison. They came so near getting me that they got 8 of my company. That was my first run & I hope it will be the last.

I have not time to give you any of the particulars of the fight. I sent Capt Dohoney a list of the casualties in the company knowing that you & every body else would be "quite miserable" untill you heard from me & learned that I am yet, as "Grand Da" would say, on the land amongst the living, &c. I send you this merely to convey the glad tidings.

My best wishes to Miss Mary, Mat & all "inqurin friends"—& accept the assurance of my continued esteem.

J.C. Bates

Oct 17th/62 I open this letter to say that all missing from my company are safe[.] they were captured in the fight at the bridge on Hatchie on Sunday—have been paroled & will be exchanged in a few days. They have about a hundred more prisoners than we have. Sam Griffith says they don't claim any great victory at Corinth & admit they were beaten at Hatchie. Sam Says that in attempting to cross the bridge after us our own batteries (we had two which enfiladed the bridge) literally mowed them down & they admit a loss of *450* killed there[.] our loss in killed & wounded was not more than 25. We lost however about 300 prisoners there. Bragg's victory has been confirmed—& if the enemy come against us here we will be able to record another—we are prepared for them.[29]

JCB

28. Mootie's brother, a soldier in the 7th Texas Infantry, had indeed been exchanged and was on his way home to Paris on furlough.

29. Braxton Bragg's invasion of Kentucky ended with the Battle of Perryville, southeast of Louisville, just three days after the fight at Hatchie Bridge. Although Perryville was a tac-

Very few of the letters Bates received from Texas survived his travels and the trip back to Paris for safekeeping. One that did survive was from his minister, C. J. Bradley of the Cumberland Presbyterian Church in Paris. Bradley's letter was primarily a response to news of the Battle of Corinth. Like Bates's mother, his pastor worried that Bates and the men of Lamar were perhaps too aggressive and too willing to risk their lives for the cause. The reader may rightly wonder whether Mrs. Bates had put Reverend Bradley up to his admonitions.

Paris Texas
Oct 26, 1862
Capt J.C. Bates
D[ea]r Jim,

I have enjoyed the peculiar pleasure of receiving and reading two letters from you since I have written. I should have answered promptly but there seemed so little prospect of getting a letter to you, that I awaited a more certain opportunity of conveyance. I read your letters with a great deal of pleasure, and hope you will not wait for answers.

We have just received some very mournful intelligence from your company, in the late Corinth battle, and fear that it is too true. I truly sympathize with you and those who, in that terrible battle, through God's mercy, were spared. Oh, how deeply it hurts me that so many of our good, brave men have been sacrificed in this cruel and unjust war. Some men will be held responsible for this fearful waste of precious life, and wreck of morals. We receive a very gratifying account of yourself and company, in that fight, as in all others. In it you have abundantly met the expectations previously raised.

In the midst of such dreadful havoc, it is not a little gratifying to learn that you have nobly dared to do your duty. I hope however that no morbid ambition moves any of you to such daring. Although I have great confidence in your prudence, I cannot say that I fully approve the *full* extent of your daring, if correctly informed, of leading your men up to, and over a breastwork which perfectly protected the enemy, largely outnumbering you, and shooting at you through port holes. If ordered, by a superior, to charge it, unless under most desperate circumstances, I cannot at all approve his wisdom or

tical draw, Bragg withdrew from the field and from Kentucky, so Bates's initial evaluation is off the mark.

prudence. Perhaps my judgement is the result of an earnest anxiety for your deliverance from the dangers to which you are so imminently exposed, and will therefore be pardoned for an opinion that may seem to be rash. This much I may say with impunity, that you will take all the care of yourself that may be consistent with your responsible position, committing yourself, your men and your cause to the protection of the Almighty avenger of the just. We still continue to pray for you all, and hope ere long to worship with you again around the same altar of religion.

We were long hoping you would return west of the Mississippi river, but have almost despaired of this, and fear you will be detained on that side. Our forces on this side seem to be doing little or nothing. One gentleman from Titus County told me that he and many others were sworn into the service on Feb'y last, and that they had been marching and countermarch[ing] ever since, and that he is now farther from home than he had been during the whole service. I believe there are many such. Several regiments, raised last winter & spring have just left Texas. This is certainly very inexcusable conduct in those who have the authority to put them to their work. I am certain that there are men enough mustered into the service west of the river, who, if they had a good leader, would be able to march right through Missouri. I refer you for the news and "Matters about Town," to Mr Bramlette and to friends writing to you.

We are all well.

Please write as often as you have the leisure to do, assured that your letters are read with peculiar interest,

My love and best wishes to all the dear friends, yours truly

C.J. Bradley

Captain Bates had performed well since his company's transfer to Stirman's regiment of sharpshooters. His company was well drilled, his men considered him a good leader, and he had weathered the thickest of the storm with them at Corinth and Hatchie Bridge. Still, he was doubtless pleased in late October when his company was sent back to the 9th Texas Cavalry, now brigaded with three other Texas units, and his men were remounted for service as cavalry. This was the type of war they had signed up to fight. The other three units in the new brigade (the 3rd Texas, 6th Texas, and John W. Whitfield's Texas Legion—later known as the 27th Texas Cavalry) received their horses in early November, but the 9th had to wait until early December before the men were reunited with their beloved mounts. In the meantime, the 9th Texas was temporarily detached from the brigade and sent with the rest of the army to Abbeville, about twenty miles south of Holly Springs.[30]

Bates's next letter to Mootie informs her of the new brigade assignment and brings her up to date on the regiment's activities. He reemphasizes his determination to fight on until victory is achieved, even as his friends are leaving the company and the Confederacy appears to be isolated in international affairs. He teases Mootie about the rumor that her sister Mary has finally married Eb Dohoney and hints broadly that he and Mootie may one day enjoy the same marital happiness. Bates has seen the horrors of war and is no longer a naive young man, but he can still flirt like a teenager when he writes to Mootie.

Abbeville Miss
Nov /62
Miss Mootie Johnson
Dear Friend

As Lieut Gibbons leaves tomorrow for home I take the opportunity of writing by him. You may consider this an answer to two or three letters which I have — *not* received of late but which are and have been for some time due.

I regret very much that Jno has to leave us.[31] He has been a good officer—a good friend to all & we will miss him much. Especially will I miss him as he is the last one of my mess who started with me from Paris. Now, I am the only officer who started originally with the company. When Jno leaves I will feel like the last friend is gone. Well! as they say in obituaries: "What is our loss will be his (and your) gain." Let me recommend Jno particularly to your care—as I believe you can do more to effect a cure than a Regt of M.D.s. I am very sure I would have more faith in a prescription from *the* (not *a*) Dr.s daughter than from the Dr himself.[32]

Within the last week or so our forces have all been withdrawn from Holly Springs & that place is now in the possession of the enemy. Here I think we will make a stand and give the enemy battle whether we will be able to repulse them is more than I can undertake to say just now. If we do not receive reinforcements from some

30. Kerr, ed., *Fighting with Ross' Texas Cavalry*, 48, 93.
31. John Gibbons, Bates's friend from prewar days, was released from the army owing to a long-term illness.
32. Bates is referring to Mootie, the daughter of a physician.

source I am *afraid* we will be forced to abandon this part of the State. It is generally understood that the enemy are moving against us, from Corinth, Jackson [Tennessee] & Grand Junction [Tennessee] and their force in the aggregate will not fall short of 75,000 men.[33] We have a strong position—& if the Yanks come against us here I predict we will fall back finally to Vicksburgh & as soon as there is sufficient water in the Miss[issippi River]—to allow gun boats to come down—the place will be attacked by land and water & one of the bloodiest of the many bloody battles of this revolution will be fought there.

I hope we may not be forced from here but fear we will. A battle may be fought here in a week or ten days—it may be a month or six weeks and there may be no general engagement here at all.

We have no news of interest from either V.A. or E. Tenn. Lord Lyons the British minister has arrived at Washington & will it is said visit Richmond in a week or so. A thousand rumors are afloat as to the probable course of England & France—but I predict that they will offer neither negotiation[,] ask for a cessation of hostilities[,] nor recognize the Confederate States before spring if then. Our hopes of mediation and intervention have so often proved groundless, and we have so often been deceived on that point that I place no reliance on any rumor that I hear. If they recognize us, all well and Good; if not, we should be prepared to fight on unassisted by any one.

My Co[mpany] is once more in the 9th Texas. Our old Brigade has been broken up and a new one formed of the 3d (Maberry's) 6th (Ross') 9th (Townes) & Whitfield's Texas Legion—under command at present of Whitfield.[34] We thus have a Brigade composed

33. After Van Dorn and Bragg turned back from Corinth and Perryville, General Grant went on the offensive in northern Mississippi. He gathered an army of forty thousand men at Grand Junction in southwestern Tennessee in October and began moving south toward central Mississippi in early November. Edwin Cole Bearss, *The Campaign for Vicksburg* (3 vols.; Dayton, Ohio: Morningside, 1985–86), 1:28–36; McPherson, *Battle Cry of Freedom,* 577.

34. Hinche P. Mabry had commanded the 3rd Texas Cavalry at Iuka, where he was captured. Lawrence Sullivan Ross commanded the 6th Texas Cavalry and later, the entire brigade. Nathan W. Townes was still the colonel of record for the 9th Texas Cavalry, but he had been absent from the regiment since the spring of 1862. John W. Whitfield, commander of Whitfield's Legion (later known as the 27th Texas Cavalry), had been seriously wounded at Iuka, but he was given command of the new Texas brigade. Biographical sketches of Mabry, Ross, and Whitfield are in Tyler et al., *New Handbook of Texas,* 4:359–60, 5:688–89, 6:945.

entirely of Texans which I think will fully sustain the character for bravery & daring that the Texas troops have every where obtained.

I was in the 7th Texas several weeks since, but did not see your brother as he had gone home a few days before. I learned your uncle was there but I did not see him. I congratulate you on the safe return of a brother from a long and irksome captivity.

Shall I also congratulate you that a sister has been *led captive* to a (to me) far distant state (matrimony). The brother returned only in time to see the sister made a prisoner for life. Let me hope that her captivity may be a more pleasant one than was Tom's. I regret that I was not present to say a last goodbye to the "poor captive" for I am afraid it will be a long time before I will be permitted to see her, *in the same state.*

You however, who I understand, *are living on the border* will see her sooner than I will as you are nearer the aforesaid "State." It may be that what I have written above is premature. If the "reliable gentleman" who wrote me that they were married, was mistaken I have gotten myself into a fix. For I have no "official information" that such is the fact (*They* in the second sentence above I suppose you will understand as referring to Miss Mary & Eb, or if you did'nt so understand it I will now tell you I referred to them.) I am in a "mighty" big hurry—as you see—therefore excuse my unintelligibility (get your spelling book). I have no doubt that if my informant was mistaken it was only as to the time. Tell Miss (or shall I say *Mrs*) Mary & E [that] I think they have treated me badly in not giving me a hint even of the fact that they intended to commit matrimony.

Well the Yankees and some pretty girl willing I will have a wedding of my own some of these days—and will eat my own cake, and have all the fun generally to myself not forgetting to kiss the bride often or oftener. Speaking of kissing, tell Mat [Mootie's younger sister] that I went home on furlough last night (in imagination) and that she was the only one amongst all my good friends in Paris who welcomed me with a kiss. I was sadly disappointed to find it "all a dream."

My compliments to Miss Mat & Mary.
Truly Your Friend
J.C. Bates

E. L. Dohoney, skeptical as always about the competence of Confederate leaders, nevertheless rejoined the army in late 1862 by raising a company of conscripts.[35] His letter in late November brings Bates up to date on military and political affairs in Texas and includes a dose of Dohonian gloom. He also informs Bates of some pending legal matters and spins out an extended play on words involving Bates and his suit in a "moot court," referring to the captain's suit of Miss Mootie Johnson. Dohoney's use of legal terminology to describe Bates's courtship of Mootie also implies that Dohoney himself is not yet married, contrary to the rumor in Bates's camp.

Paris Texas
Nov 20th 1862
Capt James C. Bates
Dear Friend,

Your letter giving the casualties in your Company was duly received. I was truly glad to learn it was no worse, & that all the wounded except one, would recover; also that the Missing had all returned, & would be exchanged.

The order for the [return of the regiment's] horses was so sudden that owing to the negligence of the friends of some of the boys, or want of friends no horses were sent to several of them. I regretted this exceedingly but am of opinion, that there are horses enough sent for all the men you have fit for service. I tried to get you another horse, but could find none you would have, at a price your Mother felt justified in giving considering all the hazard of getting it across the Miss[issippi River]. I got your saddle bags made by the very hardest the day after the horses started, & they had to be sent over the day following.

I expect to go into the Service again very soon. I have authority to muster my Company & will do so next Monday. We organized the 4th of November—myself Capt—P.A. Lin[,] 1st Lieut—T.H. Perkins 2 Lt, & Lin Buford 3rd Lieut. We are Company A of John- son' Regiment of Infantry for the Indian Department, & will move over the river very soon to Goodwater some 35 or 40 miles from here.

Nov 25th 1862

I mustered my men on yesterday, but we have no orders to march yet. Our General [Albert] (Pike) is under arrest & we are conse-

<hr>

35. Dohoney, *Average American*, 123.

quently in a quandary for the present.[36] Some of the commanders in Ark had him arrested from malicious motives. We will make every thing right as soon as he gets to Little Rock, & gets a trial. The Generals on this side the river are all the time in a sweat & quarreling with each other; & had better all be removed, & some body of some sense sent to command our troops. The *citizens of Lamar hold a meeting in a few days to send Wright (W.B.) to tell Jeff Davis to send Gen Maxey here at once, or Texas will be lost.*[37] As Wright is one of Davis' principal advisors, there is no doubt but that [he] will at once comply; & that with such [a] General as Maxey we will be perfectly safe against the two Armies of invasion that are to be led in on us very soon. Viz one by Jack Hamilton by way of the East & one by Martin Hart from Kansas.[38]

The aforesaid Hart some two months since escaped from Hunt County with 40 or 50 new conscripts & scoundrels from Hunt[,] Hopkins[,] Fannin [Counties] &c & got to the Federal Army — drawing rations as he went from the Confederate Commissaries in the Nation. And it is reported that he is proposing to lead an Army into northern Texas.

And by the way there is little to prevent their coming if they are a mind to do so. Hindman & his Army have been whipped over Boston Mountain, & are now eating the little corn raised on the Ark river.[39] And very soon this Army (if not driven) may be on Red River

36. After Elkhorn Tavern, General Pike engaged in several squabbles with fellow officers, some of whom considered him insane. General Thomas C. Hindman had Pike arrested at one point, and Pike's resignation from the army was accepted in early November 1862. Warner, *Generals in Gray,* 240; Neal and Kremm, *Lion of the South,* 126–27.

37. W. B. Wright was the Confederate congressman whom Bates had denounced in an earlier letter. Samuel Bell Maxey, thirty-seven years old, was a native of Kentucky, an 1846 graduate of the U.S. Military Academy, a veteran of the Mexican War, and a resident of Lamar County. He had organized the 9th Texas Infantry in 1861 and served as its colonel. By the fall of 1862, he was a brigadier general. Tyler et al., *New Handbook of Texas,* 4:580.

38. Andrew Jackson Hamilton, a forty-seven-year-old Alabama native, had opposed Texas's secession and was forced to flee the Lone Star State in 1862. President Lincoln appointed him military governor of Texas during the war, after which Hamilton worked hard to lead an army of occupation into the state. Martin D. Hart, a wealthy lawyer from Hunt County in northeast Texas, had openly and loudly opposed secession in 1860–61 and slipped through the lines to join the Federal army in 1862. Within two months of Dohoney's letter, Hart would be captured, tried, convicted of murder, and hanged by Confederate authorities in Arkansas. Ibid., 3:427, 491.

39. Major General Thomas C. Hindman's army of ten thousand men had not yet been

for subsistence. Hindman had already taken all the troops out of the Nation, & that country is now perfectly exposed. The Creek & Cherokee Nations are now in the hands of the Federals, & most of the Indians gone to them for protection, & the balance fleeing to Texas for something to eat; already many Indians have crossed Red River—Col [Chilly] Mcintosh's family is in the country near Paris.

Unless the defenses at Vicksburg can be held & your Army can hold its position at or above Jackson [Mississippi]—we are gone up the spout in Texas, as well as elsewhere; for so soon as the Mississippi is opened the programme is for [Major General John A.] Mcclernand to strike for Texas up the valley of Red River—while Jack Hamilton will lead Banks & his Army from Galveston to Austin & thence wherever their interest may lead them.[40] I am very apprehensive about the fate of your Army in Miss—it is too small—the great central purpose of the federal avalanche is against your column. That gallant Army must be cracked, in order that Vicksburg may fall & the Miss[issippi River] be opened. But thank God the Battle is not always to the strong, & I have high hopes that you will demoralize your vaunting & overwhelming foe.

If you cannot whip Grant or hold him in check, Vicksburg is gone, & the Miss is open, & the country is overrun & Texas too comes in for her share of the war, & the horrors of an invading foe. And before Spring will be heard the federal troops on Texas' fair prairies. And I awfully fear that such is our fate—that such is manifest destiny—God has brought this war to humble a wicked & corrupt people, & until the country & all its inhabitants are ruined I fear we will have no peace.

We have today *reliable news* that England & France have recognized us, & some believe it, but I do not believe a word of it. The common people of Europe doubtless desire it, but the governments will never act until we establish ourselves beyond question. The Northern Democracy may get the majority, but Lincoln & the

---

"whipped." Hindman would fight a Federal army to a tactical draw at Prairie Grove in northwest Arkansas on December 7, but his postbattle retreat and the desertion of much of his army made the engagement a strategic defeat. Neal and Kremm, *Lion of the South*, 145–54; Current, *Encyclopedia of the Confederacy*, 3:1246–47.

40. McClernand, a general by virtue of one of President Lincoln's unfortunate political appointments, would capture Arkansas Post in January 1863 and lead a corps in Grant's final drive on Vicksburg in the spring of 1863. McClernand never did lead an offensive up the Red River. Warner, *Generals in Blue*, 293.

Abolition Car have attained such a momentum that it will take many cogs to stop the wheels. We must sweat it out in our own fight. And when we have suffered until we are sufficiently humbled before God, we will get peace. Peace after [illegible word] with some sort of a government. It may be a democracy after *a sort*. It may be Anarchy—*it may be military despotism*. I tell you the future is gloomy. But as they say the darkest hour is just before day. I cannot but hope for peace, and occasionally think there are indications of it within the coming six months. But can only say "God's will be done."

Well supposing I have said enough of the Military & will turn briefly to the civil authorities. First we beat Todd for Judge most scandalously. Greg of Mt Pleasant was elected by about 4 votes to 1 in the district. Todd says the *Churches* the *Union men* & the *Conscripts* conspired against him, and formed a secret sworn society throughout the District. Josh Stevens is again the District Attorney. F Miles is our County Judge. Henry Moore County Court Clerk. Hamlin Williams Dis Clerk, beating Dick Barns by only a few votes. Norvill Beauchamp is Sherriff—Esq Farrer Treasurer, & A Rodgers Assessor & Collector. Spain & Esq Shearon magistrates.

But I find I have strayed far from burning matters. H[enry] Moore says that an act has been passed by the confederate Congress providing for paying for taking the census but the act is not to be found here; he has however ascertained that he can get it by applying to the Confederate Court at Tyler, which he intends doing for himself & you.[41] I should think that Bramlette could not attend to it for you without inconvenience as he is Chief Deputy Marshall himself, & will be much about the Court. *Jim Mosely* being the most *talented* & *best educated man* in the last Texas Legislature was unanimously recommended by that body to Pres Davis for the office of Confederate Marshall, & has used the opportunity [of] making Bramlette his chief deputy to do the business. *Oh wont the Cliques curse Jim as most ungrateful.*

As to your case with the *Conscript Father* Peterson[,] that is hung by the Hay-law till the end of the war. Howe ran off & Bramlette neglected getting out an attachment until his Jewelry &c was confiscated & sold. I saw the Receiver & he says that this law requires him to collect the money of all confiscated property & pay it into a general fund. Your claim in common with all others, must after being

41. Moore and Bates had been census marshals in 1860.

established in a Commissioners Court at Richmond,—come in for payment, or prorates. I don't believe any such tomfoolery, but have never seen the law & cannot tell. If such is the law it is inequitable & unjust. Every confiscated Estate ought to pay its own individual debts first, & then the balance go to the Government. He however made no claim on the house & lot, which still secures your debt. Bramlette will get a copy of the Confiscation law if he can.

As to your case in *Moot Court* I attended a sitting of *that Court on last night* purposely to ascertain how the case stands. But was charged by the Hon Judge with coming into Court not so much to look after your suit, as to get a *writ of Execution issued* in a case of my own in which it was alleged I had *already obtained Judgement.* However that might have been I find that as the Hay-law had hung up your Peterson case until the end of the war so has the Conscript law hung up this *Moot Case* until a like period elapses—nertheless the suit is still pending. And I also found out that although *final judgement* could not be taken in this case until the end of the war— yet the *statute of limitations* does not run against it during that time, & there is no *danger* whatever of your claim being *barred,* but it may be prosecuted as a new case at the end of that time & as *summarily* as you may see proper. Rest assured that the case will not be dismissed; but the Court seriously objects to your *prosecuting* by *attorney,* & prefers that *you appear in proper person* as soon as said court *is open for the trial of such causes.*

Contrary to your orders I produced not the whole of *your Document,* but extracts from it in said case, & among others read your interview with Miss Helen Lowell to see what effect it would have on the Court. The Court adjudged that the effect produced on you was attributable partly to the music, but mainly to the "contrabands." To counteract the effect of Miss Nelson's music the Court proceeded to perform the same pieces & even more, & *charged me* to inform you that not only ["]Lone rock by the sea's Lone Star[,]" Juniata &c were played, but also "Do they Miss Me at Home" *especially for you*; & that I might say here—well performed—which I proceeded to do by saying that a much better looking woman had performed the same music & more, much more admirably than Miss Helen or any body else could possibly do.

As to my own case, having never liked Moot Court much & prosecuted in a different branch of Judge Cupid's Court & before a different Judge—obtained a Special Term for the trial of my cause—

have obtained Judgement & am now thinking of taking out a *Writ of Execution soon*. The only fear is that before my *execution can be satisfied*—I may be taken from Cupid's bailiwic to *that of Mars,* on a writ of Conscript from Lord Perersoris Court, & not get the *full benefit* of my *Execution* for many days hence, & may be never, But *my Court* & myself have come to certain conclusions that obviate that old-fogey idea entirely, for instance we have concluded that a man is no man & a woman is no woman until they get married[,] that public opinion give them no rights—that a poor bachelor must go to the war & stay no matter what age he may be—he is considered of less note than even a conscript. And that if a gal gits her bachelor lover killed in the war she cannot mourn for him without being ridiculed by a busy public. In short my Court has decided that a woman had better marry a man if he starts to the wars the next day, for even if he gets killed it is better for her to be a "soldier's widow" than an old maid. And I have decided that a fellow had better do so 1st for fear he may never marry *at all*. And because he will have more to fight for viz a wife & will in fact *be* & *feel himself* a *real man*. And if he gets killed he will leave *his name* and a *remote possibility* at least of *his race* behind him in the world. These & *others* have been conclusive considerations with me, so you may listen & not be astonished at any story you hear from the trans-Miss District.[42]

As to the *Infantry Recruits* of which you advised me. I have resolved that they may like Dr Manklin's hounds *take care of themselves*. There may be no *war in their generation* in which they will be required *to bare arms*. Attest "sufficient unto *the day* is the evil thereof."[43]

My *regards* to all the boys. *Ladies send their love*. Write soon & often, Tell Gibbons [illegible] to write.

Yours truly

E L Dohoney

While Grant's Federal army moved slowly south from west Tennessee, Lieutenant General John C. Pemberton, Van Dorn's replacement as Confederate commander in Mississippi, held his army between Grenada and Abbeville in northern Mississippi, blocking the road to Vicksburg. During

42. In this letter Dohoney clearly implies that he is not yet married, but in his 1907 autobiography he wrote that he had been married on October 7, 1862. Why he dissembled is not clear. Dohoney, *Average American*, 172.

43. Dohoney is quoting from Matthew 6:34.

these relatively inactive weeks in late October and November, Bates had time to write another letter to his brother-in-law, summing up his understanding of the progress of the war. The captain puts the best light possible on Bragg's retreat from Kentucky, emphasizing the war materiel that the Confederates have hauled out of Kentucky. And now that President Lincoln has issued his preliminary Emancipation Proclamation, Bates again rails at the duplicity of the Yankees. They pretended to fight for the restoration of the Union, he fumes, when their real purpose is to undermine slavery.

Camp Rogers [near Abbeville] Miss
Nov 1862
Will,
    Yours of the 3d inst was received this morning—& [I] reply immediately as Capt [J. W.] Sims [quartermaster of the regiment] leaves this evening to meet our horses. He goes to forage them through [from Texas to Mississippi]. We have no news of interest. Both armies here are laying in perfect quiet. No signs of another engagement soon—have occasional skirmishes with scouts.
    Genl Bragg at last accounts had fallen back to Cumberland Gap. Although his move into Ky is in some respects a failure—it has been successful in others. He has captured & paroled near 20,000 prisoners—captured at least that many arms—large quantities of Q.M. Comissary & Ordnance Stores—1,500 or 2,000 wagons & teams & as much bacon & flour as Kirby Smith's immense trains could haul away. Genl Bragg reached the Gap with about *5,000* wagons—quite a valuable acquisition to our Q.M. Department. He also obtained clothing sufficient to fit the army out comfortably for the winter.[44] Besides this his recruits will more than cover our losses & Bragg therefore comes out of Ky with a larger force than he entered with.[45]
    If we had had any other commander here than Van Dorn I think

44. Generals Bragg and Kirby Smith had indeed captured many prisoners and tons of supplies, but Bragg's retreat back to east Tennessee after a tactical draw in Kentucky disappointed authorities in Richmond. Connelly, *Army of the Heartland*, 273–80; Foote, *Civil War*, 1:740, 743.
45. Bragg had expected Kentuckians to flood into Confederate ranks during his invasion, but, contrary to Bates's information, the general brought very few new recruits back to Tennessee—2,500 of the 30,000 he expected. Connelly, *Army of the Heartland*, 273–76; Foote, *Civil War*, 1:742.

we would now be with Bragg & Bragg's army in Ky. From all I can gather it was intended that Van Dorn show
[page(s) missing]
that they could not get them south if they wished to. If they submit to the [Emancipation] proclamation they lose only their slaves—if they attempt to run them off & are detected they lose all their property—& they will therefore choose the least of two evils.

If Lincoln had at first avowed the object of this war to be the abolition of slavery, hundreds of thousands of men at the north would have refused to fight for such a cause—but the union was then the plea & the leaders & politicians at the north will still tell the *people* that the union is what they are fighting for—that the abolition of slavery is necessary to the salvation of the union—that it is a military necessity—that every slave we have in our corn & cotton fields puts a soldier in the army—that as long as we can maintain our armies as at present—& keep all the whites who are able to bear arms in them—it will be impossible to subjugate us & restore the union. We hear but little said nowadays of peace—if we do not have it this winter it will be a long while before we do. I do'nt expect it for three or four years not untill the north & South are both exhausted.

I send you a few items of news. You see Rosencrants [Rosecrans] pays a compliment to the Texas troops in the battle at Corinth.[46] The boys who were captured at Corinth say it was a common expression with the Yankee's that the Texans fought more like devils than men. Be sure and write every opportunity. I will not let a chance pass.
Your Brother
J.C. Bates

We ca'nt get postage stamps here.
Boys are all well—but one case of sickness in the Regt.

The horses for the 9th Texas Cavalry finally returned to camp on December 8, fat and sleek from their long holiday in Texas. Private Sparks, one of

46. George Griscom, now assistant adjutant of the 9th Texas Cavalry, noted Rosecrans's message as well: "General Rosecrans (fedl) sends in a flag of truce to Van Dorn with his compliments assuring him that the wounded are all cared for & at Iuka the dead buried & a soldier's tribute paid to all who fought & died as bravely as some of Maury's Division did [at Corinth]—quite a new feature in the war for our enemy to compliment us." Kerr, ed., *Fighting with Ross' Texas Cavalry*, 48.

those who led the mounts from Texas, remembered that Monday as a special day indeed: "We carried clothing and letters for the boys, and that day
was spent in a general rejoicing."[47] The next day, Dohoney, in faraway
Paris, scribbled another letter to Bates. It includes Dohoney's usual acid
observations but also the long-awaited news that he and Mary Johnson
have been married. He apparently enclosed this letter with his earlier communication of November 20.

Paris Texas
Dec 9th 1862
Dear Friend
    I will now close my long (being written) letter. I delayed mailing
to add more & have delayed until now. But I know that you will excuse any seeming indifference: a *newly married man* is *not responsible for all he does.*
    Jno Gibbons, Fowler, Griffiths & Johnson arrived a few days
ago—all except Gibbons looking better than I ever saw them before.
Was glad to learn that the health of Company was good—hope it
may continue so. Fowler says he will take horses for the other boys
if their friends will get them. They shall have notice.
    Our Regiment is not yet organized. Everything is so disorganized
in the Nation &c Ark, that we may be all Spring get[ting] out. [The
29th Texas Cavalry under Colonel Charles] Demorse yet lies in Red
River. [The cavalry battalion of Robert S.] Gould is ordered to
[Monroe?]. Demorse was ordered to Ark but like Maxey wants to go
to the coast. Hindman & all his officers above Lieut (except Capt
Bovine) are drunk, & the Army in west Ark going on badly.
    Travis Henderson arrived last night, & reports [Theophilus]
Holmes & [Trans-Mississippi] Army ordered to your assistance. The
whole Army in Ark is doing no good, & should be taken at once to
reinforce Pemberton.[48]
    Capts Bill [torn spot] & Buck Moore are here *recruiting.* Also
[torn spot] Truman & Mayo Spears for clothing for their Compa-

47. Sparks, *War Between the States,* 59–60; Kerr, ed., *Fighting with Ross' Texas Cavalry,* 50.
48. Dohoney's sense of strategy was sound. President Jefferson Davis repeatedly suggested to General Theophilus Holmes that regiments west of the river should be transferred
to the east side to defend Vicksburg. Holmes resisted, Davis did not insist, and the result was
that no troop transfer was made to buttress Pemberton in Mississippi. See Steven E. Woodworth, " 'Dismembering the Confederacy': Jefferson Davis and the Trans-Mississippi West,"
Military History of the Southwest 20 (Spring 1990): 1–22.

nies. Ben Famey was beaten for Lt Col & Jim Wortham for Major in Benson's Regt. Capt Welch & Lieut Carroll of Cooper's Choctaw Regt were elected to fill said offices. R. Peterson (*the aforesaid*) late Enrolling Officer is trying to keep out of Service under cover of old Col Fowler's cattle. He sold your place to Marsells a little time ago but I informed the latter of its condition which broke up the trade. Nothing local except that Miss White married a Campbellite preacher the other night.

Bramlette has not yet arrived—is staying with his wagons. Your Ma has been puny but is now well. Also Sister & family. Drs [Dr. Johnson's] folks all well, except Moot has cold. Tom has been fine but returned to Marshall. My family are *all well*. Write soon.
Yours Truly
E L Dohoney

Soldiers from the Lone Star State were proud of their reputation as ferocious and deadly fighters—sure of aim, brave of heart, and sound of body. But Bates and the 9th Texas Cavalry had so far fought in only five engagements, the two most important of which—Elkhorn Tavern and Corinth—were defeats. Moreover, Round Mountains had been a questionable victory because the Texans had been surprised, driven back, and nearly beaten before the Indians melted into the darkness. Chustotalasah had been a tactical victory, to be sure, but Opothle Yahola's fugitives had remained in the field after the fight. Even Hatchie Bridge was no clear-cut victory. Although the Texans had helped to save Van Dorn's army by holding off four times their number, their side was retreating, not advancing. But if Bates and his comrades had any doubts about their reputation as warriors, the events of December 1862 would lay them to rest. The men of Lamar were about to ride off on the most successful cavalry raid of the entire war.

8 Holly Springs and Thompson's Station

In the autumn of 1862, the federal high command in Washington was focusing on control of the Mississippi River as the Union's highest priority in the western theater of the war. With the entire Mississippi in its power, the federal government would realize some important goals: the Confederacy would be split in two, thereby preventing the rebels from transferring men and supplies from one theater to another; northern commerce would have an outlet into the Gulf of Mexico for the first time since the war began; and Confederate morale would surely plummet with the loss of its last strong points on the river.

The U.S. Army and Navy had taken control of most of the river by the late spring of 1862. New Orleans and Baton Rouge surrendered at the southern end of the stream in April, and Memphis fell under Federal control in early June. Thus, United States gunboats ruled the whole waterway except for the stretch between Port Hudson, Louisiana (just north of Baton Rouge), and Vicksburg, Mississippi, about 120 miles in a straight line and 250 miles by water.

Federal river fleets from Memphis and New Orleans had tried to reduce Vicksburg with heavy bombardments the preceding summer, but the city was well situated on high bluffs, and the naval officers had finally given up on taking Vicksburg from its river side. General Ulysses S. Grant, once he could stop worrying about Braxton Bragg in Kentucky and Earl Van Dorn at Corinth, then determined to capture Vicksburg by marching an army of forty thousand from west Tennessee, south through the center of Mississippi, and approaching Vicksburg from the high, dry ground to the east.

The new Confederate commander in Mississippi, John C. Pemberton, countered by placing his army (essentially, the three divisions that had fought at Corinth plus about five thousand exchanged soldiers—maybe twenty-two thousand men) in northern Mississippi, across Grant's path to Vicksburg. Bates and the 9th Texas Cavalry were part of this blocking force, first at Holly Springs and then at Abbeville, as Pemberton fell slowly back before Grant's larger army. Pemberton assigned his cavalry to patrol the space between the two armies, slowing Grant's advance but making no real difference in the campaign. By early December, when Grant reached Oxford, Pemberton's army had backtracked to Grenada, about forty-five miles south on the Yalobusha River.[1]

This repeated backstepping was annoying to some Confederate horsemen, especially Lieutenant Colonel John S. Griffith, the commander of the Texas Cavalry Brigade.[2] Upset over the steady withdrawals before Grant's army, and looking for a more aggressive role for the cavalry of Pemberton's army, Griffith pored over maps of northern Mississippi. On December 6 he proposed a daring raid around the flank of Grant's army to strike the supply line sustaining the Federal invasion. If the scattered Confederate cavalry brigades in northern Mississippi were consolidated into a large striking force, Griffith wrote to General Pemberton, an aggressive leader might "penetrate to the rear of the enemy, capture Holly Springs, Memphis, and other points, and, perhaps, force him to retreat."[3]

The supply line Griffith proposed to cut ran from the Mississippi River at Columbus, Kentucky, down a railroad to Jackson, Tennessee, and from there down the Mississippi Central Railroad through the center of Mississippi via Holly Springs, Oxford, Grenada, and Jackson. Holly Springs was an especially tempting target because Grant had planted a huge supply depot at that point, about twenty miles south of the Tennessee border. The little town was overflowing with Federal army supplies—commissary stores, ordnance by the ton, quartermaster and medical supplies, hundreds of bales of cotton seized from local plantations, and an abundance of the luxuries that Union armies seemed to carry wherever they went.[4]

---

1. Bearss, *Campaign for Vicksburg,* 1:21–76.

2. Thirty-three years old, Griffith was a Maryland native who had moved to Texas with his family in 1839. He was a merchant and cotton farmer in Kaufman County east of Dallas when Texas seceded. He had raised a company for the 6th Texas Cavalry in 1861 and then served as that regiment's lieutenant colonel. Tyler et al., *New Handbook of Texas,* 3:339.

3. Griffith's proposal is reprinted in Rose, *Ross' Texas Brigade,* 131–32. Also see Bearss, *Campaign for Vicksburg,* 1:287–88.

4. For descriptions of Holly Springs in December 1862, see A. F. Brown, "Van Dorn's Operations in Northern Mississippi—Recollections of a Cavalryman," *Southern Historical Society Papers* 6 (July–December 1878): 154–61; J. G. Deupree, "The Capture of Holly Springs, Mississippi, Dec. 20, 1862," *Publications of the Mississippi Historical Society* 4 (1901):

At about the same time that Griffith proposed the raid on Grant's supply line, Grant was planning to strike behind Pemberton. On December 8 Grant instructed Major General William T. Sherman to take still another Federal army—more than thirty thousand men—down the Mississippi River from Memphis to attack Vicksburg from the bluffs a few miles northeast of the city. With Grant pushing south along the railroad in front of him and Sherman preparing to slip behind him by water, Pemberton would have to handle his army with great skill. If the Confederate commander focused all his resources on Grant for an extended period, Sherman might march into Vicksburg almost unopposed.[5]

General Pemberton read Griffith's proposal well before he learned of Sherman's strike downriver. On December 12 Pemberton approved the Texan's plan and assigned Earl Van Dorn to lead three brigades of 3,500 horsemen on the raid around Grant's left. Van Dorn, beaten at Elkhorn and Corinth, had been moping about his recent defeats and about public criticism of his professional and private life. This new assignment offered him a chance to redeem his name.[6]

Captain Bates had an inkling that some type of scout to the rear of Grant's army was in the works, but he presumed that his regiment, remounted only a few days earlier, would not be in on the fun. The men were still making the adjustment to mounted service; horses had to be shod, equipment repaired, and recruits added to the ranks. As unprepared as they were, though, Bates was certain that Texas horsemen would be infinitely more valuable to the army than the amateurish horsemen of Mississippi whom he saw around him.

Camp near Granada
Dec 11th 1862
My Dear Sister,

I wrote to you & Ma a few days ago, but as A. A. Walker leaves in the morning for Paris I write again. We have been mounted but are not quite in fighting trim, as many horses are unshod, rigging broken &c. We are at present detached from our Brigade & will

49–61; Rose, *Ross' Texas Brigade*, 85–90; Hartje, *Van Dorn*, 256, 261–64; William R. Brooksher and David K. Snider, "A Visit to Holly Springs," *Civil War Times Illustrated* 14 (June 1975): 4–9, 40–44.

5. McPherson, *Battle Cry of Freedom*, 577–78; Foote, *Civil War*, 1:62–64.

6. Hartje, *Van Dorn*, 248–49, 255; Rose, *Ross' Texas Brigade*, 84, 133; Bearss, *Campaign for Vicksburg*, 1:290–91.

probably remain so for some time as Genl Maury wishes our Regt to do the scouting for his Division.

The Genl drilled the officers of our Regt this morning & complimented us by saying that we had fought as bravely & scientifically as ever regular infantry had done & he knew that if the opportunity were presented we would [lose?] nothing of our good name by being mounted. Most of the cavalry here are Mississippians & worthless. The Texans have given them the name of "hominy beaters" from the fact that they bounce up & down while riding like a pestle. A great deal is expected of the Texas cavalry that have recently been mounted & I am a little afraid we ca'nt come up to the mark that had been made for us. Our Brigade has however made a good beginning having been successful in two fights & captured two pieces of artillery. Our Brigade starts in a day or so on a Scout to the rear of the federals to be gone probably a couple of weeks. Our Regt will probably remain in camp to recruit a while.

It is generally believed that our retreat has caused the federals to change their programme. It is certain that they are not now advancing on us here but where they will next turn up is hard to say—probably on the Miss river somewhere.[7] The latest news we have from V.a. is that Burnsides has recrossed the Potomack. If this is true either a winter campaign in V.a. is given up—or another route has been chosen which they think presents fewer obstacles to their "on to Richmond."[8] Or it may be that a desperate effort will be made to open up the Miss[issippi River] this winter & Lincoln may transfer a few hundred thousand of his minions to this department. A great many federal troops have passed down below Memphis & landed at different points on the Miss. Some of these have been operating in the vicinity recently—but they betook themselves to the river on our approach.

The probabilities of an engagement here at present are rather remote & growing less every day. There is no telling however what a day may bring about. Our troops are in fine health. I have two men in hospital besides five who have not yet recovered from their wounds.

7. Bates could not have known about Sherman's downriver expedition to Vicksburg. The Federals were just beginning to gather in Memphis for the trip.

8. Two days after Bates wrote these lines, Major General Ambrose Burnside's Federal army smashed itself against Robert E. Lee's almost impregnable position at Fredericksburg, Virginia, ending yet another attempt to reach Richmond overland from Washington.

Mr Walker is waiting & I must close. Perkins will probably get a transfer & be going home in a day or so & I will write by him.
Your brother
J.C. Bates

To the delight of Bates and his comrades in the 9th Texas Cavalry, General Van Dorn included them in the column of 3,500 horsemen assigned to break up Grant's supply line. In addition to Griffith's Texas brigade (roughly 1,500 men), the strike force consisted of Colonel William H. "Red" Jackson's brigade of Mississippi and Tennessee regiments (about 1,200 troopers) and Colonel Robert McCulloch's brigade of Missourians and Mississippians (about 800).[9]

Before dawn on December 16, the men of the 9th Texas left their scouting duties and joined the rest of the brigade gathering at Grenada. General Van Dorn then led the entire column to the east on their wide swing around the left of Grant's army. By December 18 they had turned north and were thirty miles east of Grant's headquarters at Oxford. So far, their raid had gone completely undetected by the Federal army. In fact, General Grant was more concerned with another cavalry raider that day— Nathan Bedford Forrest was raising hell behind Union lines again. With 2,500 horsemen, Forrest had darted from middle Tennessee on December 15 and headed west toward the Mobile & Ohio Railroad, part of Grant's lifeline to the rear. While Van Dorn's column trotted north, Grant, expecting the worst from Forrest, fired off numerous telegrams to his subordinates in west Tennessee, ordering them to close in and destroy the elusive Forrest. With Federal eyes turned elsewhere, Van Dorn moved closer and closer to his target at Holly Springs.[10]

Although General Grant had no idea that Van Dorn's horsemen were sweeping to his rear, the citizens of the village of Pontotoc were well aware that Van Dorn was drawing near. By the time his column reached them on the eighteenth, they had prepared food of every description for his hungry troopers. Almost every surviving firsthand account of the raid mentions Pontotoc as a highlight of the expedition. One of the raiders had fond memories of the women of Pontotoc even forty years later: "Here the good ladies and sweet maidens stood on the streets with baskets and dishes filled to overflowing with all manner of edibles, which we seized in our hands as

9. Rose, *Ross' Texas Brigade*, 84, 133.
10. Kerr, ed., *Fighting with Ross' Texas Cavalry*, 51; *OR*, Vol. 17, Pt. 2, pp. 426–29; Wills, *Battle from the Start*, 85–96; Bearss, *Campaign for Vicksburg*, 1:300.

we rapidly passed along." Snatching and gobbling the prepared food as they rode through the streets, Van Dorn's horsemen moved on through the town, no doubt thinking that raiding was much more fun than retreating.[11]

By the next afternoon the Confederate column had ridden as far north as Ripley, about thirty miles east of Holly Springs. That night they rode silently to the west, creeping to the outskirts of Holly Springs before stopping for a few hours' rest. Late that same afternoon, Grant had finally received word that a rebel cavalry force was moving rapidly toward the Mississippi Central Railroad, but still the Federals were not sure who was in command or where the Confederates would strike. General Grant sent out streams of telegraph messages, warning commanders of posts along the railroad to be on the lookout. Finding the slippery rebels was easier ordered than done, however, for General Grant admitted that "they traveled as fast as the scouts who brought the news" of their movements. Fortunately for Bates and his friends, the commander in Holly Springs bungled his orders, and the garrison of about 2,200 Federals in the little town was completely unprepared for visitors.[12]

At dawn on December 20, Van Dorn's troopers came crashing through the Federal camp on the eastern edge of town. One brigade rode directly through the tents and campfires, not pausing to fire shotguns or take prisoners. Its target was the Union camp around the courthouse in the center of town. Another brigade stayed behind to mop up the startled and confused Federals near the railroad depot. The third brigade raced around the eastern edge of Holly Springs to attack the Union cavalry camp at the fairgrounds north of town.[13]

In less than an hour, Van Dorn's horsemen had completely neutralized the Federal defense of Holly Springs, capturing between 1,500 and 2,000 Union soldiers and chasing most of the rest out of town to the north and west. Then, after the ragged Confederates had taken everything they thought they might need from Grant's supply depot, the destruction began. Entire railroad cars of commissary and quartermaster stores were torched; immense piles of boxes and sacks were doused with coal oil and

11. Deupree, "Capture of Holly Springs," 52; Rose, *Ross' Texas Brigade,* 84–85. Also see Kerr, ed., *Fighting with Ross' Texas Cavalry,* 51.

12. *OR,* Vol. 17, Pt. 1, p. 477; Pt. 2, pp. 439–40; John Y. Simon, ed., *The Papers of Ulysses S. Grant* (20 vols. to date; Carbondale: Southern Illinois University Press, 1967–), 7:74–101.

13. Deupree, "Capture of Holly Springs," 55–56; Rose, *Ross' Texas Brigade,* 86; Kerr, ed., *Fighting with Ross' Texas Cavalry,* 51; W. P. M'Minn, "Service with Van Dorn's Cavalry," *Confederate Veteran* 27 (October 1919): 385; Barron, *Lone Star Defenders,* 133–37.

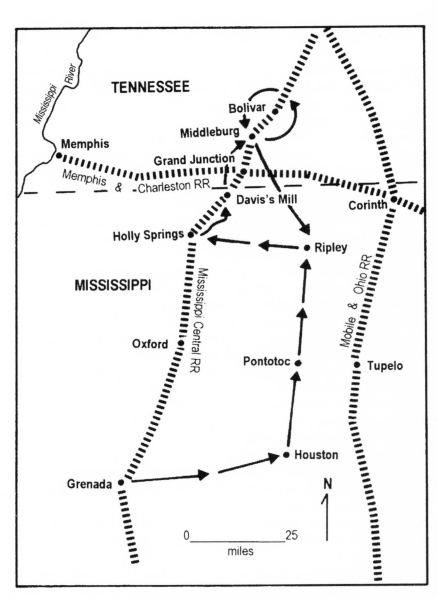

The Raid on Holly Springs

burned; a mountain of ordnance was stacked near the courthouse and blown up. For ten hours the demolition continued, until the Federal supply base was totally wrecked.[14]

A correspondent for the *New York Times* described Holly Springs shortly after Van Dorn's visit. The writer found "cars and once splendid depots, and the large secesh armory just handsomely fitted up as a hospital for our sick, in ashes; and approaching the square, windows shattered in houses and churches, and all the buildings on the east and most on the north side destroyed; the old Courthouse, in the centre, bored through windows and walls by shot and shell, the old clock in the tower still sublimely ticking on." Some of the Federal soldiers who had been "gobbled up" by the rebels were still trying to explain their lack of preparation: "Yes, gobbled up, but *we* aren't to blame. We didn't know anything about it till the town swarmed with secesh. Our officers neither didn't anticipate it. They rushed into our camps before we were up . . . the road was black with their cavalry."[15]

By 4 P.M., with the destruction complete and the prisoners paroled, Van Dorn led his horsemen out of Holly Springs to the north. They spent the next several days weaving back and forth across the Mississippi Central Railroad, tearing up the track, cutting telegraph lines, and spreading alarm throughout northern Mississippi and west Tennessee. The raiders bumped into two Federal commanders along the railroad who had heeded Grant's advice to prepare for an attack. Well fortified in boarded-up buildings and behind cotton bales, they held off the Confederates long enough to convince Van Dorn to ride on—he could not afford to stay too long in one place because Grant's cavalry was not far behind him now.[16]

On Christmas Eve, with Federal columns dogging his tracks, Van Dorn decided to reverse course, slip between his pursuers, and streak home to the safer confines of his starting point at Grenada. Federal cavalry chased after the southern horsemen for several days, occasionally making contact with the Confederate rear guard, but Van Dorn wiggled away each time. After twelve days and nearly five hundred miles on horseback, the weary riders from Texas, Mississippi, Missouri, and Tennessee trotted into the safety of their own lines at Grenada on the night of December 28. Van Dorn's raid was over.

---

14. Deupree, "Capture of Holly Springs," 56–58; Rose, *Ross' Texas Brigade,* 87–90; Brown, "Van Dorn's Operations," 159; Bearss, *Campaign for Vicksburg,* 1:312–15.

15. Eton to *Times,* December 27, 1862, in *New York Times,* January 21, 1863.

16. Secondary accounts of Grant's attempt to run down Van Dorn's raiders include Bearss, *Campaign for Vicksburg,* 1:319–47, and Bruce J. Dinges, "Running Down Rebels," *Civil War Times Illustrated* 19 (April 1980): 10–18.

Although they may not have fully realized at the time just what they had accomplished, in the words of historian Edwin Bearss, "For the first and only time during the Civil War, cavalry and cavalry alone was the decisive factor in a major campaign." Van Dorn's 3,500 raiders, along with Nathan Bedford Forrest's cavalry in Tennessee, had brought the entire Federal war machine in the western theater to a halt. With his supply line fractured and vulnerable, General Grant was forced to abandon his overland movement toward Vicksburg and backtrack all the way to Memphis. This allowed General Pemberton to move his forces south to meet and throw back William T. Sherman's river-borne assault on Vicksburg. Van Dorn and Forrest had delayed the fall of the river city at least six months and the fall of the Confederacy even longer.[17]

The day after he dragged into Grenada, Captain Bates wrote one of his famously long letters to Paris, describing his adventures during the preceding two weeks. This letter is especially significant because it is one of the few Confederate accounts written immediately after the raid on Holly Springs. Several other histories of the expedition appeared in print later, but most of them were composed long after the fact. Bates's letter, in addition to describing the main events of the expedition, also adds a few details not mentioned by other writers and, of course, expounds on the war as a whole.

Dec 29th 1862
My Dear Ma

We this morning returned from the Scout we were about starting on when I wrote you last—& I avail myself of the few leisure moments I have this evening to write you again.

As some accounts of our trip may not be without interest to you I will give you some of the particulars. At 2 oclk on the morning of the 16th our Regt left camp & at daylight arrived at Grenada where we found the remainder of our Brigade, together with another cavalry Brigade awaiting us.[18] At 8 a.m. the two Brigades, commanded by Genl Van Dorn, were on the march. Crossing the Yazoo [Yalobusha] river some distance above Grenada we proceeded to Houston & from Houston to Pontotock.[19] Amongst the crowds of ladies

17. Bearss, *Campaign for Vicksburg,* 1:345.
18. Bates apparently did not realize that the smaller units commanded by Colonels William H. Jackson and Robert McCulloch were separate brigades.
19. The Confederate column crossed the Yalobusha River, a tributary of the Yazoo, rather than the Yazoo itself.

who thronged the streets to welcome us I found *one* familiar face—
Mrs Row[?] at the latter place. She did not recognize me & I did not
make myself known. I never saw such wild demonstrations of joy as
were exhibited by the ladies of Pontotock & in fact of every little
town we passed through. At almost every door you might have seen
a crowd of soldiers receiving meat & bread milk &c.

From Pontotock we proceeded northward twenty five miles. An
hour or so after we left Pontotock a considerable force of abolition
cavalry which had been down the Mobile [& Ohio] RR on a plun-
dering expedition came in to town—but as soon as they learned that
we were in the vicinity they set fire to their plunder & made for Oxford on double quick.[20] They had a large train & wagons which they
had stolen from citizens & these were filled with every species of
property imaginable—harness, household furniture, table ware, negroes, &c. We proceeded without molesting these scoundrels, as our
designs on Holly Springs might have been frustrated if we had
stoped to thrash them.

When 30 miles from Holly Springs & east of the place we turned
our course west & on the evening of the 19th halted 15 miles from
the place, at 10 oclk P.M. we were again on the move. Six miles from
the place we again halted & lay down to earth an hour or two, [to]
sleep as best we could without fire. The night was intensely cold, the
ground was frozen hard & Sleep was therefore almost out of the
question although we had slept but 4 or 5 hours each night for a
week past. At 5 AM we were again in the Saddle—moving noise-
lessly along.

The first plan of attack was as follows—our Brig was to dismount
a short distance from town, form our lines & move in with [Colonel
William H.] Jackson's Cavalry [brigade] on our right & [Colonel
Robert] McCulloch's [cavalry brigade] on our left, get in musket
range if possible before daylight & make the attack just at break of
day—a company being sent above & below town to cut the rail road
& telegraph. The Surprise however was so complete that it was not
necessary for us to dismount & just at daylight we charged on the
Yankee encampment from two points. Some of them were not yet
out of bed[,] some were making fires—others getting breakfast &

20. Four days earlier Colonel T. Lyle Dickey had taken eight hundred cavalrymen from
Grant's army into eastern Mississippi to wreck as much of the Mobile & Ohio Railroad as
possible. Dickey was leading his men back to Oxford when he ran upon the rear guard of Van
Dorn's column. Bearss, *Campaign for Vicksburg*, 1:279, 285, 294–95.

still others just sitting down to eat. As soon as they heard our yells & the clatter of our horses' feet most of them took to their heels— a few officers tried to rally their men—but as soon as it was known that "The *Texas* cavalry are on us" they even fled. Every man for himself & we for the hindmost was now the order & such another "Skeedaddle" I have never before seen. The first Regt we came on was captured almost entire—a few making their escape through adjoining houses & yards. The next two Regts being on the opposite side of town heard the alarm & got formed. Two thirds or more of these threw down their arms without firing a gun. The only resistance made of consequence was by a Regt of Cavalry—which had just mounted & were about starting on a scout. Our Regt was sent to wait on these gentlemen—a few shots were fired by our men on horse but as the Yankees were in line on a hill above us in a vacant lot, & had full play at our whole colum and as we could only present a front the width of the street—we were fighting under great disadvantages—so we dismounted, turned our horses loose & in less time than it takes me to write this we were in line in the same lot with the Yankees & in five minutes we saw the backs of all who had not been brought down by our Rifles. This ended the fighting.

Our next business was to destroy all the government property which we could not carry away. Wagons—ambulances—harness Q.M. & Comissary Stores—Medical & hospital stores, Sutlers goods &cc to the amount of at least four or five millions of dollars were burned.[21] Our whole Division helped themselves to as much clothing as they could wear & carry. Almost every man fitted himself out in Yankee uniforms—boots, hats, caps, pants, shirts, overcoats &c & as far as uniforms went we were transformed into Yankee Cavalry. Besides the above we captured not less than 600 or 800 horses & mules—burned some 300 wagon loads of ammunition & after our men had picked out such arms as they preferred instead of their own we destroyed 6,000 or 7,000 stand of Enfield & Springfield Rifles— Six Shooters & Sharp's rifles went almost begging. The fact is I have never seen such destruction of property in so short a time. After the soldiers had taken as much as they could carry—the citizens helped themselves to whatever was wanted.

21. None of the raiders had time to list or even estimate the value of the supplies they captured and destroyed, so the exact measure of their destruction was unknown. General Van Dorn estimated a figure of $1.5 million; General Grant, only $400,000. *OR*, Vol. 17, Pt. 1, pp. 478 (Grant's estimate), 503 (Van Dorn's estimate).

I got all I wanted in the way of clothing—a hat, coat, shirts & a pr of cavalry boots—worth here fifty Dollars—a fine pr spurs & a horse—also a splendid silk sash—(military)—& sword—the last belonged to a Col[onel] of cavalry[.] fresh fruits—pickles, preserves, jams, oysters, Tobacco, cigars &c were strewn by our men all over town.

After the town and vicinity had been scoured and all stragglers brought in the business of paroling them began and was finished about night[.] 1,800 privates & 140 officers were paroled—making one entire Brigade & two Battalions.[22] But [I] have devoted more time to this part of our raid than I intended. The remainder however would possess but little interest to you. If Van Dorn had been satisfied with this, and loaded the wagons & ambulances with the most valuable arms & other property—& returned with it to Grenada it would have been one of the most brilliant feats of the war. He was, I suppose, intoxicated with this success & ambitious to do something else.[23]

[From] Holly Springs we proceeded up the [Mississippi Central] RRoad to within 3 miles of Lagrange [Tennessee] when Van Dorn dismounted our Brigade, and sent us on [to] capture a Regt of Yanks who were guarding a bridge [at Davis's Mill, Mississippi]. We found them strongly fortified & on the *opposite side* of the Hatchie river. After fighting them several hours we withdrew having lost 40 or 50 killed & wounded & accomplished *nothing*. Proceeding northward, Our Brigade was again dismounted to capture Middleburgh [Tennessee], but found the enemy posted in brick houses, the doors and windows barricaded & port holes cut in the walls. We had no artillery, and of course could do nothing without sacrificing 200 or 300 men, & again withdrew without accomplishing our purpose— this time however with but trifling loss & the only Yankees killed were by my company. They were thrown in advance as Skirmishers. At this latter place & at the Bridge referred to above we were pushed

22. Adjutant George L. Griscom of the 9th Texas Cavalry recorded in his diary that 2,200 men and 140 Federal officers were paroled. General Grant again estimated a lower figure, about 1,500. See Kerr, ed., *Fighting with Ross' Texas Cavalry*, 51; *OR*, Vol. 17, Pt. 1, p. 478.

23. Having fought—and lost—with Van Dorn on two previous occasions, Bates questioned the general's judgment. He did not know that Van Dorn's orders were to continue north and destroy as much as possible of the Mississippi Central and Memphis & Charleston Railroads.

forward without even knowing where or how the enemy was situated, or what their strength. This was however only in accordance with Van Dorn's acts generally. The object of proceeding as high up as Bolivar was to form a junction with Forrest, who was somewhere in that section—but all the couriers sent to him—four in all [—] failed to return—& we could not in consequence ascertain his exact whereabouts.

Turning our course homeward we reached Riply without molestation. Here the federal cavalry came up with us. Our Regt although in the rear the day previous, was detailed to cover our rear which we did successfully. It seems Van Dorn has more confidence in our Brigade than all the other cavalry—as we were invariably put in front, or rear when fighting was expected. And in fact we did all the fighting on the whole scout.

The boys have a good story on the Mississippi "Joels[?]."[24] They say Genl Grant sent a flag of truce into Grenada telling Genl [William W.] Loring he must remove the women and children & the *Miss Cavalry* out of danger as he was going to shell the place. The Yanks followed us but a short distance this side of Riply. We had some sharp skirmishing with them there with which they seemed satisfied.

As I have to muster & inspect the Regt today I will not have time to finish my letter but will do so tomorrow.

Jany 8th—As the gentleman by whom I intended sending my letter left before I had an opportunity of finishing I thought it best to await another opportunity of sending by hand—as there is probably no mail communication across the [Mississippi] River. A few days after our return from above we received orders to proceed to Vicksburgh. We reach[ed] Lexington 60 miles below here when the order was countermanded—& we were turned back. We now have orders to prepare three days rations preparatory, I suppose, to another scout. I am in utter ignorance of which direction we will take—but *guess* we will move round towards Helena.[25]

We have had cheering news from our armies everywhere for the past week or so. First was the great battle at Richmond, in which, according to their own account, the Yankees suffered a terrible defeat.

24. It is not clear exactly what Bates meant by the term "Joels," but the context suggests that it was not a complimentary term.

25. Helena was on the opposite bank of the Mississippi River in Arkansas.

Their official reports place their loss at 13,050 whilst ours did not exceed 800.[26] This is the first time since the battle of Bull Run that they have acknowledged total defeat. Following the battle of Fredericksburgh was our raid on Holly Springs. Then came the news of the repulse of the federals at Vicksburgh—the capture of Trenton & Lexington Tenn by Forrest—& a Brigade of feds at the former place.[27] Next was the second repulse at Vicksburgh—& now we hear that Bragg has completely routed Rosencrants.[28] I have some fears that this may prove untrue. The latest report that we have, is that Bragg had repulsed all but the left wing of Rosencrants's army capturing 4,000 prisoners & 30 pieces of cannon but the same report says that the federals are still in line of battle only three miles from Murfresboro, which would seem to indicate that no very decided victory had been won.

After the last repulse of the federals at Vicksburgh they reembarked all their troops & moved off up the river. Whether they have given over the capture of Vicksburgh for the present remains to be seen. I think they found our works stronger than they anticipated—& have drawn off for the purpose of making a feint on some other point in order to draw our forces off, or else they intend to make an effort to reach the place by some route which presents fewer obstacles.

It is hardly probable that they will give up the place without another effort. But come when or where they may we are prepared for them.

Aside from the good reports we have from our armies, we have encouraging news, both from the north & from Europe. Since the battle at Fredericksburgh many of the leading men of the north are in favor of an armistice of 3 or 6 months. The New York Herald—Tribune—& Cincinnatti Times—favor it. The New Jersey M.C.s

26. Bates wrote the word Richmond in error; he clearly meant Fredericksburg. Federal losses at Fredericksburg, fifty miles north of Richmond, were nearly 13,000; Confederate, about 5,300. Boatner, *Civil War Dictionary,* 313.

27. General Sherman's river-borne expedition to take Vicksburg had failed when his army was thrown back from the bluffs northeast of the city in late December. The reference to Forrest recalls his recent raid through west Tennessee, simultaneous with Van Dorn's raid.

28. From December 31 to January 2, Bragg and Rosecrans had fought to a bloody stalemate near Murfreesboro, southeast of Nashville, in the Battle of Stones River. Again Bragg had retreated after the engagement, so the news that the Federals had been routed is wrong.

[members of Congress] proposed an armistice: that the constitution be so remodeled as to satisfy every Southern man that our rights shall be forever secured. Valandingham of Ohio & Several members from Ky favor the same.[29] France too it is said proposes an armistice for 6 months during which time the Southern ports shall be left open.[30] These reports are all very fine & pleasant to listen to, but we have heard so much of this kind of stuff of late that no reliance *should* be placed on such rumors, but at the same time we can't help thinking they *may* be true. Taking every thing into consideration—our success at home—the quarrels & jealousies of the Yankees amongst themselves—&cc I think our cause is brightening up—& that we have no cause for despondency at present. Our independence may be a long way off—but I am as confident that we will *finally* succeed, as that tomorrow's sun will rise.

Jany 15th The fates seem determined that this letter shall not reach you, or rather that I shall not finish it soon. We were ordered to strike tents & move while I was writing, & I had to leave it unfinished. We are now encamped 15 miles north of Grenada.[31] Will probably start in the morning on another scout, & be out 15 or 20 days. There is no enemy of consequence now this side of Holly Springs, probably none there now. What the intention of their retrograde move is it is hard to divine. I cannot believe that it is their intention to abandon this country or to give up the capture of Vicksburgh. The federal fleet have left that place & gone up the river, to return again soon I predict, with an overwhelming force.

Since the first of this letter was written we have had reliable intelligence from Bragg—& he certainly defeated Rosencrantz capturing 4,000 prisoners—26 pieces brass & steel cannon[,] 5000 stand of small [arms] & 200 wagons & teams. Rosencrantz was subsequently reinforced & Bragg retreated back towards Knoxville. We

29. These rumors of northern defeatism are exaggerated. Clement L. Vallandigham, an Ohio Democrat, was the unofficial head of the northern peace movement. Sifakis, *Who Was Who*, 670.

30. The French emperor Napoleon III had indeed suggested a six-month truce and the opening of southern ports, but the British government rejected the idea, and nothing came of it. D. P. Crook, *Diplomacy During the American Civil War* (New York: John Wiley and Sons, 1975), 100–101.

31. As Grant pulled his army back to Memphis in the aftermath of the raid on Holly Springs, the Confederates moved north into the spaces abandoned by the Federals.

have a *rumor* today that he was met by reinforcements from V.a. & again gave Rosencrantz battle & again defeated him.[32] This last report is very probable, but needs confirmation. There has also been a considerable fight in N Carolina in which we were again victorious.[33]

But I expect you are tired of reading "war news" & may be tired of this long letter. You asked me several times to send you my Daguerreotype. I will do so as soon as I have an opportunity of having one taken. I received a letter from Sister, also one from Capt D[ohoney], written the 5th of *July*—just 6 months on the way. If you can send letters *direct* by hand do so, but if not, send by mail. We sometimes receive letters by mail only ten or fifteen days on the way—at other times they are several months.

The health of my Co is very good at present. The paroled men have not been exchanged as yet but I suppose will be soon. We had an election this morning for two Lieuts, J.W. Smith & Jno Fowler were elected.[34] Both are good soldiers and will make good officers. You need not look for me home this winter. I have no idea that furloughs will be granted except in cases of sickness. Many are of opinion that our Brigade will be exchanged for an Infantry Brig west of the Miss, but I do not think so. If this exchange *should* be effected we will be sent to Kansas, it is understood & I believe I would prefer remaining here.

I will close this, promising to write again soon, I have not time to write to all, or in fact, any of my friends at home at present. Tell them I will always be glad to hear from any & all of them. Enquire of Mr Hatcher if he has received forty five ($45) Dollars I sent him by a Dr West living, I believe, in Grayson County. I also sent you two hundred (200$) Dollars by Lieut Gibbons which I suppose you have received.

My love to Aunt Tenn & best wishes to "our neighbors" & Capt Wright if he still lives.[35]

Say to Col Townes we are all impatient to see him with us again.

J.C. Bates

32. This is another unfounded rumor.

33. No large-scale military actions occurred in North Carolina in late 1862 or early 1863.

34. J. W. Smith was a nineteen-year-old Tennessee native and carpenter from Lamar County. J. L. Fowler, a native Texan, was a college student who had lived with his parents in Lamar County before the war.

35. The neighbors were doubtless the Johnsons, including Mootie.

The Texas Cavalry Brigade remained in northern Mississippi through January, scouting in all directions from Grenada. The winter was unusually bitter for Mississippi, and Bates and his comrades had to suffer through every form of frozen precipitation—snow, sleet, and hail—as well as frequent rains. Writing under weepy skies along the Mobile & Ohio Railroad in early February, Adjutant Griscom complained that "this black land is worse than black prairie for mud & we are Camped in it."[36]

While the cavalry slogged through a wet January and early February, they were reorganized into two divisions of a single corps. The new corps commander, Earl Van Dorn, had finally found his element—as a cavalry leader. His success on the Holly Springs raid seemed to promise a great future in that arm of the service. The Texans who had fought in the Indian Territory, Elkhorn Tavern, Iuka, Corinth, and Holly Springs composed the second brigade of his second division. This brigade, 1,500 strong, consisted of the 3rd, 6th, 9th, and 27th Texas Cavalry Regiments. In early February the entire corps of 7,500 horsemen was ordered to middle Tennessee, there to join with Nathan Bedford Forrest in protecting Bragg's western flank and harassing the Federal army that had turned Bragg out of Kentucky. This Union army was now commanded by an old adversary of the Texans, William S. Rosecrans.[37]

Captain Bates fired off a few short letters to Paris in early February, just as his brigade was beginning the march to Tennessee. He was not certain about their exact destination or precise orders, but he did understand that they were leaving Mississippi. His predictions about Federal operations around Vicksburg—especially his idea that Union armies would get below the city and cross the Mississippi River to the high ground on the east bank—were exactly on the mark.

[Feb. 7?, 1863]
[From Bates to his mother]
[page(s) missing; first line of page torn]
course of a day or so will proceed to East Tenn, where it is probable we will join Forrest & Morgan. If we should do this you may expect to hear from us soon in Middle Tenn or Ky.

I have no news of special interest to write you. Northern Miss is now clear of the enemy except at Corinth & Grand Junction. The

36. Kerr, ed., *Fighting with Ross' Texas Cavalry,* 56.
37. *OR,* Vol. 24, Pt. 3, p. 614; Vol. 17, Pt. 2, pp. 832–33, 844; Thomas Lawrence Connelly, *Autumn of Glory: The Army of Tennessee, 1862–1865* (Baton Rouge: Louisiana State University Press, 1971), 116; Foote, *Civil War,* 2:176.

federal forces have all been withdrawn from here to Memphis, with a view I suppose, of taking them to Vicksburgh. If they succeed in making a channel sufficiently large to admit their transports, which I have no doubt they will do, these will be run down the canal & the Gunboats run past the batteries on the river. I think they will then land their forces on this side some ten or fifteen miles below Vicksburgh & attack the place simultaneously by land and water. This is only what I think about it, but mind if my predictions are not verified. They know quite as well as we do that Vicksburgh is weaker on the South than any where else & will be sure to take advantage of it.

One of my Company, Robt Sykes, who was wounded at Corinth, came in yesterday. He was taken to the Iuka hospital, and remained there some time when he [first line of next page frayed] me very much & wrote me a letter, but I have never received it. Another man in the Regt who was also wounded at Corinth was at his [Bates's uncle's] house for several weeks. He says uncle F[letcher] told him *he raised me* & that *I owed all that I was to him.* We will probably pass through Tuscumbria [Alabama, on the way to Tennessee] & as Sikes tells me he [the uncle] has several fine horses, I will most likely owe him for one of them if there is any chance.

Sikes' wound is not well yet & will probably not be for a long while. His ankle is stiff & will always be so. I intend trying to have him discharged & if there is a probability of succeeding, he may go with us to Athens & from there home. Van Dorn will furlough no one now no matter how badly they may be wounded, so you see there is but a slim prospect of well men getting home. You need not *expect* me although I intend to try for a furlough if I should live to get back from the next scout. You need not, however, be uneasy if you should not hear from me for several months as it is generally believed we will be gone untill April or May.

I have been offered the position of Quarter Master in our Regt & think I will accept it for a month or so at least, as I will be better able to take care of myself during the winter. If I go in to that department it will only be for [first line of next page frayed] Walker. The reason I said nothing in that letter was, that I had written to you but a short time before, about the clothing. But I will say again, that I received it all, & as I wrote before was prouder of it than I would have been of the finest uniform. In fact the grey cloth & pants make as nice a uniform as I wish to wear. The clothing all fit well, the pants being large enough. I also received the visor you sent by Jno Fowler,

& don't see how I could well do without it in these cold windy snowy days. Every body allowed I must have the best mother in Texas, & I was of that opinion myself.

I have not time to write more just now. Will write again before we leave here if possible. If Sikes gets a discharge I will send two or three hundred dollars home by him. I want you to use all my money you wish, I send it home more for your benefit than for my own. My love to all the family & to Aunt Tenn & family.
Affectionately Your Son
James C. Bates

[torn spot] Miss
Feb 8th / 63
Dear Sister,

I wrote to Ma a few days ago, but having another opportunity I write again, as so few letters reach you. I have only time to say I am well and the co[mpany] are generally well. We leave this morning for East Tenn—or at least I think that is our destination. Will write again the first opportunity.
Your Son [*sic*]
J.C. Bates

I take the Q. M. Department this morning for a short time.

Miss
In Camp Monroe Co[38]
Feb 9th 1863
My Dear Ma,

If all the letters I wrote you are received you ca'nt complain of negligence on my part,—I wrote you yesterday, the day before another, & still another a few days previous to that, So amongst all you will certainly receive some of them. We are now in Monroe Co on our way to Tenn. Will go by way of Florence Ala,—think I will call & see uncle Fletcher if I have time. I send you by the bearer of this, Mr John Wheat, of Lamar Co, one hundred dollars[.] Would send more, but am a little afraid he might fall into the hands of the feds, & the money be lost.

This leaves the co all well, Sikes did not get a discharge & has gone to the hospital—or rather started to the hospital but will go

---

38. Monroe County is in northeastern Mississippi, southeast of Tupelo.

into the country [i.e., to a private home for recuperation] the first opportunity. Billy Wilson (of Paris) went with him. I will write every opportunity.
Your affectionate son
J.C. Bates

Van Dorn's new cavalry corps left northeast Mississippi on February 8 and cut across the corner of northwest Alabama. Their route crossed innumerable streams and rivers, many with no bridges, and they consequently made slow progress. At Florence, Alabama, the 9th Texas Cavalry waited two days before it could ferry all its men and horses across the half-mile-wide Tennessee River. Slowing the pace further were freezing rains and muddy roads. Finally, on March 2 Van Dorn's column reached its destination, a railroad stop on the Central Alabama Railroad about thirty miles south of Nashville. Here Van Dorn shielded the left of Braxton Bragg's army, strung out over fifty or sixty miles across middle Tennessee.[39]

The Texans marveled at the richness of the Tennessee countryside. For men who had eaten acorns in the Nations and scrambled for food and forage in Mississippi, middle Tennessee was a paradise. As usual, Private Sparks was more expressive than most: "There was no scarcity of provision or forage, corn or meat, not the stinted little pile of tythe corn, and the few thin bacon sides that we had been accustomed to see, but corn is plenty—great houses of corn, corn for sale for Confederate money, corn to feed to cavalry horses, corn for the mules, great houses of corn, and bacon shoulders, sides and hams, yes, enough of hams to get a full ration of ham for all—even the privates. Glorious country!"[40]

Almost as soon as they unsaddled, the recently arrived horsemen got their first taste of war in Tennessee. On March 4 General Rosecrans sent two columns of Federal infantry in their direction. One, under Major General Philip Sheridan, set out from Murfreesboro, about twenty-five miles east of Van Dorn's headquarters. The other, led by Colonel John Coburn, left Franklin, ten miles north of Van Dorn. The two Federal forces intended to converge at Spring Hill, a few miles south of Van Dorn, and from there push farther south to Columbia.[41]

Alerted by his scouts, Van Dorn was waiting for Coburn's column the

39. The route of the march to Tennessee may be traced in Griscom's diary; see Kerr, ed., *Fighting with Ross' Texas Cavalry*, 57–59. Also see Connelly, *Autumn of Glory*, 116, and Foote, *Civil War*, 2:175–77.
40. Sparks, *War Between the States*, 74.
41. Foote, *Civil War*, 2:176–77.

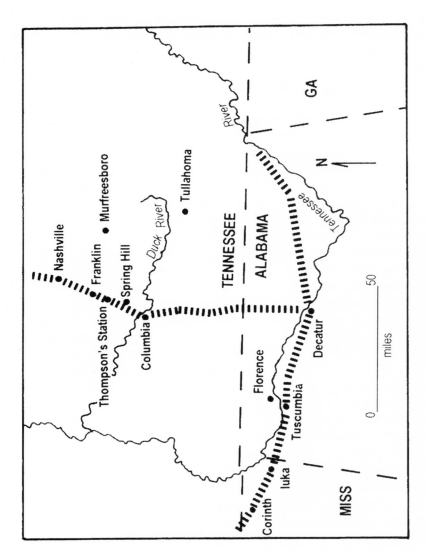

Middle Tennessee

next day at Thompson's Station, a few miles north of Coburn's intended point of convergence with Sheridan. Coburn's 2,800 Federals were outnumbered twice over by Van Dorn's cavalry, now reinforced by Nathan Bedford Forrest himself. Van Dorn threw his dismounted horsemen, including the 9th Texas Cavalry, at the front of Coburn's column while Forrest tore in from Coburn's left and rear. Although this was a much smaller engagement than Corinth, it must have reminded some of the Texans of the carnage of the preceding October because they made repeated charges on foot across open ground against the Federal battle line. Forrest's troopers soon dismantled the left and rear of Coburn's line and drove the Federals from the field just as Bates and his comrades made another charge on foot from the front. Van Dorn captured nearly half of Coburn's whole force, including the colonel himself, and chased the remainder off to the north. His blood up, Van Dorn then turned to deal with Sheridan's column, but that element of the Federal advance had already retreated.[42]

Bates began two letters to Paris the day after arriving at the new camp in Tennessee. Before he could finish either, his regiment had fought at Thompson's Station, so he added a postscript to his mother and several more pages to his letter to Mootie. In addition to describing the fight, he expresses his happiness at leaving Mississippi and returning to the state of his birth.

I send this to Tom Johnson to be forwarded to you. If you have mail communication with Port Hudson send via that place.

In Camp Near Franklin [Tennessee]
March 3*d* 1863
My Dear Ma:
Now, for the first time I write you from our old native state Tenn. I sincerely hope I may never write another letter from *Miss,* but that each succeeding letter may be dated a little further north until we get to the Ohio River. We arrived at this camp on yesterday evening, will probably remain here for a day or two, Franklin is eighteen miles south of Nashville & we are seven or eight miles south of F. The federals at F. are supposed to number 5 or 6,000. Our force is about ——— [six thousand] large enough to thrash out all the feds at

42. Battle reports are in *OR,* Vol. 23, Pt. 1, pp. 85–91 (Coburn), 116–19 (Van Dorn), 122–23 (William H. Jackson, Bates's division commander), 123–24 (J. W. Whitfield, Bates's brigade commander), and 124–25 (Dudley Jones, Bates's regimental commander). Also see Barron, *Lone Star Defenders,* 147–49.

Franklin; provided they don't get reinforcements. Our pickets have been skirmishing for several days, & a general engagement of all the forces here may be looked for soon. Our forces here compose the extreme left wing of Bragg's army, his right rests near Shelbyville & Tulahoma on the Nashville & Chatanooga Rail Road—some thirty or forty miles from here.

I have no news of interest to send you. I send you some news copied from northern papers of the 20th of last month. I had a few of later date but they have been misplaced. The Cincinnatti Enquirer, Chicago Times, New York Tribune, (Horace Greeley's paper) & many others come out boldly & say the North *must have* peace on any terms that it is folly & madness to continue this war longer, that the South is today stronger than ever before, & the North weaker.

I did not see uncle Fletcher as I expected as we came up. He lived some 25 miles off our route—it was raining, the roads were in bad condition & I concluded it would'nt pay. I however saw the brotherinlaw who told me they were all well—& that uncle F was making a fortune speculating in leather. I received a note a few days since from Isaac Wolsey & MB Wood saying they would call to see me the first opportunity.[43] They are in the Eighth Tenn Cavalry Regt. Woolsey is Capt & Wood 1st Lieut of the Co.

Don't fail to write every opportunity. I have not heard from home for several months[.] with the exception of Newt Stephenson, Jo Price & Jim Perkins who were left sick on the road, the Co. are all well.[44]

I will close as I wish to write several other letters & have but one hour or two in which to write.

Your Affectionate Son,

J.C. Bates

Since writing the above we have had a fight with the Yanks routing them completely. They sent out five Regts to take in our cavalry & were themselves taken in, the whole five Regts being captured by us. Our loss in killed or wounded 169—federal about 300[45]—They

43. Wolsey and Wood, friends of the Bates family, were from Overton County, Tennessee, birthplace of Bates and his mother.

44. Stephenson and Price have been identified earlier. Perkins could not be identified from the company's military records.

45. In skirmishing on March 4 and the fight at Thompson's Station on March 5, Colonel

afterwards sent down a very heavy force & we were compeled to cross to the S[outh] side of Duck river.[46] A general engagement is expected here soon. Jno Smith [in] my Co was killed in the last fight.[47] Nobler boy or better soldier never lived. Henry Rogers & Sam Bridges slightly wounded—remainder all well.[48]

Tenn
In camp near Franklin
March 3d 1863
Miss Mootie Johnson,
Dear Friend,

As I promised to write "every opportunity" I must fulfil my promise, tho' several letters are still due from you. We are once more in the Volunteer State & I hope we will not make another retrograde movement at least during the war unless Miss is first shoveled into the ocean. After reflecting on the subject for nearly two years I think I have at last found the true cause of this war. You remember about two years ago the Confederate States sent Commissioners to treat with old Abe. Well—everything went on finely until Abe noticed that Miss was left out when our Commissioners called over the states they desired Whereupon old Abe swore he'd have nothing to do with Miss—but finally agreed to compromise by taking half of her. After deliberating on the matter our Commissioners concluded that a few years civil war would be no worse for the C.S. than to take *half* of Miss. So that ended their negotiations & commenced the war. But without jesting the people of Miss have less kindness than patri-

---

Coburn lost about 400 men killed or wounded and 1,150 captured. Confederates losses were much lighter, about 360 total. The 9th Texas Cavalry lost 3 killed, 3 mortally wounded, and 15 wounded. *OR*, Vol. 23, Pt. 1, pp. 75, 91, 117, 119; Kerr, ed., *Fighting with Ross' Texas Cavalry*, 60.

46. About twenty thousand Federals chased Van Dorn's troopers out of Spring Hill and nearly trapped the Confederates on the banks of Duck River on March 10, but the slippery Confederate horsemen eluded their enemy and survived the scare. Connelly, *Autumn of Glory*, 119.

47. John Smith, a twenty-year-old native of Tennessee, was a Lamar County carpenter before the war.

48. Henry Rogers, a twenty-three-year-old private, survived his wound and served until he was wounded again and captured near the end of the war. Sam Bridges, a Kentucky native and farm laborer in Lamar County before the war, also survived but deserted the company five months later.

otism—less christianity & *less to* eat than any other people I have ever been amongst.[49]

We are now about 25 miles south of Nashville—about 6 or 8 south of the Yanks, with a fair prospect of being in musket range of them in the course of a few days. It may be however that we will have no fight of consequence here. From present indications I think we will Make an attempt to gain the rear of Nashville & cut off supplies from the federal army. But as Genl Van Dorn has'ent informed me of his plans as yet, I cant say positively where we may go probably into Ky. I am of opinion that if this army were today in Ky with a prospect of being able to hold the state that two thirds of the people would be with us.[50] The Kentuckians of Rosencrants army are deserting daily & when they get home are not permitted to be arrested by the citizens. A Democratic convention composed of delegates from all the counties in the state was dispersed at Frankfort as being treasonable in its designs according to the Louisville Journal from which I get the above "the state is ripe for rebellion."

Many papers in the North boldly advocate peace. They have long since been convinced of the folly of attempting to subjugate the South & are now being forced to acknowledge it as evidence of the great change being brought about in the sentiments of the people of the North—if newspapers had spoken out against Lincoln & for peace three months ago as they now do, it would have been sufficient cause for Lincoln to have consigned their editors to a dungeon in Fort Lafayette.[51] Although these papers do not reflect the feelings of a majority of the people of the North it is conclusive evidence that a peace party is rapidly growing up there & are determined to make themselves heard & their opinions respected. Notwithstanding all these signs of peace I cant think the war will end soon—not before the close of Lincoln's administration.[52]

49. Bates has apparently forgotten about the Indian Territory, where he was reduced to eating acorns.

50. Bates is apparently unaware of the cool reception Kentuckians had given Bragg a few months earlier.

51. Federal authorities confined many northerners considered disloyal to the Union at Fort Lafayette in New York. Faust, *Historical Times Illustrated Encyclopedia*, 275.

52. Many Confederates, especially diehards such as Bates, looked forward to the 1864 elections as an opportunity to replace Abraham Lincoln with a more reasonable and accommodating president who might negotiate with the Confederacy. Richard E. Beringer, Herman Hattaway, Archer Jones, and William N. Still, Jr., *Why the South Lost the Civil War* (Athens: University of Georgia Press, 1986), 347–49; McPherson, *Battle Cry of Freedom*, 721.

Tenn is emphatically the State of beautiful women—& Miss[is-sippi] of ——— women that are *not pretty*. I would dislike to say that I had ever seen a woman that was *ugly*—but I have seen them in Miss that wouldn't compare favorably with an orangutang. It may be however that I form my opinion from the old adage that "Handsome is who handsome does". I have heard, probably from you that there are several very pretty girls in Paris. More than when I was last there. I am anxious to see some of these, but still more eager to see some of the pretty ones who were there before I left.

If however I should live until the close of the war and be discharged in this section of country—I very much doubt whether I would ever get home or not. At any rate I think some of these rich old chaps here abouts would find themselves Minus a pretty daughter when I left.[53] I have several very nice pieces of music which I would like to send you but cannot do so as the gentleman who takes this has as many *letters* as he can carry. The pieces are the "Morgan Rangers" "Virginia" "The Missouri Volunteer" "My Maryland" Price's March & Some others—all of them are very pretty.

I wish I knew or could imagine something to write that would interest you—but as my supply of paper & ideas are both about exausted I had better bring my letter to a stop.

My best wishes to Mr. Mrs J[ohnson]. Mr & Mrs D[ohoney,] Mat & yourself.

Truly your friend

J.C. Bates

Columbia Tenn

March [7?, 1863]

Miss Mootie

Dear Friend

The gentleman by whom I intended sending this to Texas failed to get off & as no other opportunity seems likely to present itself soon I will start it by mail.

Two days after the first of this was written five Regts of Yanks came down from Franklin with orders as the Genl (Coburn) said to capture that audacious Rebel Cavalry & proceed to Columbia. Well, they came down, attacked but instead of capturing us, were *themselves* captured. Genl Coburn said he had gone to Columbia as he

---

53. Bates often teased Mootie about the pretty women he encountered on his travels.

had been ordered, but with a different escort to the one he intended. Our loss was 169 killed & wounded. The federal loss killed & wounded about double that. We captured five regts of their infantry—one Genl four Cols & Lieut Cols, Majs & Capts &c any number.

The Ninth Texas opened the battle—& as usual our Brigade did most of the fighting. The Yanks were posted behind a high hill in the edge of the timber & had greatly the advantage of us. In the commencement of the fight our Brigade was ordered to charge them, which they did most gallantly through an open field, but were forced to retire in considerable disorder.[54] We however formed again & charged a second time, with the same result as at first. A third time we formed with about half the number of men we had at first & for the third time the order was given to "forward" which the men obeyed with as much alacrity as the first order to charge. We moved steadily forward returning the fire of the enemy until the advance of the two lines were in 20 steps of each other. Still our lines moved on & presently the enemy turned & fled. By this time Forrest had got in the rear of them & finding there was no chance of escape they surrendered.[55]

The Music refered to above I sent you by mail—but doubt your getting it. If you receive it sing "Virginia" for *me* especially will you? it is a beautiful piece.

When you write—if there is communications from Paris to Port Hudson by mail send your letters via the latter place.
Sincerely Your Friend
JC Bates

For the next two months the Texas Cavalry Brigade remained in the vicinity of Thompson's Station and Franklin, foraging in the rich farmland of central Tennessee, skirmishing with Federal cavalry, screening the main body of Bragg's army, and occasionally getting into small firefights. As long as the two main armies under Rosecrans and Bragg sat in place watch-

54. The Texans were compelled to fall back after the first charge because they had no bayonets to contend with the rallying Federal soldiers at the top of the hill. *OR,* Vol. 23, Pt. 1, pp. 116, 124.

55. Bates apparently did not lead Company H in this engagement, probably because he was serving temporarily as regimental quartermaster. Instead, 1st Lieutenant S. A. Griffith commanded the company at Thompson's Station. Kerr, ed., *Fighting with Ross' Texas Cavalry,* 59–60; *OR,* Vol. 23, Pt. 1, pp. 124–25.

ing each other in middle Tennessee, the cavalry had little else to do. Bates's letters during those weeks report the various small actions, summarize the war in general, and comment on the beauty and wealth of Tennessee.

Columbia Tennessee
March 19th 1863
Miss Mootie Johnson
My Dear Friend

I wrote a letter to you last night—but it has been "waylaid" or mislaid—& the gentleman who takes them is here waiting for this. I have not time to write another *letter*, and only send you this scribble by way of a reminder that you are not forgotten—if indeed you need to be told of that.

Present my best wishes to Mr & Mrs J[ohnson] — Capt D[ohoney] & Lady—& to Mat. Please accept this *apology* & with it the best wishes of
Your Friend
J.C. Bates

The Music about which I wrote you, I sent by mail a few days since as I did not then know of any one going to Tex Soon & I am afraid you will not get it. If not I will send other copies.

Columbia Tennessee
March 18th 1863
My Dear Ma

I wrote you on the first of this month sending the letter by hand and again mailing some letters yesterday which I had written several days previously. Several men leave in the morning for Mount Pleasant and as it seems you get but few of my letters I write by them.[56]

For the last few days we have been encamped 2 miles S.W. from Columbia.[57] As soon as our horses are shod, & recruited a little we will again take the field. This is the finest section of country I have ever seen. The citizens are almost all wealthy and consequently you rarely ever see a shabby farm or residence. The Polks & Pillows—A. O. P. Nicholson & a number of other prominent men live near

56. Mount Pleasant is about fifty miles southeast of Paris.
57. Columbia is about twenty miles southwest of Franklin.

here.[58] Andrew Polk's is said to be the Most Magnificently furnished residence in the South—& it has more the appearance inside of being the palace of a King than the residence of a private citizen. The ladies too, are as kind & as beautiful as they are accomplished.

We had a brush with the Yanks on the 5th inst in which we whipped them badly, capturing five regiments. Our Brigade as usual bore the brunt of the battle—and Genl Van Dorn complimented us by presenting us with the Yankee colors captured. Our loss 170, the enemy considerably more. Genl Longstreet is moving into the interior of Ky—& if Rosencrants is not forced by this move to fall back—a general engagement may be looked for here soon.[59]

It is growing late and I have not time to write more. My best wishes to all my friends. I would write to more of them, but when we have an opportunity of sending letters by hand, we generally have but short notice in which to write.

Affectionately Your Son

J.C. Bates

In Camp at Thompson Station

April 1863

My Dear Ma,

Another opportunity of sending a letter to you is presented & I will write a few lines hastily. As you will see from above we are encamped at our old battle ground—though I have some doubts as to whether we will be permitted to remain here long. We have occasional skirmishes with the enemy but have had no regular engagement Since the 5th ult.

On yesterday five Regts of Yanks came down. We went out to meet them but they did not show fight. We exchanged a few shots with them at "long tom" [*i.e.*, artillery]—captured a couple & re-

58. Bates refers to the Polk family that had sent James K. Polk to the White House in the 1840s, the Pillow family that had furnished a general of dubious ability to the Confederacy, and Alfred O. P. Nicholson, a former United States senator who would serve as Tennessee's chief justice in the 1870s. For General Gideon Pillow and Nicholson, see Sifakis, *Who Was Who*, 470, 508.

59. General James Longstreet, one of Robert E. Lee's corps commanders, was in southeastern Virginia in the spring of 1863, not Kentucky. Longstreet had proposed, without success, that his corps be sent into east Tennessee to reinforce Bragg, and that may have been the basis of Bates's misinformation. William Garrett Piston, *Lee's Tarnished Lieutenant: James Longstreet and His Place in Southern History* (Athens: University of Georgia Press, 1987), 42–44.

turned without loss. I would not be surprised if we had a brush with them today. Now while I write I can hear the Slow regular tap of their bass drum to which their infantry keeps time in Marching. They are coming but whether to fight us or not remains yet to be seen. If the entire force they have at Franklin Should come down we would have to "withdraw" or More plainly speaking—get up & run for it as we would not be able to meet them in a pitched battle. We have just sent our trains to the rear, ready for a fight or a foot race, as circumstances May Seem to indicate which will be for the best.

Last week Genl Forrest Made a circuit round Franklin—dashed into Brentwood—which is Midway betwixt Nashville & Franklin— or 8 miles from each—captured the entire force stationed there— 670 men—burned the depot filled with Gov Stores—& all their trains except a sufficient number to have the arms & ammunition captured[.] proceeding up the road to within a few miles of Nashville he captured upwards of one hundred more prisoners burned a rail road bridge & made good his escape South of Harpeth river.[60] Two days afterwards Col [Thomas G.] Woodward of Ky— "pitched into" Brentwood again & captured 250 more prisoners. This makes between 2500 & 3000 prisoners our cavalry have captured since we have been at this place. Add to these those captured at Holly Springs & other places & we have near 5000, or about one prisoner to each man in our command. If Genl Van Dorn Succeeds as well the remainder of the year as he has thus far, he will make full amends for his past bad success. I think he is more competent to command Cavalry than Infantry, & both officers & men are beginning to have *some little* confidence in him.

I Saw Some of My old Bethel School Mates a few days since & learned from them that cousin Ben McDonald is in the 18th Ala Regt.[61] He is Chaplain of the Regt—is in fine health. John is not in the Service[,] is said to be Union. The Yanks had Uncle Tom in jail for some time[.] he is now at liberty. I will not close this until to-morrow, as the bugle has just sounded "boots & saddles" & we may have a "skirmish" before night.

60. Forrest, recently given command of an entire cavalry division, struck Brentwood on March 25, capturing 529 Federals and losing only three of his own men. Before the end of the day, he captured 230 more soldiers nearer Franklin. Wills, *Battle from the Start*, 106.

61. Bates was related to the Tennessee McDonalds through his mother, whose maiden name was McDonald (or McDonnold in the Tennessee spelling).

Well yesterday passed without a fight *or* a foot race as far as we were concerned. I suppose the yanks merely wished to alarm us a little as they moved back to Franklin—all quiet this morning.

We have rumors every day that the Yanks are evacuating Nashville—but I don't credit them. On last week about fifty transports passed up the Cumberland, which would seem to indicate that some such move was in contemplation. We have Sent a Regt & Battalion & a couple of pieces of artillery below Nashville on the river—to attack their transports when they return. Orders have been issued by the commander at Nashville that no More goods shall be shipped there until further orders—another good evidence that the Yanks think the place *May* have to be evacuated and they consequently do not wish any goods to fall into the hands of the poor, needy, naked & half starved rebels.

Since we have been in Tenn we have lived finely—compared to our fare in Miss. In fact nothing but provisions can be had at any thing like reasonable prices. As the prices of some articles may be of some interest to you, I will give a few samples. Corn per bbl 5$[,] bbls flour pr hund—6 to 8 $—bacon per pound 25c—beef 10c pork 10 c—& dry goods very few to be had & bring any price asked. I have paid for a pr of Jeans pants 35$—for a hat 20$—for boots from 40$ to 60$. Shirts from 10$ to 15$—drawers 5$—Socks 2$—blankets from 20$ to 40$—pocket knives 15$ to 20$. Osnaburgs & Domestics 60 to 80c. Prints 2 to 3$ pr yard. Linen Hkfs [handkerchiefs] up to 6$ Silk [illegible word] 5 to 10$. Such are the prices of articles the soldier is compeled to have, & as the Gov furnishes but little clothing it is rather a difficult matter to keep decently clad. Another important item with us is horses—good ones being worth from 300 to 600$ dollars. I bought one a short time ago worth in ordinary times 150$, for which I paid 300$ & got him *cheap* as prices go here.

I would like to send some money home if I had a safe opportunity of doing so. Will send one hundred dollars by the bearer of this —though don't know whether he is reliable or not. I want you to use whatever amount you may need of the money I send home—all of it if you have need for it.

There is at present no probability of any of the corps receiving furloughs—So you need not look for any of us home. I had forgotten to say that Col Townes Office was a few days since declared vacant.[62] Lt Col Jones promoted at the same time   our Maj was dismissed as he had been absent sick over 40 days without reporting.[63] Capt Berry was promoted to Lt Col. No Maj yet appointed. I now rank as third captain in the Regt—have a prospect of ranking higher *when a Maj shall be appointed*—I regret very much that Col Townes has been thrown out but Bragg's order, that all officers absent sick over 30 days without being heard from is imperative & it could not be avoided. My love to Aunt Tenn & the family.

J.C. Bates

Bates's next letter describes an incident near Franklin that would loom larger as the war dragged on. On a reconnaissance by Van Dorn's and Forrest's cavalry on April 10, one of Forrest's subordinates allowed Federal cavalry to strike his column from the rear. The blue horsemen hit hard, capturing one of Forrest's batteries and thirty men before the Confederates recognized the threat. During Forrest's counterattack, a Federal trooper deliberately shot one of the Confederate prisoners—battery captain Samuel L. Freeman—in the head when Freeman did not move fast enough. One week later a Texan in Whitfield's 27th Texas Cavalry was also shot while a prisoner. These incidents infuriated the Texans, and thereafter they fought more brutally and with less attention to the rules of war.[64]

On a brighter note, Bates mentions that Adela's "unworthy brother" is the new major of the 9th Texas Cavalry. (His predecessor, J. N. Dodson, had been removed from that position because of prolonged absence owing to illness.) Bates was only twenty-five years old, but he had earned the confidence of his men and his superiors.[65]

Camp Near Spring Hill
April 18th 1863
My Dear Sister
    Learning that several men are to be discharged from the Legion [Whitfield's Texas Legion] in the morning & will leave for Tex, I

62. Owing to the accidental wound he received at Corinth in the spring of 1862, Colonel Townes had been absent from the regiment for more than a year.

63. Major J. N. Dodson had left the regiment in late January because of illness. Kerr, ed., *Fighting with Ross' Texas Cavalry*, 55.

64. Wills, *Battle from the Start*, 108; Judith Ann Benner, *Sul Ross: Soldier, Statesman, Educator* (College Station: Texas A&M University Press, 1983), 90.

65. Bates was promoted to major on March 24. Kerr, ed., *Fighting with Ross' Texas Cavalry*, 61; Bates file, Compiled Service Records (Microfilm M323, roll 56).

drop you a line by them. I wrote to Ma by Levi Hines & said I would send one hundred dollars by him but forgot to enclose the amount. I make this statement that you may not unjustly censure Hines. I thought the money had been enclosed in the letter until after he left.

We moved to our present camp several days since—will probably remain here some time.

A few days since [April 10] we went up and made a reconnaissance of Franklin—& found the feds still in force there. We lost a few men killed and several wounded, Genl Forrest's Division was on our right & 2 Brigades of feds from Shelbyville were on a Scout from Shelbyville happened on his rear & captured one of his guns—Forrest immediately turned on them & finding they could not make their escape with his gun and a few prisoners which they had captured they deliberately shot the Capt. of the Battery & thus made their escape. I should not be surprised if the prisoners captured by us should be made to suffer for the very cowardly acts of their men. This is the Second Man who has been murdered by the Scoundrels since we have been in Tenn.[66] It looks hard that men who may be innocent should be made to suffer, for the crime of others, but in such instances as the above I think the law of retaliation should be carried to its full extent.

We have rumours here daily of the evacuation of Nashville and Murfreesboro, but I think they are without foundation. It is true the yanks are fortifying Boling green [Kentucky] and other points in their rear, but I think these are only precautionary measures taken in case they should be defeated by Bragg.

In obedience to a recent order from Genl Bragg the Companies and Regts in our Brigade are to be consolidated, that is, two Co's are to be thrown together, requisite number of officers assigned to the new Companies thus formed, and the supernumerary officers assigned to recruiting & other special duty. The consolidation of Regts was at first contemplated but the men are so much opposed to that measure that I don't think it will be carried into effect. I think the Regt will all be reduced to Battalions & the Senior field officer sent home to Superintend recruiting. The commanders of Regts have the power to unite two Regts if they choose—but in case two Regts should be thrown together one of them from each of the two regi-

66. Bates's letters and Griscom's diary do not mention the first such incident.

ments would be compeled to remain with the Regt where as if the Regts are only reduced to Battalions the *Cols* will be thrown out, sent home on recruiting service—from the fact that a Battalion of five Companies is only entitled to a Lt Col & Maj. Hence they will work it to suit their own wishes. After they return Some of us may get to go home but that time is too far in the future to count on anything with certainty. This consolidation is understood only to be temporary.

In the recent attack on Charleston S.C. the feds lost two Gun boats & crews.[67] We did not loose a man. Our army recently surprised and captured a garrison & near 2,000 persons. Old Stonewall has been lost near a month & I look for him to turn up unexpectedly Somewhere Soon. It is rumored that he is moving into Eastern Ky.[68] It is also believe[d] here that Grant is withdrawing his forces from Vicksburgh with the intention of uniting them with Rosencrantz.[69] In consequence of Col Townes prolonged absence without being heard from he has been droped from the roll. I have no doubt but he is now on the road here & will probably be here soon—although Col Jones is a good commander & liked well by the men, Col Townes is much older, more

April 21st

experienced & therefore better qualified to fill the position.[70] Capt. T.G. Berry has been promoted to Lt Col. Maj J N Dodson has been dismissed for protracted absence and your unworthy brother promoted to Maj rank to date from the 21st April. I hope if Col Townes returns soon, that he may be restored to command. In that event I would be returned to my Co, but would be willing to [do] that in order to see Col T restored & *one or two* men in the Regt disappear. Several letters have been received here which the writers said were to be brought by Col T & we are somewhat uneasy as consequence of his non arrival.

67. On April 7 nine U.S. Navy ironclads attacked Fort Sumter in Charleston harbor. The Confederates' heavy harbor guns struck the ironclads hundreds of times, disabled five of them, and sank one. The fleet retreated from the harbor and gave up on taking Charleston by naval power alone. Long, *Civil War Day by Day*, 335–36.

68. Stonewall Jackson was not missing. He was with Lee's army in central Virginia.

69. Grant, of course, did not withdraw from Vicksburg until it fell.

70. Bates has come a long way since dismissing Dudley Jones as out of his depth a year earlier. Jones is now "a good commander," but Bates is sure that Nathan Townes would be a better colonel.

244 Texas Cavalry Officer's Civil War

I will leave this open until the bearer is ready to leave—in order to give you any additional news we may receive.

Since writing the foregoing Col Townes has sent up an application for an extension of his leave of absence. He wrote from Alexandria La.

I saw several of our old Ky & Tenn friends a few days since— amongst them were cousin Barnet McDonald & one son, Isaac Woolsey Billy Wood, Jim Reagan & several others. There are three Co's from Overton [County, Tennessee—Bates's birthplace] in the eighth Tenn. Daugherty from Livingston is Lt Col. John McDonald joined a Co of federal "Bushwhackers" & was killed. Si Served awhile in our army, then deserted & went to the feds & I have heard has since been killed.

I see in the Louisville Journal that Col Bramlette has been out of the Service for Some time. The Journal says he is to be promoted but do'nt know whether he will accept or not.[71]

April 25th & my letter not yet off. I have to go to Columbia this morning to close my Q M [quartermaster] accounts—& will put this in the hands of some of those going home to be taken when they leave.

My love to Ma, aunt Tenn and all the family
As ever your Bro
J.C. Bates

If Mr. Doak succeeds in getting a discharge, as he anticipates I will send a couple of hundred dollars by him if I can get to see him when he leaves
J.C.B.

In the third week of April, Van Dorn's corps marched for the review of General Joseph E. Johnston's inspector general. Observing the pageantry at Spring Hill was a reporter from a Mobile, Alabama, newspaper. Like many Confederates from other states, the Mobile reporter found the Texas regiments especially interesting: "Here come those rollicking, rascally, brave Texans. . . . What singular looking customers those Texans are, with their large brimmed hats, dark features, shaggy Mexican mustangs, and a *lariet* [sic] . . . around the pummel [sic] of their saddles. They are said to

71. Colonel Thomas Bramlette, Adela's brother-in-law and Will's brother, was commander of the 3rd Kentucky Infantry (U.S.). A few months later, he would be elected governor of Kentucky. Sifakis, *Who Was Who,* 69.

be unmerciful to prisoners, but are a tower of strength when there is a fight on hand."[72]

Camp near Spring Hill Tenn
April 25 1863
Dear Will;

Several days having elapsed since my letter to [blank space] was written I drop you a line. We received orders several days since to keep constantly on hand five days rations, (two cooked) and be ready, at any moment to take the field. From preparations going on and orders received, I have no doubt but we will have active work before the lapse of many days. Probably before this reaches you the great battle will have been fought and won or lost.

I have it from reliable authority that Bragg is receiving reinforcements, and also that a portion of the federal forces are being brought up from Vicksburgh some going up the Cumberland & others Tenn river. If it is true that the federals are leaving Vicksburgh I think there is no doubt that [Joseph E.] Johns[t]on, if he intends to give Rosencrantz battle at all, will do it before federal reinforcements reach Murfreesboro. Bragg's army is said to be in splendid condition, well fed, well clothed and in excellent health. Everyone here seems confident of success, and I sincerely hope they may not be disappointed.

I am confident of one thing, & that is that our corps can whip all the federal *cavalry* around Murfreesboro. Our entire corps was reviewed a few days since by Genl Johns[t]ons's Inspe[c]tor Genl. It was indeed a magnificent sight ———— thousand Cavalry all passing in review at once. Genl Van Dorn & the Inspector Genl both complimented our Brigade as being the best horsemen & most graceful riders in the corps.

Tell Capt Dohoney, as I understand Johnson's Regt has proved a failure, that we would be very glad to have him join our Regt with his company, I expect he & his company would object to crossing the Miss—but if he had remained with us until now, he would have been satisfied as most of us are, that we are better situated than we ever were west of the Miss.[73] We have more and better rations,

72. Quoted in Benner, *Sul Ross,* 91.
73. Shortly before they were to be mustered into Confederate service, the men in Dohoney's company of conscripts got themselves detailed to drive supply wagons to Mexico, leaving Dohoney with no company to command. Dohoney, *Average American,* 123.

better clothing, and not half the hard service we had while in Ark. It is true we would be nearer home, but that is always a disadvantage to an army.

Sam Griffith, for protracted absence without leave, has been dropped from the roll and I expect will be ordered to the ranks. Tell Col Fowler [that] John will be promoted to Capt. John is a most worthy young man and will make a good commander. Isaac Woolsey & several of your old friends are in the 8*th* Tenn. Woolsey I expect will write to you by some of these men going home. Write as often as convenient. Send your letter by mail if no opportunity of sending by hand occurs. Letters come by mail to almost everyone (except me).

Yours &c

J.C. Bates

In early May, Earl Van Dorn, the general whom the 9th Texas Cavalry had followed from Elkhorn Tavern to Corinth to Thompson's Station, was murdered in Spring Hill. An incorrigible ladies' man, the general had apparently been even less discreet than usual; an irate husband walked into Van Dorn's headquarters on May 7 and shot him in the side of the head as he sat at his desk.[74] Thus was the little Mississippian, who was just beginning to realize his potential as a cavalry leader, lost to the Confederate war effort. Bates, perhaps remembering Van Dorn's costly blunders at Elkhorn Tavern and Corinth, reports the murder rather casually.

Head Qrs 9*th* Tex
near Spring Hill Tenn
May 15th /63
My Dear Ma:

Mr. Tate, who promises to hand you this in person, leaves in a few minutes for his home in Fannin Co & I avail myself of the opportunity to write a line by him. I find I have not time to write much as he leaves earlier than I anticipated. I am in fine health, *and* spirits, except when I get to thinking of the "old folks at home"—and *some* folks at home who are *not* so old—at which I have the blues a little—but am generally too much engaged to indulge in such thoughts long at a time.

74. Hartje, *Van Dorn*, 307–15.

Our Brig. is still camped at Spring Hill doing picket duty, scouting &c. A few days since while the 1st Tex Legion was on picket they were surprised and 120 of their number captured. It will take the Yanks a long while to get even with us, as we have captured since the 1st March about 4,300 prisoners. Genl Forrest on the first of this month, as you may have heard before this, captured about 1,700 prisoners & four pieces artillery. This he accomplished with 750 men. He has recently been promoted to Maj Genl & will in future command our corps.

Maj Genl Van Dorn was killed at this place about ten days since by one Dr [George B.] Peters—cause Van Dorn's intimacy with his wife.

We have also gained a complete victory in V.a. & if we can whip the army here I do not look for much more fighting except on the Miss before fall.[75] Our exchanged prisoners returned report great dissatisfaction in the north on account of the conscript act—& that several riots have occurred already. If they should get up a row amongst themselves I wish them God speed for it would be our salvation.[76] Mr Tate can give you all the current news.

I wrote you by Levi Hines that I would send one hundred dollars by him to you but failed to inclose the amount. I make this correction that you may not think Levi acted dishonestly in the matter. As soon as Mr Doake goes home which will be soon I will send you a couple or three hundred dollars.

Give my kindest regards to all my friends & love to the family
Your affectionate son
J.C. Bates

Mr Tate is a very worthy young man a good soldier, & a member of the Regt. Receive him kindly

From December 1862 to the following May had been an eventful six months for Bates and the men of Lamar. They had recovered their beloved horses, helped to cripple General Grant's overland campaign to Vicksburg, won another (if less important) engagement at Thompson's Station, and returned to Tennessee, the home state of many of the men. Food and

75. The victory in Virginia was the Battle of Chancellorsville, fought in early May.
76. For an example of a draft riot in Wisconsin, see Adam J. Kawa, "No Draft!" *Civil War Times Illustrated* 37 (June 1998): 54–60.

forage in middle Tennessee were much more plentiful than in any place they had yet been, and the war in general seemed to be tilting toward the Confederacy. The future certainly looked bright. The only thing that might spoil the picture would be to return to the mud and misery of Mississippi. In May they returned to Mississippi.

Vicksburg and Home

By early May 1863, General Ulysses S. Grant had steamed his army down the Mississippi River, marched through the swamps on the Louisiana side of the river to a point south of Vicksburg, crossed the stream from Louisiana, and placed his army on the high ground south of the city. From the east bank of the river he began driving the Confederates back toward the state capital at Jackson, fighting four battles along the way, then turned back west to reduce the fortress of Vicksburg. In response, General John C. Pemberton, the city's defender, sent urgent messages to Richmond asking for reinforcements from Braxton Bragg's army in Tennessee. Bragg grumbled and fumed, but he obeyed orders and directed General William H. Jackson's cavalry division, including the Texas Cavalry Brigade, to go to Pemberton's assistance.[1]

Bates and his fellow Texans were not at all excited about the prospect of leaving the lush countryside of Tennessee and returning to Mississippi. But they had no say in the matter, and in the third week of May they turned their horses toward Vicksburg. On the way down from Tennessee, Colonel John W. Whitfield, former commander of Whitfield's Legion (also known as the 27th Texas Cavalry), received notice of his promotion to brigadier general and official command of the Texas brigade. His adjutant's records show that his unit included 1,815 officers and men in four regiments—the 3rd, 6th, 9th, and 27th Texas Cavalry Regiments. The other brigade in Jackson's division comprised more than a thousand men,

1. *OR*, Vol. 52, Pt. 2, p. 472; Connelly, *Autumn of Glory*, 125.

all Mississippians, making the reinforcements for Vicksburg about three thousand strong.[2] Rather than join Pemberton's army inside the defenses of Vicksburg, now besieged by Grant, Jackson's division joined Joseph E. Johnston's Army of Relief hovering at the rear of the Federals.[3]

Bates's letters during this period are shorter than usual, perhaps owing to the hard ride back to Mississippi and the steady round of scouting and skirmishing that awaited the regiment as soon as it reached its camps. Private Sparks wrote that "it was on the 3rd day of June, 1863, that we commenced picket duty in front of Vicksburg. It was fighting every day—sometimes a detachment or a company or a regiment, but it was fighting every day."[4] The major did have time to regret the return to Mississippi, however, and to keep the home folks apprised of the company's activities.

In Camp 15 miles S of Columbia [Tennessee]
May 21st 1863
My Dear Ma:
    Mr Doake leaves in a day or so for Texas and as I will probably not have time again to write before he leaves I do so this evening. We left our camp at Spring Hill on yesterday, and are now enroute for the "land of all abominations [Mississippi]." I hoped when we left there that we had bidden a final adieu to the hated state & yet hope we will not have to remain there long.
    I never regretted to leave any place as much as Murry [Maury] Co[unty]. Besides having much better fare for ourselves and horses, we received more kind treatment during one week of our stay there, than the whole time we were in the land of niggers and swamps. It would not be proper to write you our exact place of destination. But if Mr Doake does not leave us before we arrive there I will write you again.
    We have no very satisfactory news from Jackson. The telegraph only says we repulsed the feds, that they have retired to their gun

2. The division commander was twenty-eight-year-old William H. "Red" Jackson, a Tennessee native and an 1856 graduate of the U. S. Military Academy. He had led one of the brigades on the Holly Springs raid and had a well-deserved reputation for courage. Warner, *Generals in Gray*, 152–53; David Evans, *Sherman's Horsemen: Union Cavalry Operations in the Atlanta Campaign* (Bloomington: Indiana University Press, 1996), 224.
    3. *OR*, Vol. 24, Pt. 3, p. 947; Kerr, ed., *Fighting with Ross' Texas Cavalry*, 66; Bearss, *Campaign for Vicksburg*, 3:1010.
    4. Sparks, *War Between the States*, 79.

boats, and that the loss on both sides was very heavy.[5] Mr D will gather all the news on his way and will be able to give it to you in more detail than I can write.

Whitfield has been made Brigadier and will take command of our Brigade permanently. Genl Jackson still commands our division. As I anticipated at Genl Van Dorn's death our corps has been broken up. I very much regret this as we were just getting in condition to do good service, & win for ourselves a good name. I never saw people regret to see soldiers leave more than those living in the section where we have been stationed. They seemed to think the county would be overrun as soon as the Texans left. Some of them actually shed tears when they saw us leaving.

I send you two hundred dollars by Mr Doake. Use what you may need and give the rest to Will to be invested in land.

I saw Isaac Woolsey & Will Wood today. They both desire to be remembered to Will and to all of their old Ky friends. Woolsey is Capt & Wood 1st Lieut in the same Co. I received a note from L M Mitchell yesterday—he is in the 1st Confederate (Coxes') Cavalry. Marion as you may have heard has been dead some time.

I bought another horse today one of the finest and most beautiful dapples I ever saw. You will open your eyes a little I expect, unless you have learned to be surprised at nothing these times, when I tell you I paid 600$ for him. Any kind of an ordinary horse is worth 300$ here—and almost impossible to get them at that price. Mr Doake promised to call and see you and tell you how we are getting along. I wrote you a few days ago by Mr Tate who also promised to call & see you.

My love to all the family & to Aunt Tenn & family
Yours affectionately
J.C. Bates

I received a letter from aunt Clint a few days since. What do you suppose prompted her to write at this late day?

Decatur Ala May 24 Mr Doake leaves us this morning. We go from here to Columbus Miss. Have nothing more of interest to write.

5. Bates may be referring to the events of May 19, when General Grant's army made a general assault on the works at Vicksburg. Pemberton's army, stronger than Grant realized, threw back the attack, but the Federals did not retreat to their gunboats. Bearss, *Campaign for Vicksburg*, 3:753–73.

Jackson's camp
[May 1863?]
[Letter from Bates to his mother, probably enclosed with the pre-
ceding letter]

I had forgotten the list of clothing you asked me to make out &
hardly think it necessary for you to undertake to make any as it is
very improbable whether I could get it if you did. I will need three
prs pants two of woolen drawers two of cotton D[itt]o — 3 prs
woolen & cotton socks each — 2 pr gloves 2 undershirts — 2 overshirts *the last only* woolen & one coat. If you can make the coat &
pants a nice gray I would prefer it to any other color. Any thing however to suit yourself except *blue mixed*. Old Father Grime's Long
tailed blue &c is always associated in my mind with that color. If you
can *hire* it made do so — I do'nt want you to undertake as hard a task
yourself. I had rather buy even at present exorbitant prices, than
have you do the work yourself. Use as much of my money as
you need — if I should send home that much. As long as I am in
the Army I have plenty — and as long as I have *any* I want you to
have it.

You need not send me any more *paper*. I have an abundance and
can supply you if you need it. If you can get the material make me
two or three morning[?] overshirts.
J.C. Bates

Columbus Miss[6]
May 29 1863
My Dear Ma:

I wrote you several days since by Mr Doake. Another gentleman
leaves in the morning for Titus Co & I drop a line by him.[7]

Our command arrived at this place this morning. I was left behind to guard the trains & have just got in. We leave at 8 in the
morning on a forced march. I received a letter from you dated apr
25th on yesterday, brought by Mr Sam Long. As [Samuel B.]
Maxy's old [9th Texas Infantry] Regt is probably at Jackson Miss
I may see him before he leaves. I have not time to write more now,
as it is nearly dark. Will write again the first opportunity. I am a little

---

6. Columbus, near the Alabama border, is 130 miles northeast of Jackson.
7. Titus County is directly southeast of Bates's home county of Lamar.

afraid Vicksburgh will fall. If so you will hear it before this reaches you.

Your affectionate son

J.C.B.

[Bolton, Mississippi][8]

June 21st 1863

My Dear Ma:

A gentleman leaves this neighborhood this morning for Tex & I write a line by him as it may be some time before Tom Johnson gets off.

For a week or so past I have been a little unwell, but I believe the kindness of my hostess and her fair daughter has almost restored me.[9]

I received a letter from Sister also one from Will a few days since. Have seen Tom Johnson—he will soon be well.[10] I have no news to write you. We are expecting a fight here every day—and I am afraid of the results when it does come. Vicksburgh will be able to hold out for some time yet—until the supply of provisions is exhausted.

Sister and Will asked me if I sent any money by Jim Hines. I did not—after giving him my letters he left without my seeing him again. [torn spot] sent you some by Mr Doake.

The Regt is waiting for me to attend dress parade & I must close. My love to all.

Affectionately

Your son

J.C. Bates

Although Johnston's Army of Relief huffed and blustered at the rear of Grant's besieging Federals, it provided no relief to Pemberton's men inside Vicksburg. Jackson's cavalry division could only bother the edges of Grant's army, making small dents in the powerful war machine bearing down on Vicksburg. Bates was appalled at the suffering of the Mississippi civilians left in the wake of the Federal army but noted that those civilians

8. On June 21 the brigade was camped near Bolton, twenty-five miles east of Vicksburg.

9. Bates was apparently staying with a nearby family while he recovered from his unnamed illness.

10. Tom Johnson, a soldier in the 7th Texas Infantry, was Mootie's brother.

now seemed to appreciate their Texas defenders more than previously. As the siege and heavy artillery bombardments dragged on into late June and early July, he typically concluded that this was the time for every southern patriot to stand firm and resist all the harder.

[Bolton, Mississippi]
Hd Qrs 9th Texas
June 25th 1863
My Dear Sister

Your letter of June 2nd was received several days since. With the exception of one letter from Ma dated 25th Apr I have received none from Paris for several months. I saw Tom Johnson several days since. He will soon be with [torn spot] told me he expected to get a furlough and go home. If he goes I will send this by him. I very much doubt whether he will get a furlough. If he does not go, I suppose his uncle will & I will send by him.

We have been in Miss near a month. I regretted very much to leave Tenn—but am better satisfied than I expected to be. We have been very kindly received and treated every where since our return. In fact our men have been better treated in some instances than they deserved to be. The iron rule of the Yanks while they had possession of this country has been a wholesome lesson to some of the citizens. If I were to write you of all the acts committed by these inhuman scoundrels while in the Yazoo valley it would make a chapter of devilish cruelties that would make your heart shudder to read. You have but little idea how desolate this country looks. You must *see* it to realize it. I hope however you [torn spot] never see it. Texas has been fortunate so far & I trust an invading army may never desolate her [torn spot]. I wish every Texan could witness the ruin and devastation that has been made here. I am sure no man who had one spark of patriotism remaining would see an invading army of thieves & cut throats such as these cross her lines without shouldering his musket in her defense.

I can write you no news of particular interest. If Dr Johnson is here he will be able to tell you much more than I can write.[11] We have more at stake in the coming contest at Vicksburgh, than any

11. Mootie's father, Alfred S. Johnson, had apparently traveled to Mississippi to care for his wounded son, Tom.

battle that has been fought during the war. If we loose it the war will be made popular in the north—conscription made [torn spot] & the enemy will think of it [torn spot] place in the South may be taken [torn spot] is the only artery that connects the two halves of the Confederacy—cut it & the lifeblood of either one or the other half will soon be drained. The enemy can then concentrate their armies on either side they choose & we will be powerless to make corresponding moves to meet them. [torn spot] will have the key to the Miss valley and can overrun the adjacent country at pleasure & thousands of the north who now remain at home to keep from fighting, will then join the army for plunder. If however we hold Vicksburgh—I think this summer will end the war, otherwise it will be prolonged—possibly for years and every man *ought* to go into the fight as though the fate of the confederacy depended on his individual exertions.

I have already written twice, but for fear those letters may not reach you, will say again that I did not send any money by Hines. I expected to see him after giving him the letters but he left before I had an opportunity of doing so. I am sorry it occurred for you may have thought Hines acted dishonestly. Tell [torn spot] to explain the matter to Hines. [torn spot] several days may elapse before I can send this to Dr Johnson I will leave it open & write to you any thing that may occur of interest in the mean time.

The heaviest cannonading we have yet heard has been going on at Vicksburgh since 3 oclk this morning—but is now 10 oclk [torn spot].

[torn spot] Dr Johnson I learn had already gone home. Lt Hunt goes today or tomorrow.

July 3d I had just commenced [torn spot] were ordered to the front. I heard this morning Dr A S Johnson was at Raymond & I will send this down to him.[12] I would like to see him but will not have time to go down—as we may expect a fight at any moment. The Dr can give you all the news.

My love to all. Direct your letters to Jackson Miss.
Your Brother
J.C. Bates

12. Raymond was seven miles south of Bates's camp at Bolton and fourteen miles southwest of Jackson.

[Queen's Hill, Mississippi][13]
Hd Qrs 9th Tex
July 2nd /63
My Dear Ma;

A gentleman is starting to Tex from here & has consented to wait until I can write you that I am well—doing well & of course in good spirits. Co H are all well.

My love to all
Your son
J.C. Bates

I did not send any money by Hines.

[Queen's Hill, Mississippi]
Hd Qrs 9th Tex Cavly
July 4th 1863
Miss Mootie Johnson
My Dear Friend

"Try Try again" is an old adage that used to be impressed on my mind, by my teacher, when I was a little school boy, as being essential to final success if the first effort was a failure. But time has not brought me my reward yet—neither has the mails. In other words I have written to you very frequently during the last Six months, So often I ca'nt remember the number of times, but none of my letters have brought a reply.

We are once more in Miss. When I crossed the line into Tenn I kicked the dirt from my feet, hoping never to see this land of niggers, hard mean people & cotton again. But there's never any knowing where the Fates or Jo Johns[t]on's orders will take us. (There is *one* Johnson I'd like to have an order from—I know where I'd be ordered to)

I was at Raymond a short time since to see Tom. He was doing well—*too well* indeed to recover speedily. I was half tempted to wish for a wound myself to get to that hospital. Tom told me he expected to start home in a week or so. I would like very much to be at home with him—but even if I could get leave of absence now I would not accept it when every man who can be of any possible service will be so much needed in the coming contest before Vicksburgh—which

13. Queen's Hill was halfway between Vicksburg and Jackson.

I regard as the hinging point in the destiny of our nation. If we are successful here I believe we will have peace in six months. A defeat may result in prolonging the war for years. How important it is then that every exertion within the power of human energy should be made—and that every one should be at his post. After this fight is over—*if we win it* I intend to make an effort to obtain leave of absence. If we are defeated I will not try. However I console myself by thinking I'll get to go home *some* time "*if I ever do.*"

I have formed a much better opinion of Miss since our return than I had before—in fact better than I ever expected to have. The citizens generally & the ladies especially have treated us with great kindness. This is owing in part to the fact that the feds have had possession & given them a wholsome lesson or so.

We all regretted very much to leave Tenn, and on taking a last, longing, lingering look at Columbia I drew my thoughts up in line of battle and we held a council of war and reviewed past events about as follows—1st we were ordered to Tenn. 2nd we were well pleased thereat. 3d We went. 4th We saw the Tenn girls. 5th they were lovely—lovable loving, to be loved & *were loved*. 6th we were happy—very. 7th "old Jo" ordered us to Miss. 8th were miserable—very. 9th Have to obey orders. 10th Tenn is a great country. 11th Miss a'int. 12th Tenn girls are "regular bricks"

And no mistake

13th Miss girls are not worth sticks

And no great shakes

14th Wont have any thing to do with the whole tribe of Mississippians. But alas for all human resolves and calculations—have not been thirty days in Miss—yet have fallen in love with half a score already—and am at a loss to know which to "honor! with my choice".

We (that is "Head Qrs") were invited to & of course attended, a pic nic yesterday at which I formed the acquaintance of a young lady who bore such a striking resemblance to my sweet heart that I felt it a duty to fall in love with her and forthwith proceeded, to the best of my ability, to accomplish that task—which I found a very pleasant and not *very* difficult one. As Miss Alice gave Me a *very* cordial invitation to call again, think I'll do so merely "to keep my hand in" you know. Jest aside I did meet on yesterday, the prettiest, most accomplished & most intelligent lady I have seen in Miss & she reminded me very much of—well no matter who.

Well Miss Moot you must excuse this hastily written scribble. I learned a while ago that Dr J.—Your Dr—was at Raymond—and would probably start home soon. As he may not be here & it will be impossible for me to go to see him I will send a courier down with this. As soon as I learned the Dr was at Raymond which was after I commenced writing I proceeded "with all possible haste" as you have no doubt observed, to finish this and several others to send him before we move from here. While I write the booming of cannon can be heard on our right and I have been expecting every moment that we would be ordered to the front. I could give you some news of interest, but it would be contraband, as this might fall into the hands of the feds. If they should get it I have no doubt they would preserve it as a brilliant specimen of southern literature.

I send you a few pieces of music. "Lorena" is very pretty I think.[14] I have heard several other beautiful pieces—but have not been able to obtain copies of them. I sent several pieces some time since. Have you received them?

Very truly Your Friend

J.C. Bates

I wrote you some time ago I had no doubt I could write *poetry*. Thinking you might have some doubt about the matter I send you a specimen stanza which you will no doubt be able to find somewhere in this letter. Do'nt you think it has the genuine poetic jingle. As this is my first effort do'nt criticize to severely.

While Bates was writing his letter of July 4, twenty miles to the west General Pemberton was surrendering Vicksburg to General Grant after a seven-week siege. Having bagged Pemberton's whole army, Grant then sent General William T. Sherman and four corps to deal with Johnston's Army of Relief near Jackson. The Texas Cavalry Brigade worked hard during this period, skirmishing heavily every day along the edges of the army. On July 16 the 3rd and 9th Texas Cavalry Regiments, ranging behind Federal lines west of Jackson, captured a pioneer train, including wagons, prisoners, horses, and mules, but a more attractive target—an ammunition supply train—was too heavily defended to attack. General Johnston managed to hold onto Jackson for eight days but finally evacuated the town, or what was left of it, on July 16 and retreated to the east.[15]

14. "Lorena" was popular among the soldiers on both sides during the war. Wiley, *Life of Johnny Reb,* 151.

15. Kerr, ed., *Fighting with Ross' Texas Cavalry,* 73–75; *OR,* Vol. 24, Pt. 2, pp. 535–36, 554–55; Sparks, *War Between the States,* 79; Hale, *Third Texas Cavalry,* 182–85.

In late July, at a camp twenty-five miles east of Jackson, Bates—chin up as usual—summed up events in Mississippi in a letter to his mother. Just a few weeks earlier, fortune seemed to be shining on the Confederacy. Now, Bates predicted, Mobile, Alabama, would soon fall into Federal hands as well. Still, he wrote, the fall of Vicksburg was more a psychological blow than anything else. And, as always, the fault had not been in the soldiers but in their incompetent leaders. The men in the ranks were not the problem.[16]

One other interesting feature of the letter is Bates's use of a code to relay sensitive military information. Never knowing whether his mail would end up in Federal hands, he had provided the home folks with a simple alphabetic code they could use to decipher some words in his letter. The symbols he scrawled in his letter have been decoded below.[17]

Hd Qrs 9th Tex Cavly
Camp Pilahatchie Miss
July 25th 1863
My Dear Ma:
    A gentleman leaves today for Texas & I drop a line hastily by him. I am in very good health & notwithstanding our recent reverses, in good spirits too.
    The fall of Vicksburgh was an event I predicted, as you will remember if you have received my letters, months ago & I have not therefore been Surprised at the event. Although its fall was a heavy blow to us—one from which we will not soon recover—still I do not attach as much importance to it as some are disposed to. Regarded in a military point of view its fall was a less calamity than the moral effect it has had on both the north & the South.[18] As Soon as Jackson was evacuated nearly one half of the people West of Pearl river gave up all for lost and are now willing to submit to any thing

16. Like soldiers in the Confederate Army of Tennessee, Bates remembered vividly those moments when the enemy fled, even in battles usually considered Confederate defeats. From his perspective, for example, Texans had prevailed in the charge on the Federal battery at Elkhorn Tavern. For Bates, defeats were not attributable to poor fighting—only to poor generalship. Larry J. Daniel, *Soldiering in the Army of Tennessee: A Portrait of Life in a Confederate Army* (Chapel Hill: University of North Carolina Press, 1991), 148–50.

17. The code and its key are reproduced in Appendix 2.

18. Bates anticipates by more than a century the argument put forth by historian Thomas L. Connelly, that the blow to southern morale and boost to northern hopes resulting from the fall of Vicksburg were more important than purely military considerations. The actual military effects, Connelly believed, were minimal. Thomas L. Connelly, "Vicksburg: Strategic Point or Propaganda Device?" *Military Affairs* 34 (April 1970): 49–53.

Lincoln is disposed to put on them—and some desertions have been the consequence.[19] We lost at V[icksburg] from the best information I can get, about 23,500, prisoners near 40,000 Stand of arms, and 90 pieces artillery, all sizes.[20] Port Hudson has since surrendered 4,500 men—swelling our losses in prisoners to 28,000.[21] We fortunately have something over 30,000 federal prisoners, and an exchange will therefore soon be official. The Officers I understand are now being exchanged.

The fall of V—— is attributed here by everyone and with justice I think, to Pemberton's incompetency. Not a few are disposed to think *he sold the place* and it does seem that he was intent on sacrificing the place [torn spot] way from the fact that Genl Johns[t]on ordered him, *not* to go into V—— again from Jackson but take his army to Yazoo city—that the federals would certainly invest the place if he went there, and that it would as certainty fall as they invested it.[22] But the place is now gone and useless regrets can not mend the matter. I sincerely hope this costly lesson may be remembered by [President Jefferson] Davis, and that no more incompetent officers may be put in charge of important points.

As soon as Johns[t]on evacuated Jackson he moved leisurely back to Morton—a station 30 miles E of Jackson. The feds followed on to Brandon—12 miles from Jackson—remained a few days and are now moving back to Jackson.

I think they will leave a force at Jackson & Vicksburgh sufficient to hold those and move next on Mobile, Ala. And I predict—of it as of Vicksburgh, *that it will finally fall*—and Johns[t]on be forced to make the Tombigbee river in Ala his base of operations. These are only my predictions—but I think they are based on good reasons.

Our cavalry has been doing some hard service since the federals

19. The Pearl River runs south through Jackson to the Gulf of Mexico. Bates refers specifically to those parts of Mississippi overrun by Federal armies.

20. Confederate losses as a result of the surrender comprised about 29,500 officers and men, 172 pieces of artillery, 50,000 shoulder arms, and tons of related supplies and equipment. Bearss, *Campaign for Vicksburg*, 3:1301, 1311.

21. Port Hudson, Louisiana, the last Confederate stronghold on the Mississippi, surrendered six thousand defenders on July 9. After the victories at Vicksburg and Port Hudson, the Union controlled the river from source to mouth.

22. Johnston had urged Pemberton to come out of the Vicksburg defenses, unite the two Confederate armies, and fight Grant on open ground. While Johnston and Pemberton dithered, however, Grant kept moving, got between the two of them, and eliminated Pemberton's options. Foote, *Civil War*, 2:366–69; McPherson, *Battle Cry of Freedom*, 630.

commenced their advance from Big Black [River].[23] We fought them almost day and night from that point until we were driven into the breastworks of Jackson. In the five days and nights they were advancing to Jackson we had only *one* in which to sleep and then the rain came down in torrents nearly all night. The night before we got into Jackson I had command of the rear and it was only while bullets were whizzing about us and guns flashing in the darkness that I could keep fully awake. I would have given them every dollar I possessed for one night of quiet, uninterrupted sleep. The loss of sleep has always been the greatest hardship we have had to endure.

A few days before the evacuation of Jackson our Brigade made a dash round to the rear of the feds. Our Regt captured & burned 12 wagons, loaded[,] brought off two ambulances, 85 prisoners, also 65 horses and mules. For the last few days we have been resting and recruiting our horses preparatory to another raid. I think it quite likely the feds will fall back to Vicksburgh & make Big Black river their line until they take Mobile when they will advance from that point & V—— simultaneously.

You have probably heard that Bragg has fallen back to the Tenn river. He was forced to do this by a flank movement of Rosencrants.[24] Lee had also recrossed the Potomack and is now in Virginia. Our success at the battle of Gettysburgh was not as complete as we were at first led to believe.[25] I am satisfied however, and federal papers admit as much, that the battle was decidedly in our favor & one of the best evidences of their [this] fact the federal commander Hooker, was relieved immediately after the battle & Genl Meade put in command of the army of the Potomack.[26] Lincoln has nearly run through his catalogue of Maj Genls in the east & I ca'nt imagine who he will find to supercede Meade after the next battle. It seems to be his policy to permit no Genl to command in two suc-

23. The Federal advance Bates mentions is Sherman's movement against Johnston. The Big Black River runs generally southward between Vicksburg and Jackson.

24. In the last week of June, General Rosecrans maneuvered Bragg out of his lines along the Duck River in middle Tennessee. Bragg fell back first to Tullahoma and then farther back, behind the Tennessee River at Chattanooga, in what came to be known as the Tullahoma campaign. Connelly, *Autumn of Glory*, 113–32.

25. Bates refers to Lee's retreat from Pennsylvania after the defeat at Gettysburg. Relying on early and erroneous newspaper reports, Bates believed Gettysburg had been a Confederate victory.

26. Again, Bates had received muddled information. General George G. Meade replaced Joseph Hooker before the battle, not afterward.

cessive engagements. The oftener he changes commanders the better for us.

The principal part of Genl Johns[t]on's force is now in the vicinity of [CODE: Morton]. He has [CODE: four divisions, fourteen brigades]. His entire force is about [CODE: twenty-eight thousand].[27] It is generally understood amongst those who claim to know, that the principal part of [CODE: General Bragg's army will be brought here]. His force is [CODE: fifty-two thousand].[28] A courier just in reports no federals this side of Clinton 8 miles W of Jackson. I expect our Brigade will move down in that direction to morrow.

Lewis Means speaks of going home in a week or so as by an act of congress, he and all other Regimental Comissary will be relieved the last of this month.[29] I will write by him if he goes. I did not see Dr. Johnson & therefore sent no money by him. I will send about 500$ by Lewis which I want invested in land *as soon as possible.*

I must go on inspection and have not time to write to any one else—even if any one else wished to hear from me—which I very much doubt as I have heard from no one but you for near eight months. I have written *my last letter* to any one but home—until I hear from them.

My love to all
Your affectionate son
J.C. Bates

My old Co are *all* well. Have not time to give names. Jno Fowler will be promoted Capt.

After the fall of Vicksburg and Port Hudson, Federal military authorities consolidated their hold on the east bank of the Mississippi River from Memphis to New Orleans, leaving central Mississippi to the Confederates under Johnston. The Texas Cavalry Brigade thereupon settled into a long period of relative inactivity, staging drills and inspections under the hot Mississippi sun. On a few occasions in the second half of the year, the Texas

27. Johnston's biographer estimates that the general commanded no more than 23,000 troops at this time. Craig L. Symonds, *Joseph E. Johnston: A Civil War Biography* (New York: W. W. Norton, 1992), 219.

28. Bragg's army of 46,000 men remained at Chattanooga and was not brought to Mississippi. General Bragg still had Rosecrans to worry about. Foote, *Civil War,* 2:670.

29. Means, a twenty-nine-year-old Kentucky native and storekeeper before the war, had joined Company H of Bates's regiment in February 1862.

horsemen rode off on scouts for one purpose or another. In mid-August, for example, they galloped up toward Grenada, launching point for their earlier raid on Holly Springs, to protect 60 locomotives and 350 railroad cars left stranded there by Grant's destruction of Jackson in May. By the time the Texans reached Grenada, though, a much larger force of Federals was already at work destroying all the locomotives and cars they could not run north toward Memphis. The Confederates had to content themselves with burning trestles north of Grenada to prevent at least some of the captured rolling stock from reaching Federal lines.[30]

Bates's letter of August 22 briefly describes the unsuccessful foray toward Grenada. He also mentions the new chief of cavalry in Mississippi, Major General Stephen D. Lee. Only twenty-nine and, according to Bates, unimpressive in appearance, Lee would nevertheless prove to be a capable corps commander for the western horsemen.[31]

Bates's letter also deals with two troublesome events of August. First, on August 22 the regiment received documents from Richmond indicating that J. N. Dodson, Bates's predecessor as major, had been restored to the service and promoted to lieutenant colonel. Dodson's release from the army owing to an extended illness and absence had apparently offended him, and he spent considerable time and effort in Richmond lobbying for reinstatement. The two men serving as lieutenant colonel and major— Thomas G. Berry and Bates—then offered their resignations, the latter because his office would now presumably go to Berry. Dodson seemed to be satisfied that his honor had been upheld, however, and did not assume office or command. He resigned from the service six weeks later, and Bates continued as major.[32]

More troubling was the desertion of dozens of men from the brigade in August and September. Sagging morale owing to the fall of Vicksburg, their long absence from homes and families, a stingy furlough policy, and the dull routine of camp life apparently convinced some of the men to sneak away from their Mississippi camps, cross the river, and go home.

30. Kerr, ed., *Fighting with Ross' Texas Cavalry*, 78–80; *OR*, Vol. 30, Pt. 1, pp. 13–17; Pt. 4, p. 514; Jeffrey N. Lash, "Joseph E. Johnston's Grenada Blunder: A Failure in Command," *Civil War History* 23 (June 1977): 114–28; Hale, *Third Texas Cavalry*, 188–90.

31. Born in South Carolina in 1833, Stephen D. Lee was an 1854 graduate of the U. S. Military Academy. He had served in the artillery of Robert E. Lee's army until late 1862, when he was transferred to Pemberton's army at Vicksburg. Shortly after being exchanged, he was promoted to major general and given command of the cavalry in the Department of Mississippi, Alabama, West Tennessee, and East Louisiana. Warner, *Generals in Gray*, 183–84.

32. Kerr, ed., *Fighting with Ross' Texas Cavalry*, 80, 210.

Some indicated that they would join trans-Mississippi units; others apparently believed that the whole brigade might be transferred west of the river if enough of them took the initiative and showed the Confederate high command the way. They did not consider themselves deserters; after all, they intended to continue the fight west of the river. But to a diehard Confederate such as Bates, their disappearances were inexplicable. Even some of the men in his old company, soldiers who had proved themselves on several battlefields and countless miles of hard road, did not answer roll call in late August. He could not imagine how they could do such a thing. To make a bad situation worse, someone, presumably one of the deserters, lifted the major's wallet and stole his expensive new horse before tiptoeing out of camp.[33]

[Canton, Mississippi][34]
Hd Qrs 9th Texas
Aug 22nd 63
My Dear Ma:
    Capt [faded spot] of the 6th Tex leaves in the morning for Tex and I drop you a line by him. We returned yesterday evening from the scout on which we were about starting when I wrote you last. The Yankee force that went up from Yazoo city consisted of 800 cavalry & had two days the start of us. We pursued them as far as Grenada where they were joined by 2,000 under Col [Benjamin] Grierson from Memphis. As our force did not exceed 600 we concluded, on learning the strength of the Yanks, that our services might be needed down in this direction, so we commenced a retrograde movement & arrived safely here as when we departed[,] on yesterday. The Yanks did not follow us, and have since gone back to Memphis.
    Altogether we had a very disagreeable trip. On the night of the 18th we had one of the heaviest storms of rain & wind I have been in since the war. The darkness was so intense we could not see the sky except by the flash of lightning. A few stragglers from the Regt in front of mine led me into a wrong road which we traveled some distance before finding out we were wrong. Rousing up an old citizen near midnight I pressed him into service as guide & we at length

33. Ibid., 80–81, 100; Hale, *Third Texas Cavalry*, 194–95.
34. Canton is about twenty miles north of Jackson.

found the right road & overtook the Brig before day. Laying down in the mud with my boots full of water & clothes all thoroughly saturated with it, I had one hour's sleep as refreshing as I ever found on a feather bed. You probably think our faces on that march were rather lugubrious—but not so. Every mishap, and they were of frequent occurrence, whether of being tumbled horse & all into a gulley, loosing a hat or being pulled off by a limb were made jokes of and we were as jolly a set of fellows as you would find at any merry making. We have learned to turn all our mishaps & accidents to some good account, and even laugh at our calamities.

We move from this place (Canton) at 6 AM tomorrow & take position some twenty miles west of this. We have some sixty miles front to guard and will in consequence have little time to play. Maj Genl [Stephen D.] Lee (not a relative of Genl [Robert E.] Lee) has been assigned to the command of all cavalry in this Dept. He is a very ordinary looking man but he has the reputation of being a good officer.

Maj J N Dodson who was dropped from the rolls in March last, on account of protracted absence from his Regt, has been reinstated by order of the war Dept. I am therefore no longer Major, but Mr Bates only. It sounds right funny to me to be Mistered as I have had some sort of handle to my name for so long. Maj [Dodson] has not yet been assigned to duty in this Regt & may not be—but if he is I will send up my resignation immediately, for the reason that in my opinion he is totally incompetent to command even a company. He has been making an effort ever since his dismissal to be reinstated. I do not blame him for this. He has always said though that he would resign as soon as his "honor was vindicated." He has not yet returned from Richmond & I do not know whether he will take command of the Regt or not—& am moreover perfectly indifferent as to what course he does take. My military aspirations have been long since satisfied & since Texas is threatened I would sooner than not return home.[35]

Col [Dudley] Jones did not go home as he intended doing but has gone to Richmond. Lt Col [Thomas G.] Berry's health is now

35. It is not clear why Bates believed Texas was threatened. The first Federal attempt to enter Texas would not occur until September, and it was thrown back in the embarrassing Federal fiasco at Sabine Pass. Foote, *Civil War,* 2:774–75; McPherson, *Battle Cry of Freedom,* 683.

much improved & he will take command So I will have a little rest until sent off scouting again.

The Yanks in our front keep very quiet usually & do not often come east of Big Black.

Most affectionately

J.C. B

I got up this morning minus a pocket book & near seven hundred dollars in cash, and my finest horse. I am satisfied a scoundrel who deserted the Regt took my horse, but ca'nt tell where my money went—several pocket books were stolen. Ten men from my old Co are missing this morning. I think they left because of dissatisfaction with lt [S. A.] Griffith who was ordered on duty a few days ago. I prevailed on him this morning to decline promotion & Lt [John] Fowler will be promoted in his stead.[36] I think those men who left will return again. J.C. B

Aug 28/63

Three more letters written in the late summer continue themes mentioned in the major's previous communications: the dull routine of camp life, desertions that mystified Bates, and news from other fronts. Determined and persistent as always, Bates had by now found silver linings in the defeats of 1863: the loss of places on a map meant nothing; what really mattered was that Confederate armies were still in the field and better armed than ever. Even the expected fall of blockade-running ports such as Charleston and Mobile would not matter, really, because blockade runners brought in mostly luxury goods and inflated Confederate currency. The Confederacy might be better off without them.

Finally, Bates's letters of late August and early September reveal the increasing ferocity of the war. Men in the Texas Cavalry Brigade had apparently executed some black soldiers and their white officers without benefit of trial. Whether these killings were retaliations for the earlier murders of some of their own men held prisoner or reactions to their fear of armed, emancipated slaves is not clear, but Bates's matter-of-fact tone indicates that this was a different war from the one the Texans had begun two years earlier.

36. Twenty-three years old and a native of Tennessee, Griffith had been a clerk in Lamar County before the war. Fowler was a twenty-two-year-old Texas native who had been a student before the war.

[Vernon, Mississippi][37]
Aug 26th 1863
[letter from Bates to his mother, probably enclosed with the preceding letter]

Learning that Capt Barnhart of the Legion [27th Texas Cavalry]
would leave this evening for Tex I concluded to send this by him, as
I would be saved a ride of several miles by so doing.

We have no news of interest of late date or at least nothing reliable. The rumor of another battle in Va has been circulating for a day
or so, but I do not place much reliance on it, in the form that it
comes to us. The sum of it is that Lee has won another great victory
capturing Meade & 19,000 prisoners.[38] Charleston at last dates still
resisted the assault of the Yankees, and Beauregard is confident of
being able to hold the place. Although it still resists the assaults of
the federal fleet & may do so for some time to come I believe it will
ultimately fall.[39] Vicksburgh was admitted to be the strongest position in the Confederacy but overwhelming numbers on the part of
the enemy & bad generalship on ours, doomed the place. We have
a better Genl in command at Charleston than we had at Vicksburgh,
but still I believe the place will have to fall, and it once in the possession of the enemy they can then take up their cry of "on to Richmond" with almost a certainty of success.

Mobile being the weakest point, will certainly go up the spout as
the boys say, its fall being only a question of time, if as large an army
should be brought against it as was at Vicksburgh. Let us suppose
these places *do* fall into the hands of the enemy. What have we lost,
or have we indeed really lost anything? I think not much. True at the
beginning of the war when we had no arms comparatively, and but
little ammunition or other supplies for the army, these places were
valuable as ports through which they were received. There is now,
however, no longer a necessity for the importation of arms &c as our
arsenals now supply all that we need in that line.[40]

37. Vernon is about twenty-five miles northwest of Jackson.
38. No such engagement had taken place.
39. Charleston, besieged for 587 days, resisted every Federal effort to take it from the
east. Confederate military forces finally evacuated the city near the end of the war when General Sherman's march through South Carolina, west of the city, made it indefensible and useless to the Confederates. Current, *Encyclopedia of the Confederacy*, 1:287–88.
40. The Confederate ordnance department had indeed worked miracles in supplying

It would today be better with us if [the enemy?] had effectually sealed every port in the South & prevented the exportation of goods across the lines. Speculators in Confederate stocks & blockade runners have reduced our currency to its present value—and by so doing have done ten fold the injury to the country than if we had never received one dollar's worth of goods through the blockade. Nineteen out of every twenty ships that run the blockade are laden with goods which we can do quite as well without as with.[41] These cargoes are sold for Confederate money & this money must be sold *here* for gold. The profits of blockade running are so enormous that they can afford to pay almost any price in Confederate money for gold. Hence the high price of gold or the low price of Confederate money. If Charleston & Mobile fall blockade running will be ended, which will be in itself almost enough of good to counterbalance the evil that will result. They are worth no more to us as places for defense than any other point would be, and are valuable to the Yanks only as serving as a base for future operations—and they already have in their possession those points which would serve their purpose quite as well.

We have had more rumors recently about French & British intervention, but I suppose they are worth about as much, and as near the truth a year ago as now. I have thought all along, and still think that England and France have each one great object in view in withholding recognition. That object is, I think, with England to see the power of the old U.S. government crushed, and the longer this war continues, of course the more effectually that will be done. I think the object with France is to regain possession of her old territory—Louisiana and Texas—and although the *confederacy* may never be recognized by France, a *portion* of it will receive *French protection*. At any rate this is my prediction and I guess it is worth about as much as any one else's. But I suppose you are tired reading this—any how I am of writing.

Confederate soldiers with arms and ammunition from various sources, but southern armies still depended partly on blockade running. Stephen R. Wise, *Lifeline of the Confederacy: Blockade Running During the Civil War* (Columbia: University of South Carolina Press, 1988), 195–96, 226; Frank E. Vandiver, *Ploughshares into Swords: Josiah Gorgas and Confederate Ordnance* (Austin: University of Texas Press, 1952).

41. Blockade runners often did give more cargo space to higher-profit consumer goods than to military supplies, but their services were nevertheless vital to the Confederate ordnance office. Wise, *Lifeline of the Confederacy*, 61, 72–73.

As it is very likely men will be going home on furlough quite frequently I will try to keep you posted as to who they are & where you can send letters to them for me. My love to all the family, and do not fail to write whenever you have an opportunity of sending letters. Your affectionate Son,
J.C. B.

Hd Qrs 9th Tex Vernon Miss
Sept 3d 1863
Dear Will

I wrote to Ma three days ago, and to Sister a few days before that, but as Lt Smith goes direct to Paris, I write again by him. I have nothing however of much interest to write you. We have been laying perfectly quiet for ten days past—have not had even a skirmish to enliven these dull days. Our Scouts are continually hovering around the Yanks in the vicinity of Big Black [River] & bring in a half dozen every day or two.

Our news from the East is to the 29th ult. Meade had fallen back to the Potomack.[42] A fight at Richmond therefore is not probable for the next month or so. The Siege of Charleston still continued. Fort Sumter has been partially battered down & guns &c all removed. Battery Wagner was not expected to hold out long, the Yanks having a 350 lb gun in position within 300 yds of it.[43] None of the other forts had been injured. The news from Bragg is rather vague and contradictory. Some reports say he is evacuating Chatanooga, which I think is probably correct—another report is that he is fighting Rosencrantz at that place. [CODE: Gen Johnston's] forces have all been sent [CODE: to Chattanooga] with the exception of [CODE: two brigades], which are still in the vicinity of [CODE: Morton].[44] [CODE: Bragg's] forces now number betwixt

42. General Meade's army was in northern Virginia, but he had not retreated to the Potomac.

43. Battery Wagner, also known as Fort Wagner, was on Morris Island, only one and one-half miles from Fort Sumter, and was one of several Confederate forts ringing Charleston harbor. Confederate defenders at Wagner had thrown back assaults in late July, but Federal siege operations forced the abandonment of the fort three days after Bates wrote this letter. Boatner, *Civil War Dictionary*, 301.

44. Johnston had been sending parts of his army east since the previous summer, mostly to reinforce Bragg. By the time Bates wrote his letter, Johnston's army had dwindled to two small infantry divisions and Stephen D. Lee's cavalry, about ten thousand men in all. Symonds, *Joseph E. Johnston*, 243.

[CODE: sixty] and [CODE: seventy thousand].[45] So one of his staff informed me last week. It is generally understood that about one half
of Grant's forces have been sent to Rosencrantz—so he now has
quite a formidable army to hurl against Bragg.[46] One corps (of
Grant's army) is now at Vicksburgh—and one has been sent to
Natches. Grant himself is at V[icksburg].

The commissioners for the exchange of prisoners meet again
shortly, but I think it hardly probable that they will come to any understanding. The difficulty is, as you may be aware, that Lincoln in-
sists on *negroes* being recognized and treated as, prisoners of war,
and that when captured they shall be exchanged for white men. This
will never be submitted to by the confederate authorities & the exchange of prisoners will therefore be at an end.[47] Once quit ex-
changing and it will not be long before no prisoners are taken. The
only course left to us is to take every Negro found in arms, and every
man connected with them, into some thicket or swamp and hang
them up as soon as captured. This course *we* have heretofore pursued and our men *will continue to do so.*[48]

I send you five hundred dollars by Lt Smith—which please invest
in land. The above amount I borrowed & send because another safe
opportunity of sending money may not occur again soon—as we
have just received an order to send up no more furloughs. Some
light fingered gentleman "relieved" my pocket of near seven hundred dollars, a few nights since—& I also had a horse stolen on the
same night worth here 600$ or 700$.

Write to me by Lt Smith. What do the people of Tex think of the

45. By September, Bragg had concentrated about 66,000 men in north Georgia. Boatner, *Civil War Dictionary,* 152.

46. Bates is mistaken about Grant's army. No Federal troops from Vicksburg reached
Rosecrans before his battle with Bragg at Chickamauga (September 19–20). Peter Cozzens,
This Terrible Sound: The Battle of Chickamauga (Urbana: University of Illinois Press, 1992),
79, 523.

47. An 1861 agreement between the governments in Washington and Richmond to exchange prisoners broke down in the summer of 1863. The Confederacy's refusal to exchange
black prisoners was one of several factors that led to the breakdown. Current, *Encyclopedia of
the Confederacy,* 3:1256–58.

48. The Texans may well have hanged some black soldiers and their white officers, especially in the second, more brutal, half of the war. A systematic and painstaking search of Federal army records, however, turned up no evidence that the Texas Cavalry Brigade hanged
white officers of black units as early as the summer of 1863. James G. Hollandsworth, Jr.,
"The Execution of White Officers from Black Units by Confederate Forces During the Civil
War," *Louisiana History* 35 (Fall 1994): 475–89.

war, its termination, our prospects &cc. about 30 men have deserted this Brigade within the last two weeks—ten of them from my old co. I have no idea what reasons they had or pretend to have. Six men from the Co were sent after them the next day—and they have not yet returned & it may be that they will not. The men of this Brig are very much dissatisfied & want to get west of the Miss. I look for more desertions as soon as we move from here. They are not tired of the war but *of this state* & they have reason to be.
Your Bro JC B

Your brother Thos is elected Gov of Ky—so the Louisville Journal says—by a large majority.[49]

Hd Qrs 9th Tex Cav
Near Vernon Miss
Sept 12th 1863
My Dear Ma
    Lt Haynes leaves for Texas in the morning in pursuit of deserters, and although I have written a dozen letters home more or less, within the last six weeks I take it for granted you think of my letters as I do of yours, that they come none too often.
    We are still encamped near Vernon—and have a most tedious time in doing nothing. We occasionally burn a few hundred bales of cotton—capture a few negroes & yanks every day or so, but beyond that rarely have anything to relieve the dull monotony of camp life. On yesterday we had a little diversion in the way of a review of three Brigades of Cav'ly at this place. Our new commander Maj Genl [Stephen D.] Lee & Genl [William J.] Hardee were present.[50] Genl Lee is by no means prepossessing in his appearance and looks more like a country school master than a Maj Genl of Cavalry. I hope however that he will make up in brains and other things for his deficiency as to the outward man. Genl Hardee is a fine looking old gentleman apparently about forty-eight years old. He is about six feet high—of heavy build in this inclined to corpulency. He has grey hair, forehead

49. Will's brother, Thomas Bramlette, was elected governor on August 3 as a War Democrat and took office two days before Bates wrote his letter. Sifakis, *Who Was Who*, 69.
    50. Lieutenant General William J. Hardee, forty-seven years old, was a Georgia native, a West Point graduate, and a veteran of the Mexican War. A former commandant of cadets at the U.S. Military Academy, he was also the author of the standard textbook for infantry officers, *Rifle and Light Infantry Tactics* (1861). Warner, *Generals in Gray*, 124.

tolerably high, but not broad & a little receding—mild large blue eyes—tolerably large nose rather thick lips—upper teeth projecting a little—wore a heavy mustachio & thick grey beard on his chin. His mustachios partially conceal his lips & teeth & he is altogether a fine looking man especially at a short distance from him. But Genl [Joseph E.] Johnston came nearer up to my *ideal* of a Genl than any man I have ever seen.

You will probably hear before this reaches you of the desertions in this Regt. Thirty two of my old co have deserted—fifty three altogether from the Regt. What their reasons, or *pretended* reasons were, I have not the remotest idea. They may attempt to smooth it over as best they can, but it is *desertion,* and nothing else can be made of it. Saying they will enter the Service on that side the river does not paliate their offense, but it is on the other hand, an aggravation of it. If I had a brother I would rather see him laid in his grave than be branded as these boys will be, as a deserter. And however little they may *now* think of it the stigma will cling to them to the grave & descend to their children. I have written out a document in condemnation of their course and after having all who are present with the Regt to sign it will send it to Tex for publication. I have no doubt but most of them would be pardoned if they would return voluntarily—but there are two or three who will as certainly be hung as they are caught & without the form of a court-martial.

I have seen nothing of very late date from our armies in the east. The Siege of Charleston still continues. Fort Sumter has been reoccupied and turned into a water battery.[51] The Yanks bursted their two largest guns and have not been shelling the city for some time. About two weeks ago we received through the blocade, a monster gun carrying a 600 lb ball. I suppose it will be mounted at Charleston. Some little fighting going on at Chatanooga.[52] Grant has issued a proclamation claiming the Miss[issippi] central rail road as his line—proclaiming the negroes free, but magnanimously giving their former masters the privilege of *hiring* them. Lincoln has issued an

51. After failing to reduce Fort Sumter with a fleet of ironclads in April, the U.S. Navy attempted to capture the fort with a landing party on September 8. Confederate defenders smashed the landing party, and the navy finally gave up on capturing the fort until Charleston was evacuated late in the war. Boatner, *Civil War Dictionary,* 300–301.

52. The fighting near Chattanooga was preliminary to the bloodbath that occurred one week later at the Battle of Chickamauga. Connelly, *Autumn of Glory,* 166–93.

order for all able bodied negroes that can be gathered up within their lines to be put immediately in the army.

Well, of negroes and those who command them, we never have, and never will ask quarter. We have set a good many of them to stretching hemp & will take pleasure in "setting up" in the same business all others we catch. The day before yesterday we presented one John Buck, a citizen who piloted the Yanks through here on their last raid, with a hempen neck tie—& on yesterday a true spec- imen of the Yankee—one whose instincts are, or *were* to steal & plunder, having been caught with various silver articles gold watches &c on his person which he boasted having stolen from defenseless women—was sent with dispatches or with *dispatch* to his sable majesty which place I have no doubt he reached in safety. But I must close.

Yours affectionately

J.C. B.

I have just been informed by Scouts from Yazoo that six or eight cit- izens were *murdered* in that vicinity by some armed negroes.

Shortly after Bates wrote his letter of September 12, he received unbeliev- ably good news—he was going home to Paris. Bates, two lieutenants, and two enlisted men were ordered to round up the men who had recently crossed the river and any other soldiers of the brigade who happened to be in Texas and escort them back to service in Mississippi.[53] President Davis had recently offered pardon to deserters, so if the men could be brought back to the brigade, they had a good chance of escaping firing squads.[54] The major's spotless record as a soldier and his long absence from home doubtless played a part in the decision to send him to Texas on this im- portant mission.

Although the Federal navy now controlled the Mississippi River, small groups of Confederates frequently crossed over undetected. Where Bates and his party crossed is not known, but the nearest point to their camp was north of Vicksburg, near the Arkansas-Louisiana line. In the late summer

53. Official returns for September 16 indicated that 353 men of the Texas brigade were absent. Many, of course, were ill or wounded or on detached service, but dozens of them had slipped away to Texas. *OR*, Vol. 30, Pt. 4, p. 517.

54. Kerr, ed., *Fighting with Ross' Texas Cavalry*, 81; Faust, *Historical Times Illustrated Encyclopedia*, 12.

of 1863, the Federals had only eleven riverboats patrolling the two-hundred-mile stretch of water north of Vicksburg, so the transit going west was probably no problem at all for the homeward-bound Texans, loaded down with letters from the soldiers to their families.[55]

For six months Bates was away from the regiment, rounding up deserters and other absentees in Texas. Without the usual letters to his family and friends, it is difficult to know exactly what he did during those months, but it is safe to assume that he enjoyed the pleasures of home for a good part of his time in Texas. Visits to Mootie's parlor, hot meals prepared by his mother and sister, long conversations about the war with Eb Dohoney and Will Bramlette, reunions with former comrades such as John Gibbons—the whole experience must have seemed unreal to the hardened horse soldier.

Of course, he also tended to his assignment—finding and convincing the brigade's absentees to return to the war. Armed with an official request from General Stephen D. Lee, Bates called on trans-Mississippi officials to assist him in his work. In early October, Lieutenant General Edmund Kirby Smith, now commander of the Trans-Mississippi Department of the Confederacy, issued Special Orders No. 155 at Shreveport, directing that "all officers will give such aid to Major Bates and his officers as they can to assist in the duty with which they are charged." The major and his detail evidently had some success because Bates's later letters mention the problems involved in getting the absentees back across the Mississippi River.[56]

While Bates rounded up absentees, the Texas Cavalry Brigade remained inactive for much of late 1863, only occasionally galloping out on a scout or grappling with the enemy. On the other hand, a major change in leadership did take place—the replacement of the brigade's commander, John W. Whitfield, by the man whose name has been connected with the brigade ever since, Lawrence Sullivan "Sul" Ross. General Stephen D. Lee was convinced by late 1863 that Whitfield was an inefficient and ineffective leader. Lee believed Whitfield was too feeble to control his rowdy soldiers and urged the secretary of war to replace him with a "proper officer"; otherwise, the rest of the brigade might desert. The bureaucracy responded quickly. Whitfield left the brigade for another assignment in October, and Ross assumed command of the insubordinate Texans on December 16. Just in time, too, for one week earlier some of the men had overpowered the guards, removed the chains from some of their comrades

55. Kerr, ed., *Fighting with Ross' Texas Cavalry*, 81; Connelly, "Vicksburg," 52.
56. *OR*, Vol. 26, Pt. 2, pp. 371–72.

who had been court-martialed, and threatened any officers who attempted to stop them.[57]

When Ross arrived at brigade headquarters, he gathered the soldiers and made a speech promising to give them something to do besides guard duty. This was more to their liking, and before the day was over, the Texans were planning a serenade for their new young commander.[58] Ross was one of those legendary Indian fighters and soldiers of nineteenth-century Texas. Born in Iowa Territory in 1838, he had come to Texas with his family while still an infant. During his college days in Alabama in the 1850s, he returned to Texas for summer vacations and Indian fighting, winning the praise of regular army officers for his daring and skill in operations against the fierce Comanches of north Texas. When the Civil War erupted, Ross joined the 6th Texas Cavalry; he had risen in the ranks to colonel by 1863. His promotion to brigadier general became official five days after he took command of the brigade, known ever since as Ross's Texas Cavalry Brigade.[59]

General Ross was not long in following up on his promise of more interesting duty for his Texans. Six days after taking command, he led the brigade through rain, sleet, and snow to the Mississippi River, transporting rifles for poorly supplied trans-Mississippi Confederates. Then, in February, Ross led the brigade against a column of Federals moving up the Yazoo River toward northeastern Mississippi. The Texans shortly afterward galloped over to eastern Mississippi to assist in Confederate resistance to William T. Sherman's Meridian campaign. Before the month was over, they raced back toward Yazoo City to confront the same Federal force they had encountered before leaving to harass Sherman. This expedition turned brutal when the Texans ran up against black Federal soldiers, some of whom were apparently killed after surrendering. The Texans claimed that the African Americans had murdered two of their Texas prisoners earlier, but by this stage of the war, few could remember who had started the

57. Stephen D. Lee to J. A. Seddon, October 2, 1863, reprinted in Kerr, ed., *Fighting with Ross' Texas Cavalry*, 117–18; ibid., 103.

58. A soldier in the 3rd Texas Cavalry summed up the attitude of the Texans: Ross's "magnetic nature, and noble qualities of head and heart, made him almost the idol of the whole brigade. The boys were proud of their dashing young General, and I doubt if he would have accepted a Major General's commission, unless conditioned that the old brigade should remain with him." Rose, *Ross' Texas Brigade*, 103.

59. After the war, Ross served as a crime-busting sheriff, a state legislator, governor of Texas, and president of the Agricultural and Mechanical College of Texas (now Texas A&M University). Kerr, ed., *Fighting with Ross' Texas Cavalry*, 103; Tyler et al., *New Handbook of Texas*, 5:688–89; Warner, *Generals in Gray*, 263–64.

string of atrocities. By early March, quiet returned to central Mississippi, and the brigade camped near Benton, thirty miles north of Jackson.[60]

While Ross's Brigade bounded from one corner of Mississippi to another, Bates continued to round up deserters and other absentees in Texas. He and his detachment left Paris in late January and stayed for a while in Marshall, nearer the Louisiana border. While there, he wrote to Mootie, implying strongly that the couple had planned a marriage during Bates's recent visit, but as usual, Bates's comments about Mootie and matters of the heart were indirect. Even after their relationship had taken this important turn, he could still tease her about attractive women he encountered in his travels. Once again, the hardened soldier was as lighthearted as a boy when he wrote to Mootie.

> Marshall
> Jany 29 [1864]
> Miss Mootie Johnson
> My Dear Friend
>
> I have just returned from calling on Miss Puss and as I will in all probability leave in the morning for Miss[issippi] and not have another opportunity for doing so "I now take my pen in hand"—but you know the rest—or if you don't your School Master did not do his duty.[61]
>
> Genl W——[Whitfield?] arrived yesterday and if I had known he would have been so long in coming I certainly would have spent another week at home.[62] But what's past can't be remedied.
>
> I have spent the time since I have been here very pleasantly—called on all my old acquaintances and formed a good many new ones. last week the young ladies gave a leap year party at Mrs Peetes—at which I of course saw all the *elite* of the place. Miss Puss did me the honor to call for & take me to the party, and we had a *very* pleasant evening. But I at least would have enjoyed the party

60. Perry Wayne Shelton, comp., and Shelly Morrison, ed., *Personal Civil War Letters of General Lawrence Sullivan Ross, with Other Letters* (Austin, Tex.: Shelly and Richard Morrison, 1994), 60–62; W. A. Callaway, "Hard Service with Ross's Brigade." *Confederate Veteran* 28 (September 1920): 328–29; Hale, *Third Texas Cavalry*, 197–209.

61. Mootie's family had lived in Marshall before moving to Paris in the late 1850s, and she still had kinfolk in Marshall. The flirtatious Miss Puss was her cousin. Neville, *History of Lamar County*, 105.

62. When General Whitfield left the Texas brigade, he transferred to the Trans-Mississippi Department. Rose, *Ross' Texas Brigade*, 103.

more if this "shadow" next my heart had been replaced by a face more substantial.[63] I do'nt meant that I wished that face in my *pocket* exactly or even against it "right before all the folks" but somewhere in the vicinity.

I have no doubt there was an immense amount of courting done that evening, but that do'nt concern you & me *now* you know. I expect you would like me to tell you who were there, how they were dressed, how they wore their hair &cc but as you are aware I have'nt a very nice perception of different kinds of dress—and as well as I now remember they were all dressed just alike. As to the matter of hair I only remember some wore qu[eu]es, some wore *knots* on the back of their heads—I mean the *hair* was in knots—some wore *shingles,* and one or two dozen wore *splinters*—but which were really intended for curls. If you do'nt know what I mean by splinters I'll say *strings.* But taking strings, splinters, shingles knots &c and their owners, and every thing else into consideration I "kalkilate" we had quite as nice a time as need be.

What a delicious sensation flattered vanity is—I've *felt* it. Do you wonder that I felt a little "stuck up" when Miss N with a blush just perceptible and the sweetest grace imaginable asks, "Maj Bates will you give me the pleasure of dancing a set with you" and Miss T "will you take my arm for a promenade, Maj," & Miss J "Let me help you to a glass of wine" &cc. But you are used to all this and of course ca'nt properly appreciate my "felinks" [feelings] on that momentous occasion. Well I've said enough about *that* party but don't know what to say about any thing else so turn over and lets think a little.

But I can think of no one just now but yourself—and your fair cousin. Its lucky for you—or most likely unlucky—that I didnt know her first for I certainly would have fallen in love with *her*—and in fact I don't know but I have any how. The fact is I am so entangled in Cupid's meshes that I don't exactly know where I'm located. Would you be so kind as to straighten me out again when you wish. Seriously I am very much pleased with Miss Puss—but havent told her so with my tongue or pen either but cant answer for my eyes.

Don't you think it is time to stop foolishness for a while and write a little sober sense. Well I'd do it in a minute or less if I *knew* any thing that *was* sensible. You see I've been nearly or quite sick for several days & momentarily threatened with an attack of the ———

63. Bates is referring to the picture of Mootie he carried with him throughout the war.

blues and I have just been trying to get rid of them—at your expense and some others—very generous, aint I? Have you been having the blues any lately. If so you must not do so any more. You see I say you *must*—& my orders must be obeyed.

Well, I'd give a Lincoln half dollar—would give more if I had it & it was necessary—to be in Paris this evening—nearly morning now 11 o clk—and have a good talk with you. I believe the purest happiness of a man's life—except that derived from religion—is when he receives an avowal of affection from a pure virgin heart. If I were with you tonight *words* might not give me this happiness—though I am sure I would receive it through a Source not less intelligible—to those interested at least. But I have had that so often I need not wish it again.

I said awhile ago it was 11 o clk but it is past 12 & I must write *something* in Miss Jo's album yet, tho cant imagine what it will be as I cant feel a bit "inspired" and I must also get a little sleep. I want you to write to me immediately directing your letters to Brandon Miss. If you have no opportunity of sending by hand send with Ma or sister to Capt G G Griff. I will direct them to send letters to John as he will have frequent opportunities of forwarding them.

Will you write something every day or so making your letter as long & consequently as interesting as you can. Do not fail to write immediately as several men leave here for the Miss in a month from now.

Please excuse this letter for being too short—too long—too foolish—too profound—too prosy?—or whichever it is. In fact please excuse me generally—and at the same time receive the assurance of my continued high regard.

J C B

Don't fail to write immediately.

After leaving Marshall, Bates and his party probably rode forty miles east to Shreveport, Louisiana, then down the Red River to its confluence with the Mississippi. The major apparently had collected several dozen absentees, but he discovered how unruly his fellow Texans could be when he tried to cross them to the east side of the river—some of them deserted again while waiting for Bates to arrange transportation. A few even went over to the Federals to be paroled. Controlling these men was like trying to herd cats.

Complicating the whole project were Federal gunboats steaming up and down the Mississippi and Red Rivers, making a crossing too dangerous. Bates had to wait at least a week, probably longer, before he could get his men into Mississippi. He was fortunate to get across at all. If he had waited a few more days, he would have been caught in the middle of Federal general Nathaniel P. Banks's Red River campaign. In fact, the largest Federal river fleet to be assembled in the entire war gathered at the mouth of Red River—Bates's exact crossing point—on March 12 as part of the campaign. If his timing had been only slightly different, the major might have been forced to spend the next few months fighting with Richard Taylor's army in northwestern Louisiana rather than riding with Ross's Texas Brigade in Mississippi, Alabama, and Georgia.[64]

Marksville La[65]
Feb 28th 1864
My Dear Sister:
   From various causes we have not yet crossed the river. I left the men in charge of Capt Cook at Shreveport & went on myself to the Miss river and made arrangements for crossing. At Alexandria about half the men deserted and went back again. As soon as I learned this I went back to meet them, but they had gone on by a different road and I missed them. I sent a dispatch to Genl [Kirby] Smith to arrest the deserters, and started again for the Miss & met Cook & twenty five men at this place returning saying they could not cross. I will start again this morning & make another effort to get them across. If Cook had not delayed so much on the road we could have crossed ten days ago with perfect ease and safety. Now however we will have a good deal of difficulty. The boats in which I intended crossing, and in fact all in reach of here have been broken up. I intend to lay on the river until an opportunity occurs if it is a month.
   A Lieut—the same who deserted from our Regt with forty men—& three privates went to a gun boat to be paroled. The men were paroled but the federal officer refused to parole the Lieut, whereupon he put spurs to his horse & made his escape. He is now in the guard house here, awaiting his trial.
   We have had a rumor for some time that Longstreet had captured

   64. Ludwell H. Johnson, *Red River Campaign: Politics and Cotton in the Civil War* (Baltimore: Johns Hopkins University Press, 1958), 89–91.
   65. Marksville is near the right bank of the lower Red River.

Knoxville & several thousand prisoners, but I don't believe the report.[66] It is also said that Sherman & his corps are at Meridian Miss
& [General Leonidas] Polk in his rear at Jackson.[67] If this is true I
am of opinion that Polk & not Sherman—as is generally believed—
is in danger. If Sherman is at Meridian it is only a ruse to entrap Polk
& I would not be surprised if a large force were at Vicksburgh to
close in on his rear while Sherman attacks him in front. I will write
again before crossing the river. My love to all
Affectionately your brother
JC Bates

Simsport La[68]
March 4th 1864
My Dear Friend [Mootie]

Are you getting impatient for a letter from me. From various
causes "too numerous to mention" I have not written as often as I
should have done, but as apologies are usually pretty good evidence
of neglect I will make time for the last week or so. I have been "laying around loose" watching for an opportunity of crossing the
"branch" but as yet none has been presented. I have sent to Alexandria for arms for my men & when I get them will lay on the bank of
the Miss until I do get over, and in the mean time if these pesky Yankees don't quit bothering me as they have been doing Some of them
will get hurt that is, if they get near enough to me.

I have just seen a gentleman from Richmond who says Mobile is
not invested, but is being shelled by gunboats, that Longstreet has
not captured Knoxville, but in stead a few wagons and prisoners,
that Genl Polk was at Demopolis [Alabama] and Sherman at Meridian with 25 or 30,000 men, that two corps of the enemy crossed the
Rapidan & were driven back with some loss by Lee, that Forrest and
Grierson had a fight in north Miss in which the latter was badly

66. Lieutenant General James Longstreet's twenty thousand Confederates besieged
Knoxville in November and December 1863 but finally gave up the siege and returned to
Virginia in the spring of 1864. Current, *Encyclopedia of the Confederacy*, 2:895–97.

67. Sherman did carry out his campaign against Meridian in eastern Mississippi, but
Polk's forces were not in the Federal rear. Rather, they were falling back into Alabama before Sherman. Foote, *Civil War*, 2:924–25.

68. Simmesport, Louisiana, is at the head of the Atchafalaya River, near the point where
the Red, Atchafalaya, and Mississippi Rivers converge.

beaten.[69] five gun boats & several transports have gone up Black river & we hear firing at Fort Beauregard.[70]

I have been stopping for a day or so with Capt Sadbury who is on out post duty here. I have made the acquaintance of some very nice ladies in this Section, but the one I like most is always near me & though I occasionally speak to *her* she never replies. Did I ever write you as short a letter as this before—but this is all the paper I have & it contains quite as many good wishes & as much esteem as if it were longer. So with the usual promise of doing better in future, I am sincerely,
Your friend
JCB

I am on the bank of the river & will cross tonight providence & the federals permitting. There seems to be no doubt from all the information I can get, that Sherman has been badly whipped at Selma alabama & is retreating towards Vicksburgh.[71]

On Miss[issippi River]
Mar 6th 1864
My Dear Ma

At last I am on the bank of the Miss & if nothing unforeseen occurs will cross tonight. I have secured a boat & am only awaiting for my horse to eat grist awhile before starting across. From gentlemen just from the other side I learn we will have but little difficulty on the other side.We have reliable information from Federal sources that Sherman has been badly whipped by Polk at Selma Alabama. I learn this evening that he is retreating to Vicksburgh. The story that

69. Most of Bates's information is correct. Neither Forrest's successful raid into west Tennessee in December nor his victory at Okolona, Mississippi, in February had included a battle with Benjamin Grierson's cavalry, however. Wills, *Battle from the Start,* 150–56, 158–68.

70. The Black River emptied into the Red twenty straight-line miles north of Simmesport. Fort Beauregard was another thirty-five miles farther north. On March 1–4 a Federal river fleet exchanged fire along the Black River with Confederate infantry. This was doubtless the firing Bates heard to the north. *OR,* Vol. 34, Pt. 1, pp. 155–58.

71. General Sherman had not even fought at Selma. After ripping up railroads and eastern Mississippi in general, he returned to Vicksburg as planned. Foote, *Civil War,* 2:924–26, 934–35.

Mobile has been invested is not true.[72] The enemy are however shelling it from the gulf and all noncombatants have been ordered to leave the place in anticipation of a general engagement.

I was informed this evening by a lady just from New Orleans that Banks with a force estimated at from 10 to 15000 men are on the point of moving from Texas via Berwicks Bay [Louisiana].[73] Six gunboats went up Black river the other day but did but little damage and have returned. It is reported that the raft in Red River had been washed away mostly. If this is the case our army will probably fall back above Alexandria. I think it would do this anyway as the fort (De Rusy) [Fort De Russy, near Marksville] can be flanked I think on either side.[74]

If anything happens that I don't cross I will write again. If I don't write again take it for granted that I am safely over.

J.C. Bates

Major Bates finally got his absentees—at least, those who had not deserted again—over the river, probably on March 6 or 7. Within a couple of weeks, he had escorted them back to the brigade near Benton, north of Jackson. He had missed a great deal of action while in Texas and Louisiana, but he probably regretted not a minute of the time he had spent in Paris. Besides, there was still plenty of fighting left to do east of the river.

72. Federal forces would not capture Mobile, Alabama, until the last month of the war.

73. General Nathaniel P. Banks's Federal army of seventeen thousand men, many of whom had recently returned from the lower Texas coast, began marching from South Louisiana toward the vicinity of Bates's camp the day after Bates wrote this letter. Johnson, *Red River Campaign*, 98.

74. General Richard Taylor's Confederate army, concentrated around Alexandria and Marksville, did fall back north of Alexandria, and Fort De Russy near Marksville was taken by the Federals on March 14. Ibid., 91–96.

10 Alabama, Georgia, and Hospitals

While Major Bates was shepherding his band of absentees back to camp, Ulysses S. Grant, conqueror of Vicksburg, was promoted to lieutenant general and appointed general in chief of all United States armies. At about the same time, President Lincoln and General Grant agreed on an all-out simultaneous advance of the various Federal armies—George G. Meade's in Virginia, William T. Sherman's in north Georgia, and smaller armies on other fronts. The Confederates might be able to scrounge up enough resources in one or two areas to stymie the Union's offensives, but the rebels could not deal with all of them. A breakthrough must happen somewhere. Joseph E. Johnston, Bates's ideal image of a general, now commanded the army formerly led by Braxton Bragg, and it was Johnston's job to stop Sherman's advance from Chattanooga into central Georgia.[1] Ross's Texas Cavalry Brigade, which had spent nearly all of the preceding two years in Mississippi, would be drawn into the maelstrom of north Georgia in the spring of 1864.

Bates's first few letters after rejoining the brigade were written from the camps near Benton, thirty miles north of Jackson. In addition to providing general war news to the home folks, Bates also complained that after all his efforts to round up deserters and return them to service, he had been arrested as soon as he reached camp! One of his fellow officers, a major in the 3rd Texas Cavalry, had accused him of "continued absence without sufficient excuse" and of being drunk and encouraging the desertions while Bates was in Louisiana. For a man like Bates, who had little

1. McPherson, *Battle Cry of Freedom*, 721–22; Connelly, *Autumn of Glory*, 281.

patience with drunken rowdyism or desertion, such accusations were out-rageous, and he challenged his accuser to provide evidence. Bates prevailed in this imbroglio and was soon released from arrest and restored to command.

Hd Qrs 9th Tex Cavly
March 29th 1864
My Dear Ma

After so long a time I am again with my command & am truly glad of it. It seems a good deal like I had just got home. I find things going on about as usual. The same round of camp duties—parades, inspections, reviews, picketing, scouting &c.

Our Brigade has had two severe fights recently, in both of which they were victorious. In one about 60 negroes & yankees were killed—in the other about 40—our loss about forty altogether.[2]

I had a good deal of difficulty in crossing the Miss but got over without accident. I don't think I ever did a harder days work than I did that night. I came over with the last boat load & reached this bank just at day break, as soon as the last were over the river[,] twelve miles & back at least.[3]

I had a good deal of trouble with my horse after leaving Texas on account of lameness produced by serving. He is now however well but not in good order. I find horses here *very* high—such as mine worth 1,500 or 2,000$ & but few to be had. I find a good many of my Regiment dismounted & impossible to get horses. We sent a Lieut into Alabama for the purpose of pressing & after Securing a Sufficient number to mount the Regt they were taken from him by Genl [Leonidas] Polk for artillery.[4]

The last Congress as I anticipated they would, enacted the conscript law.[5] The same officers & organizations win victories. I fear we

2. Bates refers to the recent engagements with the Federals near Yazoo City, about ten miles west of Benton. See Barron, *Lone Star*, 181–84, for accounts of the brigade's actions in late February and March.

3. Bates must have crossed and recrossed the river on successive trips to travel twelve miles.

4. "Pressing" was essentially "taking" horses from civilians for military purposes. Those civilians considered loyal to the Confederacy probably received receipts for later reimbursement.

5. The Confederacy's third conscription act, adopted in mid-February, extended the term of service for most soldiers from three years to "the duration" (i.e., the end of the war).

will have a good deal of trouble with the men when our three years expire.[6] Unless a change occurs or some arrangement is made to furlough them a great many will desert. If a Regt at a time should be furloughed I think most of them will return. They will desert not to get out of the service, but to get home for a time. And it does seem hard that men whose families are in reduced circumstances should be denied the privilege of visiting them. Once in three years, on the other hand, each Regt. is furloughed at the expiration of its term. Our army will be almost broken up in the process.

On my arrival in camp I was placed under arrest for "continued absence without sufficient excuse" but subsequently released by Genl Ross explaining the cause of my excursions in Texas. I intend however as soon as I can get the evidence of Genl. Whitfield, to demand a court of inquiry.[7]

The slanderous representations of one major J.N. Coleman (who has always disliked me, for the reason I suppose that I gave him once my opinions of his sort) to Genl [William H.] Jackson was the cause of my arrest.[8] He is generally reported to have said "we (myself & men) were all drunk in La,["]—that I told the men I did not intend to return & was making no effort to do so &c. I have just addressed a letter to Genl Jackson to know what was said to him by Coleman and will in the morning send up a statement from all the men & officers under my charge at that time proving Maj Coleman's statement deliberate falsehoods, in every particular.

[one line illegible] that land patent I received a short time before

---

Congress also stretched the draft to include men as young as seventeen and as old as fifty, closed various loopholes in the conscription system, and authorized the employment of twenty thousand black southerners as laborers in the army. Moore, *Conscription and Conflict,* 308–309; Current, *Encyclopedia of the Confederacy,* 1:398–99.

6. The men in Ross's brigade had originally signed up for twelve months of service. Then their terms were extended to three years by the first draft law in 1862. Now, when the end of the three-year period was in sight, the men were told they would have to stay in the army indefinitely.

7. Bates had apparently worked with General Whitfield while in Texas and expected Whitfield to provide good reasons for his prolonged absence.

8. Coleman, a twenty-eight-year-old Georgia native, had been a Harrison County merchant before the war. He had worked his way up from private to major in the 3rd Texas Cavalry and served on General Ross's staff. Jackson was commander of the cavalry division that included Ross's Texas Cavalry Brigade. Hale, *Third Texas Cavalry,* 44, 115; Joseph H. Crute, Jr., *Confederate Staff Officers, 1861–1865* (Powhatan, Va.: Derwent Books, 1982), 168.

leaving home.[9] Write to me *immediately* sending the letters to Capt. Grigg at Marshall as I before directed you.

I must close and be ready for review. Has Dohony sold my pistol yet. If not let him do so & pay Moore. My love to all the family.
Your affectionate son
JC Bates

Hd Qrs 9th Tex Cavly
April 1st 1864
My Dear Ma,

I wrote you a few days ago but as some others are going home on furlough I drop a line by them. Since I have been with the Regt we have done nothing but picket duty—the [Federal] army having kept themselves pretty close to Vicksburgh.

The general character of the news from the north is encouraging to us. The bitter feelings existing betwixt the Copperheads & abolitionists is growing stronger every day, & if we can believe the reports of federal papers[,] frequently result in serious riots and fights betwixt the citizens & soldiers.[10] The news from Ky is that Gov Bramlette has written Lincoln that he will resist, by force if necessary, the enlistment of negro troops in that state.[11] A Maj Gnl of cavly in Ky whose name I do not recollect, is reported by a chicago paper to have said in a speech to his troops that if Lincoln insisted on the enlistment of negro troops in Ky, he was henceforth a rebel. There may be, and doubtless is some truth in these reports but I am afraid resistance in Ky will never be sufficiently formidable to be of any benefit to us.

Genl Grant who has been made commander in chief of the Yankee army, had pledged himself in a speech in Washington, if left untrammeled by Lincoln, to have possession of Richmond, Mobile &

9. While in Texas rounding up deserters, Bates had transferred title to 640 acres of land northwest of Fort Worth from himself to his mother. The transfer document, dated January 11, 1864, is in the Bates Papers.

10. Copperheads were conservative northern Democrats, sometimes known as Peace Democrats, who hoped to end the war as soon as possible with an armistice and negotiations rather than through military action.

11. Will's brother, governor of Kentucky, may not have openly threatened to resist the enlistment of black soldiers, but he certainly did complain to President Lincoln about such recruiting in his state. Roy P. Basler, ed., *The Collected Works of Abraham Lincoln* (9 vols; New Brunswick, N.J.: Rutgers University Press, 1953–55), 7:272, 272n, 283n.

Charleston by christmas. But this is of a kind of the braggadocio we usually hear from the great Yankey nation.[12]

Our Division commander complimented our Brig very highly in recent order & ordered "Yazoo" and "Liverpool" to be inscribed on our banner which already had on it the batles of Corinth, Hatchie Bridge, Iuka Holly Springs, Thompson's Station, Elkhorn & Davis' Mills.[13] We can therefore boast of *four* more hard fought battles than any other troops in our cavalry. Application has been made to furlough our Brig by Regts, but I think it will be disapproved. Do not fail to write often. My regards to friends & love to sister & the family.
Affectionately,
J.C. Bates

Less than a week after Bates wrote his first letter home following his return, Ross's Texas Cavalry Brigade, as part of William H. Jackson's cavalry division, was ordered into northern Alabama. Confederate authorities were worried that Federal troops along the Tennessee River in the north might dash down on the iron and coal fields of central Alabama, and Jackson's horsemen were to keep an eye on them and report to General Leonidas Polk, commander in Mississippi and Alabama. As long as the gray troopers were in north Alabama, they were also to send out "expeditions against the deserters and tories of North Alabama."[14] The cavalry's commander, General Stephen D. Lee, "will arrest them [Tories and deserters], and will deal with all such as may be banded together for resistance in the most summary manner."[15]

The brigade set out from central Mississippi on April 4, crossed into Alabama on the fifteenth, and settled into a new camp near Tuscaloosa on

12. In General Grant's only speech in the spring of 1864, he made no such remarks about the capture of Richmond, Mobile, and Charleston by Christmas. Bates must have read a Confederate account of Grant's speech. John Y. Simon (editor of the Ulysses S. Grant Papers) to Richard Lowe, September 11, 1997, in possession of the recipient.

13. Yazoo and Liverpool were the two engagements fought shortly before Bates returned to active duty with the regiment. Davis's Mill was one of the small fights along the Mississippi Central Railroad during the Holly Springs raid in December 1862.

14. Confederates often referred to white southern Unionists as Tories, recalling the term used for loyalists during the American War of Independence. More than three thousand Alabamians, mostly from the northern counties, joined the Federal army during the war. Richard Nelson Current, *Lincoln's Loyalists: Union Soldiers from the Confederacy* (Boston: Northeastern University Press, 1992), 103–107, 217.

15. *OR*, Vol. 32, Pt. 3, p. 785; Hale, *Third Texas Cavalry*, 211–12.

the eighteenth. The next day Colonel Dudley Jones led three hundred troopers (parts of the 3rd, 6th, and 9th Texas Cavalry Regiments) on an expedition to hunt down deserters and Tories in Marion County in northwestern Alabama. The woods and hills in that part of the state were honeycombed with hideouts for deserters, draft dodgers, and Unionists, estimated by some Confederate officials to number between eight and ten thousand men. Some of these fugitives had assassinated conscription officers, burned courthouses, overpowered law officers to liberate friends from jail, and robbed civilians. In retaliation for outrages committed against them by Confederate supporters, the pro-Union fugitives had hanged one Confederate home-guard leader by his feet and then built a fire directly beneath his head, roasting him to death. General Polk ordered the cavalry to punish armed deserters and Tories "with death upon the spot."[16]

Major Bates commanded the troopers from the 9th Texas Cavalry on this expedition. For several days the Texans rode through the hilly back country, dodging potshots from Unionists, searching houses, and arresting deserters and draft dodgers. Private Sparks of Company I wrote that the wives and mothers of the Alabamians "were not slow to give us a piece of their minds and mostly a good large piece and [if] convenient they would emphasize that opinion with a club." One Texan, searching a bedroom, eyed a pair of shoes that appeared too large for the woman of the house, whereupon he demanded an explanation from the lady who claimed to own the size elevens. This aroused her "worser nature," and without warning "she dealt him a right-hander full in the face." After regaining his feet and declaring grandly and with a flourish that he did not make war on women, the soldier thought better of it and "finally wound up by swearing that no living person should treat him thus and go unpunished upon which he dealt her a blow in the pit of the stomach that laid her flat on the floor."[17]

General Ross, in a letter to his wife, indicated that his soldiers "have caught & hung several" of the "Robbers—Deserters &c." Major Bates did not provide details, but he did admit that this was "not a very pleasant

16. *OR*, Vol. 32, Pt. 3, p. 825. For the turmoil in north Alabama, see Moore, *Conscription and Conflict*, 211; Malcolm C. McMillan, *The Disintegration of a Confederate State: Three Governors and Alabama's Wartime Home Front, 1861–1865* (Macon, Ga.: Mercer University Press, 1986), 93–94; Alan Sewell, "The Free State of Winston," *Civil War Times Illustrated* 20 (December 1981): 36–37; Donald B. Dodd, "The Free State of Winston," *Alabama Heritage* 28 (Spring 1993): 13, 15.

17. Sparks, *War Between the States*, 80–81.

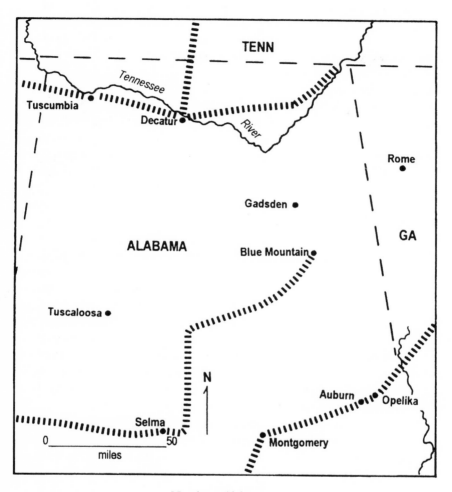

Northern Alabama

business." The Confederate cavalry's sweeps through the region must have had an effect. One Unionist leader, a cousin of Samuel Langhorne Clemens (Mark Twain), appealed to President Lincoln for protection against the gray horsemen in the spring of 1864.[18]

Bates's letter also makes it clear that General Grant's grand design for winning the war did not worry him. He was as sure now as he had been when he first left home in 1861 that the Confederacy would ultimately prevail. Confederates were still winning victories here and there, the South's armies were strong, and setbacks such as Vicksburg, Gettysburg, and Chattanooga were mere inconveniences. If he had known him, President Jefferson Davis would have loved Major Bates.

Camp near Tuscaloosa Ala
May 4, 1864
My Dear Ma,

From the want of facilities for sending letters west of the Miss I have not written to you for some time. I have just learned that a gentleman leaves in the morning for Clarksville & will send this by him provided he will take it.[19]

Soon after writing to you last from Miss we received orders to move to this point & have been in this vicinity some two weeks. What the object of placing us in here is I do not know—except it be to have us in skirmishing distance of Dalton Georgia & also of the Mobile & Ohio RR. We are about 225[?] miles from the former & [60?] from the latter.[20]

I have just returned from a ten days hard scout in the northern portion of the State catching deserters—not a very pleasant business. Deserters in the mountains of Ala are very plentiful. It seems to be the Rendezvous for them from all parts of the Confederacy.

The coming contest in Va with Grant is the subject matter here to the exclusion of all other army movements.[21] The opinion seems

18. L. S. Ross to Dear Lizzie, April 26, 1864, in Shelton and Morrison, *Personal Civil War Letters*, 62–63; Jere[miah] Clemens to W. H. Seward, May 5, 1864, Abraham Lincoln Papers, Library of Congress, Washington, D.C.

19. Clarksville is about thirty miles east of Paris.

20. This letter is faded almost to illegibility, and Bates's mileage numbers are not clear. The regiment, at Tuscaloosa, was about sixty miles east of the Mobile & Ohio Railroad and roughly 250 road miles southwest of Joseph E. Johnston's army at Dalton, Georgia. Whether that might be called "skirmishing distance" is another matter.

21. The argument that "Robert E. Lee and his soldiers functioned as the principal focus of Confederate nationalism for much of the war" seemed to be confirmed by Bates and

to be general here that if we are successful in Va this summer the war will terminate in another month or sooner—on the other hand a defeat there may result in prolonging the war from two to three years yet. I think myself that the coming summer will be the turning point in the destiny of the South. We will be able to *see* the end of this war though may not reach it for two or three years. As far as I have been able to learn, our armies everywhere are in the best of spirits & condition and we are as well or better prepared now—with men & means to meet the enemy as at any time heretofore. I have but little doubt of our success but have no doubt it will be quite sufficient. As Grant's army in Va has not been very largely reinforced as yet, & as troops are being sent from the west to Chatanooga the movement on Richmond may be only to cover their designs on Dalton. But whatever their designs I have no fears of Lee & Johns[t]on being out generaled.

I have no late news of interest. However news which we have almost forgotten may be of interest as you rarely ever hear anything more than rumors west of the river. At the battle of Plymouth N C we captured 2,500 prisoners and [illegible] cannon and a large assortment of [four illegible words] and small arms.[22] Forrest captured at union city Tenn. [Colonel Isaac R.] Hawkin's Regt Tenn Cavly (about 700 men) & 300 horses. At Paducah [Kentucky] we burned one steamer—all the comissary & QM stores.[23] At Ft. Pillow he captured 200 prisoners & near 700 mostly negroes—& recently at Somerville Tenn whiped Grissom badly.[24] It is said Grissom himself

his comrades in the western theater. See Gallagher, *Confederate War,* 63 (quotation), 72, 86–87.

22. The Union garrison at Plymouth surrendered to a combined force of Confederate infantry and the ironclad *Albemarle* on April 20 in one of the Confederacy's few recent victories in the eastern theater. Daniel W. Barefoot, *General Robert F. Hoke: Lee's Modest Warrior* (Winston-Salem, N.C.: John F. Blair, 1996), 148; Long, *Civil War Day by Day,* 487.

23. While Nathan Bedford Forrest raided western Kentucky as far north as the Ohio River in late March, he left behind one of his subordinates, Colonel W. L. Duckworth, to capture Union City, Tennessee. Meanwhile, Forrest hit Paducah, Kentucky, burned Federal supplies, captured a few dozen prisoners, and burned a riverboat. Wills, *Battle from the Start,* 174–77.

24. Bates refers to the controversial incident at Fort Pillow, Tennessee, where Forrest's horsemen shot down black soldiers who were trying to surrender. This affair, known ever since as the Fort Pillow massacre, inflamed public opinion in the North and was the subject of a congressional investigation. Ibid., 179–96; John Cimprich and Robert C. Mainfort Jr.,

was killed.[25] Since we left the Yazoo in Miss, Genl [Wirt] Adams who was left in command there repulsed a Yankee fleet going up the Yazoo, capturing one boat & 8 cannon.[26]

Application had been made for Genl Polk to furlough our Brigade [by] Regt which he has consented to do as soon as the present emergency at Dalton is passed. If it is found that our services are not needed there I think it probable our whole Brigade will be furloughed at the same time   if it is furloughed by Regt the troops of the 9th will not come until fall—as the 3rd & 6th will be furloughed.

It is getting quite late & as I did'nt close my eyes to sleep last night (was at a party) I must do it tonight & pretty soon too or they will close themselves. Give me as correct a version of the Mansfield fight as you can.[27] I can send letters to Ky if any of you wish to write. What about that land Pattent?

Most affectionately

Your son

J C B

No soldiers have ever been stationed in this section before & we consequently fare famously. Is Henry Moore paid yet?[28] Have you received anything from Capt Grigg?

Sister: I have opened this to give you a remedy for *headache*. It has frequently relieved me from a severe headache in half an hour. It is

"The Fort Pillow Massacre: A Statistical Note," *Journal of American History* 76 (December 1989): 830–37.

25. Bates is apparently misinformed about a fight at Somerville, Tennessee. No such action in March or April was reported by Forrest's biographer or in a day-by-day almanac of events in the Civil War. Wills, *Battle from the Start;* Long, *Civil War Day by Day.*

26. Brigadier General William Wirt Adams, a Kentucky native, was a Mississippi planter before the war. On April 22 his horsemen captured the gunboat *Petrel* on the Yazoo River. Warner, *Generals in Gray,* 2–3; Long, *Civil War Day by Day,* 487; Silverstone, *Warships of the Civil War Navies,* 176.

27. General Nathaniel P. Banks's Red River expedition—the one Bates narrowly escaped on his way back from Texas—got as far north as Mansfield, forty miles south of Shreveport. On April 8 Richard Taylor's Confederate army crushed Banks's leading corps and sent the Union general retreating down the Red River. T. Michael Parrish, *Richard Taylor: Soldier Prince of Dixie* (Chapel Hill: University of North Carolina Press, 1992), 338–54; Johnson, *Red River Campaign,* 126–41.

28. Henry Moore was Bates's fellow census marshal in 1860. Bates does not indicate why he owed a debt to Moore.

simply, equal parts of cloves & Seneca snake root, finely pulverized, & used as *snuff*. Don't laugh until you try it. for a half dozen kisses when I come home, I'll warrant it to cure or make you sneeze or both.

While Jackson's cavalry division, now reduced to only 2,500 effectives, milled around Tuscaloosa in early May, General Sherman's long-awaited spring campaign finally came to life near Chattanooga. With 100,000 men organized in three subordinate armies, Sherman began a four-month grind through the mountains of northwestern Georgia, aiming for the rail and manufacturing center at Atlanta. Standing in his path was Joseph E. Johnston's Confederate army of more than 60,000 men. As soon as Sherman's soldiers took their first steps southward, Confederate telegraph wires to Alabama and Mississippi buzzed with orders to concentrate all available forces at Dalton in north Georgia. Among those messages was one directing General Jackson's cavalry division to join Joseph E. Johnston as soon as possible.[29]

Ross's Cavalry Brigade saddled up and began a hard march across northern Alabama on May 6. Three days later, they received orders to leave behind their wagons and those men without horses and hurry on a forced march to Rome, Georgia, about fifty miles south of Dalton. Through heavy rains, thunder, and lightning, they pressed on under dark skies, crossing the Alabama-Georgia line on May 13 and riding into Rome the next day, Bates's twenty-seventh birthday. Most of the townspeople had fled before Sherman's army by this time. Adjutant Griscom wrote in his diary that Rome "has been a very pretty town situated on Coosa river & now looks quite forlorn[,] being fortified."[30]

Within twenty-four hours of their arrival at Rome, the Texans pitched into the fight against the approaching Federal juggernaut. Beginning on May 15, the brigade was under fire for 112 consecutive days. In mid-May they served primarily on the western flank of Johnston's army, skirmishing on foot and slowing the Federal advance as much as possible while Johnston steadily withdrew farther into the mountains of north Georgia. On May 19 the brigade rode twenty miles east of Rome, to the banks of the Etowah River, north of Allatoona. Their assignment was to guard bridges

29. *OR,* Vol. 38, Pt. 4, pp. 661–63, 691; Albert Castel, *Decision in the West: The Atlanta Campaign of 1864* (Lawrence: University Press of Kansas, 1992), 127; Connelly, *Autumn of Glory,* 326; Hale, *Third Texas Cavalry,* 214–15.

30. Kerr, ed., *Fighting with Ross' Texas Cavalry,* 141–42; Sparks, *War Between the States,* 82.

across the Etowah. Two days later, two regiments of Federal cavalry attacked the Texans in the rich, rolling farm country just south of the river, near Stilesboro, but the 9th Texas Cavalry counterattacked and drove the enemy horsemen away in a running fight.[31]

If Bates's family had seen General Ross's report of the fight on the Etowah, they would have been frozen with fear: James C. Bates was seriously, possibly mortally, wounded. At 8 P.M. on the night of the struggle, Ross reported to headquarters:

> Two regiments Yankee cavalry came up to my picket near the river, which I had reenforced with the Ninth Texas. The enemy charged twice very boldly, but were so stubbornly resisted by Colonel Jones with his gallant little regiment and Alley's company of scouts that they retired. Colonel Jones followed until too dark to see them. Major Bates, Ninth Texas, was seriously, and I fear mortally, wounded.[32]

As the Texans galloped after the Federals, Bates was hit in the face by a minié ball. The missile entered his mouth, knocked out teeth at the front and left side of his mouth, split his tongue, broke his jaw, and exited below and behind his left ear. A terrific and sudden pain wracked his face and stars danced before his eyes. His head jerked down and to the left, and blood, teeth, and tissue sprayed him and those around him. He probably lost consciousness immediately and fell from his horse.[33] Like General Ross, Bates's comrades must have thought the major would surely die from such an ugly and serious wound. Somehow, the healthy young man, wounded one week after his twenty-seventh birthday, survived long enough to be taken to a hospital in the rear. From there he was transported, probably by rail, to a larger hospital fifty miles farther south, in Atlanta.

For the next few weeks, Bates suffered terribly. For several days his mouth and tongue were too swollen for him to eat or drink. Surgeons attempted repeatedly to run a tube down his throat but failed. Finally, Bates, himself a future physician, took the tube and slid it into place in spite of what must have been excruciating pain. Four weeks after the fight on the

31. Kerr, ed., *Fighting with Ross' Texas Cavalry,* 142; Castel, *Decision in the West,* 216; Hale, *Third Texas Cavalry,* 215–21; *OR,* Vol. 38, Pt. 3, p. 986; Pt. 4, pp. 275, 729.

32. *OR,* Vol. 38, Pt. 4, pp. 731–32.

33. See Appendix 1 for an analysis of the wound and Bates's physical reaction. The author of the appendix, John C. O'Brien, is a noted oncology surgeon who has performed hundreds of head and neck surgeries at Baylor Medical Center in Dallas, Texas.

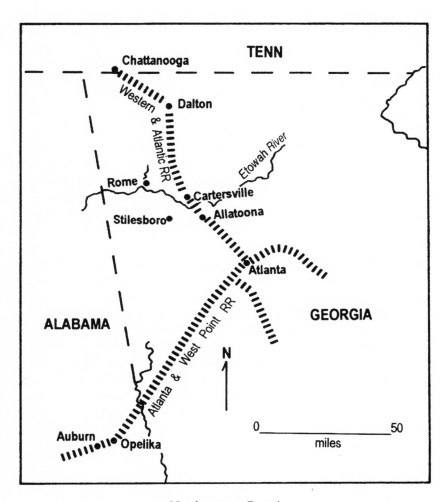

Northwestern Georgia

Etowah, the major sent his mother the bad news. As always, however, he played down the seriousness of the situation and even asked about his business affairs back in Paris.

Fair Ground Hospital[34]
Atlanta Ga
June 17, 1864
My Dear Ma:
   I wrote you a few lines several days since, but as it is doubtful whether it reached you I write again.
   I am just recovering from a very serious wound received about a month since some forty miles north of this on the Eutowa [Etowah] river. I was wounded in the mouth by a minnie ball. The ball entering my mouth & cutting my lips, but very little broken off. Four of upper front teeth are knocked entirely out by the root[,] all my lower front teeth and also *all* my lower jaw bone [teeth?] on the left side. My jaw bone was pretty badly broken also. the ball came out some three inches behind my left ear in side of my neck. Owing to the extreme care I used in dressing my jaw—bound up [torn spot] will be nearly or quite straight & my face consequently will be but little disfigured. My tongue was considerably injured being split at the end about one inch and badly torn on one side. I am a little afraid I will not have full use of it again. At present it seems that [four illegible words] paralyzed   I can talk so as to be understood very well—but can not use it in eating. I have as yet to suck all my food through a tube but I hope in a short time to be able to dispense with it. I fare very well, however as I can eat soft boiled eggs soup milk &c.
   The first [ten?] days after I was wounded my sufferings were intense, after this time they were not so severe. On account of my tongue & mouth & throat being so swollen I was not able to get anything down [my] throat until the seventh day after I was wounded. The surgeon made dismal efforts to put a tube down my

34. Army medical inspectors considered the two Fair Ground Hospitals in Atlanta equal to the best hospitals in Richmond. These Georgia facilities normally received the sick and wounded from Tennessee and Mississippi regiments only. Bates's life-threatening wound convinced doctors that he must be treated in Atlanta and not shipped elsewhere. Cunningham, *Doctors in Gray*, 61–62; James O. Breeden, "A Medical History of the Later Stages of the Atlanta Campaign," *Journal of Southern History* 35 (February 1969): 31–59; Mildred Jordan, "Georgia's Confederate Hospitals" (M.A. thesis, Emory University, 1942), 74.

throat but failed. I then took it myself & after an hour or so succeeded in getting it in my throat & had some water introduced into
my stomach. As water is the first thing a wounded man wants, you
may judge with what avidity I received this after being without it an
entire week.[35] In five minutes I was perfectly happy & dropped off
to sleep. For eight or ten days the only sustenance I received was
milk & brandy introduced into my stomach as the water was. After
that the swelling in my tongue diminished. My wound begins to heal
& has continued to do so rapidly up to this time, & though not well
yet I am very thankful that it is not worse.

Several days ago I sent up my application for leave of absence. It
has not returned yet though I am looking for it every day. I do not
expect to get more than thirty days & cannot therefore go home. It
is generally understood our Brigade are to be furloughed after this
fight—but it is hard to say when this fight will come off.

Our army & Sherman are confronting each other some 25 miles
North of this. Skirmishing goes on daily and occasionally a pretty
severe fight occurs and as yet there has been nothing like a general
engagement. I suspect [it] to have been Sherman's object heretofore
to force Johns[t]on back on this point by flank movements. Johnson
has repeatedly offered him battle but he has always declined. I think
it is his object to force Johnson back to or below this point & destroy the valuable government works here & cut our railroad communication with both the [east] & west. The rains for the past week
have retarded all military operations. As soon as the weather clears
up we will look for another effort at a flank from Sherman [torn
spot] if he fails to force Johnson any further back then a general engagement.

But the gentleman who takes this is waiting. What about that
land patent? Has Henry Moore been paid yet. Have you received
anything from Capt Grigg. Give my love to all & do not be uneasy
about me.

Affectionately your son

J C Bates

35. A healthy young man such as Bates may have been able to live for a week without
water, according to John C. O'Brien, author of the appendix on Bates's wound. It is also possible that some of the water or other fluids he attempted to consume during that week actually did trickle down his throat and that Bates did not realize it due to the numbness in his
mouth and throat caused by the wound. Passing in and out of consciousness, Bates may also
have lost track of the days.

If my leave of absence comes I will go to Crawfordsville on the Mobile & Ohio RR where I have some old acquaintances.[36]

A few days later Bates wrote to Adela, indicating that he still could not
chew. On the other hand, he was now able to swallow bread soaked in
milk, and that was better than nothing. He also altered his plans for his recuperation. At the invitation of men he must have met while in the Atlanta
hospital, he decided to go to Lafayette, Alabama, about eighty miles
southwest of Atlanta. At Lafayette, in the comfort of a hospitable home
and far from the contending armies in north Georgia, he would try to regain his strength with a view toward returning to duty. He was convinced
that a victory over Sherman north of Atlanta and another over Grant in
Virginia would result in Confederate independence within a few months.
If Sherman and Grant prevailed, however, it would not mean Confederate
defeat—not to Major Bates. In that case, the war would drag on indefinitely. The Yankees might lose heart after a couple of defeats, but the major
would not.

Fair Ground Hospital
Atlanta June 20th 1864
My Dear Sister
    Yours of April 7th was received this morning being the first and
only time I have [heard] from home since I left it. I do not however
blame you as I know you have written.
    As I have just sent two letters to Ma I have no additional news
that would interest you. My wound is still improving though not so
rapidly as a week ago. I can talk tolerable well, but still have but little use of my tongue. For the last two days I have been eating a little toast made so soft with milk that I have to make no effort at
chewing. The Drs tell me I must make no effort to chew anything
for a month or six weeks yet in order to give my jaw ample time to
heal.
    My leave of absence has not yet returned (I made application a
week ago). If it should be approved as I have no doubt it will I will
go down the rail road to Lafayette [Alabama] some eighty miles
below this.[37] Several gentlemen there have invited me to make their

36. Crawfordsville, now Crawford, Mississippi, is sixty miles west of Tuscaloosa, near the
Mississippi-Alabama border.
37. Lafayette, Alabama, was about fifteen miles west of the Georgia border and twenty
miles north of the Montgomery & West Point Railroad.

home my home as long as I choose to do so and as there has been but few soldiers there I think I will avail myself of their kind offer. I would go home but the distance is so great that I would have but few days to remain at home. Besides we are assured our Brigade will be furloughed as soon as this fight is over. It may however, and doubtless will be, two months or more before we can be spared.

Johns[t]on and Sherman are confronting each other some twenty five miles north of this. Each army has occupied their present position for the last three weeks and at present I see no indication of a general engagement soon. The continued wet weather has probably kept both armies more quiet than they would have been otherwise. It is evidently Sherman's policy to force Johnson back to below this point in order to destroy the important rail roads that unite here. If he can accomplish this without a fight so much the better for him— but if he finds he cant do this then I think he will attack Johnson.

This army is in splendid spirits and better condition every way than it has been at any time heretofore. The entire army have the utmost confidence in Johnson, and though we have retreated near seventy five miles, they are as confident now of victory whenever we fight as they were when we left Dalton. If we win this fight here & Lee in Va. is successful I believe we will have peace in six months but if we fail in this summer campaign the war in my opinion *will be protracted indefinitely.* Remember this & see if I am not a prophet for once.

I saw cousin Ben McDonald a few days since—he is chaplain in the army but not connected with any Rgt.

June 28th I commenced writing several days ago but failed to get the letter off. I have just seen a gentleman going to Tex. He will be here in a few minutes so I have not time to write more. My love to all.

Your brother
JC Bates

My wound is improving slowly. One of my Regt leaves on furlough in a few days. I will write by him.

While lying in his hospital bed or inspecting his aching, swollen face in a mirror, Bates must have wondered about Mootie's reaction. Would she still want to marry a man with a facial disfigurement, a man who could no longer speak distinctly? Perhaps he wondered whether he should even expect her to continue their relationship. Five weeks after being wounded, still so weak that his hand shook when he wrote, he gave Mootie some of the details, warning her that he would be somewhat disfigured the next time she saw him.

Fair Ground Hospital
Atlanta Ga June 22 1864
Miss Mootie Johnson
My Dear Friend

You have probably concluded ere this if you think about it at all that I have dropped you from my list of correspondents, but not so. If I were inclined to drop any I would certainly not select the best first. As it has been over two months since I wrote to you last I must try this morning to scribble you an apology for a letter notwithstanding I am so nervous, as you will see, that I can scarcely make a letter.

You will notice by the heading of my letter that I am in Hospital. I have been here since the 20th [21st] May at which time I was very severely wounded.[38] The ball entered my mouth wounding my tongue severely & as the Drs would say passed through severely fracturing the inferior maxillary on the left side and escaping upon the outer and positive aspect of the cervical region. I have lost all my front teeth above and below and all my lower jaw teeth on the left side. My tongue was badly torn up so that I will never I am afraid be able to talk distinctly. My face will be disfigured some, though how much I am not able yet to say as the swelling is not yet entirely out of my face.

But however it may appear then will I feel very thankful that it is not worse. When I entered the hospital the Drs pronounced mine a hospital case, but by the blessing of an over ruling Providence I am still alive with a fair prospect of being well soon.[39] Though I can neither talk nor eat much yet the Drs (& I hope they are correct this time) pronounce me entirely out of danger.

38. Bates had been wounded on May 21, not May 20. Given the trauma he had gone through, it is not surprising that he was mistaken about the exact date.

39. Many Civil War soldiers feared hospitals more than battlefields. Those so sick or so severely injured that they had to be hospitalized often died, either from the original ailment, incompetent physicians, or diseases contracted in the hospitals. One Alabama private summed up a common attitude: "I believe the Doctors kills more than they cour" (Wiley, *Life of Johnny Reb*, 267).

But enough about myself. Ever since daylight this morning the heaviest cannonading that had yet occurred has been going on. I have heard no reports (except the *report* of cannon) from the front this morning, and do not know whether it is a general engagement, or an artillery duel on a big scale.[40]

I must postpone finishing my letter until my nerves are a little more quiet or you will not be able to read it.

June 28th I failed to send this by the gentleman I intended. He did not succeed in getting off. One is here now waiting & I close this in order to send it as I may not have another opportunity soon. I intended writing you a *long* letter but the want of time must be my excuse. I will write again in a few days—or rather begin & continue until I meet with an opportunity of sending it. My wound is improving a little.

Most truly
Your friend
JC Bates

Bates's hand was still shaky nearly two weeks later when he wrote to Will Bramlette. As usual when writing to Will, he focused on the war and politics. His contempt for the Republican nominees in the 1864 presidential campaign, Lincoln and Andrew Johnson ("a sweet scented pair," in Bates's words), was almost palpable. As always, Bates kept close tabs on the war in general, especially now that he had time to read the latest news. Though he had been wounded fully six weeks earlier, he was still not able to leave the Atlanta hospital and was nowhere near ready to return to duty.

Atlanta Ga
July 3d 1864
Dear Will
Within the last two days I have written twice to Ma & once to Sister and as I have another opportunity of sending a letter I will try to scribble you one also—though have nothing of much interest to write you.

The news from our front each day is almost a repetition of that which preceded it. Skirmishing goes on almost every day & night and the dull booming of cannon has become almost as familiar to

40. The artillery Bates heard that day was associated with General John Bell Hood's unsuccessful attack on Sherman's army near Kolb's Farm, about eighteen miles northwest of Atlanta. Castel, *Decision in the West,* 291–99.

the people of Atlanta as the striking of the town clock. Occasionally a sharp artillery duel will take place and for half an hour or more the roar is continuous & about the time anxiety is raised to the highest point and the most excitable are confident the long expected conflict has at last begun, this thunder of the artillery will die die away and all will be again quiet for a time.

William this last two weeks the enemy have made several attempts to break our lines where they supposed we were weak, but have been invariably repulsed with considerable loss. A week ago they made a very determined assault on [Major General Benjamin F.] Cheat[h]am's and [Major General Patrick R.] Cleburn[e]'s Divisions and were driven back with a loss of about 2,500 killed & wounded & some 150 prisoners & three stand of colors.[41]

I will have to delay finishing my letter until my hand gets a little steadier. Our loss in the above engagement was nearly 250.

July 4th A heavy cannonading was commenced at day light this morning & kept up for several hours until many were induced to believe that Sherman had determined to see what effect whiskey and the "glorious old fourth" would have in sustaining the courage of his men or a general assault on our bases. The firing is again getting pretty heavy & I am a little inclined to think something more than an artillery duel is going on. For the last month every body had been anxiously looking for a general engagement but when it may occur I have no idea. It may be today, or it may be a month hence.[42]

A report has been current for a day or so that [Stephen D.] Lee & Forrest were in Sherman's rear. If this be true I think he will be forced either to give battle to Johnson or retreat—for he cant long keep his communications free with a heavy cavalry force in his rear.[43] Prisoners captured in the last day or so report his army on half rations for ten days past.

The latest news we have from V.a. Grant has succeeded in transferring his army to the south side of James River & was in front of

41. Bates is referring to Sherman's failed attack on Johnston's army at Kennesaw Mountain, about twenty miles northwest of Atlanta. Ibid., 303–16, 320.

42. The two armies would continue to batter each other on the outskirts of Atlanta through July and August.

43. Bates is reporting hopeful rumors, not facts. Neither Stephen D. Lee, commander of Confederate cavalry west of Georgia, nor Nathan Bedford Forrest was anywhere near Sherman's rear in July. They were still in Mississippi, taking on one Federal column or another, while Sherman pressed toward Atlanta. Wills, *Battle from the Start*, 216–46.

Petersburgh.[44] A number of large raiding parties had been sent out to cut the different rail roads leading to Richmond & some of them had been successful. The most important roads except the Danville are still open.[45] From Grant's operations since he has been on the South side [of the James River] his purpose seems to be to force Lee out of Richmond by cutting off his supplies and I have some fears that he may be eventually successful in this. I have no fears that he will ever take Richmond in any other way.

You will hear probably before this reach[es] you of the presidential nominations north. The Baltimore republican convention nominated honest old Abe for pres and Andy Johnson of Tenn for vice-pres—a sweet scented pair to save the union. The Cleveland convention, which claims to be more conservative (& I think is) than the Baltimore affair nominated Freemont for pres and Jno Cochrane of N.Y. for vice.[46] I send you, with a lot of other papers, the platforms of the two parties.

The Chicago Convention (Copperhead) has been postponed until 27th Aug.[47] I suppose their object is to be enabled to make nominations & adopt a platform to suit the times. If Grant and Sherman both fail they will have an out & out peace man, if both succeed a war man, if only one succeeds then they will be non-committal.— So I think.[48] Valandingham has returned to Ohio & defies Abraham

44. After the bloody month of May, when Grant and Lee fought repeatedly north of Richmond, the Federal general crossed the James River and curled around to Petersburg, about twenty-five miles south of Richmond, where he was forced by Lee's strong earthworks to begin a ten-month siege. Noah Andre Trudeau, *The Last Citadel: Petersburg, Virginia, June 1864–April 1865* (Boston: Little, Brown, 1991), 14–25.

45. Bates is mistaken about the railroads to Danville, about 125 miles southwest of Richmond. They would be the last to be captured by Grant's army, several months later. McPherson, *Battle Cry of Freedom*, 844–45.

46. John C. Frémont, a disgruntled general without a command, gathered some abolitionists and radical German Americans at Cleveland, Ohio, in May to nominate him for the presidency. Bates may have considered this group more conservative than the regular Republicans because Frémont's platform denounced Lincoln's suppression of free speech and suspension of the writ of habeas corpus. In other ways, however, the Frémont platform was much more radical than Lincoln's. Ibid., 715–16.

47. Bates is referring to the northern Democrats, who opened their convention in Chicago on August 29.

48. Bates's prediction that the northern Democrats would waffle, depending on the fortunes of war, was echoed by other southerners. See, for example, the *Richmond Examiner,* September 1, 1864; Allan Nevins, *Ordeal of the Union* (8 vols.; New York: Charles Scribner's Sons, 1947–71), 8:101.

Africanus to molest him.[49] I hardly think old Abe will dare to stir up such a row as would follow an attempt to arrest Valandingham. He & McClellan will probably be the most prominent men before the Chicago convention.[50] The Democrats of Ky have nominated McClellan for Pres and Thos E Bramlette for vice-Pres.[51] But you will find more news in the papers I send than I can write. I will keep this open & if anything of interest occurs will keep you advised.
Your Bro
JC Bates

A few days later Bates wrote a joint letter to his mother and sister. Still in Atlanta, he did not mention his wound, but he remained under the care of army physicians. He complimented the women for their recent strong spirits, especially since he had evidently lectured them about defeatism during his long stay in Paris several months earlier. He also sent news that must have provided great relief to his mother: he had undergone a religious conversion that many soldiers described as "taking religion." Bates had always been a Bible-reading, churchgoing Presbyterian, but in the weeks he spent among the wounded and dying—not sure whether he would survive another week—he pondered his place in the universe and gave himself over to his God. He was certain now that even if he did not live through the war, he would meet his family in heaven.

Atlanta Ga
July 8th 1864
My Dear Ma & Sister
    Your joint letter of April 21st is just received—although I have written several times to each of you in the last two weeks, and also to Will, I will not let this pass unanswered for that reason. I am glad

49. Clement L. Vallandigham of Ohio, the most prominent Peace Democrat in the North, had been banished from the United States in May 1863 by President Lincoln—Abraham Africanus, in Bates's characterization. Thirteen months later Vallandigham surreptitiously returned to Ohio and played a leading role in the Democratic nominating convention of 1864. Frank L. Klement, *The Limits of Dissent: Clement Vallandigham and the Civil War* (Lexington: University Press of Kentucky, 1970), 190–200, 270–72, 280–87.
50. Bates predicted correctly that Vallandigham and George B. McClellan, the former leader of the Army of the Potomac and the Democratic nominee in 1864, would be the most prominent figures in the 1864 nominating convention. Ibid., 280–87.
51. Kentucky Democrats may have pushed Will's brother, then governor of Kentucky, for the vice presidency, but the national party nominated George H. Pendleton of Ohio as McClellan's running mate. Ibid., 286.

indeed to see by the tone of your letter that you are both in better spirits & more hopeful of the future than you were when I was at home & I do hope not only you but the people of the Trans Miss may remain so through whatever changes the future has in store for us.

Nothing of interest has transpired here since my letter to Will—except the fact that Genl Johns[t]on has withdrawn his lines to the Chatahoochie [River]—as I said in my letter to Will I thought he would do.[52] I am very much afraid Atlanta will fall into the hands of the enemy, & it will be a most serious loss to the Confederacy—both on account of the rail road & the extensive manufactories here. The news from Va this morning is very cheering. Grant had been re-pulsed with terrible loss in [his?] advances on our works at Peters-burgh.[53] [Major General David] Hunter had also been defeated in the valley & was retreating.[54] No particulars given.

But I have something else to tell you which I believe will give you more pleasure than anything I have written. When I bid you good bye on leaving home & received the parting injunction to meet you in heaven if we should not meet again on earth—I resolved *that I would try,* and now through the mercy of the great & good God I feel that *"my sins are forgiven me,"* and that although we *may* never meet *here* again, I *will* meet you in Heaven where partings are not known. Oh I would not exchange the *peace* & *happiness* that this "blessed hope" gives me, for the wealth of all the world. God grant me strength ever to "keep the faith."

Ma, you need not make any coat for me. If I go home I will get you to make me a jacket. You ask how I came out of the difficulty Maj Coleman got me in,—I was released as soon as I made a state-ment of the matter to Genl Ross. Sister I will try to keep a diary as you request, but will not promise. Give my love to all the family &

52. Johnston withdrew to the Chattahoochee River, only eight miles northwest of At-lanta, in early July. Castel, *Decision in the West*, 332–34.

53. In an attempt to get astride a major railroad into Petersburg, Grant had sent two corps south of the city in late June. Vicious counterattacks by three Confederate divisions battered the Federal advance and kept open the lifeline to Richmond. Foote, *Civil War,* 3:442–45.

54. With fifteen thousand men, Hunter had burned his way south through the Shenan-doah Valley of Virginia in early June. When he ran up against equal numbers of Confederate veterans at Lynchburg, about ninety miles west of Richmond, however, Hunter blundered by retreating into West Virginia, leaving the Shenandoah Valley open for a Confederate raid toward Washington. McPherson, *Battle Cry of Freedom,* 737–39; Foote, *Civil War,* 3:445.

Aunt Tenn & family. I will write to Capt. Grigg to know whether he
has collected any thing for me.
JC Bates

During the second week in July, Bates was transported, probably by rail,
from the hospital in Atlanta to a large hospital for Texas troops on the cam-
pus of East Alabama Male College in Auburn (later Auburn University),
one hundred straight-line miles southwest of Atlanta on the Montgomery
& West Point Railroad.[55] Safe in a region undisturbed by contending
armies, and surrounded by solicitous citizens, Bates enjoyed higher spirits
than he had in many weeks. Although the voyage must have weakened
him, he got some relief from physical pain when an abscess on his wound
was lanced and one of his broken teeth was extracted from his neck.
Mootie had apparently written to complain of his flirting with his nurses
and to remind him that her confidence in ultimate victory was not as
strong as his. Bates tried to lift her spirits but continued to tease her about
the "kind and obliging" ladies of Alabama.

Auburn Ala
July 15th 1864
Miss Mootie Johnson
My Dear Friend
    Although I have written to you *four* times within the past month,
I will drop you a line hastily this morning not because I have anything of interest to write, but as you say you have received but *one*
letter from me since I left Tex, of the five or six I had written. I hope
you may receive at least *one* of the five (including this) that I have
written during the last month.
    About the time I wrote you last from Atlanta, the hospitals there
were ordered to be moved and I came down to this place which is
on the Montgomery and west Point R.R. some 125 miles from the
former. The Texas genl Hospital is at this place.[56] I find the citizens
here very kind & obliging—the ladies especially—as indeed *they* are
everywhere. Some half dozen were in to see me yesterday—and

55. Evans, *Sherman's Horsemen*, 139; W. J. Donald, "Alabama Confederate Hospitals
(Part II)," *Alabama Review* 16 (January 1963): 67.
    56. The Texas Hospital was a four-story Italianate brick building with an impressive
arched entrance, a spacious balcony, an exterior clock, and several chimneys. Mickey Logue
and Jack Simms, *Auburn: A Pictorial History of the Loveliest Village* (Norfolk, Va.: Donning,
1981), 27.

their bright smiles and sparkling eyes left sunshine enough in my heart to make it glad a week. God Bless *all* the women of the South (do'nt get jealous now).

I feel much better today than I have for some time. An abscess which had been forming on my throat for some days, was opened yesterday, and a piece of bone, or rather a piece of one of my teeth taken out & gave me considerable relief. I hope in the course of a couple of weeks to be able to leave the hospital, & find some good old cit [citizen] in the community to stay with[,] with a pretty girl or two, to whom I can talk sense or nonsense, or whatever else the mood happens to inspire—even *love* if it should be found agreeable to both parties.

You ask me for a specimen of my poetry. Well, the "machine" is not in order this morning but as soon as I can "get the thing ago-ing" I will practice a little on some of these pretty girls and then give you a sample.

With the hope that you may have no farther acquaintance with the "green-eyed monster," & that you may not have the blues once where you seem to have had them forty times heretofore; and that you may receive all the letters I write hereafter; and that you may be in *better spirits* when you write again; *and remain so*—I am most sincerely
Your friend
JCB

Bates had promised his sister that he would keep a diary and send it to Paris for his family and friends to read. In his next letter he enclosed his diary entries from mid-July to early August, including a colorful account of the flight of hundreds of hospital patients from their beds in Auburn to the nearby woods to avoid Yankee cavalry. Federal Major General Lovell Rousseau's cavalry column of 2,700 troopers raided south through Alabama in mid-July in one of several Federal strikes at the railroads feeding into Atlanta. Rousseau's men destroyed nearly thirty miles of track between Montgomery and Opelika, including the line at Auburn, only six miles southwest of Opelika. Major Bates and his hospital comrades, weak from wounds and disease, made a "masterly retreat" into the woods until the Federals galloped off toward Union lines north of Atlanta.[57]

The major's wound continued to extrude teeth and pieces of bone in

57. Evans, *Sherman's Horsemen*, 99, 137, 153, 158.

July and August as his body attempted to slough off the foreign matter floating in the tissues of his neck. Each extraction must have been painful, but at least he had evidence that his body was fighting back from the terrible wound he had suffered two months earlier.

Hospital
Auburn Ala
July 16th 1864
My Dear Sister

According to your request I will keep a sort of journal to send you occasionally, and will promise you in the outset that it will *not* possess many items of interest. If I were able to be at the front with my command I might probably pick up something occasionally worth putting down—but not so in hospital.

We have a rumor this morning that a yankee raiding party is making for this rail road. A good deal of excitement amongst the citizens is the result. Several ladies in to see me bringing a variety of good things in the way of eatables. Got another piece of bone out of my neck.

[July] 17th The raiders 2,500 strong struck the rail road 12 miles below this place *&* are moving in this direction tearing up the road as they come. Excitement increasing[.] citizens have organized a small Co[mpany] to meet them. Convalescents in hospital being organized for resistance by order of Post com[mander]. Think that gentleman very near akin to a fool if he sends 50 dismounted men to meet 2,500 mounted[58]—4 Btn—Raiders only 5 miles below here. Have sent for my horse to try to get out of the way.

[July] 19th Night before last just as I had gone to bed, hoping the azure Stomachs would not molest us before the morning, [illegible word] of the college bell rang out loud and clear on the night air.[59] This was the signal previously agreed on that the yanks were about entering the town—and all was immediately hurry & confusion & all who were able to walk were ordered to take care of them-

58. The post commander in Auburn, Captain T. H. Francis, could scrounge up only eighteen convalescents able or willing to resist the blue raiders. The captain's little army, armed with shotguns, skirmished with Rousseau's Federals until Francis ordered them to scatter and hide, every man for himself. *OR,* Vol. 38, Pt. 3, p. 974.

59. The "Azure stomachs," of course, were the "blue bellies," a common Confederate term for Federal soldiers.

selves as best they could. As my horse had come in, I sent Horace for him, But the old Scamp in whose stable I had put him had mounted him and gone.[60] Not liking the idea of being captured & forced to walk before yankee bayonets or do worse I concluded to take to the woods.[61] In company with Mitch Hancock I left the hospital & striking across a cornfield entered the woods.[62] As we were both very weak we could only walk a few hundred yards at a time without resting. Over 200 convalescents had left the hospital and as we groped our way in the dim moonlight we were continually stumbling on some luckless wight, who like us was seeking a temporary resting place possessing more attractions than Auburn.

About 2 oclk A.M., we had managed to put some 2 miles betwixt us and Auburn and concluding we were at a safe distance entered a pine thicket hard by, & perfectly exhausted dropped on the ground to rest till morning. Although we were tire[d] enough to "Sleep without rocking" our Sore Sides testified in the morning that Mother earth had "rocked" us to some purpose.

Sun up found us looking & listening for some signs of life that would lead us to any charitaby minded old cit[izen] who might have a desire to accommodate a couple of destitute rebs to a warm breakfast. We were not long in finding a house & having made a reconnaissance to see if the enemy were about, sent Horace up to negotiate. He soon returned with a smoking pan of meat bread eggs &c & a couple of canteens of milk. Having breakfasted we lay down & slept until noon & woke to find a good dinner ready for us to which we did ample justice. At night it began to rain with a prospect of continuing all night, and as no yanks had been visible in our vicinity during the day I determined to risk sleeping in the house of our friend. This morning we learned the enemy had left & as my wound needed attention I started immediately on a borrowed horse, but could not ride. Next tried a wagon, but after having my head nearly

60. Horace must have been an enlisted man or a servant.

61. Although they could not have known it, Bates and his fellow patients would not have been marched off to northern prisons; the Federal cavalry column was traveling fast and light and had no time to escort slow-moving hospital patients. Indeed, General Rousseau paroled patients at another Confederate hospital along the railroad earlier the same day. Evans, *Sherman's Horsemen,* 152.

62. Hancock was probably a fellow Texan whose name Mootie would recognize, but he was not a member of the 9th Texas Cavalry.

jolted off, got out & walked in—got here [the hospital in Auburn] at noon & found the yankees had been gone two or three hours. Had my wound dressed—took a nap & feel some better.

[July] 20th All quiet this morning. Yanks seven miles above here still tearing up rail road. All the Stores here broken open & robbed—but little private property injured—some few Negroes left with them—one citizen killed & three yankees. Negroes all been run off from hospital & have no cook & nothing to eat. Several of my roommates came in. Now that we are safe again, can afford to laugh at the "masterly retreat" of the Tex Genl Hospital.

[July] 21 Not well last night—wound very painful. Yankees left the rail road today & make in the direction of Sherman's army, [Brigadier] Genl [James H.] Clanton in pursuit with a Small force.[63] We have a rumor that Genl Johns[t]on has been relieved from the command of the army of Tenn.—cant believe it yet.[64] Had nothing I could eat today until a kind lady friend sent me some milk & toast.

[July] 22nd Yankees have made their escape & our forces are re-turning—some 25 miles of road have been torn up. This road is very important & the break here will give our army at Atlanta some in-convenience until wagons are supplied. All the Negroes in the coun-try ou[gh]t to be pressed to work on it—but suppose the powers that be will wait a week or ten days & then do what they could as well do today. Had the abscesses in my neck opened afresh & a piece of silk drawn through from one side to the other. Rumors today of a general engagement & a victory for us at Atlanta.[65]

Sunday [July] 23 Don't feel able this morning to go to church. Read two or three books in Testament. The news of yesterday from Atlanta confirmed today. Enemy attacked our positions were re-pulsed and driven over two lines of their works. 3,000 prisoners cap-tured and about 30 cannon. Loss reported heavy on both sides. This evening I left the hospital & came out with Mr. Hurt, the gentleman

63. James H. Clanton, a Georgia native and a veteran of the Mexican War, had been a lawyer before the war. His tiny brigade of only two hundred horsemen dogged the heels of Rousseau's column all the way through Alabama, but Clanton's small force could only annoy the Federals. Warner, *Generals in Gray*, 50–51; Evans, *Sherman's Horsemen*, 110–14, 141, 152–53, 157.

64. In one of his most controversial decisions, President Jefferson Davis removed John-ston from command of the army at Atlanta on July 17 and replaced him with Lieutenant Gen-eral John Bell Hood. Castel, *Decision in the West*, 360–63.

65. By this time, Sherman's army had swung around to the eastern suburbs of Atlanta, and heavy fighting was a daily occurrence. Ibid., 365–410.

who was kind enough to feed us while on our "retreat."[66] Dr Yates one of my roommates came out & will remain with me.

[July] 24th Find this place very quiet & much more to my liking than the hospital. Have plenty of peaches & vegetables prepared to suit my *lame* teeth & jaw. Mr & Mrs H show me very kind attention. Think I am improving already.

[July] 30th Have been here one week today & have gained strength very fast. Several young ladies from Town have been out for several days—have had a gay time. Another severe fight at Atlanta. Drove the enemy from two lines of works & were in turn driven back our loss about 3,000, Enemy report their loss at 2,500. News this morning of a raiding party under Stoneman on their way to Macon.[67]

Aug 7th Have had nothing of interest to write for several days, have an abundance of rumors but nothing reliable. Came in to the Methodist church yesterday—had a very good sermon. Dined & Spent the evening with the Misses R.—went into Auburn this morning & had my neck lanced—got a small piece of bone out.

[August] 8th Have reliable news this morning of the capture of a raiding party on the West Point & Atlanta [rail]road. From 8 to 12 hundred prisoners & 1,500 horses. Stoneman & 800 of his men also captured near macon. 21 pieces of artillery & their trains (a small one) also captured. Enemy attacked our works at Atlanta on 1st & were driven back with heavy loss. Latest news from Petersburgh Grant had mined about 100 yards of our works killing several. He at the same time assaulted our works & was repulsed with 300 killed & 1,500 prisoners.[68]

66. More than two months after his injury, Bates finally left the hospital to recuperate in the home of a friendly civilian family. Plentiful and healthful food in his new location helped him recuperate faster than previously. See Appendix 1 for the importance of nutrition to wounded men.

67. On July 27 General Sherman sent two columns of cavalry to cut the last railroad supporting the city from the south. The Federal commanders, Major General George Stoneman and Brigadier General Edward McCook, botched the two-pronged raid completely and were defeated within three days by Major General Joseph Wheeler's Confederate horsemen. Ross's Texas Cavalry Brigade, including Bates's regiment, played a leading role in the Confederate victory. Castel, *Decision in the West,* 417, 436–42; Evans, *Sherman's Horsemen,* 217–354; Hale, *Third Texas Cavalry,* 233–38.

68. Willing to consider almost any idea for breaking through Lee's entrenchments south of Petersburg, Grant had approved a plan to dig a tunnel under the ground between the two armies. At the end of the tunnel, directly beneath the Confederate earthworks, Fed-

[August] 9th No farther news. A gentleman leaves today for Tex by whom I send this. A Capt who was wounded in the fight tells me that the capture of the raiders on the West point road was made by our Brigade with less than half the number of men than were captured.[69]

Mr Hurt's carriage is waiting for me & I must "shut up." Don't fail to write often.

Your Brother

JC Bates

Don't show this scribbling to everybody.

Before he finished his diary for Adela, Bates sent another letter to his mother. His wound was still festering, and doctors continued to extract pieces of bone, teeth, and dead tissue from the hole in his neck. Still, he was feeling much better now that he had plenty of nourishing food and an opportunity to rest in the comfort of a friendly home in the countryside near Auburn. He also reported the great dissatisfaction among the troops around Atlanta when General Johnston was replaced by John Bell Hood. Some soldiers even threatened to quit the war and go home rather than give up a general they considered superior to his replacement. A soldier in Ross's brigade grumbled that "our hearts were filled with sadness. We loved him [Johnston], we were proud to be commanded by so great and gifted a soldier." In fact, "this change of commanders when we were in line of battle had an effect on the army that was hard to overcome."[70]

---

eral engineers placed four tons of gunpowder. The charge was ignited on July 30 and sent tons of dirt and hundreds of Confederate soldiers into the air in a spectacular explosion. The Federals bungled the assault through the gap, however, and Lee's lines quickly closed over the wound, inflicting nearly four thousand casualties on the attackers. Trudeau, *Last Citadel*, 102–27; Faust, *Historical Times Illustrated Encyclopedia*, 190.

69. Bates is describing one part of the two-pronged Federal cavalry raid turned back by Wheeler's Confederate horsemen in late July. Ross's Texans hammered the western prong near Newnan, Georgia, on July 30, capturing artillery, wagons, horses, and arms. Sparks, *War Between the States*, 100–102; Barron, *Lone Star Defenders*, 200–204; Kerr, ed., *Fighting with Ross' Texas Cavalry*, 161–62; Evans, *Sherman's Horsemen*, 252–77; Hale, *Third Texas Cavalry*, 236–38.

70. Douglas John Cater, *As It Was: Reminiscences of a Soldier of the Third Texas Cavalry and the Nineteenth Louisiana Infantry* (1981; reprint, Austin, Tex.: State House Press, 1990), 185; Castel, *Decision in the West*, 363–65.

Auburn Ala
July 30th 64
My Dear Ma

Another opportunity of sending a letter is presented & I send you a line in haste.

For the past few days I have been staying in the country and have improved very rapidly in health. The people with whom I am staying are very kind Rec'd [illegible word] & I am consequently doing finely. I come into the hospital every day to have my wound attended to—pieces of bone still come out occasionally. Two or three pieces are still to come out. I can feel them with the probe but cant get hold of them. They will work out of the inside after a while.

Gen Johns[t]on has been removed from command of the army at Atlanta & Genl Hood Succeeded him. Great dissatisfaction is the result[,] this not only in the army but in the whole country. A heavy engagement occurred a few days ago in which our loss was about 8–9,000 killed & wounded, the enemy's much greater. We captured 3,000 prisoners, about 30 cannon, several hundred weapons & 13 stands of colors.[71] Our army occupies a position immediately around Atlanta. The enemy position isn't far out[.] *Atlanta will fall* is my prediction. Dispatches to the 25th [of July] represent all very quiet in Va. Grant still in front of Petersburgh fortifying.

I have not time to write more as the mail carrier is ready.

My love to all
Affectionately,
JC Bates

One year earlier, Bates had been downplaying the fall of Vicksburg in his letters to Paris. Optimistic to a fault, he had been certain of eventual victory, Vicksburg or no Vicksburg. Now, Grant was at the back door to Richmond and Sherman was tightening his grip on Atlanta. His mother, sister, and sweetheart had sometimes expressed despair and lamented the loss of so many men in an apparently doomed cause—but not Major Bates. True, he was out of the fight and mangled in body, but he was also hopeful that he could return to his regiment and continue his war against the

---

71. Bates is probably referring to the bloody clash on July 28 at Ezra Church, two miles west of downtown Atlanta. General Hood lost nearly three thousand men that day, almost five times as many as the Federals. Castel, *Decision in the West*, 425–36.

Yankees. The fall of Atlanta would be a blow to the Confederacy, certainly, but Bates was still sure that renewed commitment and hard service would ultimately win the contest. The end of the war and defeat were only nine months away.

11 Decline and Defeat

While Bates recuperated in eastern Alabama, his regiment and brigade fought General Sherman's Federals almost constantly in the vicinity of Atlanta. In the four months after they arrived in Georgia, the 9th Texas Cavalry lost eleven officers, seventy-nine men, and sixty-seven horses in nine battles and eighty-one skirmishes, according to the records of the regimental adjutant. For sixteen long weeks, from mid-May to early September, Ross's Texas Cavalry Brigade fought every day, only to see Atlanta occupied by Sherman's army on September 2. In mid-September, Bates's regiment was still near Atlanta, seventeen miles to the southwest, screening General Hood's army while he pondered what to do next.[1]

Major Bates still had not recovered sufficiently to return to duty, but he hoped to do so soon. In late August he moved from Auburn, Alabama, to Brownsville, Mississippi, about twenty-five miles northeast of Vicksburg. His surviving letters do not indicate why he moved, but the threat of Sherman's advancing army may have convinced him that recuperation was more likely in a friendly southern home than in a northern prison. The major regretted the loss of Atlanta, but after all, it was impossible to defend, and all the Confederacy had lost was a railroad. Besides, Hood's army would doubtless cut Sherman's supply line and force the Federal army to turn back into Tennessee. Bates could find the thinnest of silver linings.

1. Kerr, ed., *Fighting with Ross' Texas Cavalry,* 170–71; Hale, *Third Texas Cavalry,* 248.

Mrs. Smith's near
Miss River
Sept 19 1864
My Dear Ma:

A much longer time—nearly a month—has elapsed since I wrote to you last than I usually suffer to pass without writing to either you or Sister. I have been during that time at Brownsville Miss—some 25 mile East [actually, northeast] of Vicksburgh—& being entirely off the route usually taken by persons going across the river, I have had no opportunity of sending letters. I came out to the Miss a few days since for the purpose of getting some clothing I have not succeeded as yet, in getting much out[.] think in a day or so I will be able to procure as much as possible.

There has been but little trading going on on the river for the past two months until a few days past two trading boats came down with clothing and plantation supplies. The restrictions heretofore existing have been partially removed and citizens can now buy goods for family use. A number of six shooters and a quantity of powder and caps have been smuggled out on the boat here which is pretty good evidence that the owners of the boat are not as loyal as Abe would like them.

I suppose you have heard before this of the fall of Atlanta. I wrote to you some time since that you might expect to hear of it at any time, because from its position it was almost impossible to defend it. The only serious inconvenience resulting from its fall is the loss of the principal Rail road leading to Richmond. I do not think Sherman will be able to hold Atlanta. If his line of communication with his rear, which is nearly 400 miles in length, can not be cut and *kept* cut we had almost as well give up the struggle.

A heavy fight has recently occurred on the Weldon rail road near Petersburgh in which the Yankees were badly beaten. The telegraph reports it the worst slaughter of the war. No particulars of the fight yet received.[2]

My wound is improving[,] throat still very sore on account of pieces of bone coming out occasionally. Am a little tongue tied yet, but will soon get over that. I will return to my Regt in a few days—will not be able for field service for a month probably, but

2. In late August, General Grant's infantry struck the Weldon & Petersburg Railroad south of Petersburg and proceeded to destroy the track. See James M. McPherson, ed., *The Atlas of the Civil War* (New York: Macmillan, 1994), 184–85, for maps and narrative.

can do light duty. Will write again before I leave the river. My love to all.

Affectionately,

JC Bates

I will send money to pay the hire of that negro by the first one that passes. Has Henry Moore been paid yet.

On Miss River
Sept 22nd 1864
Miss Mootie

Although I have not had the pleasure of a line from you (but once) since leaving Texas, in fulfillment of my promise to write regularly I send you a Short Scribble very hurriedly this morning. I am now on the half way ground to home and feel a very strong inclination to travel westward the other half & would certainly do so if I had a rail road to go on. As it is I am not able to travel so far on horseback.

I have been out on the Miss for Several days trying to get clothing—have succeeded in getting some & sent to Memphis for another bill. For a month past I have been stopping at Brownsville Miss where live my Miss Sweethearts. I need hardly tell you I have had a most pleasant time. You will remember my old sweetheart—Miss Alice—(who sent you the music) lives near there & of course I saw her often. I Spent my time pretty equally betwixt her and three other young ladies living in B[rownsville], that is I "boarded around with the schollars."

I have written to you so often without getting a reply that I am at a loss what to say. One thing, however, I will *not* do; and that is to *scold* and complain because *I* do not get letters. I think you *have* written & if I do not get the letter I do not attribute the blame to you. I will return to the command in a day or so & hope to find some letters there.

My wound is not well yet & will probably not be for a month or so. It does not however pain me much. My neck is yet stiff but I hope in time it will be all right again.—Mr. [A. J.] Petty who takes [this letter] is waiting & I have yet to write a few lines to Ma, so you must excuse this short scribble.[3] If I have an opportunity of writing

3. A. J. Petty was a private in Company I of the 9th Texas Cavalry. Kerr, ed., *Fighting with Ross' Texas Cavalry*, 234.

again before I leave the river I will do so. Mr. P. may deliver this in person. If he does you can send a reply by him.

Very truly
Your friend
JC B

Direct to Lovejoy, Georgia
Hood's army
be sure to write by Petty

[On the Mississippi River]
Sept 22nd 1864
[letter from Bates to his mother][4]

Mr Petty leaves this morning for Texas & I send my letter by him, I also send two hundred dollars by him with which pay the hire of that negro. As I have never heard from you but once since leaving home—I do not know whether Henry Moore has been paid or not. I want *him paid before any one else.* If Mr Petty himself goes to Paris treat him with all kindness. He is a member of my Regt & a very clever gentleman. I have sent to Memphis for a bill of clothing but will not wait here for it. There are some 25 men from my Brig on the river as Scouts & I will get some of them to attend to my clothing when it comes down.

Hood & Sherman have had a truce for ten days to remove the non combatants from Atlanta.[5] I have seen McClellans letters of acceptance.[6] He *is* in favor of reconstruction peaceably if possible. If peaceable means fail he is for war. I would much prefer Lincoln to McClellan. Lee has again whipped the enemy on the Weldon R Road.[7] No other news.

JCB

4. This letter was probably enclosed with the earlier letter, dated September 19, to Bates's mother.

5. On September 7 Sherman ordered all civilians out of Atlanta, a move that brought howls of protest from southerners in general and John Bell Hood in particular. Castel, *Decision in the West,* 548.

6. Bates is referring to George B. McClellan's acceptance of the Democratic Party's nomination for the presidency.

7. Bates is probably referring to the Federal defeat at Reams Station, south of Petersburg, on August 25. The Federal Second Corps lost more than 2,700 men when Lee's Confederates hammered them away from the Weldon & Petersburg Railroad. McPherson, ed., *Atlas of the Civil War,* 184–85.

At some point in early October, Bates left Mississippi and returned to Auburn, Alabama, on his way to rejoin his regiment. He was still too weak to resume normal service, but he thought he might be able to contribute in a less active role. In the hospital at Auburn he found his colonel, Dudley Jones, recovering from an ankle injury suffered when he was thrown from his horse. The two officers planned to return to duty together.

Bates, as always, sent the latest war news in his next letters to his mother and Mootie. For the first time, he began to express regrets about the terrible cost of the war. The loss of Atlanta, Vicksburg, New Orleans, Memphis, Nashville, and other strong points must have suggested, even to a diehard like Bates, that the Confederacy was tottering. More regrettable, though, were the deaths of so many men he respected and admired. The news of Lieutenant Colonel Thomas G. Berry's mortal wound hit him especially hard. Could victory ever compensate for the loss of so many good men? Bates began to wonder.

Auburn Ala
Oct 10th 1864
My Dear Ma,

I have just returned from Miss & will remain here a day or so & then go on to my Regt. Col Jones is in hospital here. He was thrown from his horse some time since & had his ankle badly hurt—we will return to the Command together.

I received a letter from you, dated 25th of Aug, on yesterday—being only the second time I have heard from you since I left Tex. I wrote to you some ten days since from the Miss River & also sent you two hundred dollars by A. J. Petty. You say in your letter that you are expecting me home as Jim Crooks told you I was going home. I told Jim I was *not* going home, but he probably did not understand me. If I had been able to ride on horseback so far I would have gone home, when I first went to Miss—but by the time I was able to ride my leave of absence had nearly expired—& although I am not yet able for duty in the field I deemed it best to return to my command as I can do post or office duty.

My neck has not yet healed up & probably will not for two months. I have no doubt I could get another leave of absence by applying for it—but I think the present is an emergency that calls for the services of every man who is able to do anything whatever—and even if I had a leave of absence I would not go home *now* as badly as I want to see you all. So you need not look for me at present or in fact at any time until I tell you I am coming.

On the 4th inst Genl Hood began one of the boldest movements of the war. Our army was quietly withdrawn from Sherman's front and thrown rapidly across the Chatahoochie—around his right and on to the State road in Sherman's rear. Up to the 6th we had captured several trains loaded with supplies & about 300 prisoners & were destroying the road northward. I feel a good deal of anxiety as to the result of this move, and am afraid it will fail in its principal object i.e. in forcing Sherman to abandon Atlanta. I think Sherman will leave a portion of his force to garrison Atlanta and move the rest back to meet Hood and either give him battle or throw his forces betwixt Hood and his base of supplies (Blue Mountain [Alabama]) & force him to abandon the State road.[8] I don't think Hood will do this however until the last extremity as the complete destruction of that road will insure Sherman's defeat or at least force him to evacuate Georgia. But it is useless to speculate on what may be the result of this daring & I hope wisely planned move.[9]

Genl [P. G. T.] Beauregard is for the present in command of the army—having gone to the front day before yesterday.[10] Pres Davis was also with the army just before it moved & said in a speech that he was confident 30 days would not elapse before we would see Sherman on a retreat more disastrous than that of Napoleon from Moscow. But that I think impossible. Forrest is doing noble work in Tenn having captured at last accounts 3000 prisoners, as many small

8. General Sherman did lead most of his army out of Atlanta in early October to chase Hood away from the Federal supply line to Tennessee, but the Federal general soon gave up pursuing the retreating Confederates and returned to Atlanta. Federal troops in Tennessee would have to deal with John Bell Hood. Castel, *Decision in the West,* 552–53.

9. Bates would have been stunned to learn that General Sherman had an even bolder idea—to plunge deeper into Georgia's unprotected center, leaving Hood behind for another Federal army to worry about. Without Hood's army in his front, Sherman could easily drive across the middle of Georgia, all the way to the Atlantic Ocean, capturing Savannah and splitting the Confederacy a second time. Ibid.

10. In response to widespread calls for the removal of Hood as army commander, President Jefferson Davis refused but appointed Beauregard, hero of Fort Sumter and Manassas, to head a new Military Division of the West, comprising Hood's army and Confederate forces in Mississippi. Beauregard's office was nearly powerless, however, because he could only advise, not command. Ibid., 552.

arms & large amounts of stores & was moving on the Nashville and Chattanooga rail road.[11]

As Mr Chance does not leave until tomorrow I will leave this open with the hope of hearing more from Hood's army.
JC Bates

The mail brought no additional news—last night—a report came down on the cars that Forrest has captured Sherman and as he had gone to Washington City some two weeks since and was expected back about this time the report may be true.[12]

Since I wrote you last the Lt Col of our Regt [Thomas G. Berry] has been killed.[13] His death will be a heavy blow to our Regt. He was one of the best & bravest men I ever saw & a truer patriot cannot be found in the army. I felt when I heard of his death that I had lost the best friend I had on this side the Miss.

Oh how long will such men have to be butchered before this inhuman war will have an end. It is *sometimes* hard to think that our success will compensate for the loss of thousands of brave men whose lives have been sacrificed during the past three years. But regrets are useless—though natural. We have come too far to think of retracing our steps now even if we desired. The first gun that fired in this war shut out forever all hope of reconciliation and even if Grant were not [torn spot] we have had enough of Lincoln's cruelty & acts of oppression to satisfy us fully with that government.

But I must close as Mr Chance will be leaving in a few minutes. Give my good wishes to my friends there.
Most affectionately your son
J C B

11. Forrest had indeed created havoc along the railroads in middle Tennessee in late September and early October, but he was not able to cut the vital line between Chattanooga and Nashville. Wills, *Battle from the Start,* 250–60.

12. Forrest, of course, did not capture Sherman, but the Confederate cavalry leader was an infuriating irritant to the Federal general. At one point in 1864, the exasperated Sherman wrote bitterly that "Forrest is the very devil," and he promised to order his subordinates to "follow Forrest to the death, if it cost 10,000 lives and breaks the Treasury. There never will be peace in Tennessee till Forrest is dead." *OR,* Vol. 38, Pt. 4, p. 480.

13. A native of Alabama, Berry moved to Tarrant County, Texas, near Fort Worth, before the war. He began his military career as captain of Company A, 9th Texas Cavalry, and was promoted to lieutenant colonel in October 1863. Mortally wounded in a charge the day before Sherman entered Atlanta, Berry died the next night. He was widely admired among the men in the regiment. Kerr, ed., *Fighting with Ross' Texas Cavalry,* 169.

Auburn Ala
Oct 10th 1864
Miss Mootie Johnson
My Dear Friend

I must try this morning, although it is Sunday to write you a short letter—I don't mean I must *try* to make my letter short. It has so happened how I don't know—that every time I have written to you for the last two months I have either had the blues a little or been out of sorts in some other way and my letters have been no doubt as dull and as much out of sorts as myself. If it requires as much patience for you to read as for me to write I know you are glad when the end comes. I believe I will quit writing go to church and try again this evening. maybe a look at the pretty girls will help me. Monday Morning   I have waited until I have but a short time to write in with the hope of hearing some news of interest by last nights mail but nothing in the way of news came but a rumor that Genl Forrest had captured Sherman on his return from Washington City. I do not credit the report. On the 4th of this month our army was moved from Sherman's front & thrown around his right into his rear. The last definite news from Hood he was some 40 miles above Atlanta—had captured two trains & several hundred prisoners & was destroying the rail road northward. This movement of our army to the rear of Sherman is the most hazardous yet undertaken, but if successful it will prove very disastrous to the enemy. The only thing I fear is that Sherman will get betwixt Hood and his base of supplies at Blue Mountain which I do not think it will be difficult for him to do.[14] The next ten days will decide the fate of Georgia & I will wait the results with more anxiety than I have ever felt for any movement heretofore. Genl Forrest is in Tenn doing good work has captured some 3000 prisoners large amounts of stores, destroyed rail roads &c & is still going on with the good work.

The Col of my Regt (Jones) is in hospital here. He had his ankle severely hurt by a fall from his horse some time since. About the 1st of Sept Lt Col Berry was mortally wounded in a charge on the enemy. He only lived one day. In his death the Regt sustained a loss that can never be replaced. He was in every sense one of nature's

14. Blue Mountain, Alabama, two miles northwest of present-day Anniston, is eighty-four straight-line miles west of Atlanta.

truest noblemen & when dangers thickened most & bullets were flying fastest he was the bravest & coolest of them all.

I was very much pained to learn of the death of Lt Croy But none
of us know how soon we too may fall as he did. I sometimes think
that the lives already lost, and yet to be sacrificed in this war were
worth far more than we will ever gain. But I must close. Do not fail
to let me hear from you often. Direct to the Army of Tenn at Atlanta
or Palmetto Geo. My regards to all.
Most truly yours,
JCB

I sent you some music about a month since—have you received it.

While waiting to go on with Colonel Jones to rejoin the regiment, Bates
found time to send another letter to his brother-in-law. Following his usual
practice when writing to Will, the major spent little time on small talk and
focused on war news and politics. He did show his playful side when he
asked Will to tell him everything he knew—"it won't take you long."

Auburn Ala
Oct 13th 1864
Dear Will,

I wrote to Ma several days since but as I have an opportunity of
sending a letter direct to Paris, I avail myself of it. I will leave for my
command tomorrow & expect to find them on the Atlanta &
Chatanooga RR about the Etowah River or probably above there.
We have no definite news from Hoods army later than the 7th at
which date our forces stormed and carried the Alatoona hills, capturing 4,000 prisoners & large amounts of stores.[15] Our loss not
stated. The rail road had been completely destroyed for 25 miles &
the work still going on northward.

It is impossible to conjecture what may result from this daring
move of our forces. It is generally believed that Sherman has 15 or
20 days rations in Atlanta & by issuing only half rations he will be
able to hold out probably a month allowing that Hood can maintain
his present position which I very much doubt. Hood's base is Blue

15. Bates had received faulty information. Three thousand Confederates did attack the
Federal supply base at Allatoona, north of Atlanta, on October 5, but they were driven off.
Foote, *Civil War,* 3:609–12.

mountain, the terminus of the rail road leading north from Selma & sixty miles or better south of west from Rome, Ga. Hood is now east of Rome some 20 or thirty miles. I predict that Sherman will leave about one corps to garrison Atlanta & either offer Hood battle in his present position, or what is more likely throw his forces in Hood's rear & compel him to leave the railroad. The opinion prevails here generally that Sherman will be forced to evacuate Atlanta immediately. But I hardly think he will give it up after so hard a struggle to obtain it, except as a last resort to save his army.

I was confident Atlanta would have to be given up finally by our forces, & wrote as much to Ma long before it fell—but I thought then, as I still think, that Sherman will be forced to retrace his steps to Chatanooga before many months roll round. If Hood can maintain his present position for 20 days I see nothing to prevent Forrest from making a complete wreck of the road from Chatanooga to Nashville & with the damage already done by Hood & what he may still be able to inflict it seems to me that it would be almost an impossibility for Sherman to remain in Georgia any length of time. Genl Beauregard is at present with the army of Tenn & I suppose directs its movements[16] Genl Hardee has been relieved from command of his old corps & assigned to command of the Dept of South Carolina.[17]

There has been considerable fighting around Petersburgh during the last ten days. We captured some 15,000 prisoners & lost but few men.[18] The defeat of Early in the valley of Va. turns out to be much less serious than was generally believed at first. We have regained possession of Staunton & Early I believe occupies nearly the same ground he did before his defeat.[19] In an attack on Saltville west Va.

16. Beauregard, as noted earlier, had little influence over the war in Tennessee and Georgia. He was there only to advise.

17. Unhappy serving under a man he considered his inferior, General Hardee escaped the embarrassment of following any more of Hood's orders and took command of Confederate defenses on the south Atlantic coast. Castel, *Decision in the West*, 552.

18. Again, Bates had received poor information. In fact, in late September and early October, Grant's army seized important points north of the James River and southwest of Petersburg. For the closest study of these actions, see Richard J. Sommers, *Richmond Redeemed: The Siege at Petersburg* (Garden City, N.Y.: Doubleday, 1981).

19. After racing north and crossing the Potomac River in the summer of 1864, Major General Jubal Early's small Confederate army reached the northern outskirts of Washington, D.C., on July 11. Too weak to assault the reinforced works of the capital, Early returned to the Shenandoah Valley in late July and was defeated by Philip Sheridan in three successive en-

on the 4th inst, by a body of 10,000 of the enemy under [Brigadier General Stephen] Burbridge, they were repulsed & completely routed.[20] Affairs at Mobile are comparatively quiet—the enemy making no other advances since the capture of Fort Morgan.[21] The bombardment of Charleston still continues with the usual result—which is no result.

Will, who are you trans-Miss rebs going to vote for for Pres of the "glorious old union"? Public opinion here seems to favor the election of McClellan, but for my part I think I'll vote for honest(?) old Abe i.e. I prefer him to little Mac. As I have no more news of interest to write you I will bore you with my reasons for preferring Lincoln & what I think will be the result of the election of either. As to why I prefer Lincoln.

1st His policy of confiscation and emancipation will unite the South & forbid division of any consequence among us & thus finally secure our independence for if we remain united we are *bound to succeed.*

2nd His incompetency has been shown by almost all his acts. His emancipation proclamation—his "penchant" for decapitating every genl so unfortunate as to lose a battle—his acts of diplomacy from the Trent affair to the present—&c

3d If elected he will have to contend with all the elements of opposition in the north united in one party against him. That party is now organized & will use every exertion to defeat his war policy if he should be reelected.

4th McClellan's election would give a new impetus to the war

gagements in September and October. See Frank Vandiver, *Jubal's Raid: General Early's Famous Attack on Washington in 1864* (New York: McGraw-Hill, 1960), and Jeffry D. Wert, *From Winchester to Cedar Creek: The Shenandoah Campaign of 1864* (Carlisle, Pa.: South Mountain Press, 1987).

20. Saltville, nestled in the mountains of far southwest Virginia, was the scene of a brutal massacre on October 3. General Burbridge's Federal column of 4,500 men unsuccessfully assaulted a smaller Confederate force at Saltville and was thrown back on October 2. The next morning, some of the Confederates combed the battlefield, shooting at least forty-six of the wounded, especially black soldiers. See Thomas D. Mays, *The Saltville Massacre* (Fort Worth: Ryan Place Publishers, 1995).

21. On August 5 Rear Admiral David G. Farragut led a U.S. fleet past Fort Morgan, guarding the entrance to Mobile Bay. After a vicious and famous fight, the Union navy took control of the bay and Fort Morgan, ending Mobile's role as a major blockade-running port. See Current, *Encyclopedia of the Confederacy,* 3:1059. Arthur W. Bergeron, *Confederate Mobile* (Jackson: University Press of Mississippi, 1991), is the best study of wartime Mobile.

feeling of the north for even the Abolitionists have confidence in McClellans "military ability."

5*th* His (McC) policy of conciliation with a promise to guarantee all the rights of the South, only on the condition that we return to the union under the old constitution will have a tendency to raise up a reconstruction party in the South—as was indicated recently by the actions of the Ala legislature.[22]

These are some of the reasons I would rather have Lincoln than McClellan. Then as to what will follow—I predict that if Lincoln is elected the war will go on as it has done with probably more opposition to Lincoln's policy.

If McClellan should be elected he will propose an armistice for 60 or 90 days with a view to the adjustment of our difficulties—and the appointment of commissioners to meet others from the confederacy. His commissioners will be instructed to listen to no terms unless based on a reunion of all the states under the old constitution. Ours will be instructed to accept nothing but final separation and independence. Nothing will be accomplished by them & at the expiration of the truce or before, hostilities will be resumed. Then by May or June McClellan will have nearly or quite a million men in the field. *Then* will come the tug of war for us. But I have no fears of McC election. Still if he should be just listen to my predictions & see if they are not correct.

Let me hear from you soon & when you write tell me everything you know, "it wont take you long," & every thing thats going on in Texas. heard from home only twice since I left there. I send you some extracts containing the latest news—would send you papers but the gentleman who takes this seems to have as much as he can carry without

My love to all the family & to aunt Tenn

JC Bates

While Bates and Colonel Jones prepared for their trip north to rejoin their regiment, General Hood devised a bold plan to neutralize Sherman's victory at Atlanta. Hood would move from north Georgia into Alabama, cross the Tennessee River, and strike north into Tennessee. He could at least tear up the railroads running to Atlanta, and he might even capture

---

22. Bates may be referring to the recent introduction of resolutions for peace in the Alabama legislature. Current, *Encyclopedia of the Confederacy*, 4:19.

Nashville, invade Kentucky, and cross the Ohio River. A Confederate flag over Cincinnati would make everyone, North and South, forget the Union flag over Atlanta.[23]

Sometime in mid-October, Bates, still not completely recovered, left Auburn to join his regiment. Colonel Jones, apparently not ready to travel as soon as Bates, left the hospital about two weeks later. Bates's surviving letters do not indicate the route he took, but he caught up to the regiment about sixty miles northwest of Atlanta, near Cedartown, Georgia, on October 22. Two days later Ross's cavalry brigade rode west into Alabama, crossed the Coosa River at Gadsden, and then moved rapidly to the northwest, reaching Decatur on the Tennessee River by October 29.[24]

On this swing into north Alabama, part of Hood's general movement from Atlanta to Tennessee, the 9th Texas Cavalry could count only 110 soldiers fit for duty. Ninety percent of the original roster of roughly 1,000 men was no longer with the unit. Disease, death, desertion, and wounds had taken most of them out of the war. The entire brigade, originally numbering about 4,000, could muster only 686 troopers in November 1864.[25]

Even if Bates took the most direct route to his regiment, he would have ridden about 265 miles from the time he left Colonel Jones at the hospital until his regiment arrived at Decatur two weeks later. For a man still not completely back to normal strength, twenty miles on horseback every day for two weeks must have been exhausting. Indeed, the ride convinced Bates that he was not ready to resume active duty. To his dismay, he was still too weak to make any contribution to the regiment.

In Camp Near Tenn River
Nov 8 1864
My Dear Ma,

Some ten days have elapsed since I wrote you last, and as I have an opportunity of writing and also of sending a letter across the river I avail myself of them to drop you a note hastily.

Our Brig is encamped tonight 12 miles west of Decatur. We passed in sight of Decatur coming up, and saw the hateful old *gridiron* flaunting in the breeze as we came on. Genl Hood halted awhile in front of the place, but I presume either did not care to take the place or concluded it was not worth the sacrifice of the lives the

23. Richard M. McMurry, *John Bell Hood and the War for Southern Independence* (Lexington: University Press of Kentucky, 1982), 161–62; Connelly, *Autumn of Glory*, 483.
24. Kerr, ed., *Fighting with Ross' Texas Cavalry*, 187; *OR*, Vol. 45, Pt. 1, p. 768.
25. *OR*, Vol. 45, Pt. 1, p. 768.

taking would cost.[26] From the best information I can get Genl
Hood's forces are in the vicinity of Tuscumbia. There is no doubt
but a portion of his forces are already across the Tenn River—but
what number are across I have no idea.

Various opinions are entertained as to what his next move will be.
Some think his object will be to make a feint on Nashville & strike
for Memphis whilst others are of opinion that He will plant himself
at Corinth. I think he will either throw his forces across the Tenn
River and make for the Nashville & Chatanooga R Road, or else run
his forces by rail around to Blue mountain and from there to the rear
of Atlanta again. But whatever may be his object the next ten or fifteen days will tell. I have heard no news for V.a. or in fact from anywhere, for some time, as we have been completely shut out from the
"civilized world" for two weeks.

I have not yet decided whether or not I will go home. I have
however remained in camp long enough to be convinced I am not
able for active duty yet. I have made application for sixty days leave.
If it does not come in a few days I will go to Miss or somewhere else
until I get well. Genl Ross has offered me an unlimited pass which
will answer me as well to stay in the country as a leave of absence.

If I have opportunity I will write again soon.
My love to all
Most affectionately
Your Son
J. C. B.

I will write again in a few days & inform you whether I will be at
home this winter or not. Hood's forces are crossing the Tenn.

The surgeons of the Texas Cavalry Brigade agreed that the major was not
ready for duty in the field and issued a sixty-day medical leave of absence
at about the time Bates wrote his letter of November 8. Thus he missed
the brigade's hard service during Hood's campaign into Tennessee. Acting at times as the vanguard to Hood's army, and as rear guard at other
times, the Texans clashed frequently with Federal cavalry as Hood's Army
of Tennessee marched to its destruction at Franklin and Nashville in

26. Hood had considered crossing the river at Decatur, but the little town was strongly
fortified, so the general led his army west about forty-five miles to Tuscumbia. McMurry,
John Bell Hood, 164; Connelly, *Autumn of Glory*, 485–87.

November and December. After Hood's disastrous defeat at Nashville in mid-December, the Texans, now serving under Nathan Bedford Forrest, were one of two cavalry brigades that covered the Confederate retreat into Alabama. The 9th Texas Cavalry lost twenty-two more men and the brigade lost eighty-seven, on Hood's doomed campaign.[27]

Where Bates spent those months is not indicated in his letters. In fact, numerous letters have not survived—his next extant letter is dated April 2, five months later. He may have returned to Texas during that period, but more likely he rode to Mississippi to continue his recovery from the wound he had received nearly a year earlier. Meanwhile, the Texas brigade spent late December and early January around Iuka and Corinth, Mississippi, then moved down toward Yazoo in central Mississippi in mid-February. These early months of 1865 were uneventful for the brigade, and few of the Texans left accounts of their activities during this period.[28]

By contrast, the war was grinding to a close in the eastern theater. General Sherman by this time had made his march from Atlanta to Savannah and was in early 1865 tearing up South Carolina on his way into North Carolina. General Grant closed the vise ever tighter on Richmond, stretching Lee's tattered lines to the breaking point. On the very day that Bates wrote his next surviving letter, Lee abandoned the works around Petersburg and Richmond and retreated west on his army's last march of the war. A week later the Army of Northern Virginia surrendered at Appomattox Court House southwest of Richmond, ending all meaningful resistance to Federal control of the dying Confederacy.

Bates of course did not know of the disaster in Virginia when he scrawled his letter of April 2. He had apparently just rejoined his regiment, then stationed about thirty miles north of Jackson. By this time he had been appointed lieutenant colonel, effective September 2, 1864 (the day of Lieutenant Colonel Berry's death), and was in command of the regiment while Colonel Jones directed the brigade. Nearly eleven months after his injury, Bates and the Texas surgeons still had doubts about his ability to serve in the field. His lighthearted description of a wedding near camp reveals much about his racial views.

---

27. Compiled Service Records, James C. Bates file (Microfilm M323, roll 56); Tyler et al., *New Handbook of Texas*, 5:692; Connelly, *Autumn of Glory*, 512; "Minutes of the Proceedings of the Association of the Survivors of Ross,' Ector's and Granberry's Brigades, U.C.V.," in Bates Papers.

28. Kerr, ed., *Fighting with Ross' Texas Cavalry*, 198, 202; Hale, *Third Texas Cavalry*, 268.

Hd Qrs 9th Tex Cavly
Madison Co, Miss
Apr 2nd 1865
Miss Mootie Johnson,
My Dear Friend,

After a very lonely and toilsome trip I am at last in camp again, and I assure you I was glad enough to reach here. If there were not so many & such strong inducements at home, I doubt whether I would start there tomorrow if I had a final discharge from the army.

I found very few men in camp. More than half as you have doubtless heard before this have been furloughed. Just before these men were furloughed near one hundred & fifty of the Brig deserted (only *one* man from my Regt left). Gen Ross has gone home on 90 days leave. Col Jones commands the Brig which leaves me in command of the Regt. I have not yet made up my mind as to whether I will remain in the field or not. The surgeons advise me not, and I think I will take their advice. But if I do not go on duty you need not look for me home until you hear from me again as I think it very likely that I will be assigned to post duty somewhere.

I have just returned from Brownsville where I have been for several days past on a visit to see my old friends.[29] Had quite a pleasant time and by the way did something which is not laid down in the army Regulations as being the duty of an officer. Just stop here and see if you can guess what it was. Well I see you can't guess it so I will tell you. *I united a couple in the holy bands of matrimony.* You needn't look incredulous. I married them in regular *magisterial* style—as tight as a parson could do it.

It happened in this wise—while in Brownsville I was invited to attend a wedding & on the appointed evening in company with a couple of ladies we went out to the bride's house a mile from town. All went on swimmingly until the arrival of the groom about 8 o clk when it was ascertained the parson could not be present—was very sick. This was an unfortunate dilemma. The supper was all ready the guests in attendance. But no preacher or magistrate in reach. What was to be done. It would not do for the happy couple to be disappointed after so many preparations had been made—but who could marry them was the question.

29. Bates is doubtless referring to the civilian friends with whom he had stayed while recuperating the previous September. Brownsville is about twenty-five miles northeast of Vicksburg.

After debating the question for some time "Mine Host" who is a fat, jolly round faced, fun-loving sort of a [gentleman?], took me by the button *a la Gibson* and suggested that I should "play the parson". Well, this was a new item in my experience. I knew all about Hardee's, Maury's and Wheeler's tactics and something of the army regulations, reviews &c, but no form for a case of this kind was laid down in my books. I knew how to unite companies, squadrons, & columns but how to unite a man & woman in wedlock was a poser.

However, after Some hesitation I concluded to retrieve the "blushing couple"(?) from their embarrassing situation provided a methodist or episcopal prayer book could be found, but nothing of the kind could be produced. Here was an awkward fix *I* had got in. I had agreed to marry them, but for the life of me could not tell how the thing was to be done. after thinking over all the ceremonies I had ever seen or heard or read, and failing to remember enough of any of them to answer the purpose a bright idea occurred to me. *I'd write it down.* So taking out my memorandum book, with Miss *Alice* to assist, I went to work—supplying omissions where we could not remember the usual forms   in ten minutes or less I announced myself as being in readiness to make the twain one.

In a moment all was buster [bluster?]—the guests took their places—the bride & groom with their attendants entered—silence was restored. I opened my book—read the ceremony—the responses were made, and with due solemnity I pronounced them "husband and wife." The friends and relatives of the happy couple offered their congratulations "and all went merry as a marriage bell."

I believe I neglected to tell you that the couple were "American citizens of African des *scent.*" I did not as preachers sometimes do claim the privelege of *kissing the bride.* After partaking of a Splendid Supper prepared for the "white folks" present, we returned home perfectly satisfied with our evenings enjoyment.

But enough of this "nigger weddin"—tho' I have nothing else to write about. As I said above I have not decided whether I will go in the field yet or not. If I should be assigned to post duty I will ask to be ordered to the trans Miss. You need not therefore write to me until you hear from me again. If I go on post duty here you will have to direct your letters differently. I will write again as soon as opportunity offers.

Truly your friend &c

J.C.B.

While General Sul Ross enjoyed a leave of absence in Texas, Colonel Dudley Jones commanded the brigade at Canton in central Mississippi. The Texas brigade was apparently ordered to retrain as infantry about this time, and the Texans were put through their paces in a brigade drill on May 1. As always, Lieutenant Colonel Bates had his men ready for the contest: "The prize was awarded by the appointed judges to the Ninth Texas Cavalry Squadron, commanded by Lieut. Col. J. C. Bates, as being the best drilled in the various movements."[30] The world of the Confederacy may have crumbled to dust farther east, but Bates remained at his post, drilling his men and preparing for any eventuality. Significantly, the 9th Texas Cavalry Regiment was now referred to as a "squadron."

The pitiful remnants of the Confederate army in Mississippi were only going through the motions, however. While they milled about their camps near Canton in mid-April, Federal forces had marched into Mobile, Alabama, effectively ending the war in the western theater. On May 4, three days after Bates accepted the drill prize for his regiment, the commander of Confederate forces in Alabama, Mississippi, and eastern Louisiana, Lieutenant General Richard Taylor, surrendered his army at Citronelle, Alabama, forty miles north of Mobile, on the same terms as Lee in Virginia and Joseph E. Johnston in North Carolina.[31]

When confirmed reports that Lee and Johnston had surrendered reached the Texas brigade near Jackson in early May, some of the men suggested breaking up into small bands and fighting a guerrilla war west of the Mississippi. Cooler heads prevailed, however, and some of the officers, perhaps including Bates, rode sorrowfully into Jackson with their muster rolls to surrender to the Federals. Union officers generously allowed the Confederates to return to the brigade alone and issue paroles to the men. These paroles promised that the soldiers would not take up arms against the United States again unless properly exchanged, something that would never happen. Thus, without a single Federal soldier among them, Ross's Texans gave up the fight. In the words of Private Sparks, "Our artillery was parked and arms stacked to be taken to Jackson. The old flag was taken from the staff and folded up as a relic. Our side arms were all retained with horses, saddles and all other equipage and the only difference that the writer really saw was the officers ceased to command or to advise, and the command was disbanded."[32]

Bates's war was over. Despite his optimism, his efforts to prop up

30. *OR,* Vol. 49, Pt. 2, p. 1277.
31. Parrish, *Richard Taylor,* 441–42.
32. Sparks, *War Between the States,* 117.

morale, and his will to win—despite giving everything he could give, watching his best friends die, and having his jaw shot to pieces—his Confederacy had declined into defeat. The dark bitterness and deep disappointment that invaded his soul after the surrender left him confused and disoriented. He did not want to stay among the Yankees now swarming over Mississippi, he did not want to go home, he did not want to do anything. All he wanted was to get away from everything.

Vicksburgh Miss
May 19th/65
Miss Mootie Johnson
My Dear Friend

A few months ago I little thought that I would write you a letter from this place. More especially while it was in the possession of the Yankees & myself a prisoner. But it is well for us that we cannot raise the veil that hides the future from our view   How dark and gloomy in all probability would be the future to us. As it is *Hope* bids us look for a better and brighter day—but at the same time I must admit that the chances *for a better day* seem to me very remote. The dark clouds which have been for the past few months, gathering over our national horizon, have finally shut out the last ray of hope in *this* Dept. Will it be otherwise in the Trans Miss? I fear not.

I see in this morning's paper an official report by Maj Gnrl [James H.] Wilson of the capture of Pres Davis and staff. Whether true or not I am unable to say[.] I am afraid it is.[33]

I wrote you a long letter a few days ago & you must consequently expect little now. I am *in no condition* to write—or do anything else—I feel as though an other month or so such as the past would positively run me mad I am consequently anxious to get away from every body (except of course my friends) & everything exciting where I can have some rest mentally as well as physically. I will be at home soon but in the mean time be assured of my sincere and unwavering friendship.
J.C.B.

Bates could not steel his nerves sufficiently to return to Paris for several

---

33. A detachment of Wilson's cavalry corps captured Jefferson Davis in southern Georgia on May 10. Michael B. Ballard, *A Long Shadow: Jefferson Davis and the Final Days of the Confederacy* (Jackson: University Press of Mississippi, 1986), 140–44; William C. Davis, *Jefferson Davis*, 635–57.

months after the surrender. He remained in Mississippi at least through the summer, but he promised his mother he would eat Christmas dinner with her.[34] His family must have wondered at his prolonged absence. What had happened to him that he would turn away from the warm embrace of his mother? He had ridden off to war a mere boy only four years ago. Now he was a man, scarred by war and aged by failure. His surviving letters do not indicate exactly when he traveled back to Paris, but it was a day he wanted to put off as long as possible. The humiliation of defeat, the blasted hopes, the gloomy future, his disfigured face, the prospect of meeting the families of the dead—it was all too much.

34. Bates to My Dear Ma, July 17, 1865, Bates Papers.

Epilogue

James C. Bates, former lieutenant colonel, C.S.A., returned to his home in Paris, probably in late 1865, keeping his promise to eat Christmas dinner with his family. He and his mother owned some land in north Texas, and Bates had repeatedly advised her and his brother-in-law Will Bramlette to buy land and livestock during the war, so perhaps Bates lived for a while as a grain farmer or stock raiser. Within a few months, however, he had determined a different course for his life—he would become a physician. No one else in his family was a doctor, but his apparent respect for Mootie's father, a successful small-town physician, and his extensive experience with the surgeons in the Atlanta and Auburn military hospitals may have inspired him to move in that direction.

By the fall term of 1866, Bates was a student in the medical school at the University of Virginia in Charlottesville. After his training in Virginia, he traveled north, into the land of his former enemies, and attended clinical lectures at Bellevue Hospital in New York City. If Bates wondered whether his facial wound and speech impediment might make him less attractive as a potential mate, Mootie put his mind to rest. In January 1868 he married his longtime sweetheart, and a year later he began his medical practice in his home town.[1]

James and Mootie started a family almost immediately. When the census marshal visited their home in 1870, the couple had a one-year-old son. Living with them, and doubtless doting on the baby, was his mother, then fifty-six years old. Bates at that time was combining his medical practice with the life of a gentleman farmer. He operated a Lamar County farm of 70 improved and 240 unimproved acres, worth two thousand dollars. The land produced 30 bushels of wheat and 1,500 bushels of corn in 1870, supplementing the young couple's income from his medical practice.[2]

Ten years later another census marshal recorded seven children in the

1. N. C. Bates to Dear James, October 30, 1866, Bates Papers; James C. Bates obituary, ibid.

2. Schedules I and III, Lamar County, Beat 3, Ninth Census of the United States, 1870,

Bates family, including two sets of twins. Five sons and two daughters, ranging in age from eleven years to one month, must have made for a lively household.[3] Dr. Bates still operated a small farm in Lamar County in 1880, but the family must have relied primarily on his medical income, because the farm included only nine improved acres and $1,200 worth of farm animals.[4]

Shortly after the census taker closed his books on the Bates household in 1880, Dr. Bates moved his family 170 miles southwest to Palo Pinto (in Palo Pinto County) for reasons of health. Bates suffered from chronic diarrhea for many years after the war, probably a result of his service in the army, and he believed that a different climate might help him cope.[5] Despite his weakened physical condition, Bates took an active role in veterans' affairs, serving as vice president of the Ross Brigade Association, United Confederate Veterans, in the middle and late 1880s.[6] He continued to practice medicine and to farm on the western plains of Palo Pinto County, but his ailment continued and in fact grew worse. The family's standard of living doubtless declined along with his health. His taxable property in 1890, at the end of his medical career, was worth less than one-fourth of his property in 1871, when he was just beginning.[7]

His enfeebled condition eventually forced Bates to abandon his medical practice altogether, and he moved his family back to Paris in 1887. But nothing seemed to help. He consulted one of his medical-school professors for the latest remedies for chronic diarrhea in early 1891, but it was too late. On August 11, 1891, thirty years to the month after he had

---

Records of the Bureau of the Census, Record Group 29, National Archives, Washington, D.C. (Microfilm M593 and T1134).

3. Two other offspring died in childhood. Interview with Henry Fink, September 19, 1997.

4. Schedules I and III, Lamar County, Precinct 3, Tenth Census of the United States, 1880, Records of the Bureau of the Census, Record Group 29, National Archives, Washington, D.C. (Microfilm T9 and T1134).

5. While studying medicine in New York, Bates suspected he might have tuberculosis. At that time he discussed moving to western or southwest Texas for its superior climate, but his symptoms apparently abated, and he and Mootie began their married life in Paris. B[ates] to My Dear Moot, August 18, 186[7?], Bates Papers.

6. "Minutes of the Proceedings of the Association of the Survivors of Ross,' Ector's and Granberry's Brigades, U.C.V.," Bates Papers.

7. James C. Bates obituary, Bates Papers; Records of the Comptroller of Public Accounts, Ad Valorem Tax Division, County Real and Personal Property Tax Rolls (Lamar County), Record Group 304; interviews with Bates descendants.

joined his cavalry company, James C. Bates died in his bed at home in Paris at the age of fifty-four.[8]

On the day he died, his former comrades from Ross's Texas Cavalry Brigade were celebrating a reunion 120 miles to the southwest in Fort Worth. A telegram announcing his death was read to the aging former horse soldiers, and they stopped business to draw up a memorial to their former lieutenant, captain, major, and lieutenant colonel:

> While we bow in humble submission to the will of God, we sincerely mourn his death; and affectionately cherish the memory of our deceased comrade, his noble soldierly example, his unflinching devotion to duty and his cheerful endurance of the trials and suffering on the field and in the hospital.[9]

Bates's obituary, published in a Paris newspaper a few weeks later and possibly written by his old friend Dohoney, indicated that the lighthearted young man of 1861 had been transformed by the war, his wound, and his long-term illness: "being of a modest and reserved disposition, [he] was not understood or appreciated by any but his intimate acquaintances." His mother lived nearly five more years, and Mootie nearly sixteen. The bodies of all three are buried near each other in Evergreen Cemetery in Paris, surrounded on all sides by the remains of family members, friends, and twelve other soldiers of Company H.[10]

James C. Bates was the very best sort of soldier for the Confederacy and the worst sort of enemy of the Union during the Civil War. He was deeply committed to Confederate victory, intelligent, well educated, diligent, disciplined, and physically courageous. Although he had no military training before he joined the army, he quickly learned the manual of drill, and his company was repeatedly praised for its mastery on the drill field. He made extra efforts to see that his men were well fed, well supplied, and well clothed, even spending his own money to care for them. When a wounded comrade was stranded on the field at Chustotalasah, Bates rode back into a storm of minié balls to carry him off. The fall of Memphis, New Orleans,

8. James C. Bates obituary, Bates Papers; J. E. C. to J. C. Bates, March 27, 1891, Bates Papers.

9. Memorial of the Ross' Brigade Association, August 11, 1891, Bates Papers.

10. James C. Bates obituary, Bates Papers; Bates genealogical chart, Bates Papers; interview with Nancy McKnight Fink, September 19, 1997; Ron Brothers, comp., "Confederate Veterans Who Died or Are Buried in Lamar County, TX," Lamar County, Texas, World Wide Web page on the Internet (http://gen.1starnet.com/civilwar/csadead.htm).

Vicksburg, and Atlanta did not discourage him; he only fought harder. His nearly fatal wound kept him out of the war for almost a year, but he returned to duty even before he was capable of contributing to the war effort and served with his regiment to the very last days of the war. All things considered, it was probably best that the regiments of the Confederacy were not composed entirely of men like Bates. The tragic, fratricidal war of the 1860s would have been even longer and bloodier.

Appendix 1

The Wound of James C. Bates

John C. O'Brien, M.D., Baylor Medical Center, Dallas

The moment he was hit by a minié ball, Major James C. Bates experienced severe, sharp pain and saw stars. His head probably jerked down and to the left, and blood, teeth, bone, and tissue sprayed from his wound, splattering Bates and anyone close to him. He probably passed out immediately, but he might have struggled to his feet, in "shock," and stumbled to the rear (if he could identify that direction), or a comrade might have helped him reach safety.

He was shot through the mouth, with little damage to the lips. This indicates that his mouth was open at the time of impact. His jaws must have been in apposition (i.e., teeth touching) or close to apposition because he lost the four upper front teeth and suffered damage to the lower teeth and jaw. The missile passed through the tip of the tongue and shattered the left side of the mandible (lower jaw bone) and exited the left side of the neck below the ear.[1] This indicates either that Bates was leaning over with his head down (as a cavalryman might lean forward over his horse's neck) or that the Federal soldier who wounded Bates was at a higher elevation and shooting down while Bates was in an upright position.

The tip of the tongue was lacerated (about one inch) and the left side of the tongue, the floor of the mouth, and the mandible were injured. Such wounds were not uncommon in this war. Two similar cases were reported in the *Confederate States Medical and Surgical Journal*.[2] W. M. Wyatt, a private in Page's battery, 1st Virginia Artillery, suffered loss of the entire lower jaw when struck by a fragment of a shell.[3] The anterior por-

1. E. L. Howard, "The Effects of Minié Balls on Bone," *Confederate States Medical and Surgical Journal* 1 (June 1864): 88–89.

2. H. L. Thomas, "Cases of Gunshot Injury Requiring Ligation of the Artery," ibid., 1 (November 1864): 184–86 (cases 4 and 6).

3. C. B. Gibson, "Operations in Reparative Surgery," ibid., 1 (July 1864): 104–106.

tion of the tongue is innervated by two nerves—the lingual, which is sensory, and the hypoglossal, which is motor. Hence, the left side of Bates's tongue was numb and paralyzed, although it was possible that the function of the nerves could later return. In view of the severe damage to the jaw, however, this would be doubtful. A third nerve, the inferior alveolar nerve, passes through the substance of the mandible, exits at the chin, and is the sensory innervation of the side of the chin and lower lip. Injury to this nerve causes anesthesia (numbness) of the chin and lip. These results are similar to the defects created after the removal of fairly advanced cancers from the side of the tongue, the floor of the mouth, and the mandible in which a portion of the jaw is removed. Patients who have undergone such surgery are able to speak with some impediment, and to eat, but with some difficulty because they must use the unaffected side of the mouth. This side is sensate and the location of the food is apparent; whereas on the affected side, there is anesthesia and food can get "lost" and fall out of the mouth. Patients are also prone to drool until they become accustomed to the altered sensation. As Bates's wound healed, his chin probably deviated to the left side because the strut support of the mandible on that side had been lost. This caused a cosmetic defect, but such defects are normally not severe. The teeth usually come into occlusion when the jaws close. Thus, chewing is still possible on the unaffected side, although this does not happen in all cases. The major had a fairly good prognosis as far as eating and speaking, but he would have had a deformity on the left side of his face. This may explain why he grew a beard after the injury.

Bates was shot with a relatively slow-moving missile, which would have lost much of its velocity by passing through the jaw bone and then passing under, over, or through the sternocleidomastoid (SCM) muscle.[4] Several important structures are located under this muscle: (1) the carotid artery (which branches to the brain [internal carotid] and the jaws, face, scalp, etc. [external carotid]), injury to which can cause major hemorrhage, hematoma (a collection of blood in the tissues and spaces), stroke, and death; (2) the internal jugular vein, which carries blood from the above structures and is less likely to cause severe hemorrhage, hematoma, etc.; (3) the vagus nerve, which contains the nerve to the muscles of the left vocal cord; and (4) the XI (eleventh) cranial nerve (or spinal-accessory nerve), which is the innervation to the trapezius—the muscle that holds up the shoulder. Since Bates did not mention suffering from hoarseness,

4. M. Legouest, "Motion of Balls, and Ball Wounds," ibid., 1 (August 1864): 120–24 (originally published in French in *Chirurgerie Militaire*).

his vagus nerve probably was not injured. Because he did not complain of left-shoulder pain, it is unlikely that the spinal-accessory nerve was transected or contused (bruised). Transection or contusion would cause loss of function, so the shoulder would droop and hurt. Thus, the ball probably passed over or through the SCM. Today, a patient suffering a similar wound would be stabilized, evaluated thoroughly, taken to the operating room, and placed under anesthesia. The wound would be debrided (i.e., bone and tooth chips and necrotic [dead] flesh would be removed) and the course of the missile discerned in order to ascertain the integrity of the major structures of the neck. (Apparently, Bates did not experience a neurovascular injury as he had no neurologic symptoms—such as paralysis, stroke, etc.—or hemorrhage.) The patient would also be fed intravenously or through intestinal tubes, and pain medication would be administered intramuscularly or intravenously.

As his letters make clear, Bates struggled mightily to obtain fluids and nutrition. His efforts to pass a tube through his swollen mouth and throat testify to his great thirst. Nutrition is very important to healing, and Bates improved rapidly once he was able to eat an adequate amount of good food. (See his letter of July 30.) It is amazing that any soldiers lived at all after some of the wounds they suffered, especially when nutrition could not be taken. Today, physicians use intravenous fluids and TPN (total parenteral nutrition—high-calorie feedings through a large vein) to maintain fluid balance and nutrition. When possible, surgeons insert a tube into the intestinal tract to feed the patient directly, thus helping to maintain the intestinal barrier against infection.

Not only did Bates have to fight to get fluids and nutrition; he also was treated in a time when injections for pain control were relatively new and not generally available.[5] A patient with his wound would normally need strong pain medication for one to two weeks. Usually, healthy young men such as Bates need less medication, and for a shorter duration, than do physically and emotionally weaker men. Alcohol (such as the brandy mentioned in his letter of June 17) and laudanum (tincture of opium) or morphia (morphine) were the pain medications available at the time.

The occasional suppuration (expression or flow of pus) and extrusion of bone that Bates mentions in his letters is a natural response of the body to a foreign body (dead bone or tooth fragments), similar to a splinter in

5. J. Julian Chisolm, *A Manual of Military Surgery, For the Use of Surgeons in the Confederate States Army* (3rd ed.; Columbia, Ga.: Evans and Cogswell, 1864), 221–25, makes it clear that the use of hypodermic needles to inject morphine for pain control was a "new" process available only to "fortunate" physicians.

a finger.[6] Generally, this situation is heralded by a boil (abscess), redness and warmth in the area, and pain. Bates had odynophagia (pain on swallowing) when the boils developed.

Wounded Civil War soldiers had many adversities to overcome: poor nutrition, unsanitary conditions, viruses (measles, chicken pox, yellow fever), malaria, dysentery (*E. coli* and typhoid among others), a generally ill-equipped medical profession (some doctors were excellent, others poorly educated and trained), lack of clothing and blankets, and on and on. Wounds were expected to become infected, and "laudable pus," a widely accepted sign of healing, was often spread from soldier to soldier by those caring for them. Few wounds healed by primary intention (without infection); this was so uncommon that a number of cases were noted in a report by the Confederate surgeon M. Michel.[7] The use of phenol (carbolic acid) for antisepsis was studied by Joseph Lister of England in the early 1860s but not used frequently until 1865. This information was not available in North America during the Civil War, and of course, there were no IVs, antibiotics, etc., although a few medications, such as quinine, were available. The survival of some seriously wounded men in the Civil War may be more a testimony to heavenly intervention and luck than to the great skill of the physicians.

6. W. S. Savory, "On the Absorption of Dead Bone," *Confederate States Medical and Surgical Journal* 1 (November 1864): 187–89 (originally published in England in *Royal Medical and Chirurgical Society,* April 1864).

7. M. Michel, "Healing of Gun-Shot Wounds by First Intention," *Confederate States Medical and Surgical Journal* 1 (July 1864): 99–102.

Code Used by James C. Bates
in Correspondence with His Family

The code key shown below was enclosed in an undated letter from Bates to Mootie Johnson. Bates used the code in his letters of July 25 and September 3, 1863, to transmit information about the numbers and locations of various Confederate forces in the western theater of the war.

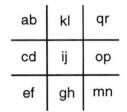

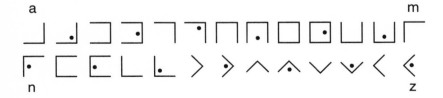

Bibliography

PRIMARY SOURCES

Manuscripts

Bates, James C. Papers. Private collection of Henry and Walter Fink, Dallas, Texas.
Lincoln, Abraham. Papers, 1833–1916. Manuscripts Division, Library of Congress, Washington, D.C.
Neville, A. W. Papers. Texas A&M University at Commerce Library, Commerce, Texas.
Rawlins, F. A. Diary. University of North Texas Library, Denton, Texas.
Regimental Files (9th Texas Cavalry). Confederate Research Center. Hill College, Hillsboro, Texas.

Government Documents

National Archives, Washington, D.C. Compiled Service Records of Confederate Soldiers Who Served in Organizations from the State of Texas. War Department Collection of Confederate Records (Microfilm M323, rolls 56–60, 9th Texas Cavalry), Record Group 109.
National Archives, Washington, D.C. Seventh Census of the United States, 1850. Records of the Bureau of the Census (Microfilm M432), Record Group 29.
National Archives, Washington, D.C. Eighth Census of the United States, 1860. Records of the Bureau of the Census (Microfilm M653, T1134), Record Group 29.
National Archives, Washington, D.C. Ninth Census of the United States, 1870. Records of the Bureau of the Census (Microfilm M593, T1134), Record Group 29.
National Archives, Washington, D.C. Tenth Census of the United States, 1880. Records of the Bureau of the Census (Microfilm T9, T1134), Record Group 29.
Texas State Library and Archives Commission, Austin. Records of the Comptroller of Public Accounts, Ad Valorem Tax Division. County Real and Personal Property Tax Rolls, 1860–1890, Record Group 304.
United States War Department. *The War of the Rebellion: A Compilation of the Official Records of the Union and Confederate Armies.* 128 vols. Washington, D.C.: Government Printing Office, 1880–1901.

Newspapers and Magazines

Dallas Herald, 1861–62
Harper's Weekly, 1861–65
Houston Tri-Weekly Telegraph, 1861–65
New York Herald, 1861–65
New York Times, 1861–65
Paris (Tex.) Herald, 1861–62, 1891
Tyler (Tex.) Reporter, 1861–62

Books

Barron, Samuel B. *The Lone Star Defenders: A Chronicle of the Third Texas Cavalry Regiment in the Civil War.* 1908. Reprint, Washington, D.C.: Zenger, 1983.

Basler, Roy P., ed. *The Collected Works of Abraham Lincoln.* 9 vols. New Brunswick, N.J.: Rutgers University Press, 1953–55.

Blessington, Joseph Palmer. *The Campaigns of Walker's Texas Division.* Introductions by Norman D. Brown and T. Michael Parrish. 1875. Reprint, Austin, Tex.: State House Press, 1994.

Brown, Alonzo L. *History of the Fourth Regiment of Minnesota Infantry Volunteers During the Great Rebellion, 1861–1865.* St. Paul, Minn.: Pioneer Press, 1892.

Carr, Pat, ed. *In Fine Spirits: The Civil War Letters of Ras Stirman.* Fayetteville, Ark.: Washington County Historical Society, 1986.

Cater, Douglas John. *As It Was: Reminiscences of a Soldier of the Third Texas Cavalry and the Nineteenth Louisiana Infantry.* 1981. Reprint, Austin, Tex.: State House Press, 1990.

Davis, James Henry. *The Cypress Rangers in the Civil War: The Experiences of 85 Confederate Cavalrymen from Texas.* 2d ed. Texarkana, Tex.: Heritage Oak Press, 1992.

Dohoney, E. L. *An Average American: Being a True History of Leading Events in the Life of Lafayette, Who Was Born in Ky.; But "Went West to Grow Up with the Country."* Paris, Tex.: n.p., 1907.

Hewett, Janet B., Noah Andre Trudeau, and Bryce A. Suderow, eds. *Supplement to the Official Records of the Union and Confederate Armies.* 47 vols. to date. Wilmington, N.C.: Broadfoot, 1994–.

Kerr, Homer L., ed. *Fighting with Ross' Texas Cavalry Brigade, C.S.A.: The Diary of George L. Griscom, Adjutant, 9th Texas Cavalry Regiment.* Hillsboro, Tex.: Hill Jr. College Press, 1976.

Rose, Victor M. *Ross' Texas Brigade, Being a Narrative of Events Connected with Its Service in the Late War Between the States.* Louisville, Ky.: Courier-Journal Book and Job Rooms, 1881.

Shelton, Perry Wayne, comp., and Shelly Morrison, ed. *Personal Civil War Letters of General Lawrence Sullivan Ross, with Other Letters.* Austin, Tex.: Shelly and Richard Morrison, 1994.

Simon, John Y., ed. *The Papers of Ulysses S. Grant*. 20 vols. to date. Carbondale: Southern Illinois University Press, 1967–.

Sparks, A. W. *The War Between the States As I Saw It. Reminiscent, Historical and Personal*. Tyler, Tex.: Lee & Burnett Printers, 1901.

Articles and Essays

Barron, Samuel B. "Van Dorn at Holly Springs." *Confederate Veteran* 10 (October 1902): 455–56.

Billingsley, William Clyde, ed. " 'Such Is War': The Confederate Memoirs of Newton Asbury Keen." *Texas Military History* 6 (Winter 1967): 239–53 (Part 1); 7 (Spring 1968): 44–70 (Part 2); 7 (Summer 1968): 103–19 (Part 3); 7 (Autumn 1968): 176–94 (Part 4).

Blanton, J. C. "Forrest's Old Regiment." *Confederate Veteran* 3 (February 1895): 41–42.

Brown, A. F. "Van Dorn's Operations in Northern Mississippi—Recollections of a Cavalryman." *Southern Historical Society Papers* 6 (July–December 1878): 154–61.

Callaway, W. A. "Hard Service with Ross's Brigade." *Confederate Veteran* 28 (September 1920): 328–29.

———. "Hard Times with Ross's Cavalry." *Confederate Veteran* 28 (December 1920): 447.

———. "Incidents of Service." *Confederate Veteran* 28 (October 1920): 372.

"Col. Erasmus I. Stirman." *Confederate Veteran* 22 (May 1914): 226.

Deupree, J. G. "The Capture of Holly Springs, Mississippi, Dec. 20, 1862." *Publications of the Mississippi Historical Society* 4 (1901): 49–61.

"Dismounted Cavalry." *Confederate Veteran* 37 (November 1929): 411–12.

M'Minn, W. P. "Service with Van Dorn's Cavalry." *Confederate Veteran* 27 (October 1919): 384–86.

Rosecrans, William S. "The Battle of Corinth." In *Battles and Leaders of the Civil War*. 4 vols. Edited by Robert Underwood Johnson and Clarence Clough Buel, 2:737–57. New York: Century, 1887–88.

Searcy, M. W. "Gen. Van Dorn's Holly Springs Victory." *Confederate Veteran* 15 (May 1907): 229.

Stevenson, W. R. "Capture of Holly Springs, Miss." *Confederate Veteran* 9 (March 1901): 134.

"Vivid War Experiences at Ripley, Miss." *Confederate Veteran* 13 (June 1905): 262–65.

SECONDARY SOURCES

Books

Abel, Annie H. *The American Indian as Slaveholder and Secessionist.* Cleveland: Arthur H. Clark, 1915.

Allardice, Bruce S. *More Generals in Gray.* Baton Rouge: Louisiana State University Press, 1995.

Ballard, Michael B. *A Long Shadow: Jefferson Davis and the Final Days of the Confederacy.* Jackson: University Press of Mississippi, 1986.

Barefoot, Daniel W. *General Robert F. Hoke: Lee's Modest Warrior.* Winston-Salem, N.C.: John F. Blair, 1996.

Bearss, Edwin Cole. *The Campaign for Vicksburg.* 3 vols. Dayton, Ohio: Morningside, 1985–86.

Benner, Judith Ann. *Sul Ross: Soldier, Statesman, Educator.* College Station: Texas A&M University Press, 1983.

Bergeron, Arthur W. *Confederate Mobile.* Jackson: University Press of Mississippi, 1991.

Beringer, Richard E., Herman Hattaway, Archer Jones, and William N. Still Jr. *Why the South Lost the Civil War.* Athens: University of Georgia Press, 1986.

Boatner, Mark Mayo III. *The Civil War Dictionary.* Rev. ed. New York: David McKay, 1988.

Buenger, Walter L. *Secession and the Union in Texas.* Austin: University of Texas Press, 1984.

Campbell, Randolph B., and Richard G. Lowe. *Wealth and Power in Antebellum Texas.* College Station: Texas A&M University Press, 1977.

Castel, Albert. *Decision in the West: The Atlanta Campaign of 1864.* Lawrence: University Press of Kansas, 1992.

Chisolm, J. Julian. *A Manual of Military Surgery, For the Use of Surgeons in the Confederate States Army.* 3rd ed. Columbia, Ga.: Evans and Cogswell, 1864.

Connelly, Thomas Lawrence. *Army of the Heartland: The Army of Tennessee, 1861–1862.* Baton Rouge: Louisiana State University Press, 1967.

———. *Autumn of Glory: The Army of Tennessee, 1862–1865.* Baton Rouge: Louisiana State University Press, 1971.

Cozzens, Peter. *The Darkest Days of the War: The Battles of Iuka and Corinth.* Chapel Hill: University of North Carolina Press, 1997.

———. *This Terrible Sound: The Battle of Chickamauga.* Urbana: University of Illinois Press, 1992.

Crook, D. P. *Diplomacy During the American Civil War.* New York: John Wiley and Sons, 1975.

Crute, Joseph H., Jr. *Confederate Staff Officers, 1861–1865.* Powhatan, Va.: Derwent Books, 1982.

Cunningham, Horace H. *Doctors in Gray: The Confederate Medical Service.* Baton Rouge: Louisiana State University Press, 1958.

Current, Richard N., ed. *Encyclopedia of the Confederacy.* 4 vols. New York: Simon & Schuster, 1993.

———. *Lincoln's Loyalists: Union Soldiers from the Confederacy.* Boston: Northeastern University Press, 1992.

Cutrer, Thomas W. *Ben McCulloch and the Frontier Military Tradition.* Chapel Hill: University of North Carolina Press, 1993.

Daniel, Larry J. *Soldiering in the Army of Tennessee: A Portrait of Life in a Confederate Army.* Chapel Hill: University of North Carolina Press, 1991.

Davis, William C. *Breckinridge: Statesman, Soldier, Symbol.* Baton Rouge: Louisiana State University Press, 1974.

———. *Jefferson Davis: The Man and His Hour.* New York: HarperCollins Publishers, 1991.

Debo, Angie. *The Road to Disappearance: A History of the Creek Indians.* 1941. Reprint, Norman: University of Oklahoma Press, 1967.

Duncan, Robert Lipscomb. *Reluctant General: The Life and Times of Albert Pike.* New York: Dutton, 1961.

Evans, David. *Sherman's Horsemen: Union Cavalry Operations in the Atlanta Campaign.* Bloomington: Indiana University Press, 1996.

Faust, Patricia L., ed. *Historical Times Illustrated Encyclopedia of the Civil War.* New York: Harper & Row, 1986.

Fisher, Noel C. *War at Every Door: Partisan Politics and Guerrilla Violence in East Tennessee, 1860–1869.* Chapel Hill: University of North Carolina Press, 1997.

Foote, Shelby. *The Civil War: A Narrative.* 3 vols. New York: Random House, 1958–74.

Franks, Kenny A. *Stand Watie and the Agony of the Cherokee Nation.* Memphis: Memphis State University Press, 1979.

Gaines, W. Craig. *The Confederate Cherokees: John Drew's Regiment of Mounted Rifles.* Baton Rouge: Louisiana State University Press, 1989.

Gallagher, Gary W. *The Confederate War.* Cambridge, Mass.: Harvard University Press, 1997.

Geary, James W. *We Need Men: The Union Draft in the Civil War.* DeKalb: Northern Illinois University Press, 1991.

Hale, Douglas. *The Third Texas Cavalry in the Civil War.* Norman: University of Oklahoma Press, 1993.

Harris, William C. *With Charity for All: Lincoln and the Restoration of the Union.* Lexington: University Press of Kentucky, 1997.

Hartje, Robert G. *Van Dorn: The Life and Times of a Confederate General.* Nashville: Vanderbilt University Press, 1967.

Hennessy, John J. *Return to Bull Run: The Campaign and Battle of Second Manassas.* New York: Simon & Schuster, 1993.

Holmes, Richard. *Acts of War: The Behavior of Men in Battle.* New York: Free Press, 1985.

Johnson, Ludwell H. *Red River Campaign: Politics and Cotton in the Civil War.* Baltimore: Johns Hopkins University Press, 1958.

Josephy, Alvin M., Jr. *The Civil War in the American West.* New York: Alfred A. Knopf, 1991.

Klement, Frank L. *The Limits of Dissent: Clement L. Vallandigham & the Civil War.* Lexington: University Press of Kentucky, 1970.

Logue, Mickey, and Jack Simms. *Auburn: A Pictorial History of the Loveliest Village.* Norfolk, Va.: Donning, 1981.

Long, E. B. *The Civil War Day by Day: An Almanac, 1861–1865.* Garden City, N.Y.: Doubleday, 1971.

Lowe, Richard G., and Randolph B. Campbell. *Planters and Plain Folk: Agriculture in Antebellum Texas.* Dallas: Southern Methodist University Press, 1987.

Lowry, Thomas P. *The Story the Soldiers Wouldn't Tell: Sex in the Civil War.* Mechanicsburg, Pa.: Stackpole Books, 1994.

McCaslin, Richard B. *Tainted Breeze: The Great Hanging at Gainesville, Texas, 1862.* Baton Rouge: Louisiana State University Press, 1994.

McMillan, Malcolm C. *The Disintegration of a Confederate State: Three Governors and Alabama's Wartime Home Front, 1861–1865.* Macon, Ga.: Mercer University Press, 1986.

McMurry, Richard M. *John Bell Hood and the War for Southern Independence.* Lexington: University Press of Kentucky, 1982.

McPherson, James M. *Battle Cry of Freedom: The Civil War Era.* New York: Oxford University Press, 1988.

———. *For Cause and Comrades: Why Men Fought in the Civil War.* New York: Oxford University Press, 1997.

———, ed. *The Atlas of the Civil War.* New York: Macmillan, 1994.

Magill, Frank N., ed. *Magill's Quotations in Context.* New York: Harper and Row, 1965.

Mays, Thomas D. *The Saltville Massacre.* Fort Worth: Ryan Place Publishers, 1995.

Moore, Albert Burton. *Conscription and Conflict in the Confederacy.* New York: Macmillan, 1924.

Neal, Diane, and Thomas W. Kremm. *Lion of the South: General Thomas C. Hindman.* Macon, Ga.: Mercer University Press, 1993.

Neville, A. W. *The History of Lamar County (Texas).* Paris, Tex.: North Texas Publishing Co., 1937.

Nevins, Allan. *Ordeal of the Union.* 8 vols. New York: Charles Scribner's Sons, 1947–71.

Oates, Stephen B. *Confederate Cavalry West of the River.* Austin: University of Texas Press, 1961.

Parrish, T. Michael. *Richard Taylor: Soldier Prince of Dixie.* Chapel Hill: University of North Carolina Press, 1992.

Perkins, John D. *Daniel's Battery: The 9th Texas Field Battery.* Hillsboro, Tex.: Hill College Press, 1998.

Piston, William Garrett. *Lee's Tarnished Lieutenant: James Longstreet and His Place in Southern History.* Athens: University of Georgia Press, 1987.

Randall, James G. *Constitutional Problems under Lincoln.* Rev. ed. Urbana: University of Illinois Press, 1964.

Robertson, James I. Jr. *Soldiers Blue and Gray.* Columbia: University of South Carolina Press, 1988.

Sears, Stephen W. *Landscape Turned Red: The Battle of Antietam.* New Haven: Ticknor & Fields, 1983.

Shea, William L., and Earl J. Hess. *Pea Ridge: Civil War Campaign in the West.* Chapel Hill: University of North Carolina Press, 1992.

Sifakis, Stewart. *Compendium of the Confederate Armies: Texas.* New York: Facts on File, 1995.

—————. *Who Was Who in the Civil War.* New York: Facts on File, 1988.

Silverstone, Paul H. *Warships of the Civil War Navies.* Annapolis: Naval Institute Press, 1989.

Sommers, Richard J. *Richmond Redeemed: The Siege at Petersburg.* Garden City, N.Y.: Doubleday, 1981.

Steiner, Paul E. *Disease in the Civil War: Natural Biological Warfare in 1861–1865.* Springfield, Ill.: C. C. Thomas, 1968.

Sumrall, Alan K. *Battle Flags of Texans in the Confederacy.* Austin: Eakin Press, 1995.

Symonds, Craig L. *Joseph E. Johnston: A Civil War Biography.* New York: W. W. Norton, 1992.

Tanner, Robert G. *Stonewall in the Valley: Thomas J. "Stonewall" Jackson's Shenandoah Valley Campaign, Spring 1862.* Garden City, N.Y.: Doubleday, 1976.

Texas Almanac and State Industrial Guide, 1996–1997. Dallas: Dallas Morning News, 1995.

Trudeau, Noah Andre. *The Last Citadel: Petersburg, Virginia, June 1864–April 1865.* Boston: Little, Brown, 1991.

Tyler, Ron, et al., eds. *The New Handbook of Texas.* 6 vols. Austin: Texas State Historical Assn., 1996.

Vandiver, Frank E. *Jubal's Raid: General Early's Famous Attack on Washington in 1864.* New York: McGraw-Hill, 1960.

—————. *Ploughshares into Swords: Josiah Gorgas and Confederate Ordnance.* Austin: University of Texas Press, 1952.

Warner, Ezra J. *Generals in Blue: Lives of the Union Commanders.* Baton Rouge: Louisiana State University Press, 1964.

—————. *Generals in Gray: Lives of the Confederate Commanders.* Baton Rouge: Louisiana State University Press, 1959.

Wert, Jeffry D. *From Winchester to Cedar Creek: The Shenandoah Campaign of 1864.* Carlisle, Pa.: South Mountain Press, 1987.

Wiggins, Sarah Woolfolk. *The Scalawag in Alabama Politics, 1865–1881.* University.: University of Alabama Press, 1977.

Wiley, Bell Irvin. *The Life of Johnny Reb: The Common Soldier of the Confederacy.* Indianapolis: Bobbs-Merrill, 1943.

Wills, Brian Steel. *A Battle from the Start: The Life of Nathan Bedford Forrest.* New York: HarperCollins Publishers, 1992.

Wise, Stephen R. *Lifeline of the Confederacy: Blockade Running During the Civil War.* Columbia: University of South Carolina Press, 1988.

Woodward, Grace Steele. *The Cherokees.* Norman: University of Oklahoma Press, 1963.

Wright, Marcus J., comp., and Harold B. Simpson, ed. *Texas in the War, 1861–1865.* Hillsboro, Tex.: Hill Junior College Press, 1965.

Yeary, Mamie. *Reminiscences of the Boys in Gray, 1861–1865.* 1912. Reprint, Dayton, Ohio: Morningside, 1986.

Articles, Essays, and Theses

Alverson, Allene. "E. L. Dohoney and the Constitution of 1876." M.A. thesis, Texas Technological College, 1941.

Bahos, Charles. "On Opothleyahola's Trail: Locating the Battle of Round Mountains." *Chronicles of Oklahoma* 63 (Spring 1985): 58–89.

Baker, Robin E., and Dale Baum. "The Texas Voter and the Crisis of the Union, 1859–1861." *Journal of Southern History* 53 (August 1987): 395–420.

Benner, Judith Ann. "Lawrence Sullivan Ross." In *Ten More Texans in Gray,* edited by W. C. Nunn. Hillsboro, Tex.: Hill Jr. College Press, 1980.

Berg, Richard. "The Battle of Corinth: Standoff at the Tennessee." *Strategy and Tactics* 87 (No. 1, 1981): 43–47, 53.

Black, Andrew K. "In the Service of the United States: Comparative Mortality Among African American and White Troops in the Union Army." *Journal of Negro History* 79 (Fall 1994): 317–33.

Breeden, James O. "A Medical History of the Later Stages of the Atlanta Campaign." *Journal of Southern History* 35 (February 1969): 31–59.

Brooksher, William R., and David K. Snider. "A Visit to Holly Springs." *Civil War Times Illustrated* 14 (June 1975): 4–9, 40–44.

Cimprich, John, and Robert C. Mainfort Jr. "The Fort Pillow Massacre: A Statistical Note." *Journal of American History* 76 (December 1989): 830–37.

Connelly, Thomas L. "Vicksburg: Strategic Point or Propaganda Device?" *Military Affairs* 34 (April 1970): 49–53.

Danziger, Edmund J., Jr. "The Office of Indian Affairs and the Problem of Civil War Indian Refugees in Kansas." *Kansas Historical Quarterly* 35 (Autumn 1969): 261–64.

Debo, Angie. "The Location of the Battle of Round Mountains." *Chronicles of Oklahoma* 41 (Spring 1963): 70–104.

Dinges, Bruce J. "Running Down Rebels." *Civil War Times Illustrated* 19 (April 1980): 10–18.

Dodd, Donald B. "The Free State of Winston." *Alabama Heritage* 28 (Spring 1993): 8–19.

Donald, W. J. "Alabama Confederate Hospitals (Part 2)." *Alabama Review* 16 (January 1963): 67.

Fleming, Walter L. "The Peace Movement in Alabama During the Civil War." *South Atlantic Quarterly* 2 (April 1903): 114–24 (Part 1); 2 (July 1903): 246–60 (Part 2).

Gibson, C. B. "Operations in Reparative Surgery." *Confederate States Medical and Surgical Journal* 1 (July 1864): 104–106.

Hale, Douglas. "Rehearsal for Civil War: The Texas Cavalry in the Indian Territory, 1861." *Chronicles of Oklahoma* 68 (Fall 1990): 228–65.

———. "The Third Texas Cavalry: A Socioeconomic Profile of a Confederate Regiment." *Military History of the Southwest* 19 (Spring 1989): 1–26.

Hallock, Judith Lee. "'Lethal and Debilitating': The Southern Disease Environment as a Factor in Confederate Defeat." *Journal of Confederate History* 7 (No. 1, 1991): 51–61.

Hollandsworth, James G. Jr. "The Execution of White Officers from Black Units by Confederate Forces During the Civil War." *Louisiana History* 35 (Fall 1994): 475–89.

Howard, E. L. "The Effects of Minié Balls on Bone." *Confederate States Medical and Surgical Journal* 1 (June 1864): 88–89.

Jordan, Mildred. "Georgia's Confederate Hospitals." M.A. thesis, Emory University, 1942.

Kawa, Adam J. "No Draft!" *Civil War Times Illustrated* 37 (June 1998): 54–60.

Lash, Jeffrey N. "Joseph E. Johnston's Grenada Blunder: A Failure in Command." *Civil War History* 23 (June 1977): 114–28.

Legouest, M. "Motion of Balls, and Ball Wounds." *Confederate States Medical and Surgical Journal* 1 (August 1864): 120–24.

Michel, M. "Healing of Gun-Shot Wounds by First Intention." *Confederate States Medical and Surgical Journal* 1 (July 1864): 99–102.

Rampp, Larry C., and Donald L. Rampp. "The Civil War in Indian Territory: The Confederate Advantage, 1861–1862." *Military History of Texas and the Southwest* 10 (No. 1, 1972): 29–41.

Savory, W. S. "On the Absorption of Dead Bone." *Confederate States Medical and Surgical Journal* 1 (November 1864): 187–89.

Sewell, Alan. "The Free State of Winston." *Civil War Times Illustrated* 20 (December 1981): 30–37.

Thomas, H. L. "Cases of Gunshot Injury Requiring Ligation of the Artery." *Confederate States Medical and Surgical Journal* 1 (November 1864): 184–86.

Woodworth, Steven E. "'Dismembering the Confederacy': Jefferson Davis and the Trans-Mississippi West." *Military History of the Southwest* 20 (Spring 1990): 1–22.

World Wide Web

Brothers, Ron. "Confederate Veterans Who Died or Are Buried in Lamar County, TX." Lamar County, Texas, World Wide Web page, http://gen.1starnet.com/civilwar/csadead.htm.

Index

Oxford, Miss., 211, 219
Ozark Mountains, 90, 93, 95

Paducah, Ky., 291, 291n23
Paine, Thomas, 177n
Palo Pinto, Tex., 336
Paris, Tex., xvii, xix, 1, 14, 69, 335, 336
Pea Ridge (Elkhorn Tavern), Battle of, xii,
    xiii, 70–85 passim, 88, 118–19, 142,
    151, 151n4, 185, 209
Pearl River (Miss.), 259, 260n19
Pemberton, John C., 192, 208, 208n48,
    210–11, 218, 249, 258, 260, 260n22
Pendleton, George H., 304n51
Perkins, T. A., 89, 89n, 101, 200, 214
Perryville, Ky., Battle of, 194n29
Peters, George B., 247
Petersburg, Va., 303, 303n44, 305,
    305n53, 311, 313, 316, 316n, 324,
    329
Petty, A. J., 317, 317n, 318, 319
Phifer, Charles W., 130, 130n26, 131,
    131n29, 146n, 173, 174, 175
Pike, Albert, 96, 96n, 140, 155, 167, 200,
    201n36
Pin party, 41, 41n23
Pittsburg Landing, Battle of. *See* Shiloh,
    Battle of
Plymouth, N.C., 291, 291n22
Pocahontas, Ark., 96, 96n, 99
Poindexter, James, 1, 1n
Polk, Leonidas, 280, 280n67, 284, 287
Pontotoc, Miss., 214–15, 218–19
Pope, John, 98n16, 121, 170, 171
Populist Party, xix
Port Hudson, La., 210, 231, 260, 260n21
Prairie Grove, Ark., Battle of, 202n39
Price, Joe, 232
Price, Sterling: at Pea Ridge, 70–85 passim;
    and transfer across Mississippi River,
    100n18, 102, 159, 160–61, 173n52; at
    Richmond, 135–36, 136n, 139; Bates's
    description of, 144, 144n40; and
    Corinth campaign, 154, 168, 172,
    173n52, 180; at Battle of Iuka, 180–81;
    at Battle of Corinth, 181–92 passim;
    mentioned, 146, 167

Prisoner exchanges, 270, 270n47
Prohibition Party, xix

Quayle, William: and officer elections, 6,
    6n12, 9; and early training, 10; and pur-
    suit of Unionist Indians, 21, 37, 38; at
    Round Mountains, 30; in Arkansas, 97,
    97n13; resignation of, 117, 125
Quisenberry, Si, 138

Railroads
—Atlanta & West Point, 311
—Central Alabama, 229
—Memphis & Charleston, 106, 111, 127,
    150, 180, 221n23
—Mississippi Central, 211, 215, 217, 219,
    219n20, 272
—Mobile & Ohio, 129, 131, 135, 214,
    226, 290, 290n20, 298
—Montgomery & West Point, 298n37,
    306, 310, 312
—Nashville & Chattanooga, 232, 321,
    321n11, 324, 328
—Weldon & Petersburg, 316, 316n, 318,
    318n7
—Western & Atlantic, 323
Rains, James S., 88, 88n3, 182
Rapidan River (Va.), 280
Rawlins, F. A., 60n4, 129n24, 176n
Raymond, Miss., 255, 255n 256
Reagan, Jim, 244
Ream's Station (Va.), Battle of, 318n7
Red River, 1n, 17, 166, 201, 202, 202n40,
    277, 282
Red River campaign, 279, 282, 282n73,
    292n27
Red River County, Tex., 30
Reed, T. M., 164, 164n28
Richmond, Ky., 170n45
Richmond, Va., 131, 131n27, 135, 139,
    140, 147, 147n45, 329
Ripley, Miss., 181, 185, 215, 222
Robinson, J. T., 190, 190n22
Rogers, Henry, 233, 233n48
Rome, Ga., 293
Rosecrans, William S.: and Corinth cam-
    paign, 173, 173nn51,52; at Battle of